THE REVELS PLAYS

Former editors
Clifford Leech 1958–71
F. David Hoeniger 1970–85

General editors
David Bevington, E. A. Honigmann, J. R. Mulryne
and Eugene M. Waith

SEJANUS: HIS FALL

MANCHESTER
UNIVERSITY PRESS

THE REVELS PLAYS

BEAUMONT *The Knight of the Burning Pestle*

CHAPMAN *Bussy d'Ambois*

CHAPMAN, JONSON, MARSTON *Eastward Ho*

DEKKER *The Shoemaker's Holiday*

FORD *'Tis Pity She's a Whore*

JONSON *The Alchemist The Devil is an Ass Poetaster
Sejanus: His Fall*

LYLY *Campaspe* and *Sappho and Phao Endymion*

MARLOWE *Doctor Faustus Edward the Second The Jew of Malta
Tamburlaine the Great*

MARSTON *Antonio's Revenge The Malcontent*

MARSTON AND OTHERS *The Roaring Girl*

MIDDLETON *A Game at Chess Women Beware Women*

MIDDLETON AND DEKKER *The Changeling*

WEBSTER *The Duchess of Malfi The White Devil*

THE REVELS PLAYS

SEJANUS
HIS FALL

BEN JONSON

edited by Philip J. Ayres

MANCHESTER
UNIVERSITY PRESS

Manchester and New York

*Distributed exclusively in the USA
by* St. Martin's Press

Introduction, critical apparatus, etc.
© Philip J. Ayres 1990

Reprinted 1999

The right of Philip J. Ayres to be identified as the editor of this
work has been asserted by him in accordance with the Copyright,
Designs and Patents Act 1988.

First published by Manchester University Press 1990

This edition published by Manchester University Press
Oxford Road, Manchester M13 9NR, UK
and Room 400, 175 Fifth Avenue, New York, NY 10010, USA
http://www.man.ac.uk/mup

Distributed exclusively in the USA by
St. Martin's Press, Inc., 175 Fifth Avenue, New York,
NY 10010, USA

Distributed exclusively in Canada by
UBC Press, University of British Columbia, 6344 Memorial Road,
Vancouver, BC, Canada V6T 1Z2

British Library Cataloguing-in-Publication Data
A catalogue record for this book is available from the British Library

Library of Congress Cataloging-in-Publication Data applied for

ISBN 0 7190 5702 7 *paperback*

06 05 04 03 02 01 00 99   10 9 8 7 6 5 4 3 2 1

Typeset in Hong Kong
by Best-set Typesetter Ltd
Printed in Great Britain
by Bell & Bain Ltd, Glasgow

Contents

IVLIANO
FILIO CARISSIMO
D. D. D

General Editors' Preface

Clifford Leech conceived of the Revels Plays as a series in the mid-1950s modelling the project on the New Arden Shakespeare. The aim, as he wrote in 1958, was 'to apply to Shakespeare's predecessors, contemporaries and successors the methods that are now used in Shakespeare editing'. The plays chosen were to include well known works from the early Tudor period to about 1700, as well as others less familiar but of literary and theatrical merit: 'the plays included,' Leech wrote, 'should be such as to deserve and indeed demand performance.' We owe it to Clifford Leech that the idea became reality. He set the high standards of the series, ensuring that editors of individual volumes produced work of lasting merit, equally useful for teachers and students, theatre directors and actors. Clifford Leech remained General Editor until 1971, and was succeeded by F. David Hoeniger, who retired in 1985.

The Revels Plays are now under the direction of four General Editors, David Bevington, E. A. J. Honigmann, J. R. Mulryne and E. M. Waith. Published originally by Methuen, the series is now published by Manchester University Press, embodying essentially the same format, scholarly character, and high editorial standards of the series as first conceived. The General Editors intend to concentrate on plays from the period 1558–1642, and may include a small number of non-dramatic works of interest to students of drama. Some slight changes have been forced by considerations of cost. For example, in editions from 1978, notes to the introduction are placed together at the end, not at the foot of the page. Collation and commentary notes will continue, however, to appear on the relevant pages.

The text of each Revels play, in accordance with established practice in the series, is edited afresh from the original text of best authority (in a few instances, texts), but spelling and punctuation are modernised and speech headings are silently made consistent. Elisions in the original are also silently regularised, except where metre would be affected by the change; since 1968 the '-ed' form is used for non-syllabic terminations in past tenses and past participles ('-'d' earlier), and '-èd' for syllabic ('-ed' earlier). The editor emends, as distinct from modernises, the original only in instances where error is patent, or at least very probable, and correction persuasive. Act divisions are given only if they appear in the original or if the structure of the play clearly points to them. Those act and scene divisions not in the original are provided in small type. Square brackets are also used for any other additions to or changes in the stage directions of the original.

Revels Plays do not provide a variorum collation, but only those variants which require the critical attention of serious textual students. All departures of substance from 'copy-text' are listed, including any relineation and those changes in punctuation which involve to any degree a decision between alternative interpretations; but not such accidentals as turned letters, nor necessary additions to stage directions whose editorial nature is already made clear by the use of brackets. Press corrections in the 'copy-text' are likewise collated. Of later emendations of the text, only those are given which as alternative readings still deserve attention.

One of the hallmarks of the Revels Plays is the thoroughness of their annotations. Besides explaining the meaning of difficult words and passages, the editor provides comments on customs or usage, text or stage-business—indeed, on anything judged pertinent and helpful. Each volume contains an Index to the Commentary, in which particular attention is drawn to meanings for words not listed in *OED*, and (starting in 1996) an indexing of proper names and topics in the Introduction and Commentary.

The Introduction to a Revels play assesses the authority of the 'copy-text' on which it is based, and discusses the editorial methods employed in dealing with it; the editor also considers the play's date and (where relevant) sources, together with its place in the work of the author and in the theatre of its time. Stage history is offered, and in the case of a play by an author not previously represented in the series a brief biography is given.

It is our hope that plays edited in this fashion will promote further scholarly and theatrical investigation of one of the richest periods in theatrical history.

DAVID BEVINGTON
E. A. J. HONIGMANN
J. R. MULRYNE
E. M. WAITH

Preface

I am grateful to Monash University for a period of study leave in 1982, which saw the completion of the text and commentary, and to the universities, and private and public libraries, which gave me access to their copies of the original editions, most by the provision of photocopies. To the Earl of Verulam and to Mr John Wolfson of New York City, whose co-operation enabled me to collate their copies of the first edition, go my special thanks.

Ronnie Mulryne provided all the help and advice one could want from a General Editor, and I benefited from frequent discussions with colleagues, in particular Dr Peter Groves, Mr Ian Laurenson, Professor Alan Henry and Professor Gavin Betts. In Gail Ward I had a first-rate secretary and typist who can process words with skill and (less common) critical acumen. And in Patricia fortune gave me an adored wife quite uninterested in talking to me about Sejanus, who thus could never come between us.

Abbreviations

WORKS OF REFERENCE, ETC.

Arber Edward Arber, *A Transcript of the Register of the Company of Stationers of London, 1554–1640*, 5 vols. (1875–94).
B.L. British Library.
Barish J. A. Barish, ed. *Sejanus* (New Haven, 1965).
Bolton W. F. Bolton, ed. *Sejanus his Fall* (London, 1966).
Briggs W. D. Briggs, ed. *Sejanus* (Boston, 1911).
Chambers E. K. Chambers, *The Elizabethan Stage*, 4 vols. (Oxford, 1923).
D.N.B. *The Dictionary of National Biography.*
E.C. *Essays in Criticism.*
E.L.H. *English Literary History.*
E.L.R. *English Literary Renaissance.*
Gifford W. Gifford, *The Works of Ben Jonson*, 9 vols. (London, 1816).
Greneway Richard Greneway, tr. *The Annales of Corn. Tacitus* (1598).
H.&S. C. H. Herford and P. and E. Simpson, eds. *Ben Jonson*, 11 vols. (Oxford, 1925–52).
J.A.B. J. F. Bradley and J. Q. Adams, *The Jonson Allusion Book* (New Haven, 1922).
L.&S. C. T. Lewis and C. Short, *A Latin Dictionary* (Oxford, 1879).
Libr. *The Library.*
M.L.N. *Modern Language Notes.*
M.P. *Modern Philology.*
O.E.D. *Oxford English Dictionary.*
P.B.S.A. *Papers of the Bibliographical Society of America.*
P.Q. *Philological Quarterly.*
Ren.Q. *Renaissance Quarterly.*
Riddell 'Seventeenth-Century Identifications of Jonson's Sources in the Classics', *Ren.Q.*, XXVIII (1975), 204–18.
S.B. *Studies in Bibliography.*
S.E.L. *Studies in English Literature 1500–1900.*
S.P. *Studies in Philology.*
S.T.C. A. W. Pollard and G. R. Redgrave, *A Short Title Catalogue of Books Printed in England, Scotland and Ireland* ... *1475–1640*, 2 vols. (London, 1976, 1986).
Syme Ronald Syme, *Tacitus*, 2 vols. (Oxford, 1958; ed. cit. 1967).
T.L.S. *Times Literary Supplement.*
T.S.L.L. *Texas Studies in Literature and Language.*
Tilley M. P. Tilley, *Dictionary of the Proverbs in England in the Sixteenth and Seventeenth Centuries* (Ann Arbor, 1950).
Whalley Peter Whalley, *The Works of Ben Jonson*, 7 vols. (1756).
Wilkes G. A. Wilkes, ed. *The Complete Plays of Ben Jonson*, 4 vols. (Oxford, 1981–2).
Wise *Q* Ashley 3464 (B.L.)—ex-T. J. Wise copy of *Q*.

TEXTS

Alc.   The Alchemist.
B.F.   Bartholomew Fair.
C.R.   Cynthia's Revels.
Cat.   Catiline.
Conv.Drum.   Conversations with Drummond.
Disc.   Discoveries.
E.H.   Eastward Ho.
E.M.I.   Every Man In His Humour.
E.M.O.   Every Man Out of His Humour.
Ep.   Epigrams.
F   Jonson's Works (1616).
F2   Jonson's Works (1640).
For.   The Forest.
Hadd.M.   The Haddington Masque.
K.Ent.   The King's Entertainment in Passing to his Coronation.
Mort.   Mortimer his Fall.
N.I.   The New Inn.
P.Hen.Barriers   Prince Henry's Barriers.
Pan.   A Panegyre.
Poet.   The Poetaster.
Q   1605 quarto of *Sejanus*.
S.W.   Epicoene, or, the Silent Woman.
Sej.   Sejanus.
U.V.   Ungathered Verse.
Und.   Underwoods.
Volp.   Volpone.

Unless otherwise indicated, references are to the Herford and Simpson edition. Titles of Shakespeare's plays are abbreviated as in Onions, *Shakespeare Glossary*, p. x, and their line-numbering follows Peter Alexander's edition. Wherever possible I have used Loeb editions of the classical sources, giving textual rather than page references.

Introduction

Stationers' Register
Sejanus was entered in the Stationers' Register by Edward Blount on
2 November 1604, but he transferred his copyright to Thomas Thorpe
on 6 August 1605, and Thorpe published it that year. The entries in
the Register read:[1]

2 Novembris [1604]

Edward Blunt	Entred for his copy vnder th[e h]andes of Master
putt ouer to	PASFEILD and the Wardens a booke called *the*
Thomas Thorp	*tragedie of SEIANVS* written by BENIAMIN
6 *Augusti* 1605	JOHNSON vj[d]

6 Augusti [1605]

Thomas Thorpe	Entred for his copy by assignement of Edward
	Blunt *the tragedie of SEIANVS* which was entred
	to the said Edward 2 *novembris ultimo* vj[d]

On 3 October 1610 copyright was again transferred, to Walter Burre:[2]

3° Octobris [1610]

Walter Burre	Entred for his Copyes by assignemente from
	Thomas Thorpe and with the consente of
	Th'wardens vnder their handes, 2 bookes th[e] one
	called, *SEIANVS his fall*, th[e] other, *VULPONE*
	or the ffoxe xii[d]

Burre did not publish it, and in 1635 his copyright to this and five
other plays was transferred to William Stansby, who had printed the
first folio of Jonson's *Works* in 1616:[3]

4° Iulii 1635

Master Stansby	Entred for his Copyes by vertue of a noate vnder
	the hand of Walter Burre and master Mathew
	Lownes warden bearing date the 10th of June 1621
	as thereby appeareth these Copies following (*vizt.*)
	by order of a Court

. . .

SEIANUS

. . .

I

Finally, on 4 March 1639 Stansby's rights were transferred to Richard Bishop,[4] who, the following year, published the second folio. This, along with the third folio (1692), lacks textual authority, and its corrections (to the Greek, for example) are not generally noted in the collation notes.

The Quarto (Q)

Sejanus was first printed in 1605—after 6 August—by George Eld (*S.T.C.* 14782). Eld's printing shop produced a number of other works by Jonson, including *Volpone* two years later, but nothing as meticulously and attractively presented as this.[5] Very few errors were made, even in Jonson's copious marginal notes, and most of those were put right in proof, a testimony to the care of Eld and of Jonson, who not only presented his printer with a scrupulously prepared fair copy but clearly supervised the printing process itself, altering in the proof tiny details that to a printer could hardly seem to need changing. A cursory examination of the collation in the Appendix is instructive: one can argue over exactly how many of the proof corrections represent authorial intrusion in the printing process, but clearly many do. The printer may have noted and inserted the missing note on H2v, but the fussy changes on sigs. ¶3v and ¶4r, and the reduction of large to small upper-case initial letters on sig. M1r, for example, are more probably Jonson's.

If the greater than normal demands this text makes on a printer by virtue of its scholarly apparatus made Jonson's presence at the shop advisable, his desire that the play in its printed form body forth the Roman-ness it achieves in language, imagery, and moral atmosphere made it essential. It is not just a matter of preferring Latin forms like ACTVS PRIMVS and FINIS to their English equivalents, though this sort of thing is significant in a Roman play, regardless of the fact that it can be found in others of Jonson's quartos. If one examines carefully the most physically Roman page in *Q*, sig. M1r (reproduced on Plate 1), one must judge it a *tour-de-force* as an exercise in making form reflect content. The central passage is like an inscription carved in stone and inserted into the text. In a marginal note, Jonson cites his principal authority for this compound of Senatorial formulae: Barnabé Brisson's *De Formulis et Sollemnibus Populi Romani Verbis* (Paris, 1583), Book II, in which all the formulae are set out in inscriptional fashion. Jonson's scrupulous care for small details extends on this page to medial stops between the words and the use of double-V for W in the inscriptional passage, since of course the Latin

SEIANVS.

Sᴀɴ.

Sᴀɴ. I, and get more. Lᴀᴛ. More Office, and more Titles.   Dio. *ibid.*
Pᴏᴍ. I will not loose the part, I hope to share
In thefe his Fortunes, for my *Patrimony.*
Lᴀᴛ. See how *Arruntius* fits, and *Lepidus.*
Tʀɪ. Let 'hem alone, they will be markt anone.
Sᴇɴ. Ile doe, with others. Sᴇɴ. So will I. Sᴇɴ. And I.
Men grow not in the ftate but as they are planted
Warme in his fauors. Cᴏᴛ. Noble *Seianus.*
Hᴀᴛ. Honor'd *Seianus.* Lᴀᴛ. Worthy and great *Seianus.*
Aʀʀ. Gods! how the Spunges open, and take in!
And fhut againe! Looke, looke! Is not he bleft
That gets a feate in eye-reach of him? more,
That comes in eare, or tongue-reach? O but moft,
Can claw his fubtle elbow, or with a buzze
Flieblow his eares. Pʀᴀᴇᴛ. Proclaime the *Senates* peace;
And giue laft fummons by the Edict. Pʀᴀᴇ. Silence.
In name of Cᴀᴇsᴀʀ, and the Sᴇɴᴀᴛᴇ. SILENCE.

[a]MEMMIVS REGVLVS. AND. FVLCINIVS.   [a] *Vid.* Bɾ.·
TRIO. CONSVL'S. THESE. PRESENT. KALENDES. OF. IVNE. VVITH.   fonium : *c*·
THE. FIRST. LIGHT. SHALL. HOLD. A. SENATE. IN. THE. TEMPLE.   *formut.*
OF. [b]APOLLO PALATINE. ALL. THAT. ARE. FATHERS. AND.   *liu.2.*
ARE. REGISTRED. FATHERS. THAT. HAVE. RIGHT. OF. ENTRING.   Et Lipfium
THE. SENATE. VVE. VVARNE. OR. COMMAVND. YOV. BE. FREQVENT-   Sat. Menip
LY. PRESENT. TAKE. KNOVVLEDGE. THE. BVSINESSE. IS. THE. COM-   [b] *Palatinus.*
MON. VVEALTHES. VVHOSOEVER. IS. ABSENT. HIS. FINE. OR. MVLCT.   *à monte*
VVILL. BE. TAKEN. IIIS. EXCVSE. VVILL. NOT. BE. TAKEN.   *Palatin.*
                                                      dictus.

Tʀɪ Note, who are abfent, and record their names.   [c] *Solemnis*
Rᴇɢ. [c]Fᴀᴛʜᴇʀs Cᴏɴscʀɪᴘᴛ. Mᴀʏ Wʜᴀᴛ I Aᴍ Tᴏ Vᴛᴛᴇʀ,   *prefatio*
Tᴠʀɴᴇ Gᴏᴏᴅ Aɴᴅ Hᴀᴘᴘʏ Fᴏʀ Tʜᴇ Cᴏᴍᴍᴏɴ Wᴇᴀʟᴛʜ.   *Confulum*
And thou Aᴘᴏʟʟᴏ, in whofe holy Houfe   *in relatio-*
We here are met, Infpire vs all, with truth,   *nibus.*
And liberty of Cenfure to our thought.   *Dio. pa*
The Maieftie of great *Tiberius Cæsar*   *718.*
Propounds to this graue *Senate,* the beftowing
Vpon the man he loues, honour'd *Seianus,*
The [d] *tribuniciall* dignity. and power;   [d] *Vi*·
Here are his Letters, figned with his fignet: Tib·
                    M   Wʜᴀᴛ

PLATE I *Q*, sig. M1ʳ

SEIANVS.

ACTVS PRIMVS.

SABINVS. SILIVS. NATTA. LATIARIS. CORDVS.
SATRIVS. ARRVNTIVS. EVDEMVS.
HATERIVS. &c.

De Caio
Silio. vid.
Tacit, Lipf.
edit. 4°.
Anna. lib. 1.
pag. 11. lib.
2. pag. 28.
& 33.
b De Titio
Sabino. vid.
Tac. lib. 4.
pag. 79.
c Tac. An-
nal. lib 1.
pag. 2.
d Iuuenal.
Sat. 1. ver.
75.
e Et Sat. 3.
ver. 49. &c.
f De Latia-
ri, cōf. Tac.
Annal. lib. 4
pag. 94. &
Dion. Step.
edit. fol. lib.
58. pag.
711.
g De Satrio
Secundo, &
h Pinnario
Natta,
Leg Ta-
cit. Annal.
lib. 4. pag.
83.
Et de Sa-
trio. conf.
Senec. cō-
fol. ad Mar-
ciam.
i Vid. Sen.
de Benef.
lib 3 cap.
26.

SAB. HAile a *Caius Silius*. SIL. b *Titius Sabinus*, Hayle.
Yo'are rarely met in Court! SAB. Therfore, well met.
SIL.' Tis true : Indeed, this Place is not our Sphære.
SAB. No *Silius*, we are no good Inginers;
We want the fine Artes, and their thriuing vfe
Should make vs grac'd, or fauor'd of the Times :
We haue no fhift of Faces, no cleft Tongues,
No foft, and glutinous bodies, that can ftick,
Like Snailes, on painted walls ; or, on our brefts,
Creepe vp, to fall, from that proud height, to which
We did by c flauerie, not by feruice, clime.
We are no guilty men, and then no Great ;
We haue nor place in Court, Office in ftate,
That we d can fay, we owe vnto our Crimes;
We burne with no e black fecrets, which can make
Vs deare to the pale Authors ; or liue fear'd
Of their ftill waking iealofies, to raife
Our felues a Fortune, by fubuerting theirs.
We ftand not in the lines, that do aduance
To that fo courted point. SIL. But yonder leane
A paire that doe. (SAB. Good Coffen f *Latiaris*.)
SIL. g *Satrius Secundus*, and h *Pinnarius Natta*,
The great *Seianus* Clients; There be two,
Know more, then honeft Councells : whofe clofe brefts
Were they rip'd vp to light, it would be found
A poore, and idle finne, to which their Trunkes
Had not be e made fit Organs : Thefe can lie,
Flatter, and fweare, forfweare, depraue, i informe,
Smile, and betray ; make guilty men ; then beg

B   The

alphabet does not have a W. On sig. M2r, not reproduced, Tiberius's letter opens in a formulaic manner and this section is again printed in an inscriptional form. In *F* at these points, upper case is changed to lower case for everything except a few proper nouns, italic is used to indicate that formulae are being employed, and the punctuation is normalised. Elsewhere much is lost, too. To take one more example, the unadorned, perfectly proportioned, classical simplicity of the first page of Act I in *Q*, a visible image of the Rome to which it introduces us (Plate 2), is lost in *F* through the intrusion of an ornamental device at the top and a huge ornamental H; by the insertion of three horizontal lines; by the change of 'ACTVS PRIMVS' to '*Act*. I' and the change from upper to lower case there; and by the substitution of commas for the stops between the names of the characters. It is not that Jonson had come to see his earlier edition as marred by silly pedantry: all these changes were made simply in the interests of a more or less standard-ised lay-out in *F*.

Q instructs us that there is a third category of 'signs' in some texts that we should add to or fuse with our two (not always clearly dis-tinguishable) categories of substantives and accidentals, and which might, somewhat pompously, be called the iconographic. It is not commonly met with, but it is met with in this quarto where it has an important function to play in physically imaging the Roman-ness of this most Roman of English plays.[6] *Q*'s inscriptional passages in Act V are preserved in this edition.

Q collates ¶4, A-M4, N2, fifty-four leaves unnumbered. Despite the demanding nature of this text, copy seems to have been cast off and the play set by formes, since the discrepant length of the text (excluding running-title and catchword) on sig. K4r—10 mm shorter than the (38-line) average—is best explained by inaccurate estimation in casting-off resulting from an over-allowance for the very great number of marginal notes in the area of sigs. K3v–K4r, where they overrun large areas of what would normally be the text proper. Sig. L1r is also shorter, and this again may have something to do with its large number of notes. Also pointing to casting-off is the fact that a note is never continued on a following page.[7]

Because the printing was so carefully supervised, compositor iden-tification is more than usually hazardous, and Peter B. Murray has shown that 'for the most part Eld's workmen simply reproduced the forms they found in the manuscripts presented to them for printing'.[8] Indeed so even is the product that the whole text could have been set up by one compositor using one stick with two slides, fixed throughout, for setting text and (where required) parallel marginal notes. That the preliminaries were set up last, a normal procedure, is suggested by variant watermarks on sheet ¶ in some copies.[9]

Twenty-three of the twenty-eight copies of *Q* known to me were collated by me in Australia using a Lindstram stereoscopic comparator and working with photocopies. I was provided with information on three of the other copies, allowing me to assign their formes to the categories 'uncorrected state', 'first corrected state', and 'second corrected state' on the basis of my collation of the twenty-three. Press correction was four times more extensive than Herford and Simpson realised—they collated only seven copies non-mechanically. The Newberry Library copy proves that the author of the final commendatory poem is Ev. B., not (as *H.&S.*, XI, 317 conjecture) ED. B.; certain formes exist in more than two states; what they identified as corrected states are in some cases uncorrected states (sig. M3r, for example); and what they identified as the uncorrected state of the title-page is in fact the most corrected state—this page having three, not two, states (see Appendix B). The two large-paper presentation copies bearing inscriptions in Jonson's hand (B.L., Ashley 3464, ex-Wise; Huntington, ex-Huth) have their title-pages in the most corrected state. The B.L. ex-Wise copy has a number of manuscript corrections to spelling and punctuation, generally accepted to be in Jonson's hand.

The First Folio (F)
Sejanus occupies sigs. Gg4r-Oo3v, pp. 355–438 in *F* (the *Works*, 1616—*S.T.C.* 14751/14752). *F* added the epistle to Aubigny, and the page giving members of the original cast; omitted 'To the Readers'; shortened Chapman's commendatory verse and moved it, along with Holland's, to the head of the folio; dropped the other verses; and cut the supplementary paragraph to 'The Argument'. *Q*'s marginal annotations disappeared. The text of the play in *F* was set up from a marked-up copy of *Q*, and further changes were made during the printing. Stage directions, scarce in *Q*, were added; the number of inverted commas, used in *Q* to indicate 'sentences' or maxims, was heavily reduced; exclamation marks were used more liberally, sometimes replacing question marks in *Q*; a few of *Q*'s metrical apostrophes, which Jonson used between unelided syllables to indicate that they are metrically equivalent to one syllable but should still be slightly distinguished when spoken (see *H.&S.*, IV, 338–42, and IX, 50) were accidentally dropped; and emphatic pauses, already prominent in *Q*,

were made more prominent. Proper names in the text were changed from italic to small capitals. Substantive changes of a fairly clearly authorial kind include the intriguing one at IV.438—from *Q*'s 'POM. By *Castor*, that's the worst. (ARR. By *Pollux*, best.)' to 'POM. By POLLVX, that's the worst. (ARR. By HERCVLES, best.)', made in the proof in *F* because Jonson now realised what he had not in 1605, that only women swore by Castor. The second of the following lines in *Q*,

> so soone, all best Turnes,
> With *Princes*, do conuert to iniuries
> In estimation, when they greater rise,
> Then can be answer'd   (sigs. F3*v*–F4*r*)

reads in *F* 'With doubtfull Princes, turne deepe iniuries'—less generalised and less offensive. This change represents self-censorship on Jonson's part and is also verbally inferior since it introduces a chiming 'Turnes ... turne'. Other changes, most of them minor, can be traced in the collation notes. The physically Roman appearance of *Q*, as already noted, was completely lost in *F*. Press corrections were, as in the case of *Q*, more extensive than Herford and Simpson knew (see Appendix B). Many of them were undoubtedly Jonson's. But while *F* is an authoritative text, it is not in all respects—not even in most respects—superior to *Q*.

The changes introduced in *F* are a mixture: many substantive alterations are clearly authorial or too inconsequential to be the work of compositors. They include an example of self-censorship that hardly counts as a gain. A considerable number of metrical apostrophes, a Jonson hall-mark of permanent interest and value, disappear. *F*'s accidentals must be considered less reliable, being one remove further from Jonson's manuscript. Occasionally *F* follows the uncorrected rather than the corrected form of *Q* (sigs. M2*v*, M3*r*, for example), leading modern editors astray (V.636 and V.666). And last, but certainly not least, as a text *F* lacks the unique physical beauty and interest of *Q*.

This edition
The present edition uses *Q* as copy-text, generally accepting its authority on accidentals and emending from *F* selectively where substantives are concerned, normally incorporating what seem to be authoritative changes and additions (but not the self-censorship). The editors of the Yale and New Mermaids *Sejanus*, Jonas Barish and W. F. Bolton, used *F* as copy-text; Herford and Simpson did like-

wise, with more justification, since they were not editing the play
alone but with all the Works. W. W. Greg pointed out that 'In the
case of a work like *Sejanus*, in which correction or revision has been
slight, it would obviously be possible to take the quarto as the copy-
text and introduce into it whatever authoritative alterations the folio
may supply; and indeed, were one editing the play independently,
this would be the natural course to pursue'.[10] It is the course pursued
in this edition. Fredson Bowers and G. Thomas Tanselle have en-
dorsed this procedure—for a play like *Sejanus*, the proper, conservative, and logical procedure.[11] Variants with substantive or metrical
value, between *Q* and *F* and between copies of each, are recorded in
the collation notes.

Q's marginal annotations are useless to most modern readers, who
cannot go to the early editions Jonson cites, and may not read Latin.
This edition gives, in its commentary, every one of Jonson's citations
and a translated form of every significant annotation, but with
references (for the most part) to Loeb editions, reproducing the Loeb
translation of the passage directly quoted or echoed in *Sejanus*. Acts
are not divided into scenes in *Q* and *F*, and of course Jonson's theatre
followed the convention of continuous staging within the Acts. In
following *Q* and *F* here, this edition breaks with normal Revels
series practice. Earlier editors' notes on location are left where they
belong, in the collation notes. Jonson's massed 'entries' at the head of
each Act are distributed according to the characters' entries.

As this is a modern-spelling edition, 'strooke' becomes 'struck',
'shittles' becomes 'shuttles', though words like 'illustrous', 'ventrous'
and 'adscribe', where modernisation would add a syllable or eliminate
a consonant, are kept. I have reluctantly dispensed with Jonson's
Latinate spellings—his 'tyran' becomes 'tyrant', 'aequal' becomes
'equal', and so on. When pronunciation is clearly affected, the change
is noted. Punctuation has been lightened, but in a discriminating way:
an editor should take care to lighten punctuation only when so doing
will not puzzle or mislead the reader. Where modern practice will
allow a choice of whether or not to use a comma, and caesural effect
or emphatic pause is involved, I generally keep the comma. Tiberius
often speaks very deliberately, with a good deal of parenthetical side-
tracking, and the effect of this can be lost if the punctuation is
routinely lightened. Even where a comma cannot be kept, there may
be a way of preserving its effect—an example is *Q*'s 'Those, bounties'
which this edition renders as 'Those 'bounties'' (see III.532n.).
Where Jonson's colons anticipate a consequence or further definition,

I keep them or use dashes, depending on the context. Jonson's indication of asides by parentheses is silently dispensed with. Where *F* changes a *Q* question mark to an exclamation mark, I follow *F* only if the exclamation cannot have a questioning note, and record the variant. Jonson's metrical apostrophes are an aid, not a distraction, to the proper reading of the play, and are kept. Herford and Simpson added two or three where they are clearly required, and I follow them, with an acknowledgement. These apostrophes are certainly idiosyncratic, but they were idiosyncratic in 1605.

Despite the need of a modern edition to alter typography in many instances, I have done what I can to pay tribute to the 'iconography' of *Q*, preserving features like ACTVS PRIMVS and the 'inscriptions', which serve to remind us of how literary a play this is, and of how important Jonson considered it that this work, of which he was so proud, appear well and appropriately dressed.

2. DATE, AND PLACE IN JONSON'S CAREER

Jonson may have been working on *Sejanus* for something like two years before its appearance on the stage, having declared in the 'apologeticall Dialogue' at the end of *Poetaster* (printed 1602) his intention to 'trie/If *Tragoedie* haue a more kind aspect', where popular acclaim was concerned, than comedy. The title page of *Sejanus* in *F* gives '1603' as the year of the play's first production (by the King's Men)— that is to say, between 25 March 1603 and 24 March 1604, the old-style dates for the beginning and end of the year. As E. K. Chambers pointed out, because the theatres were closed on account of Elizabeth's death on 24 March 1603, and almost certainly remained closed because of the plague until 9 April 1604, the 1603 production to which the title page of *F* refers 'may have been at Court in the autumn or winter of 1603', with the most likely dates being 26, 27, 28 and 30 December 1603, 1 January 1604, and 2 and 19 February 1604.[12] The unsuccessful performance of the play at the Globe, where it was greeted by the hostility of its audience (see the commendatory verse by Ev. B.), must have taken place later in 1604, probably soon after the opening of the theatres on 9 April 1604.[13].

Sejanus represents a crucial point in Jonson's development as a dramatist.[14] The pervasive optimism of the earlier comedies, the faith in the ability of good men to keep in check, if not thoroughly control, the criminal, the selfish or the merely foolish elements in their society is finally dead by the time Jonson writes his deeply disillusioned 'apologeticall Dialogue' attached to *Poetaster*, where he rejects both his audience and comical satire. Considerable attention has recently been paid to the relation of *Sejanus* to the comedies that follow.[15] It is the first play of Jonson's to express a thoroughly pessimistic outlook on the human condition, and the first to concentrate its action exclusively about a central intrigue. Like Volpone, Sejanus appears to derive his greatest pleasure from the intrigue itself, joying more in the quest than in the conquest ('Is there not something more than to be Caesar?'), and like Volpone, Sejanus is matched with a skilful partner who turns adversary. It is the criminal or quasi-criminal mind, in *Sejanus* as in *Volpone* and *The Alchemist*, that now fires Jonson's imagination. The Germanicans may constitute a model of virtue, but it is an uninspiring and socially ineffective one in contrast with that of Horace in *Poetaster*. In *Sejanus*, as in *The Alchemist*, the fall of a criminal or criminals is no guarantee of future order: Macro follows Sejanus, and Tiberius still reigns. The trial scenes in *Sejanus* and *Volpone* are comparable—neither offers an unalloyed justice. Arruntius may speak at times for Jonson, but he exercises no real control over events, merely a verbal authority. The villains have the power in *Sejanus*, and in this respect it anticipates the more popular *Volpone* and *The Alchemist*. In distinction to the earlier comedies, Jonson is no longer a strong presence on his own stage.[16]

3. SOURCES, INFLUENCES AND CHARACTERISATION

The sources from which Jonson drew in writing *Sejanus* are cited in the commentary, and where a source is incorporated (even loosely) in the language of the play, a translation of that source is provided, generally from Loeb editions. Jonson's principal debt is to the *Annals* of Tacitus, particularly the fourth book. Most of the fifth, which would have covered the final three years of Sejanus's life, is lost, and for this period Jonson turned to a later account, that of Dio Cassius in his *Roman History*, Books LVII–LVIII, and to the life of Tiberius in Suetonius's gossipy, sensational, and probably not always reliable history of the 'twelve Caesars'. Juvenal's tenth satire is the chief source for the death of Sejanus at the hands of the Roman mob. Other major classical sources, not all of them having to do with Sejanus but each providing substantial material that Jonson turned effectively to his purposes, include Seneca's *To Marcia on Consolation* and *On Benefits*, Claudian's *Against Rufinus* and *On Stilicho's Consulship*, Pliny's *Natural History*, Juvenal's *Satires*, Persius's *Satires*, Martial's

Epigrams, Lucan's *The Civil War*, and the plays of Seneca. In addition
to these there are dozens of minor classical sources.

This material is handled creatively, and Hazlitt's description (in his
lecture on Beaumont and Fletcher, Ben Jonson, Ford and Massinger)
of the play as a 'mosaic' of 'translated bits' does it an injustice. It has
been estimated that no more than a quarter of the play is translation or
paraphrase,[17] and what has been translated has generally been deftly
rearranged. A good example of Jonson's skilful 'cutting-up' of his
source material is provided if one compares the passage of Tacitus
quoted in the commentary on I.218–37 with the appropriate passage
in *Sejanus*. Critics have shown how Jonson takes liberties with the
historical record.[18] For instance, he compresses the trials of Caius
Silius and Cremutius Cordus, historically separated by a year, into a
single meeting of the Senate and makes Afer their accuser; he has
Silius commit suicide in the Senate rather than at home, to good
dramatic effect; and he invents the assault of Macro upon Sejanus in
the Senate. In Tacitus, the blow given by Drusus to Sejanus precedes
both the seduction of Livia and its planning, whereas in the play the
planning precedes the blow, and this subtly alters the protagonist's
motivation.[19] The long, equivocating and strategically brilliant letter
from Tiberius which so effectively destroys the former favourite is
worked up by Jonson from the merest hints in Juvenal and Dio.[20] The
character of Tiberius is far more complex in Tacitus than in *Sejanus*,
where he has no introspective soliloquies that might engage our
sympathies but would detract from our impression of him as the
epitome of astute Machiavellian manipulation and cool cunning. His
hesitant speech rhythms and the parenthetical side-tracks that mark
his thought processes are from Tacitus, where they heighten the sense
of his complexity and self-doubt, but Jonson probably kept them only
because in his play they effectively reinforce our impression of
Tiberius as a devious 'enginer'. The virtue of the Germanicans is
presented more equivocally in Tacitus—for instance, any criticisms of
Agrippina in the play come from characters we distrust. Drusus is
relieved of the cruelty that compromises him in Tacitus, no one re-
peats Tacitus's admission that Silius was guilty of extortion, Jonson's
Sabinus is a stronger character than his model in the *Annals*, and
Lepidus loses much of his neutrality. In ways like these Jonson
shapes or reduces his sources better to suit his dramatic or didactic
purposes.

Little shaping of the Tacitus was required for the title character,
since in his case Tacitus has nothing but criticisms to make. Jonson

might, however, have added more psychological interest to his
character if he had so desired, and based this on classical authority.
The Roman history by Velleius Paterculus, a friend of Sejanus,
whatever its limitations, succeeds (as the Loeb editor has pointed out)
'in clothing the bones with real flesh', thanks to Velleius's 'own
enthusiastic interest in the human side of the great characters of
history'.[21] Writing shortly before the fall of Sejanus, Velleius likens
him to other 'new men' raised to eminence for their personal qualities
(Marcus Agrippa, Statilius Taurus), mentions Sejanus's illustrious
connections on his mother's side, and discusses Sejanus's character in
terms of paradoxes that would have interested a Shakespeare. Jonson
admits only a few: 'stern but yet gay, cheerful but yet strict; busy, yet
always seeming to be at leisure', and 'his mind is sleeplessly alert'
offer features discernible in Jonson's protagonist; but 'calm in expression and in his life' is passed by, as is the claim that Sejanus's 'estimate
of himself is always below the estimate of others'.[22] For Jonson's
moral and satiric purposes, the 'new man' must have all the unbear-
able qualities of the *arriviste* (for instance the insistence on being
addressed as 'my lord', I.278), and his bombastic rhetoric (II.139–62,
for example, or V.1–24) must be there to reveal the upstart egotist for
the overblown criminal he is. The result is a stage presence of great
force and moral clarity—and one with whom any sympathetic engage-
ment is rigorously denied.

Jonson also drew upon some of the best sixteenth-century classical
scholarship. The edition of Tacitus he employed was that of Justus
Lipsius, one of the most eminent classicists of the day, who, in his
1600 Antwerp edition of the Works, provided not only the most
authoritative text but a wealth of annotations and references to relevant passages in other Latin and Greek authors. Jonson incorporates
(without acknowledgement, in most cases) some of these notes and
references in the critical apparatus of his 1605 quarto edition: they
saved him time and effort by sending him directly to the secondary
sources, but the procedure involves an element of pretence.[23] Besides
Lipsius, Jonson consulted such scholars as Budé (on the value of
Roman money); Brisson (on the formulae of Senatorial procedure);
Giraldus, Stuck, and Panvinio (on Roman religion); and Rosinus (on
the strength of the night watch).

Seeming to pervade the entire play and define the terms of its
political commerce is the spirit of the two principal works of Machiavelli, *The Prince* and *The Discourses*.[24] In the sixth chapter of the third
book of *The Discourses*, Machiavelli refers his reader to the conspiracy

of Sejanus as one of the best-known attempts by a favourite to usurp power. It teaches the prince an important lesson: he should guard against his favourites even more than against those he has injured, since the latter lack the opportunities the former find everywhere at hand. The relevant passage from Machiavelli is reproduced in the commentary to III.637–42. Machiavelli advises the prince to be as much the fox as the tiger—he should know how to recognise traps. Jonson's Tiberius has learned these lessons: a 'good fox', he is 'Princelike, to the life' (V.593; I.395), and operates in accordance with Machiavelli's advice that a prince who suspects a conspiracy to be building against him should wait quietly until he is ready and able to crush it, meanwhile simulating ignorance. The respect Tiberius shows for the gods (I.375–8) is consistent with Machiavelli's advice to the prince to don the mask of piety. However, whether all of these and other 'Machiavellian' features of the play come directly from Jonson's reading of Machiavelli is not clear. Many might as well be derived directly from Tacitus, who provides them with a common source.

The figure of Fortune who, in person or in spirit, is a presence throughout the play, is both Roman and medieval. Jonson's play combines, in the attitudes of the Germanicans, a Juvenalian attitude to 'the vanity of human wishes', which is essentially contemptuous of the goddess Fortune, with a frequent insistence upon her influence on the affairs of men. That influence is made crystal clear by the animated statue of the goddess whose miraculous vitality confirms her divinity for an audience at the same time as it (paradoxically) converts her most devoted worshipper into her chief contemner. If it is man who makes Fortune a deity (as Lepidus claims at V.743–5), how does one account for the miracle, which even Sejanus accepts as genuine? If Fortune, as that miracle plainly shows, is a deity indeed, why does the play seem to insist that men are responsible for their own actions?—that Sejanus owes his fall not to some desertion on Fortune's part but to his fatal error of judgement in the third Act when he imprudently seeks Tiberius's consent to an alliance with Livia? Jonson satirises the attempt to cater to Fortune's whims, yet (because he must—the miraculous statue is in Dio) insists on her 'real presence'. The medieval tragic concept of the wheel of Fortune, and the *contemptus mundi* attitude, are undeniable influences on the play, but they are complicated and, I would say, confused and jangled by their combination with the classical source material. It is a problem that Jonson has not satisfactorily resolved.[25]

Jonson and Richard Greneway

Something should be said about an unacknowledged and generally unrecognised source.[26] In the same paragraph in which he notes the edition of Tacitus he used, Jonson tells us that all of the classical texts he has consulted are 'in the learned tongues, save one, with whose English side I have had little to do'. This text, which he does not name, is Richard Greneway's translation, *The Annales of Corn. Tacitus* [with the *Germania*], first printed in London in 1598. He also referred to this text in conversation with William Drummond in 1619: 'The first foūr bookes of Tacit' ignorantly done in Englishe'.[27] This has been enough to discourage any comparison of Greneway and the relevant passages in *Sejanus*, with one exception. Sir Israel Gollancz wrote a brief note for *T.L.S.* in 1928 on Jonson's debt to Greneway, but his few examples failed to convince Percy Simpson.[28] I have compared them carefully, and it is clear that Jonson had Greneway's translation beside him in writing *Sejanus*, that—his derogatory comments notwithstanding—he glanced at it from time to time, in three instances introducing serious errors into his play as a consequence, and that in a number of cases he reproduced distinctive wording in Greneway. In each of the following three examples of the importation of Greneway's errors into *Sejanus*, I give the Latin context, italicising the key phrase (and, as there are no variants in the passages quoted, I cite the Loeb Latin text for convenience rather than that of Lipsius[29]); Greneway's translation of this key phrase, citing page numbers of the 1598 edition; and Jonson's phrasing in *Sejanus*.

I. *et minui sibi invidiam adempta salutantum turba*, sublatisque inanibus veram potentiam augeri (*Annals*, IV.xli) (... *while [Sejanus's] own unpopularity would diminish with the abolition of his great levées*, and the realities of his power be increased by the removal of its vanities (Loeb translation)); and that the enuie borne to himself should be diminished, accesse to the Prince being lesser (Greneway, p. 104). And these that hate me now, wanting access / To him, will make their envy none, or less (*Sejanus*, III.619–20). As Herford and Simpson point out, '*Wanting accesse to him* [i.e. Tiberius] is not what Tacitus here says: the "salutantum turba" was Sejanus' own crowded receptions; when these stopped, the envy they excited would cease or at any rate be less'.[30] What Herford and Simpson fail to realise is that Jonson's error has a source, Richard Greneway, whom Jonson follows in thinking it is Tiberius's rather than Sejanus's receptions that are being referred to here. In Tacitus, Sejanus is supposed to be calculating that by removing the vanities of power (his own 'receptions') the reality of that power will be enhanced.

II. et Rhodi secreto vitare coetus, recondere voluptates *insuerat* (*Annals*, IV.lvii) (... while, in the seclusion of Rhodes, he *had acquired the habit* of avoiding company and taking his pleasures by stealth (Loeb translation)). Tacitus is here referring to Tiberius's early 'exile' at Rhodes, during the principate of Augustus. The reference comes in the context of Tiberius's leaving Rome for Capreae in A.D. 26—hence the pluperfect 'insuerat'. Greneway translates this as 'And at Rhodes he was wont ['he had been wont' is called for by the Latin] to shun companie, liue secretly, and hide his lasciuious dissolute life' (Greneway, pp. 109–10). At this point, Jonson makes a major error:

> [Sejanus] is all, does all, gives Caesar leave
> To hide his ulcerous and anointed face,
> With his bald crown, at Rhodes, while he here stalks
> Upon the heads of Romans (*Sejanus*, IV.173–6)

Herford and Simpson, following W. D. Briggs, comment on this: 'Jonson ... overlooked "insuerat". The exile at Rhodes had taken place in the reign of Augustus; Jonson speaks of it as if it were taking place at the moment'. But the *reason* Jonson did this is that he was misled by Greneway's use of the imperfect 'he was wont ...' where the pluperfect 'he had been wont ...' was called for.

III. Compositum inter ipsos, ut *Latiaris, qui modico usu Sabinum contingebat*, strueret dolum (*Annals*, IV.lxviii) (The arrangement among the four was that *Latiaris, who was connected with Sabinus by some little intimacy*, should lay the trap. (Loeb translation)); *Latiaris*, who was somewhat allied to Sabinus (Greneway, p. 113); He'is allied to him (*Sejanus*, IV.110). Because 'allied' could mean 'related', editors of Sejanus claim that Jonson has turned what in Tacitus is only slight friendship—the italicised Latin phrase would normally be understood thus—into kinship. So, at I.21 Sabinus greets Latiaris with 'Good cousin Latiaris'. Jonas Barish, in pointing out that 'This intensifies the odium of the betrayal', implies, as do Herford and Simpson, that Jonson both intentionally and fortuitously altered Tacitus.[31] This is to misrepresent what in fact occurred. Jonson almost certainly thought he was rendering Tacitus faithfully—for at this point he is simply following the translation of Richard Greneway, taking Greneway's 'allied' to mean 'related'.

From these instances, and others where Jonson reproduces distinctive wording in Greneway (e.g. 'thrust in': Greneway, p. 95, *Sejanus*,
III.179; 'To watch and travail': Greneway, p. 102, *Sejanus*, III.510;
'Augustus' nephew's sons' (where 'great-grandsons' would be expected): Greneway, p. 92, *Sejanus*, III.75), it is clear that Jonson used
Greneway from time to time as a check on his own rendering of
Tacitus. At times he was not above using Greneway's phrasing if it
seemed apt, and three times he repeated Greneway's errors. He was
only human, and the source is notoriously difficult.

4. *SEJANUS* AND THE PRIVY COUNCIL[32]

'Northampton was his mortall enimie for brauling on a St Georges day
one of his attenders, he was called befor ye Coūncell for his Sejanus &
accused both of popperie and treason by him.'[33] William Drummond's slightly ambiguous note is usually taken to mean that Lord
Henry Howard, from 13 March 1604 the Earl of Northampton,[34]
detected 'treason' in *Sejanus* and brought Jonson before the Privy
Council for that reason, adding the charge either that the play was
'popish' or, more likely, that Jonson was a Catholic—a not very well-
hidden fact, in any case. Apart from Drummond's note we know
nothing about the matter, and there has been very little in the way of
speculation.[35] It is discouraged by the fact that Jonson changed the
play before its first appearance in print in 1605 to the extent of cutting
out the work of the 'second Pen', probably Chapman's, which had
originally 'had good share' in the play.[36]

The revision was therefore quite radical, and it is generally assumed
that whatever particularly offensive lines there had been in *Sejanus* in
its original form that gave offence in late 1603 or early 1604 were
carefully removed before the 1605 printing, the one possible exception
being the reference at III.303 to princes, noted above. Nevertheless,
it is not the case, as J. Palmer claimed, that in the form in which we
have it '*Sejanus* would seem incapable of local or contemporary
application'.[37] A. R. Dutton, for instance, offering a fairly elementary
contemporary application, thinks that 'the fact that Jonson had
chosen to write a play about the fall and death of a royal favorite only
two years after the execution of the Earl of Essex made it virtually
inevitable that parallels would be drawn'.[38]

Herford and Simpson pointed to another factor that must have
reinforced the suspicions of seekers after parallels: in his previous
play, *Poetaster*, Jonson 'had just used the Court of Augustus as a

vehicle for unmeasured personal ridicule of his contemporaries'. Why should one assume that in *Sejanus* he 'had portrayed the Court of Tiberius in the guileless spirit of a scholar bent only on the historical accuracy of his play'?[39] Yet that, Jonson insists, was the case. His scholarly notes in *Q* are there to affirm his 'integrity in the story', as he calls it in his prefatory address 'To the Readers': 'lest in some nice nostril the quotations might savour affected, I do let you know that I abhor nothing more; and have only done it to show my integrity in the story, and save myself in those common torturers that bring all wit to the rack; whose noses are ever like swine spoiling and rooting up the Muses' gardens, and their whole bodies, like moles, as blindly working under earth to cast any—the least—hills upon virtue'. The prefatory verses of Hugh Holland and of ΦΙΛΟΣ make the same point. See ll. 9–14 of the former and ll. 10–14 of the latter.

It is impossible to establish beyond all doubt that in *Sejanus* Jonson intentionally presented any historical analogies for specific contemporary political events or realities. It would seem, however, that he was perceived by Northampton to be doing just that. Northampton's action against Jonson only begins to make sense when considered in relation to what is known about the date of the first production of the play, and in the context of an event of late 1603 in which Northampton figures as one of the principals. Briefly, the action against Jonson is unlikely to have had anything to do with a resemblance between the theme of *Sejanus* and the Essex rebellion, which was not a burning issue when the play was first produced. It is far more likely that Northampton made a connection between *Sejanus*, much of which is about treason trials, and the big treason trials of 1603—particularly the trial of Ralegh. Ralegh was on good terms with Jonson some years later, since we know that Jonson contributed material toward Ralegh's *History of the World*, and that in 1612–13 he was travelling abroad as tutor to Ralegh's son. It is not known when Jonson's relations with Ralegh began. Northampton, Jonson's 'mortall enimie', was, with Sir Robert Cecil, the chief force bringing about Ralegh's downfall in 1602–3. In the play, the trial of the great military commander Caius Silius is especially interesting in this regard. The trial of Ralegh took place only weeks before the probable time of the first production of *Sejanus*. In short, it is highly likely that Northampton thought the play in part a comment on the trial of Ralegh and for that reason brought Jonson before the Council.

The downfall of Sir Walter Ralegh was the most significant political event in which Northampton was involved as a principal in 1603. It is

sufficient here to quote a few lines from the relevant section of the
D.N.B. article on Henry Howard, Earl of Northampton:

> After [Essex's] execution he took part with Cecil in a long secret correspon-
> dence with James of Scotland. Howard's letters of advice to the king are long
> and obscure. James called them 'Asiatic and endless volumes'. Following
> Essex's example he tried to poison James's mind against his personal
> enemies, chief among whom were Henry Brooke, eighth lord Cobham, and
> Sir Walter Raleigh. In letters written to Cecil he made no secret of his
> intention, when opportunity offered, of snaring his rivals into some
> questionable negotiation with Spain which might be made the foundation of
> a charge of treason. . . .
>
>   Northampton took an active part in political business, and exhibited in
> all his actions a stupendous want of principle. He was a commissioner for
> the trial of his personal enemies Sir Walter Raleigh and Lord Cobham in
> 1603. . . . [40]

Ralegh was imprisoned in the Tower on 17 July 1603, on suspicion of
conspiring with Lord Cobham and Count Aremberg, the ambassador
from the Archduke of Austria, to replace James I with Arabella Stuart.
After an imprisonment of four months he was tried at Winchester on
17 November by a commission which numbered among its members
the man who had done most to compass his downfall. Ralegh defended
himself with wit and skill in the face of ugly provocation on the part of
the prosecutor, Sir Edward Coke. A large assembly of interested on-
lookers witnessed the trial. Despite a conspicuous lack of clear evidence, Ralegh was found guilty of conspiring, in the cause of Spain, to
kill James and of taking Spanish bribes.

This trial was the great sensation of late 1603, when Jonson was
completing *Sejanus*. In the words of a modern historian, 'It excited
the highest possible degree of interest at the time, all the actors in it
acted from the strongest possible motives, and the anonymous persons
to whom we owe the reports of the trial no doubt appreciated the
importance of the occasion.'[41] Samuel R. Gardiner, in the first of his
ten volumes on the history of England from 1603 to 1642, saw it as
marking an important turning point: 'If Ralegh's trial is remarkable
for the distinct enunciation by the judges of the harsh principles
which were then in repute amongst lawyers, it is equally worthy of
memory, as giving the first signal of the reaction which from that
moment steadily set in in favour of the rights of individuals against the
State. Many a man, who came to gloat over the conviction of a traitor,
went away prepared to sympathize with the prisoner who had defended
himself so well against the brutal invectives of Coke.'[42] The verdict of

modern legal historians on the trial is unambiguous: 'Ralegh was unjustly and wickedly convicted by the highest officers of the State exercising their most solemn functions. Of the many men who have been unjustly convicted he was perhaps the most illustrious.' The trial 'was a tragedy for all concerned; it is a disgrace to English law. But it has always served as a warning of what is to be avoided.'[43]

Depending on whether Northampton intervened after the Court or the Globe performance, the gap between the trial of Ralegh and that intervention would have been anything from two to five months. As Henslowe's diary makes clear, many plays were written in a matter of weeks, and Northampton would have had no reason to know that Jonson had been labouring over his scholarly piece for a year or two. What would have struck anyone who had taken the least interest in political events during 1603 and saw the Court production of *Sejanus* is the remarkable circumstance of a play about treasons and treason trials appearing at the end of a year of treason trials, the most sensational being that of Ralegh only weeks earlier.

However, for those with suspicious minds who would, in Hugh Holland's words, 'make our author wiser than he is' and see, as ΦΙΛΟΣ tells us they did, 'later times . . . in some speech enweaved', the obvious general analogy becomes specific in the trial of Caius Silius in Act III. Silius, like Ralegh, is a military commander on trial for conspiracy and treasonous dealings with the very enemy he had long been fighting. Throughout the relevant section of *Q* we have, of course, Jonson's scholarly marginal notes reminding us of his 'integrity in the story'—and immediately after the trial of Silius we have Cremutius Cordus, the historian accused of shadowing present times in his treatment of past times, insisting on the integrity of his presentation of history. Nevertheless, if there were any who knew their Tacitus among those determined to 'make our author wiser than he is', their suspicions would not have been allayed by noticing that the Silius of the play is a character in the mould of Ralegh and developed far beyond the Silius of Tacitus, who is not given distinct personal characteristics.[44] All that Tacitus tells us of Silius's behaviour during the trial is that he was at first very quiet, but later indicated 'whose malevolence was ruining him'. The principal characteristics that Jonson gives to Silius are impatience (III.167–8), scorn (III.176), a reputation for excessive drinking (III.270–1), a short temper (III.271), and boastfulness (III.272–6) (the last also mentioned by Tacitus)—all well-known ingredients of Ralegh's unrestrained individualism. To his enemies Silius seems 'insolent' and 'impious' (III.239–40). The spirited defence he conducts owes nothing to Tacitus. It does, however, have much in common with Ralegh's conduct of his own defence.

Before examining the parallels between the trial of Ralegh and that of Silius in *Sejanus*, it should be pointed out that there are certain non-correspondences—indeed there had to be, unless Jonson were to change the facts of Tacitus's *Annals*, and of course he prides himself, through his marginal notes, on his general fidelity to his sources. Thus Silius must commit suicide, whereas Ralegh ended his defence with a plea for mercy. In Tacitus and Jonson, Silius is confronted by his accuser, Varro, whereas Ralegh repeatedly and unsuccessfully asked for his chief accuser, Lord Cobham, to be brought into court to testify in person. The interesting point here, however, is that Varro is simply an accuser and not a witness to anything—Jonson's Silius complains that he is being condemned on mere affirmation (III.285) and circumstance (III.296), just as Ralegh complained that 'you try me by the Spanish inquisition, if you proceed only by the circumstances, without two witnesses'.[45] The correspondence is more significant than the non-correspondence. A merely apparent non-correspondence is that, whereas Ralegh stoutly maintained his innocence, Jonson's Silius seems to accept his guilt when he admits that he said that Tiberius and Rome owed their greatness to him, denouncing Tiberius for ingratitude (III.295–305). In fact this was not the original charge at all, just something thrown in as an afterthought by Afer. The charge was that Silius deliberately started and prolonged the war against Sacrovir to create fame and fortune for himself and his wife (III.179–90)—and Silius never admits to this.

The parallels between the trials are both general and specific. Both Ralegh and Silius conduct their own defences against charges of treason—in Ralegh's case because one accused of treason was not entitled to benefit of counsel.[46] Ralegh repeatedly pointed to the lack of non-circumstantial evidence, with interjections like 'prove one of these things wherewith you have charged me, and I will confess the whole indictment', 'your phrases will not prove it', 'let it be proved', 'urge your proofs'. In response Coke could only adduce circumstantial evidence.[47] In the play, Silius throws the countercharge at Varro, 'Thou liest', in response to the charge that Silius has 'been a traitor to the state' (III.190), and though Varro promises to produce tangible proof of treason, the evidence is mere hearsay. Ralegh questioned the procedures of the court, likening them to those of the Inquisition,[48] repeatedly appealing to English law: 'By the statute, civil law, and God's word, it be required, that there must be two witnesses at the least'; 'if those laws be repealed, yet I hope the equity of those laws remains still'; 'the proof of the common law is by witness and jury'; 'the common trial of England is by jury and witnesses'; 'but now, by the wisdom of the state, the wisdom of the law is uncertain'; and so on.[49] Jonson's Silius is equally insistent on the law's being observed, responding to Afer's 'He shall have justice' with 'Nay, I shall have law' (III.221)—an exchange that seems to echo, in reverse sequence, this exchange in the Ralegh trial: '*Ralegh.* O, my lord! you may use equity. *Lord chief justice.* That is from the king; you are to have justice from us'.[50] Ralegh complained to the prosecution that 'you have not proved any one thing by direct proofs, but all by circumstances.... False repetitions and mistakings must not mar my cause',[51] while Jonson's Silius complains of

> Furious enforcing, most unjust presuming,
> Malicious and manifold applying,
> Foul wresting, and impossible construction.   (III.227–9)

The general tone and substance of these complaints are almost identical, the 'unjust presuming', incidentally, reminding one of Ralegh's remarks on presumptions: 'Presumptions must proceed from precedent or subsequent facts.... If you would be contented, on presumptions, to be delivered up to be slaughtered, ... if you would be contented to be so judged, judge so of me.'[52] Especially striking is the fact that in *Sejanus* (but not in Tacitus) the accusation of impiety is hurled against Silius (III.240). During Ralegh's trial the Lord Chief Justice made a great point of upbraiding him for his notorious impiety: 'You have been taxed by the world with the defence of most heathenish and blasphemous opinions, which I list not to repeat, because Christian ears cannot endure to hear them, nor the authors and maintainers of them be suffered to live in any Christian commonwealth.'[53] Silius's citing of his many military services to his Prince and country (III.253–65) could, with a few changes of proper names, be Ralegh's, and they remind one of Ralegh's comments, during his trial, on how peculiar it is that he, who had done so much to thwart Spain over the years, should now be seen as Spain's agent.[54] Each sees his trial as a mere contrivance on the part of malicious enemies—in Ralegh's view it is obvious that the law is being manipulated in such a manner that 'if this may be, you will have any man's life in a week',[55] and the following lines of Silius capture perfectly Ralegh's view of his own plight:

This boast of law, and law, is but a form,
A net of Vulcan's filing, a mere engine,
To take that life by a pretext of justice
Which you pursue in malice.   (III.244–7)

Without questioning Jonson's general 'integrity in the story', one can easily see reasons why some of his contemporaries questioned it, especially in regard to this scene. Northampton, deeply and personally involved in the downfall of Ralegh, had particular cause to be suspicious of any play on the subject of treason trials appearing weeks after Ralegh's trial. Whether or not he knew Jonson to be a Catholic,[56] he could claim that *Sejanus*, in its perceived support of Ralegh, was not only treasonable but 'popish', since the charges against Ralegh were 'that he did conspire, and go about to deprive the king of his government, to raise up sedition within the realm, to alter religion, to bring in the Roman superstition, and to procure foreign enemies to invade the kingdom'.[57] That there are no 'popish' allusions in *Sejanus* is immaterial: the play, as Northampton perceived it, lent support to a popish treason, and for that reason its author could be 'accused both of popperie and treason'. Jonson, more successful in this respect than his character Cremutius Cordus, obviously persuaded the Council of his 'integrity', since the play, albeit in changed form, appeared in print in 1605. The text was buttressed by the scholarly notes, its author's 'proof' against people like Northampton and others of 'those common torturers that bring all wit to the rack', and preceded by prefatory matter by Jonson's friends, including, ironically but tellingly, praise of his 'mortall enimie' Northampton.[58] Yet its subject being what it is, the play as we have it still contains, if not many 'offensive' lines, quite enough material to indicate the reasons behind Northampton's calling of Jonson before the Council. The three or four specifically 'offensive' lines on the ingratitude of princes, quoted above, were printed in *Q*, only to be changed in 1616. Not surprisingly, they come from the lips of Caius Silius, during his trial on a trumped-up charge of treason.

5. CRITICAL ASSESSMENT

In spite of its initial failure on the public stage, *Sejanus* was highly esteemed among Jonson's friends and seventeenth-century admirers. William Fennor noted in 1616 the gulf between 'the multitude' who 'screw'd their scurvy jaws and lookt awry, / Like hissing snakes,

adjudging it to die', and 'wits of gentry' who 'did applaud the same, /
With silver shouts of high loud-sounding fame'.[59] During the period
to 1642 the play received high praise from many besides those who
composed the commendatory verses for the quarto. They included R.
Goodwin, Lucius Carey (Viscount Falkland), James Howell, John
Taylor, and Owen Felltham,[60] but a host of flattering references can
be found scattered through the pages of the *Jonson Allusion Book*.[61]
The number of borrowings from *Sejanus* in the works of seventeenth-
century dramatists is further testimony to the high regard in which
the play was held.[62]

During the Restoration period *Sejanus* received rather more inten-
sive—and more balanced—critical attention, principally from Dryden. Although he thought 'the Scene betwixt *Livia* and the Physician,
which is a pleasant Satyre upon the artificial helps of beauty', sat ill in
its tragic context (apparently he was unmoved by the masterful coun-
terpointing of the dispassionate language used in reference to murder
with the vocabulary of cosmetics and the frivolities of love), he praised
Jonson's classical restraint in relating rather than representing the
death of Sejanus.[63] He also praised the borrowings from classical
authors: Jonson 'invades Authours like a Monarch, and what would
be theft in other Poets, is onely victory in him. With the spoils of
these Writers he so represents old Rome to us, in its Rites, Ceremonies and Customs, that if one of their Poets had written either of
his Tragedies, we had seen less of it then in him'. The poetry, Dryden
felt, suffered from Jonson's 'a little too much Romaniz[ing] our
tongue, leaving the words which he translated almost as much Latine
as he found them'—an observation that misses the point of the
literalness of translation in *Sejanus*, namely, the achievement in
language of that same tangible Romanness Dryden identified in the
fidelity to 'Rites, Ceremonies and Customs'. A more serious criticism,
one that was to be made with increasing insistence as time passed, also
dates from the Restoration: Edward Phillips's charge that *Sejanus* and
Catiline lack 'a pathetical and naturally Tragic height'.[64] It is no good
arguing in response that *Sejanus* is a history play—in his address 'To
the Readers' Jonson claims to have discharged the 'offices of a tragic
writer'. The critics are severe in this regard. Samuel Johnson, quoting
Young in his 'Life of Young', argued that 'Jonson . . . was very learned, as Sampson was very strong, to his own hurt. Blind to the nature
of tragedy, he pulled down all antiquity on his head, and buried himself under it'.[65] Swinburne thought that 'The power of his verse and
the purity of his English are nowhere more remarkable than in his two

Roman tragedies: on the other hand, his great fault or defect as a dramatist is nowhere more perceptible.... It is want of sympathy; a lack of cordial interest'; 'not one of these scenes can excite the least touch, the least phantom, the least shadow of pity or terror'.[66] G. Gregory Smith saw it as 'an indifferent defence of him to say that, whereas Shakespeare in his Roman plays is concerned with the interpretation or creation of character, his purpose is to recover the life and setting of the ancient city.... We miss the transmutation of the scholar's dross into the gold of tragic passion. There is small opportunity for "pity and terror" in a panorama.'[67] More recently John Palmer has complained that 'always we remain aloof from the passions of the play', we never 'fear for [Sejanus] or pity him or even rejoice in the discomfiture of a bad man. We merely realize that in two moves or three checkmate is threatened'; nothing in Jonson's play 'could make up for the lack in him of tragic passion'.[68]

It is possible to defend the play against these charges by pointing out that their authors make, to bend a term from Gilbert Ryle, a category-mistake—the allocation of a concept, in this case an Aristotelian concept, to a category to which it does not belong. The play is a social tragedy on the themes of decadence, luxury, and the sacrifice of civic pride and civic virtue to selfish ambition. The tragic 'protagonist' is the city of Rome, a people fallen from an older, peculiarly Roman, virtue. In this view of things, the senate and people richly deserve their Tiberius, their Sejanus, their Macro, and over-throwing one or two individuals would solve none of Rome's problems. The fault, which is essentially spiritual, lies deep within the social fabric and has to do with luxury and cosmopolitan influences (see below, p. 31). The stoicism of the Germanicans is a realistic response to a state of affairs incurable by the exercise of a merely individual or sporadic valour. Central to this view are the speeches of Silius ('Well, all is worthy of us, ...', I.56–70) and Jonson's chief satiric voice in the play, Arruntius ('Times? The men, / The men are not the same', I.86–104). What bears them out in this, more than anything else, is the behaviour of the *Senatus Populusque Romanus* in the play's catas-trophe. An Aristotelian concept of the tragic hero—say, nobility undermined by ambition—is inapplicable to this play and not to be looked for, since Sejanus is merely an ignoble symptom of an incur-able social malaise.[69]

If we look at the play in this way, we begin to see it as a distinct type of English Renaissance tragedy, more akin than Shakespeare's to the spirit of the Renaissance in its concern for history, politics, and

civic virtue (though it will be argued later that its concern for history
is not quite that of the historian), in its affirmation that a character's
rhetoric is a measure of his moral nature (hyperbole comes naturally
to Sejanus), and in its demonstration that the classes of poet, intellectual, and scholar overlap.[70]

Once we have accepted *Sejanus* for what it is instead of criticising it
for what it is not, we are in a position to pay a less grudging tribute to
those qualities that give it dramatic power and poetic force. Chief
among these is its language, economical, like that of Tacitus, essentially plain, anti-Ciceronian, capable of conveying the rhythms of
everyday speech (though its syntax can be very Latinate: 'We not
endure these flatteries', I.375), while at the same time elevated, full of
that 'gravity and height of elocution' Jonson speaks of in the address
'To the Readers'. Its patrician restraint, however, is not always secure
and can give way to the very passions it might appear to block:
'Tyrants' arts / Are to give flatterers grace, accusers power, / That
those may seem to kill whom they devour' (I.70–2). In such apparently objective observations, metaphors like 'devour' create a dramat-
ically effective tension between intensity of feeling and restraint of
language. The restraint can collapse completely, as it frequently does
in the impatience of Arruntius:

> Death! I dare tell him so, and all his spies:
> *He turns to Sejanus's clients.*
> You, sir, I would, do you look? And you!   (I.259–60)

It is no accident that many of the play's most original and striking
metaphors, often animalistic, are found in the emotional outbursts of
Arruntius, metaphor being (as Thomas Spratt recognised) essentially
unreasonable:

> Gods! How the sponges open, and take in!
> And shut again! Look, look! Is not he blest
> That gets a seat in eye-reach of him? More,
> That comes in ear- or tongue-reach? O, but most,
> Can claw his subtle elbow, or with a buzz
> Flyblow his ears.   (V.506–11)

To a considerable extent, of course, Arruntius speaks for Jonson in
the play, and it is therefore not at all surprising that in his less self-
contained moments he sounds more like a voice from the complaint
tradition of English literature than a Roman. (In fact so insistent is
this voice of complaint that one begins to wish, with some recent

critics, that he would either act like a stoic and shut up, or actually do
something.) The important point, however, is that the play's short,
often abrupt periods can be matched to the short-tempered, passionate
Arruntius just as easily as to the calculating Tiberius, whose cautious,
deliberating mind we trace as it proceeds through interior monologue
from this side of a question to that, from first to second thoughts, then
back again:

> To marry Livia? Will no less, Sejanus,
> Content thy aims? No lower object? Well!
> Thou knowst how thou art wrought into our trust,
> Woven in our design; and thinkst we must
> Now use thee, whatsoe'er thy projects are.
> 'Tis true. But yet with caution, and fit care.
> And, now we better think—Who's there, within?   (III.623–9)

Although our sympathy may not be engaged in a soliloquy like that,
we are certainly made privy to the reflective processes of the man's
mind. A few lines later, an idea occurs to Tiberius:

> 'Tis thought—Is Macro in the palace? See.
> If not, go seek him, to come to us. [*Exit* SERVUS.]
>   He
> Must be the organ we must work by now,
> Though none less apt for trust. Need doth allow
> What choice would not. I'have heard that aconite,
> Being timely taken, hath a healing might
> Against the scorpion's stroke. The proof we'll give—
> That, while two poisons wrestle, we may live.   (III.647–54)

The 'thought' of l. 647 might seem to have been lost, but it continues
to work away beneath the surface, re-emerging in the aconite analogy.
Such passages, so perfect in their mimicry of thinking, merit high
praise. And because Jonson is offering a forensic analysis of a diseased
society, this same deliberate and precise language provides, in the
lines of the Germanicans, as ideal a vehicle for satire as for insights
into minds. It is not, however, the sort of language an impatient
audience is going to savour.[71]

    This language is at the service of a particularly fine dramatic sense
in three outstanding scenes. Nothing in Jonson's works surpasses in
intensity of moral vision the writing in the conversation of Livia and
Eudemus in the second Act. There were earlier critics like Dryden
who thought it an improper comic imposition on the tragic plot, but it
has long been recognised as a masterpiece of satiric invention. As

Eudemus assists Livia in the application of her cosmetics, their discussion of the efficacy of this ceruse, that oil, that fucus, this pomatum, proceeds concurrently with light and pleasant references to the virtues of Sejanus, the delights of new love, and the minor details of murder, punctuated here and there by the small anxieties of the lady ('How do I look today?', 'Methinks 'tis here not white'). Death is reduced to the service of sexual gratification and female vanity. The scene is important to Jonson's purposes, for it offers a distillation of that extensive moral decadence the play everywhere points up.

The two other outstanding scenes—the interview between Sejanus and Tiberius in the third Act, and the final Senate scene—are essentially Tiberius's, though in one of them he is not physically present. Each is original. In Tacitus it is in a letter, not an interview, that Tiberius refuses Sejanus's request to marry into the family—his 'tragic error'. In changing it into a direct confrontation, Jonson's dramatic instincts were perfectly correct. No other English dramatist turns the fate of his protagonist so economically upon so little as does Jonson here: in Tiberius's 'H'mh?' (III.515) *hubris* gets its subtlest come-uppance in one of the most effective scenes of dramatic irony in the language. A few lines later, left alone on stage, Sejanus is so wrong about Tiberius and blind to his own already-sealed fate that he can call his emperor 'dull' and 'heavy'. In the second Senate scene, the sources' sketchy references to Tiberius's letter (see V.545–659n.) are worked up by Jonson into a consummate exercise in the generation of suspense by remote control. To watch that control as it effectively rearranges the seating preferences of the senators, traps the protagonist in a web of equivocation, suggestion, and manipulation, and finally turns the madness of the Roman mob on, then off, is a pleasure the majority of Jonson's original public audience apparently chose to deny themselves. By that stage it is likely they had already hissed the play off the stage or were no longer listening. The play's distinguishing qualities of language and dramatic invention, evident especially in these scenes, were either too subtle or insufficient in themselves for the crowd's appreciation. Even in Renaissance England the classicists and connoisseurs could not by themselves compose a theatre audience any more than they could today (even William Poel's 1928 production—see below—was a one-night affair). For that reason, the play (at least in uncut form) is probably best represented not on a stage but in the theatre of the mind to which the 1605 quarto so attractively invites us.

It must finally be acknowledged, however, that even on its own terms *Sejanus* is a radically flawed masterpiece, one which leaves the

most fundamental questions unanswered and unanswerable. What is
to be our attitude to the obviously real and living goddess Fortune?
The difficulty here has already been touched on in an earlier section of
this introduction. It crucially affects one's view of Sejanus, for while
on the one hand the play is so insistent that our faults lie not in our
stars but in ourselves, on the other it cautions us (in the final lines of
Terentius) not to blaspheme or underestimate the powers of the gods,
who for our impiety will hurl us down from our proud pedestals
without a moment's hesitation (V.908–13). Jonas Barish first pointed
to this irresolvable problem. *Sejanus*, he claimed, 'tries to argue us
simultaneously into a belief that we are free, which we see not to be
the case, and that the gods are near, which we see equally to be not the
case'.[72] For Barish, the evidence against what Jonson was arguing
came from outside the play—from what we ourselves know. But it is
also built into *Sejanus* itself, which offers conflicting answers to such
questions. The play demonstrates to us that Sejanus falls through his
own pride, ambition, and especially imprudence—and then insists,
in the last lines of Arruntius, that the real crimes are Fortune's
(V.901–3) who, Lepidus tells us in his last lines, 'plies her sports,
when she begins / To practise 'em! Pursues, continues, adds! /
Confounds, with varying her impassioned moods!' (V.898–900).
What we are finally left with in Terentius's closing observations is the
pious contradiction of everything the play has shown us about the all-
too-human causes of a social tragedy and the fall of its towering
product.

6. JONSON'S WAY WITH ROMAN HISTORY[73]

It has been a critical commonplace that in *Sejanus* (as in *Catiline*)
Jonson assumes the dual offices of poet and historian. In affirming the
supreme importance of 'truth of Argument',[74] we are told, he took
upon himself the functions of the historian, offering in these plays 'a
great poet's illumination of two important segments of Roman history'.[75] So extensive, detailed and precise is Jonson's scholarship that
most readers who approach *Sejanus* require 'diligent preparation for
the experience'—only in this way (the argument goes) can we, like the
learned historians Camden, Speed, and Selden, whose friendship and
esteem Jonson sought and enjoyed, properly appreciate the fidelity to
historical truth the play manifests.[76] Certain minor qualifications are
admitted: careful attention has been paid to the ways in which the
dramatist deliberately introduced subtle and not so subtle changes

into the historical narrative, enhancing dramatic effectiveness.[77] 'With
few and trifling exceptions', however, 'the plot of Sejanus is built with
severe conformity to the historical record.'[78] Jonson may have put
aside the historian's recognition of the complexities of human nature
by radically simplifying the complex and tortured personality of
Tacitus's Tiberius into the scheming Machiavellian tyrant of Sejanus[79]
(and he would later simplify Catiline in a like manner).[80] But this, it is
implied, is simply a question of characterisation and takes nothing
away from the claim that Sejanus (and Catiline) everywhere reveal
'their concern for Roman history, their careful and rational buttres-
sing with historical fact'.[81] It is taken as self-evident that, in the words
of Jonas Barish, to the writing of Sejanus 'Jonson brought a scholar's
command of the historical materials, and a scholar's conscience in
dealing with them', so that the play 'constitutes in itself a piece of
historiography. It offers something like an archeological reconstruc-
tion of the epoch it deals with, and a fully worked out interpretation of
its subject, arrived at through a consideration of all relevant evidence',
it marries 'moral truth' to 'historical truth', and it shows Jonson
'fulfilling the offices of historian and poet simultaneously'.[82]

This generally-held assumption that the Roman plays everywhere
reveal a 'concern for Roman history' emerging out of a 'consideration
of all relevant evidence' is in need of severe qualification. In important
ways, Jonson displays very little interest in or concern for the larger
processes of Roman history in the periods his Roman plays animate.
One has only to ask a few pertinent questions about Jonson the
historian's treatment of Roman history to become aware that they are
somehow not the right questions. What is Jonson's position in these
plays on the respective claims of the senatorial oligarchy and the
populares (populist and reforming leaders like Marius and Julius
Caesar who in many ways prefigure the emperors)? If Jonson is a
Pompeian—as Sejanus shows he is—then is it not logical to expect
him to be more sympathetic in Catiline towards Sulla? Both were, in
different ways, defenders of the oligarchy and generally on the side of
the Senate. What were the underlying causes of the Catilinarian conspiracy? Is there not some disproportion in Jonson's offering us in
Sejanus the myth of a divine Augustus Caesar and a demonic Julius
Caesar? Does Jonson in Sejanus accept the Roman Revolution of
Augustus, and if so, with what reservations? If it was noble and
valiant of 'the constant Brutus' to 'strike / So brave a blow into the
monster's heart' (Sejanus, I.93–5), can we find reasons in Jonson's
Sejanus for the dramatist's refusal to endorse such an action if it were

to be carried out against the monster Tiberius?—or is this an un-
accountable inconsistency? If each play had offered us 'a fully worked
out interpretation of its subjects, arrived at through a consideration of
all relevant evidence', we might expect answers to such questions. In
fact, though they are certainly historical questions, to none of them
can any historically respectable answer be found in either *Sejanus* or
Catiline.

Jonson's classical scholarship issues in meticulously transcribed
and translated passages of Sallust, Tacitus, and the rest, and is at its
best in the recreation of the 'accidentals' of Roman history—the
minutiae of topography, customs, religion, the formulae of senatorial
procedure—all resulting in a great deal of Roman 'atmosphere'. The
texts of historians, the phrases of orations and the echoes of the lines
of a wide range of poets and philosophers, familiar to many in
Jonson's audience from their labours at school, are brought to life and
the impression created that the dramatic poet Jonson is not only a fine
classical scholar but a fine historian to boot, offering a more convincing re-creation of the Roman world than Shakespeare, with his 'small
Latin and less Greek', could ever have hoped to do. The truth,
however, is that to the materials of history he has so carefully sifted
and assembled Jonson brings not the subtly discriminating mind of a
historian but that same critical, simplifying eye of the moralist that
critics have detected in his handling of the central 'tragic' characters,
particularly Tiberius and Sejanus. His Roman plays may be 'archeol-
ogically' unexceptionable, but in the final analysis they are not, by
Roman or for that matter Elizabethan standards, good history. If
one's interest is in the general causes of Rome's moral decline these
tragedies will satisfy it, but neither *Sejanus* nor *Catiline* will cater for a
fascination with the play of complex historical forces and personalities.
It will be better to go to *Coriolanus*, *Antony and Cleopatra*, *Julius
Caesar*, or even to Thomas Lodge's *Wounds of Civil War*.

Any inquiry into the ways in which Jonson does characterise late-
Republican and early-Imperial history should compare his views at
certain points with the views of Elizabethan historians of Rome, and
pay particular attention to his 'position', especially as it is evident in
Sejanus, on the decline and death of the Republic. My focus here is
not upon the central dramatic characters of Catiline, Cicero, Tiberius
and Sejanus, since there is some critical agreement that in his characterisation of them Jonson at least modified the historical record, but
upon the wider historical contexts and historial personalities to whom
reference is made. By examining these we can clarify the nature of

Jonson's 'historiography'. For purposes of historico-chronological sense the Roman plays may be treated as though they were two parts of a sustained approach to Roman history—a justifiable procedure, since they embrace, in their subjects and their references to events beyond those subjects, Roman history from the Gracchi to Caligula.

Jonson, in common with historians since Polybius, traces the causes of the Republic's sickness to the second century B.C. and the increasing wealth and openness to outside (particularly Greek) influences that followed success in the Second Punic War. This process was accelerated in the first century B.C. and it constitutes the theme of the Chorus that closes the first Act of *Catiline* ('Can nothing great, and at the height / Remaine so long? ...'). It is on this theme that Jonson is most comfortable in the role of historian. Poverty made virtue before, but now Rome 'doth joy / So much in plentie, wealth, and ease, / As, now, th'excesse is her disease' (*Catiline* I.548–50). Wealth has corrupted her women (*Catiline* I.555–9) and her men (*Catiline* I.560–4). Their tastes are now unnatural (*Catiline*, I.563–4) and only novelties are in demand (*Catiline*, I.569–81). Rome has become 'her owne spoiler, and owne prey' (*Catiline*, I.586), and having conquered Asia, she finds herself conquered by Asia's vices (*Catline*, I.587–90)—and, it is implied, by the similar ones of Greece. Jonson is at one with Cato the Censor: outside influences are generally harmful. There are good things to be had from Greece (Cicero 'suck'd at *Athens*', *Catiline*, II.137), but the stress in on the bad things like 'licence' and 'lust' (*Sejanus*, III.442–3). Graecinus Laco, whose name suggests his Greek background (Lat. *Graecus*, a Greek) is even less trustworthy than the treacherous 'Greek Sinon' (*Sejanus*, IV.360), with whom he is compared. In his tastes, Tiberius, who is fond of dropping phrases in Greek (II.330), rejects Rome, preferring to spend his time on Rhodes or Capreae, surrounding himself with his 'rout' of Chaldeans. It is not only the East that provides the undesirable immigrant. Domitius Afer the orator, one of the least savoury characters in *Sejanus*, is, like Laco, given away by his name: historically, he came from Nemausus in Narbonensian Gaul, but Jonson suspects an African connection and has Arruntius call Afer 'the crocodile of Tiber' (II.424), an apt pun on his name (which means African) since crocodiles come from Africa. Already by Cicero's time we find '*Romes* faultes' 'now growne her Fate' (*Catiline*, III.847), and Tiberius and Sejanus represent a part of Rome's punishment for those faults, of which the worst is ambition (*Catiline*, III.860–71).

Central to the demise of the Republic are the Gracchi and the Civil

War. Jonson's attitude to the Gracchi accords with that of Elizabethan historians only because the historians choose unanimously in this instance not to present a balanced argument. They do this, in the face of the far more balanced discussions of the Gracchi by Plutarch and other early historians, because to them, as good Elizabethans, the attempted reforms of Tiberius and Caius Gracchus are seditious in their substance, particularly land reform. Jonson endorses this conservative view of them, presumably because it is politically germane to him and accords with his clear-cut ethical approach to history. However, in *Catiline*, the dead Gracchi inhabit the same hell as Sulla, Cinna, and Marius—an infernal co-existence of political enemies.

In regard to the period following the death of Caius Gracchus Jonson clearly parts company with the historians, who on subsequent events and personalities (Catiline excepted) generally prefer the complexity of historical cause-and-effect to the poet's morally-instructive simplification—in Sidney's words, the historian's 'what is' to the poet's 'what should be'.[83] They know that 'to acknowledge the vertues of the vicious, is such a right, that what *Historian* willingly omitteth them, therin becommeth vicious himselfe'.[84] All historians, for example, acknowledge Sulla's enigmatic character. In the Elizabethan histories of Rome one finds a diversity of views on him, none of them simply condemnatory. In N. Haward's translation of Eutropius we learn that he 'appeased and sette in order the weal publique'.[85] William Fulbecke argues that Sulla's 'medicine was worse than the maladie it selfe',[86] but the responsibility for the first civil war belongs primarily with Marius. In fact Sulla provides 'an example of a double and diuerse mind in one man'—merciful in war, cruel in peace, a man of 'vexed soul' who lacked 'true felicitie'.[87] Jonson, on the other hand is not interested in the political causes and consequences of the civil war within the 'political' framework of his plays because the points of reference are historical only in so far as they relate to moral decline. The idea, expressed in Tacitus, that Caligula could have 'all the vices of Sulla with none of the Sullan virtues'[88] is incomprehensible in the contexts of *Sejanus* and *Catiline*, for Jonson's Sulla, like Marius, Cinna, and the Gracchi, has no virtues, only vices, while Jonson's Caligula escapes serious censure. Jonson's Sulla, historically pro-Senatorial, encourages a Catiline who intends the liquidation of the Senate! Jonson could elsewhere echo Plutarch's praise of the Sulla who 'inforced frugality by the Lawes',[89] but the Sulla of *Catiline* who introduces us to his protégé is not out of Plutarch but the morality tradition. Like Marlowe's Barabas, he is a Vice figure. Had there not been such critical unanimity about Jonson's adoption of the 'office of historian' in these plays, it would hardly have been necessary to make the point. Unlike Jonson, Thomas Lodge, in dealing with the same period in *The Wounds of Civil War* (c. 1588), shows some interest in the policies of the opposing sides and gives us all the historical points of reference.[90]

By contrast with his mentor Sulla, Gnaeus Pompey, whose high-handedness in regard to the Senate he was supposed to be serving effectively demolished much of Sulla's work in shoring up the Senatorial authority against consuls-turned-*imperatores*, emerges from Jonson's plays, especially *Sejanus*, as a paragon of Republican virtue. Jonson, it would seem, is a Pompeian because Pompey supported the Senate (without indulging in Sulla's scale of bloodletting) in opposition to Caesar who, like Crassus, is a seditious *popularis*. In *Sejanus*, Pompey, seventy years dead, still has followers: the Germanicans bemoan the fact that Pompey's theatre has been defiled by the setting up within it of a statue of Sejanus, and the historian Cremutius Cordus is, like Livy, a Pompeian, though one would hope a more balanced one than Jonson.

In his presentation of the Senate's most dangerous enemy, Julius Caesar, Jonson shows little interest in him as a representative of a political or philosophical tendency. His Caesar is a Machiavellian cynic who can derisively refer to Cicero as one of the 'popular men' as if he were not one himself (*Catiline*, III.93–8). In *Sejanus* he is a 'monster' (I.95), albeit a 'spirited' one (I.151). The best that Jonson can say for Caesar in these plays is said by the Pompeian Cremutius Cordus in *Sejanus*: Caesar chose not to punish Cicero for his *Cato* but to reply in kind with his *Anticato* (III.427–30). Brutus was entirely in the right in his conspiracy, if Arruntius speaks for Jonson, for 'the constant Brutus'

> (being proof
> Against all charm of benefits) did strike
> So brave a blow into the monster's heart
> That sought unkindly to captive his country.   (I.93–6)

Cordus, in referring to Brutus and Cassius as 'the last of the Romans', underlines the point.[91]

There is no single 'position' on Caesar adopted in Elizabethan histories of Rome. He is a complex figure and the historians (pro- or con-) treat him as such.[92] The Caesar of Jonson's Roman plays, however, is little more than an emblem of tyranny held, like the main characters in these works, in the frame of a distorting 'mirror for magistrates' in which the subtle images of history are transformed into the starkest of contrasts.

From it, the picture of Augustus emerges as Caesar's antithesis. This might be expected, given the uncritical view of him already presented in *Poetaster* two years before *Sejanus* appeared, and considering the generally favourable view Elizabethan historians take of Augustus.[93] That is not to say there were no demurrers: Fulbecke argues that had Julius Caesar not been assassinated, 'though there had bene a Caesar, yet should there neuer haue bene an Augustus', without whom the Republic might still have been preserved.[94] What is so interesting about the Augustus Jonson evokes in *Sejanus* is that his system, which Tiberius has inherited, was, it is implied, made permanent by being founded in a social contract whose theoretical basis is Elizabethan rather than Roman. As Jonson sees it, Augustus changed the old constitution, in effect dissolved in civil war, with the blessing of the Roman people, and in such a way that the kind of action Brutus took against Caesar is no longer justifiable against a Tiberius. The rules have been permanently changed. Under the Republic, supreme authority rested with the Senate, and it might be argued that Brutus simply defended it against Caesar's attempt to usurp its authority; under the Principate, however, final authority rests with the *princeps*, whose *tribunicia potestas* effectively makes him supreme. The Germanicans recognise this: Republican in their sympathies, they accept nevertheless that they live under a different and properly constituted dispensation emerging out of, and finally putting to an end, a state of civil war. The 'old liberty' has been lost for good. The crucial lines are Sabinus's:

> A good man should and must
> Sit rather down with loss, than rise unjust—
> Though, when the Romans first did yield themselves
> To one man's power, they did not mean their lives,
> Their fortunes, and their liberties should be
> His absolute spoil, as purchased by the sword.   (IV.165–70)

Jonson's conception of the Augustan 'constitution' is that it was based in the consent of the governed—though Tiberius behaves as if it had been 'purchased by the sword', that is not in fact how it was established by Augustus.[95] Tiberius does not act according to the rules of the compact, but that fact can never justify rebellion on the part of the citizens. Jonson very seriously endorses what Coleridge

called the 'James-and-Charles-the-First zeal for legitimacy of descent'[96]
in Arruntius's lines:

> The name Tiberius,
> I hope, will keep, howe'er he hath foregone
> The dignity and power.
> *Silius.*   Sure, while he lives.
> *Arruntius.* And dead, it comes to Drusus. Should he fail,
>   To the brave issue of Germanicus.   (I.244–8)

In Tacitus, however, the Principate is a more flexible quantity.
While Tacitus does imply (what Sejanus assumes) that in A.D. 23 the
logical 'line of succession' ran as Arruntius has it,[97] it need not do so.
Augustus, Tacitus has earlier informed us, considered Lucius Arruntius himself for the 'succession', which did not have to be a matter of
lineal descent at all. This question is particularly important, for it
concerns the man Jonson chose as the chief commentator on the
action in *Sejanus*. In the last few years it has been claimed incorrectly
that Arruntius 'did not appear on the scene till two years after
Sejanus's death',[98] and that Arruntius does not exist in Tacitus 'in
Sejanus's lifetime'.[99] It has also recently been argued that Jonson's
presentation of Arruntius and the Germanicans is implicitly critical,
that 'the Germanicans contribute directly to the decline of their
civilization'[100] and demonstrate 'the failure of virtuous men to con-
struct a viable alternative'.[101] These statements are open to challenge.
In point of fact Arruntius does appear on Tacitus's 'scene' 'in Sejanus's lifetime'. He was consul in A.D. 6, his connections were Sullan
and Pompeian, and according to Tacitus he was a senator of great
wealth, talent, integrity, and public spirit. It is therefore not surprising that, as Tacitus informs us,

> Augustus, in his last conversation, when discussing possible holders of the
> principate—those who were competent and disinclined, who were inade-
> quate and willing, or who were at once able and desirous—had described
> Manius Lepidus as capable but disdainful, Asinius Gallus as eager and unfit,
> Lucius Arruntius as not undeserving and bold enough to venture, should
> the opportunity arise. The first two names are not disputed; in some versions
> Arruntius is replaced by Gnaeus Piso: all concerned, apart from Lepidus,
> were soon entrapped on one charge or another, promoted by Tiberius.
>   (*Annals*, I.xiii)

There are quite a few other appearances of Arruntius in Tacitus
during Sejanus's lifetime, but this one is crucial. Jonson chooses to
neglect a passage in Tacitus that is supremely flattering to his chief

commentator, and for a very good reason: the passage contradicts Jonson's neat concept of lineal descent which he makes Arruntius, of all people, proclaim. Like all Jonson's simplifications of historical truth, this one—legitimacy of descent—promotes the didactic function Jonson considered proper to literature, for it gives him an easy way out of the problem of how to account for the lack of what the spy Latiaris calls 'active valour' in the Germanicans by turning it into civic virtue. Jonson could not tamper with the historical fact that during the reign of Tiberius the Germanicans did not marry active *virtus* to their moral opposition to Tiberius. What he could and did do was to complicate and justify the fatalism which in Tacitus they share with the author by blending it with an orthodox Elizabethan attitude to 'legitimate', 'lineal' tyranny which means precisely what it says: 'A good man should and must / Sit rather down with loss, than rise unjust'. In this, Jonson was flying in the face of an intractable passage in Tacitus unsuitable to his purposes. If Jonson had wanted to present the passive stoicism of the Germanicans critically he would hardly have bothered to take such pains and liberties to 'establish' that in a tyranny-by-lineal-descent founded on good Jacobean political theory they could not justifiably do otherwise than watch and condemn.

There is another problem with the 'irresponsible Germanicans' theory: it asks us to accept that in their case Jonson has confused the moral blacks and whites he otherwise shows such fondness for, and to which he deliberately and habitually reduces the complex colourations of history. This is his way with practically every historical reference contained in *Sejanus* and *Catiline*, which are profoundly moral essays in civic virtue and civic vice in which little is allowed to spoil the clarity of the contrasts (even Cicero, perhaps, was for Jonson more clear-cut than most modern critics would want to admit). Thus the violent Drusus of history, since he is an opponent of Sejanus, has perforce to be whitewashed—to this end, Sabinus and Silius immediately 'correct' the historically valid description Arruntius gives of him ('a riotous youth') with ringing praises (I.106–16); while one would never guess the Germanican Caligula of this play had any connection with the emperor of that name—the worst to be said of him is said by Pomponius, a confederate of Sejanus: 'the young prince' has an 'appetite' for Macro's wife (IV.516–17).

There are few plays in the corpus of English Renaissance drama whose exemplars of civic virtue and vice are less open to ironic interpretation than those in *Sejanus*. Jonson is no more interested in presenting irresponsible Germanicans than he is in the positive view

of Sejanus offered in Velleius Paterculus's history of Rome, written a
year before Sejanus fell. His purpose is rather to create, out of what
Sidney calls the 'what is' of history, the dramatic embodiment of 'what
should be'. In respect to practically every detail of the historical contexts his Roman tragedies create, Jonson follows Sidney's prescription
for the poet rather than the historian. The reason is because Jonson,
like Sidney, accepts Aristotle's argument that (in Sidney's words)
'poetry is ... more philosophical and more studiously serious than
history ... because poesy dealeth with ... the universal consideration, and history with ... the particular'.[102] When Jonson speaks in
his address 'To the Readers', prefixed to *Sejanus*, of his 'truth of
argument', he ought not to be taken too literally, for much of the
strictly particular (historical) truth has been shaped and simplified in
the interests of universal (philosophical and moral) truth. He is not
taking on the role of historian but that of a poet and moralist who
turns the materials of history into poetry.

7. STAGE HISTORY

As *F* informs us, *Sejanus* was first acted in 1603 by the King's Men,
probably at Court in the winter (see above, pp. 9–10). The Globe
production came in 1604. A list of actors, in two columns, follows the
play in *F*:

Richard Burbage	William Shakespeare
Augustine Phillips	John Hemminges
William Sly	Henry Condell
John Lowin	Alexander Cooke

Burbage heads similar lists for *Every Man Out*, *Volpone*, *The Alchemist*,
and *Catiline*, and it is logical to suppose that he had the leading role in
each. Herford and Simpson therefore deduce that Burbage played
Sejanus and that Shakespeare may have played Tiberius, and point to
a contemporary poem which refers to 'Kingly parts' played by him.[103]
Insufficient is known of the special talents of the other actors mentioned for us to hazard guesses as to the roles they played in *Sejanus*.
R. B. Parker's conjecture that in *F Volpone* 'the division of the actors'
names into two columns is meant to coincide with its similar division
of the *dramatis personae*'[104] will not do service for *Sejanus*, where this
assumption would mean that the actors who played Drusus Senior,
Drusus Junior, Caligula, and Varro were named, but not those who
played the far more important roles of Arruntius, Silius, Eudemus,

and Livia. In the case of Alexander Cooke, E. K. Chambers pointed out that the fact that 'his name occurs at the end of the lists [for *Sejanus* and *Volpone*] has been somewhat hazardously accepted as an indication that he played women's parts'.[105] This would give him Livia or Agrippina—but boy actors are more likely candidates for those parts.

The play makes no great demands on the staging facilities offered at Court or at the Globe. It requires an upper gallery in which Rufus and Opsius conceal themselves in the fourth Act (see IV.95n.), but the use of an upper gallery for the meeting between Sejanus and Eudemus in the first Act is unnecessary and causes problems (see I.262.1n.). A curtained area at the rear of the stage might be used to set up in advance Fortune's statue, an altar, and the flamen's tools of trade.

Whatever the fate of the 1603 (Court) production may have been, at the Globe in the following year the play was hissed off the stage—see Jonson's epistle to Aubigny and the commendatory verse of Ev. B., a witness. William Fennor may have been another witness:

> With more than humane art it was bedewed,
> Yet to the multitude it nothing shewed;
> They screw'd their scurvy jaws and lookt awry,
> Like hissing snakes, adjudging it to die;
> When wits of gentry did applaud the same,
> With silver shouts of high loud-sounding fame;
> Whilst understanding-grounded men contemn'd it,
> And wanting wit (like fools) to judge, condemn'd it.[106]

That this initial failure was not enough to prevent the King's Men from again presenting the play seems implied by the observation of a third, anonymous, witness who 'a monst others hissed Seianus of the stage, yet after sate it out, not only patiantly, but with content, & admiration'.[107] With that one should compare Jonson to Aubigny, 'this hath outlived their malice, and begot itself a greater favour than [the historical Sejanus] lost, the love of good men', which may or may not refer to subsequent successful productions.

There is no record of any performance of *Sejanus* between its Globe production and that by William Poel in 1928, and none of a professional kind since Poel's that I have been able to discover. For a play that was a favourite of its author's and that author our second most important dramatist, this fact is astonishing. John Downes, in his *Roscius Anglicanus* (1708), mentions *Sejanus* in a list of 'Principal Old Stock Plays' acted by Killigrew's company after the Restoration, but giving no details.[108] Francis Gentleman 'adapted' the play in the eighteenth century and offered it to Garrick—the offer was declined. Gentleman had savaged it: a host of parts were cut out, and Tiberius, in the face of history, made to end the reign of terror after presiding at the fall of Sejanus and freeing his nephews.

As there is only one post-Renaissance professional production to examine, it can be examined in some detail. Fortunately, William Poel's prompt books—typescripts with sections of altered typescript pasted over the original cuts, stage directions, curtain cues, sound effects and property details—survive.[109] With the Elizabethan Stage Circle he revived the play on Sunday evening, 12 February 1928, at the Holborn Empire Theatre, and, to judge from the *Times* review of the following day, very successfully.[110] Poel constructed a large, simple, Elizabethan-type platform stage that jutted out from the proscenium edge over the auditorium level to the sixth row of the stalls. Dark curtains formed the background, and within the plain architectural sides of the stage there were arched entrances. A number of short flights of steps led on to the platform level. Within this framework 'the production achieved a remarkable effect of smooth-ness and dramatic aptness', in the reviewer's words. Robert Speaight, who played Arruntius, has described the production as 'swift in movement and elaborate in design', giving 'a rich, satiric picture of the Roman decadence.... At the beginning of the play the crowd swarmed up on to the stage from the right and left of the stalls; the front curtains opened to reveal as much of the interior stage as was required for any given scene; and behind the proscenium the palace steps led up to a balcony. This, too, had curtains in front of it.'[111] Percy Simpson told Poel he had never before 'seen an Elizabethan play done with so serene, effortless and pure a beauty, and with such a sense of quiet, spacious grandeur'.[112] Costumes were a mixture of Roman, Elizabethan, and modern—whatever came to hand. Arruntius was made up to suggest Jonson, Cordus Shakespeare. Poel felt that Jonson's play, in which the dramatist speaks through Arruntius, satirized the popular political favourite, and specifically Essex. The 'pro-Essex' Shakespeare, whose company had performed *Richard II* as 'encouragement' on the eve of Essex's abortive *coup*, was supposed by Poel to be a populist. Cordus, like Shakespeare in his *Julius Caesar*, described Cassius as 'the last of all the Romans', so in Poel's produc-tion Cordus represented a 'Shakespearian' populist line, balancing an anti-populist Jonson-Arruntius line. It is difficult to see the logic in this, since Cordus is as much opposed as is Arruntius to the 'populist' Sejanus.

Poel cut the play by roughly a quarter and added nothing: he wanted to get away from the 'literary' 1605 published version to the 'hidden' stage play. The Germanicans and Tiberius obviously seemed long-winded to him—the complaints of the former were heavily pruned, and Tiberius's letter to the Senate cut by half. Liberties were taken with extras: a crowd, monks, gaolers, pages, girls, maharajahs— even Sabinus's faithful dog made an appearance, entering under the care of Sabinus's attendant in the opening scene! Eudemus became a hairdresser, and there was a banquet scene in the first Act (I.375ff.). The stage was heavily militarised: Silius was followed about by his private retinue of soldiers carrying his trophies, while five or six others regularly accompanied Tiberius. In the final Senate scene, Laco brought in a guard of 'six Cromwellian soldiers', carrying guns. There must have seemed something very *mitteleuropäisch* about all this.

Poel's cast was as follows. Tiberius, Roy Byford; Drusus Senior, George E. Bancroft; Drusus Junior, Pat Beveridge; Nero, Lewis Shaw; Caligula, Iris Roberts; Arruntius, Robert Speaight; Silius, Gordon Douglas; Sabinus, Frank Macey; Lepidus, Arthur Brough; Cordus, Wilfred Walter; Gallus, Alan Edmiston; Regulus, Laurier Lister; Terentius, Wilfred Walter; Laco, Lionel Ridpath; Eudemus, Esme Percy; Sejanus, D. A. Clarke-Smith; Varro, Keith Pyott; Clerk, John Knox Maclean; Macro, George Skillan; Afer, Norman Claridge; Pomponius, Noel Dixon; Satrius, Charles Maunsell; Natta, Richard Coke; Agrippina, Margaret Scudamore; Livia, Viola Lyel; Sosia, Violet M. Gould.

It is certainly unreasonable to hope for a revival of an uncut *Sejanus* in the new Globe III in view of its reception in Globe I, but if a challenge of a high order is looked for, this play will provide it—and the risks will be commensurate with the rewards.

NOTES

1 Arber, III, 273; III, 297.
2 Arber, III, 445.
3 Arber, IV, 342.
4 Arber, IV, 458–60.
5 Regarding the Jonson material printed by Eld, see J. A. Lavin, 'Printers for Seven Jonson Quartos', *Libr.*, 5th ser., XXV (1970), 331–8.
6 Cf. D. F. McKenzie's observations on Congreve's collected *Works*, 'Typography and Meaning: The Case of William Congreve', in *Buch und Buchhandel in Europa im achtzehnten Jahrhundert: The Book and the Book Trade in Eighteenth-Century Europe*, ed. Giles Barber and Bernhard Fabian (Hamburg: Hauswedell, 1981), pp. 80–123, and especially p. 82: 'The

book itself is an expressive means. To the eye its pages offer an aggrega-
tion of meanings both verbal and typographic for translation to the ear;
but we must learn to see that its shape in the hand also speaks to us from
the past. The full explication of those meanings, in all their contextual
richness, is the prime textual function of historical bibliography'.

7 The fact that more than one set of running-titles appears to have been
used, to judge by the inconsistently-varying length of the running-title
through the sheets, is consistent with cast-off copy.

8 'The Authorship of *The Revenger's Tragedy*', *P.B.S.A.*, LVI (1962), 200.

9 *H.&S.*, IV, 330, argue that the variant watermark implies a cancel, but
the copies mentioned by *H.&S.* in which the variant watermark is not
found have the title-page in the most-corrected, not, as they think, the
least-corrected form.

10 'The Rationale of Copy-Text', *S.B.*, III (1950–1), 35.

11 Bowers, 'Multiple Authority: New Problems and Concepts of Copy-Text',
Libr., 5th ser., XXVII (1972), 85–6; and Tanselle, 'Classical, Biblical,
and Medieval Textual Criticism and Modern Editing', *S.B.*, XXXVI
(1983), 63.

12 Chambers, III, 367 and II, 210.

13 Bolton is confused and in error in claiming that the first production was at
the Globe (p. xi). The same mistake was made by *H.&S.*, I, 36, but
corrected (without reference to the error) at IX, 190.

14 A detailed account of Jonson's career will be found in F. H. Mares, *Alc.*
(Revels, 1969), pp. xvii–xxxi.

15 See Russ McDonald, 'Jonsonian Comedy and the Value of *Sejanus*',
S.E.L., XXI (1981), 287–305; and John G. Sweeney III, '*Sejanus* and the
People's Beastly Rage', *E.L.H.*, XLVIII (1981), 61–82.

16 See Sweeney, p. 80, for a Freudian reading of the implications here.

17 *H.&S.*, II, 11.

18 *H.&S.*, II, 12–15; A. R. Dutton, 'The Sources, Text, and Readers of
Sejanus: Jonson's "Integrity in the Story"', *S.P.*, LXXV (1978), 185–7.

19 See note to ll. 7–11, 'The Argument'.

20 See note to V.545–659.

21 Frederick W. Shipley, ed. *Velleius Paterculus* (Loeb, ed., London, 1967),
p. ix.

22 *Velleius Paterculus, History of Rome*, II, cxxvii.

23 See Daniel C. Boughner, 'Jonson's Use of Lipsius in *Sejanus*', *M.L.N.*,
LXXIII (1958), 247–55.

24 On this subject see Boughner, 'Sejanus and Machiavelli', *S.E.L.*, I
(1961), 81–100.

25 Gary D. Hamilton, 'Irony and Fortune in *Sejanus*', *S.E.L.*, XI (1971),
265–81, never really confronts this problem, though his discussion takes
us further than that of Boughner, 'Juvenal, Horace, and *Sejanus*', *M.L.N.*,
LXXV (1960), 545–50.

26 Commenting on Jonson's use of the words 'sellaries' and 'spintries' at IV,
399, Herford and Simpson, presumably after consulting *O.E.D.* 'Spintry',
which provides the information, note that 'The words "spintry" and
"sellary" are found in Greneway's translation (1598) of this passage'
(Tacitus, *Annals*, VI.i). This is the only connection they report between
Greneway and Jonson.

27 *Conv.Drum.*, I, 603, in *H.&S.*, I, 149.

28 *T.L.S.*, 1928: 10 May (p. 355); 14 June (p. 450); 21 June (p. 468).

29 *Tacitus*, III, tr. J. Jackson (Loeb ed., London, 1956).

30 *H.&S.*, IX, 618.

31 Barish, p. 199; and *H.&S.*, IX, 594.

32 The following section appeared, in a longer form, in *M.P.*, LXXX (1983), 356–63.

33 *Conv.Drum.*, item 13, in *H.&S.*, I, 141.

34 For convenience I shall refer to Howard as Northampton throughout, even when events referred to precede his assumption of the title.

35 One might, however, have expected it more in relation to *Sej.*, which we know was the cause of action against Jonson, than in regard to *Cat.*, which apparently offended no authority, but which has nevertheless been offered, not very persuasively, as a deliberate 'parallelograph' or political allegory on the subject of the Gunpowder Plot. See B. N. De Luna, *Jonson's Romish Plot* (Oxford, 1967).

36 See Jonson's address 'To the Readers'. On Chapman's share in the lost original version, see, most recently, R. P. Corballis, 'The "Second Pen" in the Stage Version of *Sejanus*', *M.P.*, LXXVI (1979), 273–7.

37 J. Palmer, *Ben Jonson* (London, 1934), p. 72.

38 A. R. Dutton, 'The Sources, Text, and Readers of *Sejanus*', p. 195.

39 *H.&S.*, I, 36–7.

40 *D.N.B.*. complete text (Oxford, 1975), I, 1014.

41 Sir Harry L. Stephen, 'The Trial of Sir Walter Ralegh', *Transactions of the Royal Historical Society*, 4th ser., II (1919), 179.

42 Samuel R. Gardiner, *History of England from the Accession of James I to the Outbreak of the Civil War, 1603–1642* (London, 1887–1904), I, 138.

43 Stephen, pp. 186–7.

44 See Tacitus, *Annals*, IV.xix.

45 *The Works of Sir Walter Ralegh*, kt., ... [edited] *by Oldys and Birch* [Oxford, 1829], I, 668; see also pp. 672, 683.

46 See Stephen, p. 184.

47 *Ralegh*, I, 657, 660, 666, 668, 683.

48 *Ibid.*, I, 668.

49 *Ibid.*, I, 668, 672, 673.

50 *Ibid.*, I, 670.

51 *Ibid.*, I, 683.

52 *Ibid.*, I, 682.

53 *Ibid.*, I, 689.

54 See *ibid.*, I, 663, 674, 682.

55 *Ibid.*, I, 675.

56 In the Consistory Court of London in 1606 Jonson denied the charge that he was 'by fame a seducer of youthe to ye popishe Religion' (*H.&S.*, I, 220–2), but he did not deny his Catholicism.

57 *Ralegh*, I, 649.

58 Chapman's verses, ll. 148–9. The flattering reference to Northampton, along with equally flattering references to other members of the Council, was clearly a tactful inclusion, and not, as suggested by Chambers (III, 367), evidence that Northampton acted after the 1605 printing. In any case, the prefatory material in the 1605 edition contains clear references, like those in the verses of Holland quoted earlier, to Jonson's troubles

over the play.

59 *Fennor's Descriptions* (1616), in *J.A.B.*, p. 98.
60 Goodwin, 'Vindiciae Jonsonianae', in *J.A.B.*, p. 163; Carey, Lord Falkland, in *Jonsonus Virbius, H.&S.*, XI, 433 and also in 'An Epistle to his Noble Father, Mr. Jonson', in *J.A.B.*, p. 171; Howell, 'To my Father Mr. Ben. Iohnson', *H.&S.*, XI, 417; Taylor, 'A Funerall Elegie', *H.&S.*, XI, 423; Felltham, in *Jonsonus Virbius, H.&S.*, XI, 461.
61 See, e.g., *J.A.B.*, pp. 283, 285, 319, 380–1, 428, 433.
62 For a detailed listing of these, see W. D. Briggs, 'The Influence of Jonson's Tragedy on the Seventeenth Century', *Anglia*, XXXV (1912), 277–337.
63 For Dryden's views on the play, see *H.&S.*, XI, 513–16.
64 Made in his *Theatrum Poetarum* (1675). See *J.A.B.*, pp. 378–9.
65 *Lives of the English Poets*, ed. L. Archer Hind (London, 1961), II, 354.
66 *A Study of Ben Jonson* (London, 1889), pp. 28–31.
67 *Ben Jonson* (London, 1919), pp. 190–1.
68 *Ben Jonson* (New York, 1934), pp. 134, 143–4.
69 This approach to the play is persuasively presented by K. M. Burton, 'The Political Tragedies of Chapman and Ben Jonson', *E.C.*, II (1952), 397–412.
70 See, in this regard, Ralph Nash, 'Ben Jonson's Tragic Poems', *S.P.*, LV (1958), 164–86; and Arthur F. Marotti, 'The Self-Reflexive Art of Ben Jonson's *Sejanus*', *T.S.L.L.*, XII (1970), 197–220, on Jonson's concern with rhetoric in the play.
71 An extensive study of the play's language is provided in the unpublished 1968 Berkeley dissertation by M. J. Warren, 'The Verse Style of Ben Jonson's Roman Plays'.
72 Barish, p. 24.
73 For a more detailed treatment of some of the issues addressed here, see my article 'The Nature of Jonson's Roman History', *E.L.R.*, XVI (1986), 166–81, which also considers *Catiline* at length.
74 *Sej.*, 'To the Readers', l. 16.
75 Joseph Allen Bryant, 'The Significance of Ben Jonson's First Requirement for Tragedy: "Truth of Argument"', *S.P.*, XLIX (1952), 213.
76 Bryant, pp. 212, 206.
77 *H.&S.*, I, 12–15; A. R. Dutton, 'The Sources, Text, and Readers of *Sejanus*', pp. 185–7.
78 *H.&S.*, I, 15, 116.
79 On the simplification of major characters in *Cat.* and *Sej.*, see K. M. Burton, 'The Political Tragedies of Chapman and Ben Jonson', *E.C.*, II (1952), 403–4; K. W. Evans, '*Sejanus* and the Ideal Prince Tradition', *S.E.L.*, XI (1971), 249; and A. R. Dutton, 'The Sources, Text, and Readers of *Sejanus*', pp. 185–7.
80 W. F. Bolton and Jane F. Gardner, eds. *Catiline* (London, 1973), Introduction, p. xv.
81 Bolton and Gardner, p. xxiv; and Ralph Nash, 'Ben Jonson's Tragic Poems', p. 185.
82 Barish, pp. 4–5.
83 *An Apology for Poetry*, in D. J. Enright and Ernst De Chickera, *English Critical Texts* (London, 1962), p. 14.
84 William Cornwallis, *Essayes of Certaine Paradoxes* (1616), C2r.

85 *A Briefe Chronicle* (1564), 14*v*, 16r.
86 *An Historicall Collection of the Continuall Factions, Tumults, and Massacres of the Romans and Italians during the space of one hundred and twentie yeares next before the peaceable Empire of Augustus Caesar* (1601), C4*v*.
87 *Ibid.*, K1r, K3*v*, L2r.
88 Tacitus, *Annals*, VI.xlvi.
89 *Disc.*, l. 1009.
90 See the Regents edn of Joseph W. Houppert (London, 1970): the tribunate, the *optimates* and the *equites*, and the Italian freemen are all part of the *mise en scène* here.
91 For a more balanced view see *Disc.*, ll. 924–31, and *Ep.*, cx.
92 See, e.g., William Fulbecke, *An Historicall Collection*, z1r–z2v; W. Traheron tr. P. Mexia, *The Historie of all the Romane Emperors* (1604), C6*v*; William Cornwallis, *Essayes* (1601), part 1, L7r.
93 As opposed to Octavius. See Robert P. Kalmey, 'Shakespeare's Octavius and Elizabethan Roman History', *S.E.L.*, XVIII (1978), 275–87.
94 *An Historicall Collection*, z2r.
95 Compare the lines of Sabinus above, especially the crucial third and fourth lines, with the phraseology of Hooker on the original social contract in *Of the Laws of Ecclesiastical Polity*, ed. Christopher Morris (London, 1907), vol. I, I.x.4: 'To take away all such mutual grievances, injuries, and wrongs, there was no way but only by growing unto composition and agreement amongst themselves, by ordaining some kind of government public, and by yielding themselves subject thereunto; that unto whom they granted authority to rule and govern, by them the peace, tranquility, and happy estate of the rest might be procured'.
96 *Lectures and Notes on Shakespeare* (London, 1914), p. 413.
97 *Annals*, IV.iii.
98 Gary D. Hamilton, 'Irony and Fortune in *Sejanus*', *S.E.L.*, XI (1971), 278.
99 A. R. Dutton, 'The Sources, Text, and Readers of *Sejanus*', p. 187.
100 Marvin L. Vawter, 'The Seeds of Virtue: Political Imperatives in Jonson's *Sejanus*', *Studies in the Literary Imagination*, VI (1973), 46.
101 Dutton, p. 189.
102 *An Apology for Poetry*, p. 17.
103 John Davies of Hereford, *The Scourge of Folly* (n.d.; Stationers' Register, Oct. 1610), Epigram 159, pp. 76–7.
104 Introduction to the Revels *Volpone*, p. 45.
105 Chambers, II, 312.
106 From *Fennor's Descriptions; or A True Relation of Certain and Divers Speeches, Spoken before the King and Queen's Most Excellent Majestie*. See *J.A.B.*, p. 98.
107 Quoted by B. M. Wagner, 'A Jonson Allusion, and Others', *P.Q.*, VII (1928), 306–8.
108 See *J.A.B.*, pp. 325–7.
109 William Poel Prompt Books, Theatre Museum, London: S. 1214–1983.
110 *The Times*, 13 February 1928, p. 18.
111 Robert Speaight, *William Poel and the Elizabethan Revival* (London, 1954), pp. 247–8.
112 *Ibid.*, p. 248.

SEIANVS

HIS FALL.

Written

by

BEN: IONSON.

MART. Non hîc *Centauros*, non *Gorgonas*, *Harpyasq́;*
Inuenies: Hominem pagina noſtra ſapit.

AT LONDON
Printed by *G. Ellde*, for *Thomas Thorpe.* 1605.

PLATE 3 Title-page of *Q*

SEJANUS HIS FALL

TO THE NO LESS
NOBLE BY VIRTUE
THAN BLOOD:

Esmé

L. AUBIGNY.   5

MY LORD,

If ever any ruin were so great as to survive, I think this be one I send
you: The Fall of Sejanus. *It is a poem that, if I well remember, in*
your lordship's sight suffered no less violence from our people here
than the subject of it did from the rage of the people of Rome; but   10
with a different fate, as (I hope) merit: for this hath outlived their
malice, and begot itself a greater favour than he lost, the love of
good men. Amongst whom, if I make your lordship the first it
thanks, it is not without a just confession of the bond your benefits
have, and ever shall hold upon me.   15

Your lordship's most faithful honourer,

BEN. JONSON.

TO THE ... BEN. JONSON.] *F; not in Q.*   4. Esmé] Esme *F.*   9.
lordship's] *F2; Lo. F.*   13. lordship] *F2; Lo. F.*   16. lordship's] *F2; Lo. F.*

4–5. *Esmé/L. AUBIGNY*] Esmé Stuart (1579–1624), seventh (not 'eighth'
—D.N.B. *article on Ludovick Stuart) Seigneur d'Aubigné and third Duke of
Lennox (succeeding his brother Ludovick in 1624, shortly before his own death, not
1583 as H.&S.,* IX, 591, have it). Jonson pays tribute to him in *Ep.,* CXXVII,
and to his wife in *For.,* XIII. The epithalamium in *Und.,* LXXV, is on his
daughter's (not 'sister's'—*H.&S.,* IX, 591) marriage to Jerome Weston in
1632. Jonson lived in his home for five years (*Conv.Drum.,* ll. 254–5),
sometime after Esmé Stuart took up residence in London in 1603, but for
precisely which period is unclear.
   9. violence ... here] This more probably alludes to the play's unfavour-
able reception at the Globe than to 'the accusations which led to Jonson's
appearance before the Privy Council' (Wilkes, II, 233). See Introduction, and
cf. the remarks of 'Ev. B.' on 'the people's beastly rage' in his commendatory
verse, below, and William Fennor's 'Description of a Poet', from *Fennors
Descriptions* (1616)—see Introduction, p. 38.
[Q title-page motto: from Martial, X.iv.9–10, 'Not here will you find
Centaurs, not Gorgons and Harpies: 'tis of man my page smacks'. Loeb ed., tr.
W. C. A. Ker (London, 1950)]

To the Readers.

The following and voluntary labours of my friends, prefixed to
my book, have relieved me in much, whereat (without them) I
should necessarily have touched. Now I will only use three or
four short and needful notes, and so rest.

First, if it be objected that what I publish is no true poem in   5
the strict laws of time, I confess it; as also in the want of a proper
chorus, whose habit and moods are such, and so difficult, as not
any whom I have seen since the ancients—no, not they who have
most presently affected laws—have yet come in the way of. Nor
is it needful, or almost possible, in these our times, and to such   10
auditors as commonly things are presented, to observe the old
state and splendour of dramatic poems, with preservation of any
popular delight. But of this I shall take more seasonable cause to
speak, in my observations upon Horace his *Art of Poetry*, which,
with the text translated, I intend shortly to publish. In the   15

To the Readers ... opimum.] *Q; not in F.*   9. of] off *Q.*

5–22.) Not only the ideas, but many of the phrases here were copied by
Webster in his own preface ('To the Reader') to *The White Devil* (Revels Plays,
2nd. ed., 1966).

6. *the strict ... time*] The classical 'unity of time' required that the action
represented by a dramatic 'poem' or tragedy should be confined to one day,
but in the Renaissance some scholars narrowed it to the time the play takes
to present.

6–9. *the want ... way of*] These lines suggest that Jonson aspires to be the
first 'since the ancients' to succeed in the 'so difficult' task of incorporating a
'proper chorus' into a tragedy. Although he had planned to include a chorus in
the incomplete and probably early *Mort.*, it was not until he came to write *Cat.*
(1611) that he felt adequately equipped for the task. That play's chorus
represents a faithful following of Horace's prescription in the *Ars Poetica.*
Choruses, not all of them classical in form, had been used by a number of
Elizabethan dramatists, including Marlowe (*Faustus*) and Shakespeare (*H5*).

7. *habit and moods*] characteristic behaviour and modes (or 'tunes'). 'Mode',
O.E.D. sb. 1a and 1b—a musical scale—was often spelled 'mood' in the
early seventeenth century. In the *Ars Poetica* Horace discusses the traditional
chorus's degeneration 'numerisque modisque'—'Both in their tunes, the
licence greater grew, / And in their numbers'–Jonson's translation (*H.&S.*,
VIII, 319).

9. *presently affected*] recently sought to put into practice.

13. *popular*] of the ordinary people.

14. *observations ...* Poetry] Although Jonson's translation of the *Ars
Poetica* survives, the commentary was lost in the fire in Jonson's library, 1623
(see *Und.*, XLIII, ll. 89–91).

meantime, if in truth of argument, dignity of persons, gravity
and height of elocution, fulness and frequency of sentence, I
have discharged the other offices of a tragic writer, let not the
absence of these forms be imputed to me, wherein I shall give
you occasion hereafter, and without my boast, to think I could   20
better prescribe, than omit the due use for want of a convenient
knowledge.

The next is, lest in some nice nostril the quotations might
savour affected, I do let you know that I abhor nothing more; and
have only done it to show my integrity in the story, and save   25
myself in those common torturers that bring all wit to the rack;
whose noses are ever like swine spoiling and rooting up the
Muses' gardens, and their whole bodies, like moles, as blindly
working under earth to cast any—the least—hills upon virtue.

Whereas they are in Latin, and the work in English, it was   30
presupposed none but the learned would take the pains to confer
them, the authors themselves being all in the learned tongues,
save one, with whose English side I have had little to do: to which

23. lest] least Q.

---

16. *truth of argument*] Aspiring to be something more than the dramatic
poem 'whose subject is not truth, but things like truth'—Chapman, Dedication to *The Revenge of Bussy D'Ambois* (1613), A3v, glancing at Jonson—*Sej.*
offers to present literal historical truth, grounding itself in the great Roman
historians.

17. *fulness and frequency*] abundance and constant use.

17. *sentence*] *sententia*, aphorism—frequent in Seneca's tragedies.

21. *convenient*] proper.

23. *nice*] fastidious.

23–4. *the quotations ... affected*] the marginal notes (of *Q*) might smell of
affection. Marston, in his preface to *Sophonisba* (1606), glances critically at
these: 'I have not laboured in this poem to tie myself to relate any thing as an
historian, but to enlarge everything as a poet. To transcribe authors, quote
authorities, and translate Latin prose orations into English blank verse, hath,
in this subject, been the least aim of my studies.' *Works*, ed. A. H. Bullen
(London, 1887), II, 235.

25. *integrity ... story*] fidelity to history—but also *political integrity*: the
marginal notes are there to refute any charge that Jonson tampered with
history for some political purpose. See Introduction.

26. *in*] in regard to.

26. *wit*] learning.

30. *they*] the classical sources.

31. *confer*] compare (*O.E.D. confer*, 4).

33. *save one ... to do*] Richard Greneway's translation, *The Annales of Corn. Tacitus* [with the *Germania*] (1598; six edd. to 1640).

it may be required, since I have quoted the page, to name what
editions I followed. *Tacit. Lips.* in 4°. *Antwerp. edit.* 600. *Dio.*   35
Folio. Hen. Step. 92. For the rest, as *Sueton. Seneca.* etc., the
chapter doth sufficiently direct, or the edition is not varied.

Lastly, I would inform you that this book, in all numbers, is
not the same with that which was acted on the public stage,
wherein a second pen had good share; in place of which I have   40
rather chosen to put weaker (and no doubt less pleasing) of mine
own, than to defraud so happy a genius of his right by my loathed
usurpation.

Fare you well. And if you read farther of me, and like, I shall
not be afraid of it though you praise me out.   45

> *Neque enim mihi cornea fibra est.*

But that I should plant my felicity in your general saying
'Good', or 'Well', etc., were a weakness which the better sort of
you might worthily contemn, if not absolutely hate me for.

> BEN. JONSON and no such,   50
> *Quem palma negata macrum, donata reducit opimum.*

---

35. editions] Editions *Q.;* Edition *H.&S., Barish, Bolton.*   44. farther]
farder *Q.*   49. contemn] coutenme *Q.*   50. such,] such. *Q.*

Despite what he says here and in *Conv.Drum.*, l. 603 ('ignorantly done'),
Jonson made use of it. See Introduction.

35. Tacit ... 600.] The Lipsius edition published at Antwerp in 1600.

35-6. Dio ... 92] The reference is to the *Roman History* of Dio
Cassius published in twenty-five books in 1592 by Henry Estienne at
Geneva.

36. Sueton. Seneca] see Introduction, p. 10.

38. *numbers*] lines, verses.

40. *a second pen*] possibly that of George Chapman (1559-1634). *H.&S.* (II,
3-5, IX, 592-3) suggest that the passages which Jonson replaced with his own
in the printed play may well have been those that had most worried the Privy
Council, and that when Chapman praises its members in his commendatory
verses he certainly seems to be associating himself with Jonson.

42-3. *loathed usurpation*] offensive arrogation (of the material) to myself.

44-8. *I shall ... weakness*] From Persius, *Satires*, I, 45-9: 'I am the last
man, I say, to be afraid of praise. My heart [literally, *fibra* = entrails] is not
made of horn! [the sentence Jonson quotes in Latin.] But I decline to admit
that the final and supreme test of excellence is to be found in your "Bravo!"
and your "Beautiful!"' (trans. G. G. Ramsay, Loeb ed. [London, 1957],
p. 321).

45. *out*] to the full.

51. Quem ... opimum] Horace, *Epistles*, II.i.181: [whom] 'denial of the
palm sends ... home lean, its bestowal plump' (trans. H. Rushton Fairclough,
Loeb ed. [London, 1961], p. 413).

SEJANUS HIS FALL

In SEIANVM
BEN. IONSONI
Et Musis, et sibi
in Deliciis.

So brings the wealth-contracting jeweller 5
  Pearls and dear stones, from richest shores and streams,
As thy accomplished travail doth confer
  From skill-enrichèd souls their wealthier gems;
So doth his hand enchase in amelled gold,
  Cut and adorned beyond their native merits, 10
His solid flames, as thine hath here enrolled,
  In more than golden verse, those bettered spirits;
So he entreasures princes' cabinets,
  As thy wealth will their wishèd libraries;
So, on the throat of the rude sea, he sets 15
  His ventrous foot for his illustrous prize,
And through wild deserts, armed with wilder beasts,
  As thou adventur'st on the multitude,
Upon the boggy and engulfèd breasts
  Of hirelings, sworn to find most right most rude; 20
And he, in storms at sea, doth not endure,
  Nor in vast deserts, amongst wolves, more danger,
Than we, that would with virtue live secure,
  Sustain for her in every vice's anger.

In SEIANVM ... *Chapmannus.*] *Chapman's verses were reprinted, in shortened form, in F,* ¶4v–5v. 1–4. In ... *Deliciis.*] Q; Vpon SEIANVS F. 16. prize] prise Q, F.

1–4. *In ... Deliciis*] On Ben Jonson's *Sejanus*—his own and the muses' favourite.
  7. travail] labour.
  7. confer] gather (*O.E.D. confer*, 1).
  8. skill-enrichèd souls] i.e. Jonson's classical sources.
  9. amelled] enamelled.
  11. solid flames] Chapman is thinking of the 'fire' in the hard jewel.
  13. entreasures] stocks with treasure.
  15. rude] turbulent.
  17. armed] furnished.
  19. engulfèd] mired. The multitude is swinish.
  20. rude] ignorant, unlearned.
  23. secure] free from care.

Nor is this allegory unjustly racked   25
   To this strange length; only that jewels are,
In estimation merely, so exact;
   And thy work, in itself, is dear and rare.
Wherein Minerva had been vanquishèd,
   Had she, by it, her sacred looms advanced,   30
And through thy subject woven her graphic thread,
   Contending therein to be more entranced;
For, though thy hand was scarce addressed to draw
   The semicircle of Sejanus' life,
Thy muse yet makes it the whole sphere, and law   35
   To all state lives, and bounds ambition's strife.
And as a little brook creeps from his spring,
   With shallow tremblings, through the lowest vales,
As if he feared his stream abroad to bring,
   Lest profane feet should wrong it, and rude gales;   40
But finding happy channels, and supplies
   Of other fords mix with his modest course,
He grows a goodly river, and descries
   The strength that manned him since he left his source;

35. sphere, and law] corr. Q, F; Sphaere and Lawe uncorr. Q.   40. Lest] Least
Q, F.

---

   25. unjustly] improperly.
   27. estimation merely] (popular) opinion only.
   27. exact] consummate, perfect.
   29. Minerva] the goddess not only of wisdom, but of poetry, and of spinning
and weaving—in fact of the arts and sciences generally. Arachne was turned
into a spider for having challenged Minerva to a trial of skill in spinning (Ovid,
Metamorphoses, vi, 5–145), and the height of presumption was 'To instruct
Minerva' (proverbial—Tilley, S.680). Chapman boldly asserts that, on this
subject, Jonson *could* have instructed her!
   31. graphic thread] the reference is to a life-like tapestry, with perhaps a
glance at the *written* thread of Jonson's plot. Use of *graphic* antedates *O.E.D.*
examples.
   32. entranced] inspired by her muse. Not in *O.E.D.*
   34. The semicircle . . . life] because Sejanus's life was cut short.
   35–6. Thy . . . strife] In treating of Sejanus, Jonson has treated of the whole
sphere of state, and the truths of the play are generally applicable to all
involved in affairs of state. The play is a powerful antidote to ambition.
   37–48.] A favourite image of Chapman's. See Phyllis Brooks Bartlett, *The
Poems of George Chapman* (New York, 1962; 1st ed. 1941), p. 469.
   42. fords] streams.
   43. descries] discovers.
   44. manned] made manly, fortified. Antedates *O.E.D.* examples.

Then takes he in delightsome meads and groves,   45
*   And, with his two-edged waters, flourishes*
Before great palaces, and all men's loves
*   Build by his shores, to greet his passages;*
So thy chaste muse, by virtuous self-mistrust,
*   Which is a true mark of the truest merit,*   50
In virgin fear of men's illiterate lust,
*   Shut her soft wings, and durst not show her spirit;*
Till, nobly cherished, now thou letst her fly,
*   Singing the sable orgies of the Muses,*
And in the highest pitch of tragedy   55
*   Mak'st her command all things thy ground produces.*
But as it is a sign of love's first firing,
*   Not pleasure by a lovely presence taken,*
And boldness to attempt, but close retiring
*   To places desolate, and fever-shaken;*   60
So, when the love of knowledge first affects us,
*   Our tongues do falter, and the flame doth rove*
Through our thin spirits, and of fear detects us
*   T'attain her truth, whom we so truly love.*

---

45. delightsome] Q; delight some F.   57–96. But as ... all degrees.] Q; not in
F.

---

46. with ... flourishes] a punning reference to fencing. Cf. Chapman's
poem 'De Guiana', l. 59: a river similarly described flows 'to ioyne battale with
th'imperious sea' (*The Poems of George Chapman*, ed. Bartlett, p. 354).

48. passages] (*a*) passage; and (*b*) 'passages-at-arms' (see prec. note).

49–56.] Cf. ll. 233–9 of the 'apologetical dialogue' To the Reader at the end
of *Poet.* (1601), where Jonson announced his intention to quit the stage for a
time and devote himself entirely to the writing of a tragedy—which appeared
two years later as *Sejanus*. On 12 February 1603 Manningham noted in his
diary that 'ben Jonson the poet nowe lives upon one Townsend and scorns the
world' (quoted in *H.&S.*, II, 3).

51. lust] appetite.

54. orgies] rites, ceremonies (*O.E.D. orgy*, 1). The 'sable orgies' are of
course tragic compositions.

56. ground] theme upon which a descant—accompanying melody—is sung
or played as an air to its base.

57–84.] These lines draw on Plutarch, *Moralia*, 'How a Man May Become
Aware of his Progress in Virtue', 77b, 81c, d, e. See Loeb ed. of the *Moralia*, I,
tr. F. C. Babbitt (London, 1960), 411, 433–5, and Bartlett, *Poems of George
Chapman*, p. 472.

63. thin spirits] watery life-blood.

63–4. of ... truth] i.e., accuses us of fear to attain her truth.

Nor can (saith Aeschylus) a fair young dame,   65
    Kept long without a husband, more contain
Her amorous eye from breaking forth in flame
    When she beholds a youth that fits her vein,
Than any man's first taste of knowledge truly
    Can bridle the affection she inspireth,   70
But let it fly on men that most unduly
    Haunt her with hate, and all the loves she fireth.
If our teeth, head, or but our finger ache,
    We straight seek the physician; if a fever,
Or any cureful malady we take,   75
    The grave physician is desirèd ever;
But if proud melancholy, lunacy,
    Or direct madness overheat our brains,
We rage, beat out, or the physician fly,
    Losing with vehemence even the sense of pains.   80
So of offenders, they are past recure
    That, with a tyrannous spleen, their stings extend
'Gainst their reprovers; they that will endure
    All discreet discipline are not said t'offend.
Though others qualified, then, with natural skill   85
    (More sweet-mouthed, and affecting shrewder wits)
Blanch coals, call illness good, and goodness ill,
    Breathe thou the fire that true-spoke knowledge fits.
Thou canst not then be great? Yes! Who is he,
    Said the good Spartan king, greater than I,   90

---

68. vein,] *vaine; Q.*   69. *truly*] corr. *Q; truly, uncorr. Q.*   80. *Losing*]
Loosing Q.

---

65. saith Aeschylus] in the *Toxotides*, quoted by Chapman's source here,
Plutarch, *Moralia*, 81d.

68. vein] inclination, desire.

75. cureful] troublesome. Not in *O.E.D.* Literally, anxiety-full (*O.E.D.
Cure*, sb., 2—care, anxiety, trouble—with the sense from Lat. *cura*, care,
anxiety.

77. lunacy] intermittent insanity.

81. recure] recovery.

82. tyrannous spleen] overbearing fit of temper.

86. affecting] assuming the character of.

87. blanch] whiten.

89–96. Who ... all degrees] from Plutarch, *Moralia*, 78d, cited by Bartlett,
p. 472. See Loeb ed., I, 417–9.

90. the ... king] Agesilaus, under whose reign Lycurgus instituted his
laws.

That is not likewise juster? No degree
  Can boast of eminence or empery
(As the great Stagirite held) in any one
  Beyond another whose soul farther sees,
And in whose life the gods are better known: 95
  Degrees of knowledge difference all degrees.
Thy poem, therefore, hath this due respect,
  That it lets pass nothing, without observing,
Worthy instruction, or that might correct
  Rude manners, and renown the well-deserving;   100
Performing such a lively evidence
  In thy narrations, that thy hearers still
Thou turnst to thy spectators; and the sense
  That thy spectators have of good or ill,
Thou injectst jointly to thy readers' souls.   105
  So dear is held, so decked thy numerous task,
As thou putst handles to the Thespian bowls,

---

94. *another whose*] *another, whose* Q.   95. *known:*] *corr.* Q; *knowne. uncorr.*
Q.   96. *degrees.*] *corr.* Q; *Degrees, uncorr.* Q.   97. *Thy poem, therefore,*] Q;
Besides, thy Poëme F.   100. *renown*] *renowme* Q, F.

---

91. degree] rank or class of persons.

92. empery] dominion.

93. the great Stagirite] Aristotle, so-called because he was born in the Macedonian town of Stagira.

96. *i.e.* the scale of intellects is different from (and confounds) the social scale which depends on birth or rank.

97. due respect] appropriate quality.

100. renown] celebrate, spread the fame of.

101. evidence] display, manifestation.

101–5.] From Plutarch, *Moralia*, 347, referring to the vividness of Thucydides' writing. See W. D. Briggs, 'Source-Material for Jonson's Plays', *M.L.N.*, XXXI (1916), 328.

105. jointly] at the same time.

106. decked] adorned, embellished.

106. numerous] comprising many separate things, with perhaps a glance at the 'numbers' of poetry.

106. task] accomplished work—a sense not recorded in *O.E.D.*

107. As] As if.

107. Thespian bowls] The inhabitants of Thespiae in Boeotia worshipped the Muses, celebrating festivals in their honour in the sacred grove on Mount Helicon, near which were the sacred fountains of Aganippe and Hippocrene. Chapman evidently has in mind the bowls (presumably lacking handles) used to quaff the fountains' waters of inspiration. That is, Jonson's poetry delights the reader.

Or stuckst rich plumes in the Palladian casque.
All thy worth, yet, thyself must patronise,
  By quaffing more of the Castalian head;   110
In expiscation of whose mysteries
  Our nets must still be clogged with heavy lead,
To make them sink and catch—for cheerful gold
  Was never found in the Pierian streams,
But wants, and scorns, and shames for silver sold.   115
  What, what shall we elect in these extremes?
Now by the shafts of the great Cyrrhan poet,
  That bear all light, that is, about the world,
I would have all dull poet-haters know it,
  They shall be soul-bound, and in darkness hurled,   120
A thousand years (as Satan was, their sire)
  Ere any worthy the poetic name—
Might I, that warm but at the Muses' fire,
  Presume to guard it —should let deathless Fame
Light half a beam of all her hundred eyes   125

---

108. casque] *Caske Q, F.*   116. What, what] *Q; What? what F.*

---

108. Palladian casque] helmet of Pallas Athene, i.e. Minerva. As represented in Greek statues, it was not, as Chapman seems to imply, always lacking in ornamentation. Jonson's dramatic poetry also profits the reader, being rich in wisdom.

109. patronise] support.

110. Castalian head] the Castalia, a fountain on Parnassus sacred to the Muses.

111. expiscation] the action of fishing out (*O.E.D.*'s first example).

112. heavy lead] presumably Chapman has in mind the heavy intellectual labours involved in the writing of poetry.

114. Pierian] of Pieria, or more specifically of Mount Pierus, in Thessaly, reputedly the birthplace of the Muses.

115. wants ... sold] the scorned and necessitous poet must sell his unappreciated work for what he can get (silver), not what it is worth (gold).

116. elect] choose as a course of action.

117. Cyrrhan poet] Apollo, god of poetry and music, and often taken for the sun. From the town of Cyrrha, where he was worshipped.

120. -bound] -bonded.

121. as Satan was] strictly, as Satan *will be*, but Chapman evidently means 'as Satan was, in Revelations XX. 2–3', where the past tense is used: 'And he ... bound him a thousand years, And cast him into the bottomless pit'.

123. warm but] only warm myself.

125. her hundred eyes] because Fame is all-seeing—and, acc. to Virgil, with as many tongues, mouths, and ears (*Aeneid*, IV, 182–3).

At his dim taper, in their memories.
Fly, fly, you are too near; so odorous flowers,
  Being held too near the sensor of our sense,
Render not pure nor so sincere their powers
  As being held a little distance thence,   130
Because much-troubled earthy parts improve them;
  Which, mixèd with the odours we exhale,
Do vitiate what we draw in. But remove them
  A little space, the earthy parts do fall,
And what is pure and hot by his tenuity   135
  Is to our powers of savour purely borne.
But fly or stay, use thou the assiduity
  Fit for a true contemner of their scorn.
Our Phoebus may, with his exampling beams,
  Burn out the webs from their Arachnean eyes,   140

130. thence,] *Q; thence. F.*   131–62. *Because . . . propagate.] Q; not in F.*

127–36. The idea, as W. D. Briggs, 'Source-Material', p. 328, points out, is from Plutarch, *Moralia*, 'Table-Talk' ('Symposiacon'), I.8.626b: 'The scent of flowers, too, is sweeter when it reaches you from a distance, but if you bring them too close, their odour is not so pure and unadulterated. The reason is that much that is earthy and coarse accompanies the scent and destroys its pleasant odour when received near by, but if from a distance, the coarse and earthy parts slip off all round and fall, while the pure and fresh part of the scent by its lightness is brought intact to the sense of smell.' Loeb ed. of the *Moralia*, VIII, tr. Paul A. Clement (London, 1969), 85.
128. sensor of our sense] the nose. 'Sensor' as a noun does not appear in *O.E.D.* Chapman also uses it in 'Ovid's Banquet of Sense', stanza 31, I. 3: 'the sensor of his sauor'—*Poems*, ed. Bartlett, p. 61.
129. sincere] true (*O.E.D. sincere*, adv., 1b).
131. troubled] agitated.
131. earthy parts] All matter was thought to consist of earth, air, fire, and water, mixed in varying proportions. As the impure and heavier earthy emanations of the flower quickly drop away, it is best savoured at a little distance.
131. improve] augment, make worse (*O.E.D., improve*, 4b).
133. vitiate] corrupt.
135. hot by his tenuity] hot on account of its rarefied condition. As air ('hot and moist' acc. to medieval physiology) became more rarefied it approached to the condition of fire ('hot and dry').
139. Our Phoebus] James I. Apollo was god of light and of poetry. See *Ep.*, IV, 'To King James' for Jonson's tribute to this 'best of *Poets*' (Apollo was also god of poetry).
139. exampling] setting an example.
140. webs] cobwebs, with allusion of course to Arachne's web.
140. Arachnean] like those of Arachne (see above, l. 29n.), perhaps because

Whose knowledge—day-star to all diadems—
  Should banish knowledge-hating policies.
So others, great in the sciential grace:
  His Chancellor, fautor of all human skills;
His Treasurer, taking them into his place;   145
  Northumber, that, with them, his crescent fills;
Grave Worc'ster, in whose nerves they guard their fire;
  Northampton, that to all his height in blood,

---

143. *grace:*] grace, Q.   144. *human*] humane Q.

---

the 'scorn' (l. 138) is as misplaced as was Arachne's when she denied that Minerva could have anything to teach her. The scorners are 'blind', as was Arachne in failing to recognize Minerva when the latter, disguised, took up Arachne's challenge to a trial of skill. Chapman's sense for 'Arachnean' is not in *O.E.D.*, though he also uses it in *Hero and Leander*, IV, 121.

141. day-star ... diadems] Like the day-star, James's 'knowledge' breaks the night and hastens the dawn (of understanding), therein setting an example to all princely authorities ('diadems'). There would appear to be an allegorical reference here to some role he played in helping to 'clear' Jonson with the Privy Council, which malicious 'scorners' were attempting to mislead with their 'knowledge-hating policies'.

142. knowledge-hating policies] i.e. cunning but ignorant political stratagems (directed against Jonson).

143. sciential grace] favourable regard for knowledge.

144. His Chancellor] Sir Thomas Egerton [1540?–1617], Lord Ellesmere. Privy Counsellor.

144. fautor ... skills] patron and protector of all the arts and sciences (the 'them' of the following lines).

145. His Treasurer] Thomas Sackville (1536–1608), first Earl of Dorset, author of the *Induction* to *A Mirror for Magistrates* and co-author of *Gorboduc*. Privy Counsellor.

145. place] office of state.

146. Northumber] Henry Percy (1564–1632) ninth Earl of Northumberland. Privy Counsellor. He protested against the punishment of Sir Walter Ralegh for 'treason', and was later suspected of complicity in the Gunpowder Plot of 5 Nov. 1605. Imprisoned in the Tower from 27 Nov. 1605 until 1621. Deeply interested in science, art, and literature.

146. his crescent] alluding to the silver crescent in the heraldic badge of the Percy family.

147. Worc'ster] Edward Somerset (1553–1628), fourth Earl of Worcester, Privy Counsellor, and patron (1602–3) of the former Pembroke's Men playing at the Rose.

147. in ... fire] in whose strength they guard their ardent spirit.

148. Northampton] Henry Howard (1540–1614), Earl of Northampton, Privy Counsellor, a commissioner for the trial of Ralegh in 1603, and Jonson's 'mortall enimie' by whom 'he was called befor ye Councell for his Sejanus & accused both of popperie and treason' (*Conv.Drum.*, item 13, in *H.&S.*, I,

Heightens his soul with them; and Devonshire,
   In whom their streams, ebbed to their spring, are flood;   150
Oraculous Salisbury, whose inspirèd voice,
   In state proportions, sings their mysteries;
And (though last named) first, in whom they rejoice,
   To whose true worth they vow most obsequies,
Most noble Suffolk, who by nature noble,   155
   And judgement virtuous, cannot fall by fortune,
Who when our herd came not to drink, but trouble
   The Muses' waters, did a wall importune,
Midst of assaults, about their sacred river;
   In whose behalfs, my poor soul (consecrate   160
To poorest virtue) to the longest liver

---

141). *D.N.B.* describes him as one who 'exhibited in all his actions a stupendous want of principle'. Chapman's reference to him here is a necessary piece of tact. See my article, 'Jonson, Northampton, and the "Treason" in *Sejanus*', *MP*, LXXX (1983), 356–63.

148. height in blood] rank.

149. Devonshire] Charles Blount (1563–1606), Earl of Denvonshire and eighth Lord Mountjoy, Privy Counsellor, a man of distinguished military accomplishments. His mistress, whom he married at the end of 1605, was Lady Rich, the Stella of Sidney's 'Astrophel and Stella' sonnet sequence. He was extremely popular with poets and dramatists, many of whom wrote poems in his praise.

150. In ... flood] The 'streams' of the arts and sciences during an ebb 'flow back', as it were, to their 'spring' or sustainer (Devonshire) which, at the very moment they reach their lowest ebb, replensihes them so that 'In' him they are 'flood'.

151. Oraculous] of inspired or authoritative utterance.

151. Salisbury] Robert Cecil (1563?–1612), first Earl of Salisbury and first Viscount Cranborne, secretary of state. Reputed to have been an excellent speaker. When Chapman and Jonson were imprisoned over *E.H.* later in this same year 1605, Salisbury and Suffolk came to their aid. See *H.&S.*, I, 38–9, 193–6; and, on the approximate date (certainly not long after the publication of *Sejanus*), *H.&S.*, XI, 578.

154. obsequies] services (*O.E.D. obsequy*, 1, *Obs.*).

155. Suffolk] Thomas Howard (1561–1626), first Earl of Suffolk, Lord Chamberlain and, like all the preceding, a Privy Counsellor.

157–9.] An obscure allegory, but probably an allusion to the 'poet-haters' with their 'knowledge-hating policies', defeated in their purposes principally through Suffolk's efforts.

158 importune] beg for urgently or persistently. The only person to whom a man of Suffolk's rank could 'importune' anything would be the king.

159. their ... river] Permessus, which rises in and flows around Mount Helicon.

His name, in spite of death, shall propagate.
O, could the world but feel how sweet a touch
   A good deed hath in one in love with goodness
(If poesy were not ravishèd so much,   165
   And her composed rage held the simplest woodness,
Though of all heats that temper human brains
   Hers ever was most subtle, high, and holy,
First binding savage lives in civil chains—
   Solely religious, and adorèd solely,   170
If men felt this) they would not think a love
   That gives itself, in her, did vanities give;
Who is, in earth though low, in worth above,
   Most able t'honour life, though least to live.
      And so, good friend, safe passage to thy freight,   175
         To thee a long peace, through a virtuous strife,
      In which, let's both contend to virtue's height,
         Not making fame our object, but good life.

Come forth, Sejanus, fall before this book,
   And of thy Fall's reviver ask forgiveness,   180
That thy low birth and merits durst to look
   A fortune in the face, of such unevenness;
For so his fervent love to virtue hates
   That her plucked plumes should wing vice to such calling,
That he presents thee to all marking states   185
   As if thou hadst been all this while in falling;
His strong arm plucking, from the middle world,

---

164. *A good deed hath in one*] Q; *The Knowledge hath, which is* F.   167.
human] *humane* Q.   170. *solely,*] Q, F; *solely,*) edd.   171. *this*) Q, F; *this*,
edd.   179–93. Come ... est] Q; *not in* F.

---

163. touch] impression on the mind or soul (*O.E.D.*, *touch*, *sb.*, 13b).
166. woodness] insanity.
167. heats] passions.
169. First binding savage lives] It was a classical doctrine that poetry (with
religion) was the first civilizing force in the development of human society.
172. in her] in poetry.
174. though least to live] *i.e.* poetry is least likely to make a living for one.
176. strife] struggle (in opposition to 'poet-haters').
183. *to*] of.
184. *calling*] position.
185. *marking*] observing.
187–8. *from ... house*] Ovid describes Fame's house as 'in the middle of the

Fame's brazen house, and lays her tower as low
As Homer's Barathrum; that, from heaven hurled,
   Thou mightst fall on it—and thy ruins grow   190
      To all posterities, from his work, the ground,
      And under heav'n nought but his song might sound.
                          Haec commentatus est
                          Georgius Chapmannus.

    For his worthy Friend, the Author.

In that this book doth deign Sejanus' name,
   Him unto more than Caesar's love it brings;
   For where he could not with ambition's wings,
   One quill doth heave him to the height of fame.
Ye great ones, though, whose ends may be the same,   5
   Know that, however we do flatter kings,
   Their favours (like themselves) are fading things,
   With no less envy had, than lost with shame.
Nor make yourselves less honest than you are,
   To make our author wiser than he is;   10
   Ne of such crimes accuse him, which I dare

---

194. *Georgius Chapmannus.*] *Q*; GEOR. CHAPMAN. *F.*   *For his* ...
HOLLAND] *Q*; *reprinted in F*, ¶6r.   0.1. *For*] *Q*; *To F*.   4. heave] *corr.*
Q; heau'd *uncorr. Q*.

world, 'twixt land and sea and sky, ... It is built all of echoing brass'. See
Metamorphoses, XII.39–63 (tr. Frank Justus Miller, Loeb ed. (London, 1968,
1971), II. 183–5).
   189. *Homer's Barathrum*] The Barathrum was a pit at Athens into which
were hurled condemned criminals, but the word was applied poetically to the
infernal regions. In Chapman's trans. of the *Iliad*, VIII, 8–14, Jove threatens
to cast any god who supports Troy or Greece 'as deepe / As Tartarus (the brood
of night) where Barathrum doth steepe / Torment in his profoundest sinks,
where is the floore of brasse / And gates of iron; the place for depth as farre
doth hell surpasse / As heaven (for height) exceeds the earth.' See *Chapman's
Homer*, ed. Allardyce Nicoll (London, 1957), I, 166.
   191. *posterities*] succeeding generations.
   191. *ground*] See l. 56n., above.
   193–4. *Haec* ... *Chapmannus*] George Chapman composed these lines.

   1. *deign*] condescend to take.
   3. *could not*] i.e. could not arrive.
   9–14.] An obvious reference to those whose inclination to read into the play
parallels with English politics brought Jonson before the Privy Council.

By all his muses swear be none of his.
    The men are not, some faults may be these times';
    He acts those men, and they did act these crimes.

                                    HUGH HOLLAND.   15

                    To the deserving Author.

When I respect thy argument, I see
    An image of those times; but when I view
    The wit, the workmanship, so rich, so true,
The times themselves do seem retrieved to me.
    And as Sejanus, in thy tragedy,   5
    Falleth from Caesar's grace, even so the crew
    Of common playwrights, whom opinion blew
Big with false greatness, are disgraced by thee.
    Thus, in one tragedy, thou makest twain;
And, since fair works of justice fit the part   10
    Of tragic writers, muses do ordain

---

13. times'] *This ed.;* Times: *Q;* times: *F.*   15. HUGH HOLLAND.] *Q;* H.
HOLLAND *follows* For . . . *Author, F.*   To the . . . *CYGNUS.*] *Q; not in F.*

---

14. *acts*] animates (*O.E.D. act, v.*, 1).
    15. *HUGH HOLLAND*] 1563?–1633, b. in Denbigh, Wales, and educated
at Westminster and Cambridge. While travelling in Europe he became a
Catholic, and was often fined for recusancy in the last years of Elizabeth's
reign. Jonson wrote a commendatory poem prefixed to Holland's *Pancharis*
(1603), in which he refers to Holland as a black swan. This is partly explained
by these lines in Holland's prefatory poem 'To My Maiden Muse': having left
Cambridge, 'Now the blacke Doune began to couer / My pale Cheekes (for I
was a Louer) / And sung Acrosticke Sonets sweetely.' Like Jonson, Holland
wrote a poem prefixed to the Shakespeare Folio. It is appropriate that his poem
on *Sej.* should be printed on the same page, A2, as that of Cygnus—another
'swan', one whose identity is unknown, but whose sonnet is of identical form
to Holland's.

    1. *respect*] consider, regard.
    1. *argument*] theme, subject.
    3. *wit*] delightfully apt association of thought and expression.
    3. *true*] accurate, right.
    4. *retrieved*] brought back.
    8. *disgraced*] put out of countenance.

That all tragedians, masters of their art,
  Who shall hereafter follow on this tract,
  In writing well, thy tragedy shall act.

CYGNUS.   15

To his learned and beloved Friend,
upon his equal work.

Sejanus, great and eminent in Rome,
Raised above all the Senate, both in grace
Of prince's favour, authority, place,
And popular dependence; yet how soon,
Even with the instant of his overthrow,   5
Is all this pride and greatness now forgot—
Only that in former grace he stood not—
By them which did his state, not treason, know!
His very flatterers, that did adorn
Their necks with his rich medals, now in flame   10
Consume them, and would lose even his name,
Or else recite it with reproach or scorn!
This was his Roman fate. But now thy muse,
To us that neither knew his height nor fall,
Hath raised him up with such memorial,   15
All future states and times his name shall use.
What not his good nor ill could once extend
To the next age, thy verse, industrious

To his ... *Th. R.*] *Q; not in F.*   0.2. equal] aequall *Q.*   3. prince's] *This ed.; Princes Q.*   11. lose] loose *Q.*   18. industrious] industrious, *Q.*

---

    14. *act*] imitate—a pun on the sense of *O.E.D.*, vb., 4, 'To ... represent in mimic action'.

    15. CYGNUS] Literally 'Swan'. Is this sonnet also by Holland?

    0.2. *equal*] just, impartial (*O.E.D. equal, a.* and *sb.*, 5)—or perhaps the 'work' is 'equal' to its author in being 'learned'.

    3. *place*] rank.

    4. *popular dependence*] dependence of the people upon him.

    8. *state*] greatness, high status.

    11. *lose*] forget.

    19. *illustrious*] perhaps a pun on Latin *illustris*, clear, manifest.

And learned friend, hath made illustrious
To this. Nor shall his or thy fame have end.   20

Th. R.

Amicis, amici nostri dignissimi, dignissimis,
Epigramma.
D.
IOHANNES MARSTONIVS.

Ye ready friends, spare your unneedful bays;   5
This work despairful envy must even praise.

Phoebus hath voiced it, loud, through echoing skies:
'SEJANUS' FALL shall force thy merit rise;

For never English shall, or hath before
Spoke fuller graced.' He could say much, not more.   10

Upon SEJANUS.

How high a poor man shows in low estate,
    Whose base is firm, and whole frame competent,

Amicis ... not more.] *Q; not in F.*   8. SEJANUS'] SEIANVS *Q.*   8–10.
'SEJANUS' ... graced.'] *inverted commas not in Q.* shall force ... graced *in*
italic in Q.   *Upon SEJANUS ... Strachey.] Q; not in F.*   3. fate:] Fate, *Q.*

---

21. Th. R.] possibly Sir Thomas Roe (1581?–1644), later ambassador to the
Great Mogul. 'T. R.' also wrote verses for *Volp.* Jonson addressed two
epigrams to Roe—*Ep.*, XCVIII and XCIX—and Roe referred to Jonson in
one of his dispatches (quoted in *H.&S.*, XI, 315).

1–4. *Amicis ... MARSTONIVS*] To the most worthy friends of our most
worthy friend, John Marston presents an epigram.
4. *IOHANNES MARSTONIVS*] The poet and playwright John Marston
(1576–1634), who collaborated with Jonson and Chapman on *E.H.* Marston
had dedicated *The Malcontent* to Jonson, but their literary relations had not
always been so friendly—witness Jonson's parody of Marston as Crispinus in
Poet. The following year, Marston covertly attacked *Sej.* for its pedantic
fidelity to its sources. See above, 'To the Readers', ll. 23–4n.

5. *ready*] willing (to praise).
5. *bays*] garland made of bay-tree sprigs.
1. *shows*] appears.
2. *competent*] fit, proper.

That sees this cedar made the shrub of fate:
  Th'one's little, lasting; th'other's confluence spent.
And as the lightning comes behind the thunder   5
  From the torn cloud, yet first invades our sense,
So every violent fortune, that to wonder
  Hoists men aloft, is a clear evidence
Of a vaunt-curring blow the fates have given
  To his forced state: swift lightning blinds his eyes,   10
While thunder from comparison-hating heaven
  Dischargeth on his height, and there it lies.
If men will shun swol'n Fortune's ruinous blasts,
Let them use temperance. Nothing violent lasts.

                           William Strachey.   15

To him that hath so excelled on
this excellent subject.

Thy poem (pardon me) is mere deceit;
  Yet such deceit, as thou that dost beguile
  Art juster far than they who use no wile;
And they who are deceivèd by this feat,

To him ... ΦΙΛΟΣ] *Q; not in F.*   3. Art] *Gifford;* Are *Q.*

    3. *this cedar*] Sejanus.
    4. *confluence*] large amount of good fortune. Cf. examples in *O.E.D.*, sb., 6.
    5. *thunder*] understood as the unseen cause of the phenomenon from which the noise and flash proceed (*O.E.D.*, sb., 1).
    9. *vaunt-curring blow*] blow announcing the soon-to-be-expected arrival of a greater blow. *O.E.D.*'s sole example of 'vaunt-currying' ('Meaning not clear') is from *Sir Giles Goosecap* (1606). Cf. Shakespeare, *Lr.*, III.ii.5, where the flashes of lightning are the 'Vaunt-couriers [forerunners, heralds] of oak-cleaving thunderbolts'; and *Tp.*, I.ii.201–2, 'Jove's lightnings, the precursors / O'th' dreadful thunderclaps.'
    10. *forced state*] status achieved through violence.
    13–14. As Briggs, 'Source-Material', pp. 328–9, points out, from Seneca, *Troades*, 258–9, 'Ungoverned power no one can long retain; controlled, it lasts'. Tr. F. J. Miller, Loeb ed. of *Seneca's Tragedies*, I (London, 1960), 143.
    15. William Strachey] possibly the colonist of that name (*fl.* 1609–18), who later wrote on Virginia, and whose account of a shipwreck in the Bermudas was used by Shakespeare in *Tp.*

More wise than such who can eschew thy cheat.   5
   For thou hast given each part so just a style
   That men suppose the action now on file—
And men suppose who are of best conceit.
   Yet some there be that are not moved hereby,
   And others are so quick that they will spy   10
Where later times are in some speech enweaved;
   Those wary simples, and these simple elves:
They are so dull, they cannot be deceived,
   These so unjust, they will deceive themselves.

                 ΦΙΛΟΣ.   15

To the most understanding Poet.

When in the Globe's fair ring, our world's best stage,
   I saw *Sejanus*, set with that rich foil,
   I looked the author should have borne the spoil
Of conquest from the writers of the age;
   But when I viewed the people's beastly rage,   5
   Bent to confound thy grave and learned toil,
   That cost thee so much sweat, and so much oil,

---

12. elves] Elfes *Q*.   15. ΦΙΛΟΣ] ΦΙΛΟΕ *Q*.   *To the* . . . Ev. B]. *Q; not
in F*.   15. Ev. B.] *corr. Q*; EDB. *uncorr. Q*.

---

5. *eschew*] avoid.

7. *on file*] perhaps 'in process'—a sense not given in *O.E.D.*

8. *conceit*] understanding—with perhaps a pun on another sense, 'imagination'.

10–11.] Cf. Holland's poem above, ll. 9–14, and Chapman's verses, ll. 141–2, 157–9.

10. *so quick*] of so ready a wit.

12. *wary simples* . . . *simple elves*] a glance back at those simpletons so guarded in their response to the play (l. 9) and to the simple or absurd 'elves' or mis-interpreting mischief-makers (ll. 10–11).

15. *ΦΙΛΟΣ*] a friend.

1–2. *When* . . . Sejanus] The first Globe performance—as distinct from the first performance in 1603 referred to on the t.p. of *F*, which was probably at court—took place in 1604, after the re-opening of the theatres on 9 April 1604. See Introduction, p. 9.

2. *foil*] in the sense of the whole setting of a jewel (*O.E.D.*, sb. 1, 5b), not just the reflective backing. The fairness of English theatres never failed to impress foreigners.

3. *looked*] expected.

7. *oil*] used for lighting the poet's study.

My indignation I could hardly'assuage.
And many there (in passion) scarce could tell
    Whether thy fault or theirs deserved most blame—   10
    Thine, for so showing, theirs, to wrong the same;
But both they left within that doubtful hell.
    From whence, this publication sets thee free;
    They, for their ignorance, still damnèd be.

Ev. B.   15

---

12. *doubtful hell*] *i.e.* the playhouse of doubters which damned the poet-along with themselves.

15. *Ev. B.*] Not, as generally assumed (e.g. by *H.&S.*, XI, 317), a misprint for 'Ed. B.', *i.e.* Edmund Bolton (*c.* 1575–*c.* 1633), who wrote commendatory Latin verse for *Volp.* Collation in fact shows that Ed. B. was altered at the press to Ev. B.—the error was picked up at an early stage. 'Ev.' could be a contraction of Everard (Everard Digby and the Catholic martyr Everard Hanse are two contemporary examples), though I have been unable to trace an Everard 'B'.

THE ARGUMENT.

Aelius Sejanus, son to Seius Strabo, a gentleman of Rome, and
born at Vulsinium, after his long service in court, first under
Augustus, afterward Tiberius, grew into that favour with the
latter, and won him by those arts, as there wanted nothing but
the name to make him a copartner of the Empire. Which   5
greatness of his, Drusus the emperor's son not brooking, after
many smothered dislikes (it one day breaking out) the prince
struck him publicly on the face. To revenge which disgrace,
Livia, the wife of Drusus (being before corrupted by him to
her dishonour, and the discovery of her husband's counsels)   10
Sejanus practiseth with, together with her physician, called
Eudemus, and one Lygdus an eunuch, to poison Drusus. This
their inhumane act having successful and unsuspected passage,
it emboldeneth Sejanus to farther and more insolent projects,
even the ambition of the Empire: where finding the lets he must 15
encounter to be many, and hard, in respect of the issue of
Germanicus (who were next in hope for the succession) he
deviseth to make Tiberius' self his means; and instils into his
ears many doubts and suspicions both against the princes and
their mother Agrippina; which Caesar jealously hearkening to,   20
as covetously consenteth to their ruin, and their friends'. In this

---

7. dislikes (it ... out)] *corr. F*; dislikes, it ... out; *Q; dislikes, it ... out,
uncorr. F.*   8. struck] *F2*; stroke *Q*; strooke *F*.   9. Livia] *F*; (*Livia Q*;
9. Drusus (being] *F*; *Drusus*, beeing *Q*.   17. in hope for the succession) he]
corr. F; in hope) he *Q*; *in hope) he uncorr. F.*

---

1. *Seius Strabo*] Lucius Seius Strabo, appointed Provost of the Praetorian
Guard under Augustus.
2. *Vulsinium*] Volsinii (now Bolsena), between Rome and Siena. The
worship of Fortuna in her Etruscan form of Nortia was strongly established
here and Fortuna is worshipped by Sejanus.
8–12. *To revenge ... Drusus*] In Tacitus, the blow precedes not only the
seduction but its planning; Sejanus's motives are thus revenge and ambition.
In the play, Sejanus is already scheming, before the blow, to corrupt Livia in
order to destroy Drusus, and the blow merely adds another motive to that of
ambition (I.580–1).
11. *practiseth*] conspires.
13. *unsuspected passage*] *i.e.* the death not creating suspicion.
15. *lets*] obstacles.
20. *jealously*] distrustfully.
21. *covetously*] ardently.

time, the better to mature and strengthen his design, Sejanus
labours to marry Livia, and worketh with all his engine to
remove Tiberius from the knowledge of public business, with
allurements of a quiet and retired life; the latter of which   25
Tiberius (out of a proneness to lust and a desire to hide those
unnatural pleasures which he could not so publicly practise)
embraceth: the former enkindleth his fears, and there gives
him first cause of doubt or suspect toward Sejanus. Against
whom, he raiseth in private a new instrument, one Sertorius   30
Macro, and by him underworketh, discovers the other's
counsels, his means, his ends, sounds the affections of the
senators, divides, distracts them; at last, when Sejanus least
looketh, and is most secure, with pretext of doing him an
unwonted honour in the Senate, he trains him from his guards;   35
and with a long doubtful letter, in one day, hath him suspected,
accused, condemned, and torn in pieces by the rage of the
people.

This do we advance as a mark of terror to all traitors and
treasons; to show how just the heavens are in pouring and   40
thundering down a weighty vengeance on their unnatural
intents, even to the worst princes: much more to those for
guard of whose piety and virtue the angels are in continual
watch, and God himself miraculously working.

22–3. Sejanus labours] *corr. F;* hee labours *Q;* he labours *uncorr. F.*   23. with
all] *F;* withall *Q.*   25. retired] *corr. F;* seperated *Q; separated uncorr. F.*
26. Tiberius] *corr. Q; Tiberias uncorr. Q.*   33. least] *F;* lest *Q.*   34.
pretext] *F;* praetext *Q.*   36. and with ... one day] *corr. F;* with one Letter,
& in one Day *Q;* with one letter, and in one day *uncorr. F.*   39–44.   This
... working] *Q; not in F.*

---

23. *engine*] cunning (*O.E.D. engine, sb.,* 2).
28. *the former*] i.e. Sejanus's desire to marry Livia.
31. *underworketh*] takes clandestine measures.
32. *affections*] dispositions.
35. *trains*] decoys.
36. *doubtful*] equivocal.
39–44. *This ... working*] Since Jonson had only recently cleared himself of
any 'treasonous' intent in his handling of the subject, these lines, which *Q*
prints in larger type, are a prudent (and perhaps a compulsory) addition, and
one that could be dispensed with in *F.* The Gunpowder Plot of 5 November
1605 seems to be alluded to here, but the precise date of *Q*'s appearance (after
6 August 1605) is unknown. It is possible that the allusion is to the Ralegh–
Cobham 'plot' of 1603.

The Names of the Actors

TIBERIUS
SEJANUS
DRUSUS SE[NIOR]
NERO   5
DRUSUS JU[NIOR]
CALIGULA

The Names of the Actors.] *Q;* The Persons of the Play. *F. Q* (and subst. *F*) disposes the names as follows: TIBERIVS. / DRVSVS. *se.* SEIANVS. / NERO. LATIARIS. / DRVSVS. *iu.* VARRO. / CALIGVLA. MACRO. / ARRVNTIVS. COTTA. / SILIVS. AFER. / SABINVS. HATERIVS. / LEPIDVS. SANQVINIVS. / CORDVS. POMPONIVS. / GALLVS. POSTVMVS. / REGVLVS. TRIO. / TERENTIVS. MINVTIVS. / LACO. SATRIVS. / EVDEMVS. NATTA. / RVFVS. OPSIVS. / TRIBVNI. / AGRIPPINA. {LIVIA. / SOSIA. / PRAECONES. LICTORES. / FLAMEN. MINISTRI. / TVBICINES. TIBICINES. / NVNTIVS. SERVVS.

Additional information on some of the characters, including appropriate references to primary sources, will be found in many of the Annotations.

2. *TIBERIUS*] Tiberius Claudius Nero, 42 B.C.–A.D. 37, stepson and adopted son of the emperor Augustus, whom he succeeded in A.D. 14. Son of Livia, father of Drusus Senior, uncle of Germanicus.

3. *SEJANUS*] Lucius Aelius Seianus (consul A.D.31), son of the Roman knight and Guard Prefect Seius Strabo, a native of Volsinii in Etruria, rose to all but supreme power under Tiberius. Condemned 18 October, A.D. 31. He was, however, more than the son of a knight: his mother was patrician, and his father's mother was sister to the wife of Maecenas and the consul Varro Murena. See Syme, I, 384.

4. *DRUSUS SE[NIOR]*] Drusus Caesar (consul A.D. 15, 21), son of Tiberius and his first wife Vipsania, second husband of his first cousin Livia (or Livilla), poisoned A.D. 23.

5. *NERO*] Julius Caesar Nero, eldest son of Germanicus and Agrippina, next in succession after Drusus senior. Banished, through the plotting of Sejanus, to the island of Pontia, where he was starved to death, A.D. 31.

6. *DRUSUS JU[NIOR]*] Julius Caesar Drusus, second son of Germanicus and Agrippina, next in succession after Drusus senior and Nero, imprisoned in the Palatine dungeons through the efforts of Sejanus, and finally, like his brother Nero, starved to death (A.D. 33) after being reduced to chewing the stuffing of his mattress.

7. *CALIGULA*] Caius Caesar, youngest son of Germanicus and next in succession after Drusus junior, was given the nick-name Caligula from his

ARRUNTIUS
SILIUS
SABINUS   10
LEPIDUS
CORDUS
GALLUS
REGULUS

---

wearing as a child the *caliga* or soldier's boot. Rumoured to have hastened the death of Tiberius, he became notorious as emperor, but is not represented unfavourably in this play.

8. *ARRUNTIUS*] Lucius Arruntius (consul A.D. 6), whose connections were Sullan and Pompeian, is Jonson's spokesman. According to Tacitus, he was a senator of great wealth, talent, integrity, and public spirit, one whom Augustus thought would make a fine emperor and would venture on the position if opportunity allowed. He committed suicide A.D. 37, convinced that the ailing Tiberius would only be followed by a worse emperor.

9. *SILIUS*] Caius Silius Caecina Largus (consul A.D. 13), a general under Germanicus, commanded the army of Upper Germany, was awarded an honourary Triumph in A.D. 15, and defeated the Aedui under Sacrovir A.D.21. Accused of extortion (with reason) and treason A.D. 24, he committed suicide, which Jonson takes the liberty of having him do in the Senate.

10. *SABINUS*] Titius Sabinus, a knight, had been a friend of Germanicus and remained close to Germanicus's widow Agrippina and her children. Betrayed by Latiaris (whom Jonson, following an error in Greneway's tr. of Tacitus, makes a cousin of Sabinus—see IV.110n.) and executed A.D. 28, for treason.

11. *LEPIDUS*] This is Marcus Lepidus (consul A.D. 6), as Jonson calls him, and not Manius Lepidus (consul A.D. 11), as *H.&S.*, IX, 594–5, argue. See Syme, II, 751–2 (Appendix G.64). This Lepidus was, according to Augustus as reported by Tacitus, capable (but disdainful) of being emperor. An honourable, sagacious senator of integrity, he yet managed to avoid alienating Tiberius.

12. *CORDUS*] Aulus Cremutius Cordus, historian, admired by Tacitus, who gives him a splendid defence of free speech which Jonson incorporates in the play. Following his prosecution (not in fact principally related to his writings) he took his own life, A.D. 25. Seneca's *De Consolatione* is addressed to Cordus's daughter Marcia. Almost all the work of Cordus is lost.

13. *GALLUS*] Caius Asinius Gallus (consul 8 B.C.), husband of Vipsania, the former wife of Tiberius. His speeches in the Senate were of an independent cast. Arrested in A.D. 30, died of starvation in 33. Dio Cassius (*Roman History*, LVIII.iii.3) points out that the letter from Tiberius denouncing Gallus arrived in the Senate on the same day the two feasted together at Capreae!

14. *REGULUS*] Publius Memmius Regulus (suffect (additional) consul A.D. 31), a man of independence who opposed Sejanus and is fulsomely praised by Tacitus. Died A.D. 62. See II.220n.

TERENTIUS   15
LACO
EUDEMUS
RUFUS
LATIARIS
VARRO   20
MACRO
COTTA
AFER
HATERIUS

---

15. *TERENTIUS*] Marcus Terentius, friend of Sejanus, he later bravely defended his friendship after his patron's fall (Tacitus, *Annals*, VI.viii–ix).

16. *LACO*] Graecinus (or Graecinius; Gracinus in *Sej.*) Laco, in A.D. 31 commander of the night watch or *vigiles*. Loyal to Macro in the overthrow of Sejanus.

17. *EUDEMUS*] Physician to Livia and in complicity with her, Lygdus, and Sejanus in the murder of Drusus senior. Later denounced by the widow of Sejanus, tortured, and executed.

18. *RUFUS*] Petilius Rufus, an ex-praetor complicit with Latiaris and Opsius in the betrayal of Titius Sabinus.

19. *LATIARIS*] Latinius (or Lucanius) Latiaris, betrayer of Titius Sabinus (see note on latter). Fell with Sejanus, A.D. 31.

20. *VARRO*] Lucius Visellius Varro (consul A.D. 24), instrumental in the fall of Caius Silius, A.D. 24.

21. *MACRO*] Naevius Sertorius Macro, Guard Prefect and the man chosen by Tiberius to undermine Sejanus. His taunting of Sejanus in the Senate in Act V is Jonson's invention. Compelled by Caligula to take his own life (after the former had appointed him governor of Egypt), A.D. 38.

22. *COTTA*] Marcus Aurelius Cotta Maximus Messalinus (consul A.D. 20), presented by Tacitus as thoroughly unscrupulous and always ready with a savage proposal—a contrast to Lepidus during the trials of Silius and Cordus.

23. *AFER*] Cnaeus Domitius Afer (suffect (additional) consul A.D. 39), from Nemausus in Narbonensian Gaul, an illustrious orator whose excessive ambition cost him a good name, became a praetor in A.D. 25 and made his reputation with the prosecution of Agrippina's cousin, Claudia Pulchra, in A.D. 26. Historically he was not connected with the trial of Silius, but Jonson cannot resist bringing him in. Syme, I, 328: 'Afer was incomparably the most impressive of all orators in that age, and worthy to rank with the ancients. . . . A great wit. His "dicta" circulated in book form'. Jonson's unflattering portrait follows Tacitus. See II.424n.

24. *HATERIUS*] Quintus Haterius (suffect (additional) consul 5 B.C.), born c. 63 B.C. and died A.D. 26, an orator noted for his style rather than the substance of his speeches. Conflated by Jonson with his son Haterius Agrippa—see below, V.456n.

SANQUINIUS   25
POMPONIUS
POSTUMUS
TRIO
MINUTIUS
SATRIUS   30
NATTA
OPSIUS
AGRIPPINA
LIVIA
SOSIA   35
TRIBUNI

---

27. POSTUMUS] *Q;* POSTHVMVS. *F.*

---

25. *SANQUINIUS*] Mentioned by Tacitus, in reference to an earlier (lost) passage, as an accuser of Lucius Arruntius.

26. *POMPONIUS*] Linked, as an underling of Sejanus, with Satrius Secundus by Tacitus—presumably there were more details in the lost books of the *Annals*.

27. *POSTUMUS*] Julius Postumus, lover of the Augusta's friend Mutilia Prisca, and used as an informer by Sejanus.

28. *TRIO*] Lucius Fulcinius Trio (suffect (additional) consul A.D. 31) took the side of Sejanus in the crucial days preceding the latter's destruction, which he survived. Committed suicide while facing prosecution, A.D. 35. A *delator* (informer, accuser) of the first rank.

29. *MINUTIUS*] Minucius Thermus, a knight and friend of Sejanus, denounced by Tiberius, A.D. 32.

30. *SATRIUS*] Satrius Secundus, client of Sejanus, is referred to by Tacitus as the divulger of Sejanus's 'plot' against Tiberius—though the plot was Tiberius's! Accuser, with Pinnarius Natta, of Cordus.

31. *NATTA*] Pinnarius Natta, client of Sejanus. Together with Satrius Secundus, he accused Cordus.

32. *OPSIUS*] Marcus Opsius, who, with Rufus and Latiaris, betrayed Sabinus.

33. *AGRIPPINA*] Widow of Germanicus, daughter of Marcus Agrippa, and granddaughter of Augustus, an intrepid woman and centre of the opposition to Tiberius and Sejanus. Exiled, A.D. 30, to the island of Pandataria, where she starved herself to death, A.D. 33.

34. *LIVIA*] Livia Julia (or Livilla in Suetonius and Dio), wife of Drusus senior and sister of Germanicus, complicit, with her lover Sejanus, in her husband's death, A.D. 23. Put to death after the fall of Sejanus.

35. *SOSIA*] Sosia Galla, wife of Caius Silius and friend of Agrippina, she fell with her husband, A.D. 23, following his trial for extortion and treason.

36. *TRIBUNI*] Military tribunes of the Guard (*tribuni cohortium praetorianarum*).

PRAECONES
LICTORES
FLAMEN
MINISTRI   40
TUBICINES
TIBICINES
NUNTIUS
SERVUS

                              THE SCENE   45
                                ROME

45–6. *THE SCENE* / ROME] *F; not in Q.*

37. *PRAECONES*] heralds.
38. *LICTORES*] lictors, who preceded magistrates through the streets,
bearing the *fasces*.
39. *FLAMEN*] priest.
40. *MINISTRI*] attendants.
41. *TUBICINES*] trumpeters.
42. *TIBICINES*] flautists.
43. *NUNTIUS*] messenger.
44. *SERVUS*] servant (*servi*, pl.).

Sejanus, his fall
Actus Primus

<hr>

[*Enter*] SABINUS [*and*] SILIUS.

Sabinus. Hail, Caius Silius!
Silius.   Titius Sabinus, hail!
   You'are rarely met in court!
Sabinus.   Therefore, well met.
Silius. 'Tis true: indeed, this place is not our sphere.
Sabinus. No, Silius, we are no good enginers;
   We want the fine arts, and their thriving use   5
   Should make us graced, or favoured of the times.
   We have no shift of faces, no cleft tongues,
   No soft and glutinous bodies, that can stick,
   Like snails, on painted walls; or, on our breasts,
   Creep up, to fall from that proud height to which   10
   We did by slavery, not by service, climb.

<hr>

ACTUS PRIMUS] *Q; Act*. I. *F;* ACT I. SCENE I *Gifford;* Act I, [Scene i] *Bolton;*
Act I *Barish.*   O.I. [*Enter*] SABINUS [*and*] SILIUS] SABINVS. SILIVS. NATTA.
LATIARIS. CORDVS. / SATRIVS. ARRUNTIUS. EVDEMVS. / HATERIVS &c. *Q;*
SABINVS, SILIVS, NATTA, LATIARIS, COR- / DVS, SATRIVS, ARRVNTIVS,
EVDE- / MVS,   HATERIVS, &c. *F;* A State Room in the Palace. / Enter
Sabinus and Silius, followed by Latiaris. *Gifford, and subst. Barish;* [*The
Palace. Enter*] SABINUS, SILIUS *Bolton.*   I. *Sabinus.*] SAB. *Q; not in F.*
3. sphere] Sphaere *Q;* sphaere *F.*

<hr>

   I. *Caius Silius*] Jonson cites Tacitus, *Annals*, I.xxxi—the army of Upper
Germany under Silius remained loyal in A.D. 14 while that of Lower Germany
mutinied; and II.vi–vii, xxv—his role in the advances of Germanicus between
the Rhine and the Elbe, A.D. 16. All refs. to the *Annals* are to the Loeb ed., tr.
John Jackson (London, 1961).
   I. *Titius Sabinus*] Jonson cites Tacitus, *Annals*, IV. xviii: Sejanus 'attacked
Caius Silius and Titius Sabinus. The friendship of Germanicus was fatal to
both'. See also *Annals*, IV. lxviii–lxx, quoted below in the note to IV.93–232.
   2. *rarely*] a pun–seldom; and very well.
   4. *enginers*] plotters, schemers.
   7. *shift*] succession.
   II. *by slavery ... climb*] Jonson cites Tacitus, *Annals*, I.ii: 'Opposition
there was none: the boldest spirits had succumbed on stricken fields or by

We are no guilty men, and then no great;
We have nor place in court, office in state,
That we can say we owe unto our crimes;
We burn with no black secrets, which can make   15
Us dear to the pale authors; or live feared
Of their still waking jealousies, to raise
Ourselves a fortune, by subverting theirs.
We stand not in the lines that do advance
To that so courted point.

                    [*Enter* SATRIUS *and* NATTA.]

Silius.   But yonder lean   20
        A pair that do.

                    [*Enter* LATIARIS.]

Sabinus. [*To Latiaris.*] Good cousin Latiaris.

---

prosription-lists; while the rest of the nobility found a cheerful acceptance of
slavery the smoothest road to wealth and office.'

  12. *then*] on that account.

  14. *we owe ... crimes*] Jonson cites Juvenal, *Satires*, I.75: 'It is to their
crimes that men owe their pleasure-grounds and palaces, their fine tables'. All
refs. to Juvenal and Persius are to the Loeb ed., tr. G. G. Ramsay (London,
1957). See also Tacitus, *Annals*, IV.lxviii, 'the complaisance of Sejanus was
only to be purchased by crime'.

  15. *We burn ... secrets*] Jonson cites Juvenal, *Satires*, III.49ff.: 'What man
wins favour nowadays unless he be an accomplice—one whose soul seethes and
burns with secrets that must never be disclosed? ... the man whom Verres
loves is the man who can impeach Verres at any moment that he chooses.'

  16. *dear*] costly—since silence is expensive.

  16. *pale authors*] fearful perpetrators of the evils to which the secrets relate.

  16–17. *feared ... jealousies*] afraid of their incessant suspicions. Each fears
the other's fears, in a climate of fear.

  17–18. *to raise ... theirs*] Line 10 has already introduced the idea of rising
only to fall, but with these words Jonson introduces the theme of one person's
rising *through* the fall of another (see also 'The Argument', 30–1, 'he raiseth
... and ... underworketh', and III.747–8 and n.). Behind the word
'fortune', of course, stands Fortuna, Sejanus's 'one deity' (V.81.).

  20. *lean*] tend or bend (this way?). Sense not recorded in *O.E.D.*

  21. *cousin*] See below, IV.110n.

  21. *Latiaris*] On the man who betrayed Sabinus Jonson cites Tacitus, *Annals*,
IV.lxviii–lxix, and Dio, *Roman History*, LVIII.1.1–3. Cited again at IV.93;
see note. All refs. to Dio are to the Loeb ed., tr. E. Cary (London, 1961).

  22. *Satrius ... Natta*] Jonson cites Tacitus, *Annals*, IV. xxxiv, 'The accusers
[of Cremutius Cordus] were Satrius Secundus and Pinnarius Natta, clients of

Silius. Satrius Secundus and Pinnarius Natta,
    The great Sejanus' clients—there be two
    Know more than honest counsels; whose close breasts,
    Were they ripped up to light, it would be found   25
    A poor and idle sin to which their trunks
    Had not been made fit organs. These can lie,
    Flatter, and swear, forswear, deprave, inform,
    Smile, and betray; make guilty men; then beg
    The forfeit lives, to get the livings; cut   30
    Men's throats with whisp'rings; sell to gaping suitors
    The empty smoke that flies about the palace;
    Laugh when their patron laughs; sweat when he sweats;
    Be hot and cold with him; change every mood,

Sejanus'; and Seneca, *To Marcia on Consolation*, XXII. 4, 'Recall that time, so bitter for you, when Sejanus handed over your father [Cordus] to his client, Satrius Secundus, as a largess'. *Moral Essays*, Loeb ed., tr. J. W. Basore, II (London, 1970).

23. *clients*] from L., *cliens*, 'A plebeian under the patronage of a patrician ... who was bound, in return for certain services, to protect his client's life and interests' (*O.E.D., Client*, 1).

24. *close breasts*] secretive hearts.

25–27. *Were they ... organs*] an 'autopsy' on their hearts would show hardly a sin to the committing of which they had not lent their persons.

28. *inform*] Jonson cites Seneca, *On Benefits*, III. xxvi, which refers to the 'common and almost universal frenzy for bringing charges of treason' under Tiberius, and to the 'notorious informers' of that time. *Moral Essays*, Loeb ed., tr. J. W. Basore, III (London, 1964).

29–30. *beg ... livings*] press for the death penalty ('beg that the lives be forfeit') in order to inherit confiscated property. Jonson might have cited Tacitus, *Annals*, IV.xx: out of Sosia Galla's estate went 'a quarter, which was legally necessary, to the accusers'.

30–1. *cut ... whisp'rings*] As Briggs points out, this echoes Juvenal, *Satires*, IV.109–10: 'more ruthless than he Pompeius, whose gentle whisper would cut men's throats'.

32. *smoke*] promises. The Romans had the phrase, *fumum vendere*, literally 'to sell smoke', to make empty promises. Cf. Thomas Nashe, *Lenten Stuff* (1599), 'that for your selling smoake you may be courtiers', in R. B. McKerrow, ed., *The Works of Thomas Nashe* (Oxford, 1904–10), rev. by F. P. Wilson (Oxford, 1958), III, 225.

33–40.] At l. 38 Jonson cites Juvenal, *Satires*, III.105, but the reference should be to the whole of III. 100–8, which he has transcribed in ll. 33–40. 'If you smile, your Greek will split his sides with laughter; if he sees his friend drop a tear, he weeps, though without grieving; if you call for a bit of fire in winter-time, he puts on his cloak; if you say "I am hot," he breaks into a

Habit, and garb, as often as he varies;   35
Observe him, as his watch observes his clock;
And true as turquoise in the dear lord's ring,
Look well or ill with him—ready to praise
His lordship if he spit, or but piss fair,
Have an indifferent stool, or break wind well;   40
Nothing can 'scape their catch.
Sabinus.   Alas! these things
Deserve no note, conferred with other vile
And filthier flatteries, that corrupt the times:
When, not alone our gentry's chief are fain
To make their safety from such sordid acts,   45
But all our consuls, and no little part

---

sweat .... being ready at any moment, by night or by day, to take his
expression from another man's face, to throw up his hands and applaud if his
friend gives a good belch or piddles straight, or if his golden basin makes a
gurgle when turned upside down.'

35. *habit*] demeanour, with perhaps a pun on the sense of 'garb'—the
following noun.

36. *as his watch ... clock*] either, 'as he checks his less accurate watch
against a public clock' (an anachronism), or 'as his guard ("watch") closely
observes the time' (on a Roman water-clock or sundial).

37. *turquoise*] precious stone, said to change its colour in response to the
health of its wearer.

41. *catch*] notice—a sense not recorded in *O.E.D.*, perhaps influenced by
'catch sight of'.

42. *conferred*] compared (Lat. *conferre*, bring together, compare).

43. *filthier flatteries*] Jonson cites Tacitus, *Annals*, I. vii: 'Consuls, senators,
and knights were rushing into slavery' in their haste to flatter the new Caesar,
Tiberius.

44–55.] Jonson cites Tacitus, *Annals*, III.lxv: 'But so tainted was that age,
so mean its sycophancy, that not only the great personages of the state, who
had to shield their magnificence by their servility, but all senators of consular
rank, a large proportion of the ex-praetors, many ordinary members even
[*pedarii senatores*—senators who had not held curule office (office of the highest
rank)], vied with one another in rising to move the most repulsive and
extravagant resolutions. The tradition runs that Tiberius, on leaving the curia,
had a habit of ejaculating in Greek, "These men!–how ready they are for
slavery!" Even he, it was manifest, objecting though he did to public liberty,
was growing weary of such grovelling patience in his slaves.'

46–8. *consuls, ... praetors, ... senators*] Two *consules ordinarii*, and several
consules suffecti, were appointed annually, officially elected by the Senate (the
supreme council of state, membership 600) as the highest magistrates in the
state. Below them in authority were twelve praetors.

     Of such as have been praetors, yea, the most
     Of senators, that else not use their voices,
     Start up in public Senate, and there strive
     Who shall propound most abject things, and base,   50
     So much, as oft Tiberius hath been heard,
     Leaving the court, to cry, 'O race of men,
     Prepared for servitude!'—which showed that he,
     Who least the public liberty could like,
     As loathly brooked their flat servility.   55
Silius. Well, all is worthy of us, were it more,
     Who with our riots, pride, and civil hate,
     Have so provoked the justice of the gods—
     We that (within these fourscore years) were born
     Free, equal lords of the triumphèd world,   60
     And knew no masters but affections,
     To which betraying first our liberties,
     We since became the slaves to one man's lusts,
     And now to many. Every minist'ring spy
     That will accuse and swear is lord of you,   65
     Of me, of all, our fortunes, and our lives.

48.] *In margin in F: Pedarij. As note in Q.*   58. gods—] Gods *Q*; gods *F*.
60. equal] *F;* aequall *Q.*

---

   50. *abject*] despicable.
   57. *riots*] debauches.
   60. *triumphèd*] conquered. L.&S. cite, as one example of its Lat. equivalent
triumphati, Ovid's *Amores*, I.xv.26, 'Roma triumphati caput orbis'—Rome,
leader of the conquered world.
   61. *affections*] passions.
   64–6. *Every ... lives*] Jonson cites several writers: Tacitus, *Annals*, I.lxxiv,
on the 'professional' informer Romanus Hispo who, with Caepio Crispinus,
'set an example, the followers of which passed from beggary to wealth, from
being despised to being feared, and crowned at last the ruin of others by their
own'; *Annals*, III.xxxvii–xxxviii—various instances of 'fictitious charges of
treason' in which 'the informers showed no fatigue'; Juvenal, *Satires*, X.87, 'let
our slaves see that none bear witness against us, and drag their trembling
master into court with a halter round his neck'; and Suetonius, *Lives*, III.lxi,
'The word of no informer was doubted'. All refs. to Suetonius are to the Loeb
ed., tr. J. C. Rolfe (London, 1960). A part of the property of the condemned
went to the informer—which practice promoted the rise of a professional class
of informers or *delatores*.
   64. *minist'ring*] obsequious, subservient—a sense not recorded in *O.E.D.*
Perhaps Latin *minister*, an inferior, influenced Jonson here.

Our looks are called to question, and our words,
How innocent soever, are made crimes;
We shall not shortly dare to tell our dreams,
Or think, but 'twill be treason.
Sabinus.   Tyrants' arts   70
Are to give flatterers grace, accusers power,
That those may seem to kill whom they devour.

[*Enter* CORDUS *and* ARRUNTIUS.]

Now good Cremutius Cordus.
Cordus.   Hail to your lordship!
Natta. Who's that salutes your cousin?   *They whisper*
Latiaris.   'Tis one Cordus,
A gentleman of Rome; one that has writ   75
Annals of late, they say, and very well.
Natta. Annals? Of what times?
Latiaris.   I think of Pompey's,

---

70. think,] *F;* thinke *Q.*   70. Tyrants'] ''Tirannes *Q;* ''Tyrannes *F.*
71–2.] *Both lines preceded by gnomic pointing, Q. F.*   74. They whisper]
Marginal s.d. in F; not in Q.   76 and 77. annals] Annal's Q, F. This is
Jonson's abbreviation for Lat. Annales.

67–8. *Our looks . . . crimes*] Jonson cites Tacitus, *Annals,* I.vii, 'all the while
[Tiberius] was distorting words and looks into crimes and storing them in his
memory'; *Annals,* III.xxxviii, 'Tiberius and the informers showed no fatigue',
and 'a charge of treason' was 'the complement now of all arraignments';
Suetonius, *Lives,* III.lxi, 'Every crime was treated as capital, even the
utterance of a few simple words'; and Seneca, *On Benefits,* III.xxvi, 'a . . .
universal frenzy for bringing charges of treason . . . seized upon the talk of
drunkards, the frank words of jesters'.

70–2. *Tyrants' . . . devour*] These lines, with the exception of the phrase
'flatterers, grace', echo Machiavelli, *The Prince,* ch. XIX, 'that princes should
let the carrying out of unpopular duties devolve on others, and bestow favours
themselves'—*The Prince and The Discourses,* ed. Max Lerner (New York,
1950), p. 70—which Jonson also cited in *Disc.,* ll. 1158–60. Machiavelli,
however, recommended that flatterers be shunned, not given 'grace' (ch.
XXIII).

73. *Cremutius Cordus*] On this Roman historian (d. A.D. 25), his offending of
Sejanus, his irreproachable life, noble suicide, and his daughter Marcia's
saving of some of his writings after his death, Jonson cites Tacitus, *Annals,*
IV.xxxiv–v (reproduced below in III.407–60n); Seneca, *To Marcia on
Consolation,* I.iii, XXII.iv–vii; Dio, *Roman History,* LVII.24.2–4; and
Suetonius, *Lives,* II.xxxv, III.lxi, and IV.xvi.

And Caius Caesar's; and so down to these.
Natta. How stands h'affected to the present state?
    Is he or Drusian? or Germanican?   80
    Or ours? or neutral?
Latiaris.   I know him not so far.
Natta. Those times are somewhat queasy to be touched.
    Have you or seen or heard part of his work?
Latiaris. Not I; he means they shall be public shortly.
Natta. O. Cordus do you call him?
Latiaris.   Aye.
                 [*Exeunt* SATRIUS, NATTA *and* LATIARIS.]
Sabinus.   But these our times   85
    Are not the same, Arruntius.
Arruntius.   Times? The men,
    The men are not the same: 'tis we are base,
    Poor, and degenerate from th'exalted strain

---

85. [*Exeunt* ... LATIARIS.]] *This ed.; Barish, Bolton om. Latiaris.*

78. *so down to these*] Jonson cites Suetonius, II.xxxv, where that author
quotes Cordus on the period of Augustus, but not on that of Tiberius.
    80. *Drusian? or Germanican?*] On the factionalism of the time Jonson cites
Tacitus, *Annals*, II.xliii, 'the court was split and torn by unspoken preferences
for Germanicus or for Drusus'; and *Annals*, IV. xvii, Sejanus warned Tiberius
that Rome 'was split in two halves, as if by civil war. There were men who
proclaimed themselves of Agrippina's party: unless a stand was taken, there
would be more'. Drusus was Tiberius's son. The popular military commander Germanicus, nephew and adopted son of Tiberius, and husband of
Agrippina, was dead, 'Germanican' referring to the interests of his family.
    82. *queasy*] hazardous.
    85. [*Exeunt* ... LATIARIS.]] Barish and Bolton leave Latiaris on stage. At
I.398.1, however, he must give letters to Tiberius, which suggests that he, like
the other presenter of letters, Haterius, has entered with Tiberius at 1.374.1.
    86. *Arruntius*] On the senator Lucius Arruntius, consul A.D. 6, Jonson cites
Tacitus, *Annals*, I.xiii—his independence in the Senate, and Augustus's
estimate of him as 'not undeserving [of the principate] and bold enough to
venture, should the opportunity arise'; *Annals*, III.xxxi—an example of his
loyalty to his Sullan connections in his defence of the young, aristocratic
Lucius Cornelius Sulla (there are other notices of Arruntius in the *Annals*
besides these); and Dio, *Roman History*, LVIII.27. 4–5, which records, as do
the *Annals*, VI.xlviii, that Arruntius, 'distinguished alike for his great age and
for his learning, took his own life' after being denounced by Macro (A.D. 37).
Though Tiberius was dying, Arruntius chose death in preference to witnessing
what he predicted would be Rome's further suffering under Caligula.
    88–9. *degenerate ... fathers*] The theme of the degeneracy of Rome and
particularly of the Senate is persistent in Tacitus, who clearly favours the

Of our great fathers. Where is now the soul
Of god-like Cato?—he, that durst be good   90
When Caesar durst be evil; and had power,
As not to live his slave, to die his master.
Or where the constant Brutus, that (being proof
Against all charm of benefits) did strike
So brave a blow into the monster's heart   95
That sought unkindly to captive his country?
O, they are fled the light. Those mighty spirits
Lie raked up, with their ashes, in their urns,
And not a spark of their eternal fire
Glows in a present bosom: all's but blaze,   100
Flashes, and smoke, wherewith we labour so,
There's nothing Roman in us; nothing good,
Gallant, or great. 'Tis true, that Cordus says,
'Brave Cassius was the last of all that race.'
Sabinus. Stand by! Lord Drusus.

DRUSUS *passeth by* [*attended by* HATERIUS].

---

96. unkindly] *F;* vnkindly) *Q, corr. in MS. to* (vnkindly) *in Wise Q.*   104.
'Brave ... race.'] *Inverted commas not in Q, F; Q, F print all but* Cassius *in
italic.*

---

traditional idea of a strong oligarchic Senate. In a series of struggles over the
previous century-and-a-half it had progressively lost out to powerful leaders of
the 'popular' party—the Gracchi, Marius, Julius Caesar—until it served under
the Principate as the emperor's rubber-stamp.

    90. *god-like Cato*] Marcus Porcius Cato Uticensis, 95–46 B.C., in urging
death for the Catilinarian conspirators, began a long opposition, republican in
principle, to Julius Caesar, which culminated in his alliance with Pompey and
his death by suicide.

    90–1. *he ... evil*] As pointed out by James A. Riddell, 'Seventeenth-
Century Identifications of Jonson's Sources in the Classics', *Ren. Q.*, XXVIII
(1975), 207, this echoes Martial, *Epigrams*, XII.vi.11–12, 'but thou, under a
hard prince and in evil times, didst have courage to be good'. Loeb ed., tr.
Walter C. A. Kerr (London, 1950).

    94. *benefits*] favours.

    95. *monster's heart*] Acc. to Caesar's physician, only the second of Caesar's
many stab-wounds—Brutus's to the breast—was fatal. Suetonius, *Lives*,
I.lxxxii.

    96. *unkindly*] unnaturally (hence 'monster's heart' at 95).

    96. *captive*] enslave. The accent is on the second syllable.

    100. *blaze*] i.e. momentary brightness, in contrast to the sustained glowing
of the 'eternal fire'.

    103–4. *Cordus ... race.'*] Plutarch later had Brutus refer to his fellow-

Haterius.   Th'emp'ror's son! Give place!   105
Silius. I like the prince well.
Arruntius.   A riotous youth,
   There's little hope of him.
Sabinus.   That fault his age
   Will, as it grows, correct. Methinks he bears
   Himself, each day, more nobly than other;
   And wins no less on men's affections   110
   Than doth his father lose. Believe me'I love him;
   And chiefly for opposing to Sejanus.
Silius. And I for gracing his young kinsmen so,
   The sons of Prince Germanicus; it shows

---

105. Stand by!] Stand by, *Q, F.*   105. DRUSUS *passeth by*] *Marginal s.d. in
F; not in Q.*   105. Th'emp'ror's son! Give place!] Th'Emp'rours son, give
place. *Q, F.*   111. lose] *F;* loose *Q.*   111. me'I] *Q;* me',I,*H.&S.;* me, I
F.   113. kinsmen] *F;* kinsman *Q, corr. in MS. in Wise Q.*

---

conspirator against Caesar, the dead Cassius, as the last of the Romans. *Lives:*
Brutus, xliv.

  105. *Drusus*] On Tiberius's son, Jonson cites Tacitus, *Annals*, I.xxiv–xxx,
which relates how in A.D. 14 Drusus was sent to Pannonia by Tiberius to quell
an army mutiny, and his ruthless success in this; Suetonius, *Lives*, III.lii,
which claims that Tiberius was 'exasperated' at his son's vices and 'loose and
dissolute life', and that 'even when he died, Tiberius was not greatly affected';
and Dio, *Roman History*, LVII.xiii.1–2: Drusus 'was most licentious and cruel
(so cruel, in fact, that the sharpest swords were called Drusian after him)'.

  105. *Haterius*] According to Tacitus, Quintus Haterius was 'a member
of a senatorial family, and master of an eloquence famous in his lifetime'—but
an eloquence that owed far more to style than the substance of his speeches.
See *Annals*, IV.lxi. Jonson conflates him with Haterius Agrippa—see V.456n.
below.

  106. *A riotous youth*] In reference to Drusus here, Jonson cites Tacitus,
Annals, III.xxxvii: 'In view of his youth, not even his laxities were too
unpopular: better he should follow the bent he did ... than live in solitude,
deaf to the voice of pleasure, and immersed in sullen vigilance and sinister
meditations.'

  109. *nobly*] trisyllabic: 'noble-y'.

  109. *other*] the previous.

  112. *for ... Sejanus*] Jonson cites Tacitus, *Annals*, IV.i–iii—Sejanus's
origins, character, influence, ambitions, and enmity towards Drusus. See
notes to I.212ff.

  113. *for ... so*] Jonson cites Tacitus, *Annals*, IV.viii: Drusus had acted as a
father to the sons of the dead Germanicus.

  114. *The sons ... Germanicus*] Jonson noted in the margin that these were
Nero, Drusus (junior) and Caius, citing Tacitus, *Annals*, I [xli] on the fact that
the last—the future emperor—was born in Germanicus's camp and nicknamed
Caligula—'little boots'. On Germanicus, Jonson at this point cites (as well as

A gallant clearness in him, a straight mind,   115
That envies not, in them, their father's name.
Arruntius. His name was, while he lived, above all envy;
And being dead, without it. O, that man!
If there were seeds of the old virtue left,
They lived in him.
Silius.   He had the fruits, Arruntius,   120
More than the seeds. Sabinus and myself
Had means to know'him, within, and can report him.
We were his followers (he would call us friends).
He was a man most like to virtue';in all,
And every action, nearer to the gods,   125
Than men, in nature; of a body'as fair
As was his mind; and no less reverend
In face than fame. He could so use his state,

---

120. fruits] *F;* fruicts *Q.*   122. know'him] *Q, H.&S.;* know him *F.*

Dio, *Roman History*, LVII), Tacitus, *Annals*, I.xxxiii–xxxiv: 'Married to
[Augustus's] granddaughter Agrippina, who had borne him several children,
and himself a grandchild of the dowager (he was the son of Tiberius' brother
Drusus), he was tormented nonetheless by the secret hatred of his uncle and
grandmother.' Republican hopes, that had centred on Tiberius's brother,
were transferred, on his death, to Germanicus, a young man of 'unassuming
disposition and . . . exceptional courtesy, so far removed from the inscrutable
arrogance of word and look which characterized Tiberius'.

   115. *straight*] strict, upright.
   116, 117. envies . . . envy] 'envy' here infers enmity.
   117. *His name*] i.e. Germanicus's—not, as the notes of *H.&S.* to ll. 124 and
132 incorrectly suggest, Drusus's.
   119. *virtue*] The Latin *virtus* implied not only moral virtue, but valour,
strength, fortitude, fitness for high, particularly military, tasks—general
excellence. This is the sense in which Jonson uses the word here—a stronger
sense than that at l. 152—and in which he defines it in ll. 124ff.
   120. *fruits*] concerning the 'fruits' of virtue cf. Cicero, *On Piso*, XXIV. 57,
on the 'iustam gloriam, qui est fructus verae virtutis honestissimus'—the
justified fame which is the most honorable fruit of true virtue.
   121–2. *Sabinus . . . within*] Jonson cites Tacitus, *Annals*, IV. xviii, 'the
friendship of Germanicus [towards Silius and Sabinus] was fatal to both'.
   124. *a man . . . virtue*] As *H.&S.* point out, this echoes Velleius Paterculus,
History of Rome, II.xxxv.2, 'homo Virtuti simillimus' (he resembled Virtue
herself). Here it is applied to Germanicus—not, as *H.&S.* falsely claim,
to Drusus.
   128–54.] Jonson cites Tacitus, *Annals*, II.lxxii–lxxiii (see Appendix A);
and also draws on Dio, *Roman History*, LVII.18.6–9, which he cites, for
Germanicus's 'striking physical beauty' and lack of ambition.

Temp'ring his greatness with his gravity,
As it avoided all self-love in him,   130
And spite in others. What his funerals lacked
In images and pomp, they had supplied
With honourable sorrow, soldiers' sadness,
A kind of silent mourning, such as men
(Who know no tears, but from their captives) use   135
To show in so great losses.
Cordus.   I thought once,
Considering their forms, age, manner of deaths,
The nearness of the places where they fell,
T'have paralleled him with great Alexander:
For both were of best feature, of high race,   140
Yeared but to thirty, and in foreign lands,
By their own people, alike made away.
Sabinus. I know not, for his death, how you might wrest it;
But, for his life, it did as much disdain
Comparison with that voluptuous, rash,   145
Giddy, and drunken Macedon's, as mine
Doth with my bondman's. All the good in him
(His valour, and his fortune) he made his;
But he had other touches of late Romans,
That more did speak him: Pompey's dignity,   150
The innocence of Cato, Caesar's spirit,

131–2. *What ... pomp*] Because Germanicus (not, as *H.&S.* and Barish claim, Drusus) died at Antioch (A.D. 19), the masks ('images') of his ancestors, kept at Rome, could not be worn, as custom normally dictated, by his relatives at his funeral.

139. *paralleled ... Alexander*] in the manner of Plutarch's *Parallel Lives* of eminent Greeks and Romans.

143. *wrest it*] contrive a parallel. Not that Sabinus questions the poisoning of Germanicus (see l. 173). However, acc. to Tacitus, *Annals*, II. lxxiii, whether the corpse of Germanicus 'bore marks of poisoning was disputable'—as is the claim that Alexander was poisoned.

147. *him*] Alexander.

148. *he*] Germanicus.

150–2. *Pompey's ... temperance*] Jonson cites Velleius Paterculus, whose compendium of Roman history contains sketches of these and many other characters.

151. *innocence*] more than blamelessness; disinterestedness, uprightness. Cf. Sallust, *Catiline*, LIV.6: Cato 'cum innocente abstinentia certabat' (vied with the upright in integrity).

Wise Brutus' temperance, and every virtue,
Which, parted unto others, gave them name,
Flowed mixed in him. He was the soul of goodness;
And all our praises of him are like streams   155
Drawn from a spring, that still rise full, and leave
The part remaining greatest.

Arruntius.   I am sure
He was too great for us, and that they knew
Who did remove him hence.

Sabinus.   When men grow fast
Honoured, and loved, there is a trick in state   160
(Which jealous princes never fail to use)
How to decline that growth, with fair pretext,
And honourable colours of employment,
Either by embassy, the war, or such,
To shift them forth into another air,   165
Where they may purge, and lessen; so was he:
And had his seconds there, sent by Tiberius,

---

152. temperance] *H.&S.;* temp'rance *Q, F.*

153–4. *Which . . . in him*] As Briggs noted, this is reminiscent of Claudian,
On Stilicho's Consulship, I.33–5, 'To all men else blessings come scattered, to
thee they flow commingled, and gifts that separately make happy are all
together thine'. Loeb ed. of Claudian, tr. Maurice Platnauer, I (London,
1963). Subsequent translations of Claudian refer to the Loeb text.

158. *and that they knew*] Jonson cites Tacitus, *Annals*, II.v, 'for Tiberius the
disturbances in the East were a not unwelcome accident, as they supplied
him with a pretext for removing Germanicus from his familiar legions and
appointing him to unknown provinces, where he would be vulnerable at once
to treachery and chance'; *Annals*, II.xxvi, 'jealousy was the motive which
withdrew him from a glory already within his grasp'; and Dio, *Roman History*,
LVII.18.9–10, 'poison was the means of his carrying off'—a 'plot formed by
[Gnaeus Calpurnius] Piso and [his wife] Plancina' but backed, it was suspected,
'by Tiberius himself'.

159. *fast*] securely, deeply.

162. *decline*] deflect (the literal sense of Lat. *declinare*).

163. *colours*] appearances.

166–72.] As his source for these lines and in particular the suspected
poisoning of Germanicus by Gnaeus Calpurnius Piso and his wife Plancina,
supposedly backed by Tiberius and his mother Livia (the 'Augusta'), Jonson
cites Tacitus, *Annals*, II.xliii, lv, lvii,lxxvii; Suetonius, *Lives*, III.lii; and Dio,
Roman History, LVII.18.9–10.

167. *his . . . dam*] Tiberius's mother Livia, the 'Augusta', widow of
Augustus.

And his more subtle dam, to discontent him;
To breed and cherish mutinies; detract
His greatest actions; give audacious check   170
To his commands; and work to put him out
In open act of treason. All which snares
When his wise cares prevented, a fine poison
Was thought on, to mature their practices.

        [Enter] SEJANUS, SATRIUS, TERENTIUS, *etc.*
                They pass over the stage.

Cordus. Here comes Sejanus.
Silius.   Now observe the stoops,   175
    The bendings, and the falls.
Arruntius.   Most creeping base!
Sejanus. I note 'em well. No more. Say you.
Satrius.   My lord,
    There is a gentleman of Rome would buy—
Sejanus. How call you him you talked with?
Satrius.   Please your lordship,
    It is Eudemus, the physician   180

174.1. SEJANUS . . . *etc.*] *s.d. follows l. 176 in Q, F.*   174.2. *They . . . stage.*]
Marginal s.d. follows l. 176 in F; not in Q.   177. *Sejanus.*] SEI. *Q; not in F.*
179. Please] *Q;* 'Please *F.*   179. lordship] *F;* Lordsh. *Q.*

---

173. *a fine poison*] Jonson cites Tacitus, *Annals*, II.lxix, which mentions
Germanicus's 'belief that Piso had given him poison', and details the
'implements of witchcraft' found in the house in which he died; *Annals*,
III.xiv, which describes Piso's trial before the senate, when Tiberius failed to
defend him, and his suicide—or murder; and Suetonius, *Lives*, IV.i–ii:
'There was some suspicion that he was poisoned' and 'that he met his death
through the wiles of Tiberius, aided and abetted by Gnaeus Piso.'
   174.1. *TERENTIUS*] Friend of Sejanus. After the latter's fall, he bravely
admitted to the Senate his earlier friendship with the man. See Tacitus,
Annals, VI.viii–ix.
   175. *Sejanus*] Jonson cites the chief sources—Tacitus, *Annals*, I–VI, and
espec, IV.i.ff; Suetonius, *Lives*, III; Dio, *Roman History*, LVII–LVIII; Pliny,
Natural History, VII.129, VIII.197 (very little here); and Seneca, *To Marcia
On Consolation.*
   180. *Eudemus*] Jonson cites Tacitus, *Annals*, IV.iii: 'Eudemus, doctor and
friend of Livia, was made privy to [Sejanus's] design [to woo Livia], his
profession supplying a pretext for repeated interviews.' His complicity in
Drusus's murder was revealed under torture—*Annals*, IV.xi. According to
Pliny, *Natural History*, XXIX.viii.20, not cited by Jonson, the relationship
between Eudemus and Livia was adulterous.

To Livia, Drusus' wife.
Sejanus.   On with your suit.
Would buy, you said—
Satrius.   A tribune's place, my lord.
Sejanus. What will he give?
Satrius.   Fifty sestertia.
Sejanus. Livia's physician, say you, is that fellow?
Satrius. It is, my lord. Your lordship's answer?
Sejanus.   To what?   185
Satrius. The place, my lord. 'Tis for a gentleman
    Your lordship will well like of, when you see him;
    And one you may make yours, by the grant.
Sejanus. Well, let him bring his money, and his name.
Satrius. 'Thank your lordship. He shall, my lord.
Sejanus.   Come hither.   190
    Know you this same Eudemus? Is he learned?
Satrius. Reputed so, my lord; and of deep practice.
Sejanus. Bring him in, to me, in the gallery;
    And take you cause to leave us there, together:
    I would confer with him about a grief.—On.   195

> [*Exeunt* SEJANUS, SATRIUS, TERENTIUS, *etc.;*
>   *manent two or three clients of Sejanus.*]

Arruntius. So, yet! Another? Yet? O desperate state
    Of grov'ling honour! Seest thou this, O sun,
    And do we see thee after? Methinks day
    Should lose his light, when men do lose their shames,

182. said—] *F; said. Q.*   190. 'Thank] *F2;* Thank *Q;* Thanke *F.*   195.
—On.] *corr. Q, F;* On? *uncorr. Q.*

---

181. *Livia, Drusus' wife*] sister of Germanicus and niece of Tiberius.
183. *Fifty sestertia*] 50,000 sesterces. Jonson—citing G. Budé, *de Asse*, p. 64,
in vol. II, *Omnia Opera* (Basle, 1557)—notes that this represents £375 in his
day.
192. *of deep practice*] expert in intrigue.
193. *gallery*] not a balcony but a long, narrow apartment common in
Elizabethan houses.
195. *grief*] ailment.
197. *honour*] Here, perhaps partly in the sense (unrecorded in *O.E.D.*) of
preferment—the sense of *L. & S., honor,* I. B. 1. Jonson's point is that honour
has been debased. The tribuneship can be bought, so that honours now reflect
only a 'grovelling honour'. Cf. I.221–3 below. 'Honor' was also a Roman deity,
and in Q the word has an upper-case H.
199–201. *When men ... living*] Gifford cites Juvenal, *Satires*, VIII.83–4,

And, for the empty circumstance of life,   200
Betray their cause of living.
Silius.   Nothing so.
Sejanus can repair, if Jove should ruin.
He is the now court-god; and well applied
With sacrifice of knees, of crooks, and cringe,
He will do more than all the house of Heav'n   205
Can, for a thousand hecatombs. 'Tis he
Makes us our day, or night; Hell and Elysium
Are in his look: we talk of Rhadamanth,
Furies, and fire-brands; but 'tis his frown
That is all these, where, on the adverse part,   210
His smile is more than e'er (yet) poets fained
Of bliss, and shades, nectar—
Arruntius.   A serving boy.
I knew him at Caius' trencher, when for hire
He prostituted his abusèd body
To that great gourmand, fat Apicius,   215
And was the noted pathic of the time.
Sabinus. And now, the second face of the whole world.

---

199. lose ... lose] *F;* loose ... loose *Q.*   212. boy.] *Q;* boy? *F.*

'count it the greatest of all sins to prefer life to honour, and to lose, for the sake
of living, all that makes life worth having'.
   202. *Sejanus*] On Sejanus's character, conduct, and power, Jonson cites
Tacitus, *Annals*, IV.i–ii (see below, notes to I.212ff. for some of this); and
Dio, *Roman History*, LVII.22.1–4 (the poisoning of Drusus, Sejanus's
schemes against Agrippina and her sons, and his ambition for supreme power).
   203. *now*] current.
   206. *hecatombs*] great public sacrifices to the gods.
   208. *Rhadamanth*] a judge in the underworld.
   212. *shades*] i.e. cool, leafy shades.
   212–16.] Jonson cites Tacitus, *Annals*, IV.i, 'Born at Vulsinii to the Roman
knight Seius Strabo [praetorian commandant], he became in early youth a
follower of Gaius Caesar, grandson of the deified Augustus; not without a
rumour that he had disposed of his virtue at a price to Apicius, a rich man and
a prodigal'; and Dio, *Roman History*, LVII.19.5—the epicure Apicius spent
his fortune on self-indulgence and, with only 100,000 sesterces left, 'became
grief-stricken, feeling that he was destined to die of hunger, and took his own
life'.
   216. *pathic*] boy prostitute.
   217. *the second ... world*] Jonson cites Juvenal, *Satires*, X. 63: the dead
Sejanus's face, 'but lately second in the entire world'.

The partner of the Empire hath his image
Reared equal with Tiberius, borne in ensigns;
Commands, disposes every dignity;   220
Centurions, tribunes, heads of provinces,
Praetors, and consuls, all that heretofore
Rome's general suffrage gave, is now his sale.
The gain, or rather spoil, of all the earth,
One, and his house, receives.

Silius.   He hath of late   225
Made him a strength too, stangely, by reducing
All the praetorian bands into one camp,
Which he commands; pretending that the soldier,
By living loose, and scattered, fell to riot;
And that if any sudden enterprise   230
Should be attempted, their united strength
Would be far more, than severed; and their life
More strict, if from the city more removed.
Sabinus. Where, now, he builds what kind of forts he please,
Is heard to court the soldier by his name,   235

---

235. heard] *Barish, following MS. corr. in Wise Q;* hard *Q, F.*

218–37.] Jonson cites Tacitus, *Annals.* IV.ii, which he has rearranged: 'The power of the prefectship, which had hitherto been moderate, he increased by massing the cohorts, dispersed through the capital, in one camp; ... His pretext was that scattered troops became unruly; that, when a sudden emergency called, help was more effective if the helpers were compact; and that there would be less laxity of conduct, if an encampment was created at a distance from the attractions of the city [225–33]. Their quarters finished [234], he began little by little to insinuate himself into the affections of the private soldiers, approaching them and addressing them by name [235–37], while at the same time he selected personally their centurions and tribunes [221]. Nor did he fail to hold before the senate the temptation of those offices and governorships with which he invested his satellites [220–23]: for Tiberius, far from demurring, was complaisant enough to celebrate "the partner of his toils" not only in conversation but before the Fathers and the people, and to allow his effigies to be honoured, in theatre, in forum, and amid the eagles and altars of the legions [218–19]'. At 225 and 238 Dio, *Roman History*, LVII.19 is cited, but the debt in this passage is to Tacitus rather than Dio.

224–5.] Briggs cites Claudian, *Against Rufinus*, I.193–4, 'a single house receives the plunder of a world'.

223. *general suffrage*] collective vote.

226. *strangely*] in an exceptional way.

228. *pretending*] alleging.

235. *heard*] *Q* and *F* have 'hard', which is difficult to justify even in the sense of 'unremitting', 'vigorous'.

Woos, feasts the chiefest men of action,
Whose wants, not loves, compel them to be his.
And, though he ne'er were liberal by kind,
Yet, to his own dark ends, he's most profuse,
Lavish, and letting fly, he cares not what   240
To his ambition.
Arruntius.   Yet, hath he ambition?
Is there that step in state can make him higher?
Or more? Or anything he is, but less?
Silius. Nothing, but emperor.
Arruntius.   The name Tiberius,
I hope, will keep, howe'er he hath foregone   245
The dignity and power.
Silius.   Sure, while he lives.
Arruntius. And dead, it comes to Drusus. Should he fail,
To the brave issue of Germanicus;
And they are three: too many (ha?) for him
To have a plot upon?
Sabinus.   I do not know   250
The heart of his designs; but, sure, their face
Looks farther than the present.
Arruntius.   By the gods,
If I could guess he had but such a thought,
My sword should cleave him down from head to heart,

---

236. Woos] *F;* Woes *Q.*   244. emperor] *H.&S.;* Emp'rour *Q, F.*

238. *kind*] nature.
241. *to*] towards, in the pursuit of; or (possibly) compared to.
244. *the name*] the name of Emperor.
244–50. Coleridge—*Works,* ed. Shedd (New York, 1853), IV, 190—and
following him, Briggs and Barish, claim that these lines are anachronistic in
the mouth of the republican Arruntius. But was Arruntius a republican at this
stage (A.D. 23)? Certainly not in A.D. 14, when Augustus, surveying possible
holders of the Principate, named him as 'not undeserving and bold enough to
venture, should the opportunity arise' (Tacitus, *Annals,* I.xiii). See also his
proposal for Augustus's funeral procession (*Annals,* I.viii). By A.D. 37, the
year of his death, however, his views were republican (*Annals,* VI.xlviii).
249. *they are three*] Nero, Drusus (junior), and Caligula, as Jonson's
marginal note points out.
252. Jonson cites Tacitus, *Annals,* IV.iii on Sejanus's forward planning: the
'plenitude of Caesars . . . gave his ambition pause: . . . violence was hazardous,
while treachery demanded an interval between crime and crime. He resolved,
however, to take the more secret way, and to begin with Drusus'.

But I would find it out; and with my hand   255
I'd hurl his panting brain about the air,
In mites as small as atomi, to'undo
The knotted bed—
Sabinus.   You'are observed, Arruntius.
Arruntius. Death! I dare tell him so, and all his spies:
            He turns to Sejanus's clients.
      You, sir, I would, do you look? And you!
Sabinus.   Forbear.   260

            [*Enter*] SATRIUS [*and*] EUDEMUS.

Satrius. Here he will instant be. Let's walk a turn.
      You'are in a muse, Eudemus?
Eudemus.   Not I, sir.
      [*Aside.*] I wonder he should mark me out so! Well,
      Jove and Apollo form it for the best.
Satrius. Your fortune's made unto you now, Eudemus,   265
      If you can but lay hold upon the means;
      Do but observe his humour, and—believe it—

---

258. You'are] *Q;* You are *F.*   259.1. *He . . . clients.*] *Marginal s.d. in F; not
in Q.*   260.1. [*Enter*] . . . EUDEMUS] SATRIVS. EVDEMVS. SEIANVS. *Q;*
SATRIVS, EVDEMVS, SEIANVS. *F;* [*Enter*] *Satrius* [*with*] *Eudemus,* [*above.*]
Barish.   261. *Satrius.*] SAT. *Q; not in F.*   262. You'are] *This ed.;* Yo'are *Q,*
F.

257. *atomi*] atoms.
258. *knotted bed*] 'the heart of his designs'—I.251 above. There is also the
suggestion that in its workings his brain resembles a bed of snakes.
258. *You are observed*] presumably a couple of clients of Sejanus remain on
stage after his exit at I.195.
261.1.] Barish (pp. 186–7) thinks that this 'scene' (ll. 261–374) 'takes place
most naturally on an upper level, that of the first gallery . . . where Eudemus
may await Sejanus in private', while 'the Germanican partisans remain on the
main stage' since the latter 'must be on hand for the arrival of Tiberius'.
However, Barish admits there are difficulties, esp. when Sejanus listens to
Tiberius at ll. 375–8 and makes his comment at l. 379, since this would defeat
the idea of the upper level as a private apartment. I prefer to have the 'scene'
take place on the main stage, on the side, well away from the Germanicans—
esp. as *F*, often quite helpful with stage directions, is silent on the question.
The long 'gallery' of an Elizabethan house was in any case not a balcony.
Gifford's 'A Gallery discovered opening into the State Room' shows little
understanding of Jonson's stage.
265.] Jonson cites Terentius's defence of his friendship with Sejanus, in
which the latter's power to make or break men is stressed. Tacitus, *Annals,*
VI.viii.

He'is the noblest Roman, where he takes—

[*Enter* SEJANUS.]

Here comes his lordship.
Sejanus.   Now, good Satrius.
Satrius. This is the gentleman, my lord.
Sejanus.   Is this?   270
   Give me your hand, we must be more acquainted.
   Report, sir, hath spoke out your art, and learning;
   And I am glad I have so needful cause
   (However in itself painful and hard)
   To make me known to so great virtue. Look,   275
   Who's that? Satrius—   [*Exit* SATRIUS.]
             I have a grief, sir,
   That will desire your help. Your name's Eudemus?
Eudemus. Yes.
Sejanus.   Sir?
Eudemus.   It is, my lord.
Sejanus.   I hear you are
   Physician to Livia, the princess?
Eudemus. I minister unto her, my good lord.   280
Sejanus. You minister to a royal lady, then.
Eudemus. She is, my lord, and fair.
Sejanus.   That's understood
   Of all their sex, who are, or would be so;
   And those that would be, physic soon can make 'em;
   For those that are, their beauties fear no colours.   285
Eudemus. Your lordship is conceited.
Sejanus.   Sir, you know it;

268. He'is] *Q;* He's *F.*   276. Who's that? Satrius—] *Q, F;* Who's that,
Satrius? *Barish.*

---

267. *humour*] mood.
275. *virtue*] ability.
278. *Sir?*] Sejanus expects more courtesy from Eudemus.
279. *Livia*] On Germanicus's sister, the wife of Drusus, grand-niece of
Augustus, Jonson cites Tacitus, *Annals*, IV.iii which mentions her beauty, and
how easily she was won to Sejanus's purposes.
284. *physic*] medical treatment (of a cosmetic kind).
285. *fear no colours*] do not fear being abandoned by an artificial complexion,
with a pun on 'fear no foe' (military colours) or rival; cf. Shakespeare's pun on
the phrase, *Tw.N.*, I.v.6.
286. *conceited*] witty.

And can (if need be) read a learnèd lecture
On this and other secrets. 'Pray you tell me,
What more of ladies, besides Livia,
Have you your patients?
Eudemus.   Many, my good lord.   290
The great Augusta, Urgulania,
Mutilia Prisca, and Plancina, divers—
Sejanus. And all these tell you the particulars
Of every several grief? How first it grew,
And then increased, what action causèd that,   295
What passion that; and answer to each point
That you will put 'em?
Eudemus.   Else, my lord, we know not
How to prescribe the remedies.
Sejanus.   Go to,
You'are a subtle nation, you physicians!
And grown the only cabinets, in court,   300
To ladies' privacies. Faith, which of these
Is the most pleasant lady, in her physic?
Come, you are modest now.
Eudemus.   'Tis fit, my lord.
Sejanus. Why sir, I do not ask you of their urines,
Whose smell's most violet? Or whose siege is best?   305

---

288. 'Pray] *F2;* Pray *Q, F*   299. You'are] *This ed.;* Yo'are *Q, F.*   305.
smell's] *F;* smels *Q.*

---

287. *read*] deliver.
291. *Augusta*] On Livia, mother of Tiberius, widow of Augustus, Jonson
cites the chief sources, Tacitus, *Annals*, I–V; Suetonius, *Lives*, III; Dio,
Roman History, LVII–LVIII.
291. *Urgulania*] favourite of the Augusta, as Jonson notes, citing Tacitus,
Annals, II.xxxiv and IV.xxi–xxii, which give examples of her influence.
292. *Mutilia Prisca*] Intimate of the Augusta and, as Jonson notes, citing
Tacitus, *Annals*, IV.xii, mistress of Julius Postumus.
292. *Plancina*] wife of Gnaeus Calpurnius Piso, as Jonson notes, citing
Tacitus, *Annals*, II, III, and IV. See note to I.166–72 above.
294. *grief*] illness, pain.
300. *cabinets*] repositories. Jonson, following Lipsius, cites Tacitus, *Annals*,
IV.iii on the pretext for intimate discussions afforded to physicians, and Pliny,
Natural History, XXIX.i, 'medicine became more famous even through sin'.
Loeb ed., tr. W. H. S. Jones (*et al.*), VIII (London, 1963). All refs. to Pliny
are to the Loeb ed.
302. *pleasant*] amusing.
305. *violet*] 'The iuice of violettes and the syrop louse the bellye by soft-
eninge of it', while 'the vinegre made of violettes slaketh wonderfullye the

Or who makes hardest faces on her stool?
Which lady sleeps with her own face a-nights?
Which puts her teeth off, with her clothes, in court?
Or which her hair? Which her complexion?
And in which box she puts it? These were questions   310
That might, perhaps, have put your gravity
To some defence of blush. But I enquired,
Which was the wittiest? Merriest? Wantonest?
Harmless intergatories, but conceits.
Methinks Augusta should be most perverse,   315
And froward in her fit?
Eudemus.   She'is so, my lord.
Sejanus. I knew it. And Mutilia the most jocund?
Eudemus. 'Tis very true, my lord.
Sejanus.   And why would you
Conceal this from me, now? Come, what's Livia?
I know, she's quick, and quaintly spirited,   320
And will have strange thoughts, when she'is at leisure;
She tells 'em all to you?
Eudemus.   My noblest lord,
He breathes not in the Empire, or on earth,
Whom I would be ambitious to serve
(In any act, that may preserve mine honour)   325
Before your lordship.
Sejanus.   Sir, you can lose no honour

306. her] *F;* the *Q.*   308. off] *F;* of *Q.*   316. She'is] *Q;* She's *F.*   321.
she'is] *This ed.;* sh'is *Q;* she's *F.*   323. on] *F;* the *Q.*   326. lose] loose *Q,*
F.

---

burninge of hote agues.' William Turner, *Herball* (1562), II, 164. Presumably
these remedies leave a heavy smell of violets in the urine.
    305. *siege*] excrement.
    307–10.] This echoes Martial, *Epigrams*, IX.xxxvii. 3–5 (which Jonson
was evidently fond of, using it also in *C.R.*, IV.i.145–9 and *S.W.*,
IV.ii.92–101): 'You lay aside your teeth at night, just as you do your silk
dresses, and you lie stored away in a hundred caskets, and your face does not
sleep with you'. Loeb ed., tr. W. C. A. Ker, I (London, 1950). Subsequent
quotations of Martial are from Ker.
    314. *intergatories*] questions ('interrogatories'). Cf. Shakespeare, *Mer.V.*,
V.i.298, and Jonson, *C.R.*, IV.iv.11.
    314. *but conceits*] simply whims.
    316. *froward ... fit*] unreasonable by temperament.
    320. *quick ... spirited*] sharp and charmingly idiosyncratic.
    321. *strange*] There may be a play on this word, as a 'strange woman' was a
harlot. See *O.E.D.*, *Strange*, a, 4, with its Jonsonian example.

By trusting aught to me. The coarsest act
Done to my service I can so requite,
As all the world shall style it honourable.
Your idle, virtuous definitions   330
Keep honour poor, and are as scorned, as vain:
Those deeds breathe honour that do suck in gain.

Eudemus. But, good my lord, if I should thus betray
The counsels of my patient, and a lady's
Of her high place and worth, what might your lordship   335
(Who presently are to trust me with your own)
Judge of my faith?

Sejanus.   Only the best, I swear.
Say now, that I should utter you my grief;
And with it, the true cause; that it were love;
And love to Livia: you should tell her this?   340
Should she suspect your faith? I would you could
Tell me as much from her; see, if my brain
Could be turned jealous.

Eudemus.   Happily, my lord,
I could, in time, tell you as much, and more;
So I might safely promise but the first   345
To her from you.

Sejanus.   As safely, my Eudemus
(I now dare call thee so) as I have put
The secret into thee.

Eudemus.   My lord—

Sejanus.   Protest not.
Thy looks are vows to me; use only speed,
And but affect her with Sejanus' love,   350
Thou art a man made to make consuls. Go.

Eudemus. My lord, I'll promise you a private meeting

330–32.] *Each line preceded by gnomic pointing, Q, F.*

330. *idle*] foolish, silly.

340. *love to Livia*] Jonson cites Tacitus, *Annals*, IV.iii ('Eudemus . . . was made privy to the design').

343. *jealous*] mistrustful.

343. *Happily*] the word has a double meaning–*happily* and *perhaps*.

350. *affect*] move.

350. *Sejanus' love*] Jonson again cites Tacitus, *Annals*, IV.iii, where it is claimed that it was the death of Drusus, not love, that interested Sejanus.

This day, together.
Sejanus.   Canst thou?
Eudemus.   Yes.
Sejanus.   The place?
Eudemus. My gardens, whither I shall fetch your lordship.
Sejanus. Let me adore my Aesculapius!   355
Why, this indeed is physic! And outspeaks
The knowledge of cheap drugs, or any use
Can be made out of it! More comforting
Than all your opiates, juleps, apozems,
Magistral syrups, or—begone, my friend,   360
Not barely stylèd, but created so.
Expect things greater than thy largest hopes
To overtake thee. Fortune shall be taught
To know how ill she hath deserved thus long
To come behind thy wishes. Go, and speed.   365
                                        [*Exit* EUDEMUS.]
Ambition makes more trusty slaves than need.
These fellows, by the favour of their art,
Have still the means to tempt, oft-times the power.
If Livia will be now corrupted, then
Thou hast the way, Sejanus, to work out   370
His secrets, who (thou knowest) endures thee not,
Her husband Drusus; and to work against them.
Prosper it, Pallas, thou that betterst wit;

354. gardens, whither] *F;* Gardens. whether *Q.*   356. physic!] *F; Physick:*
Q.   358. of it!] *F;* of it, *Q.*   359. juleps] *F2 (subst.), Iulebes Q;* iulebes *F.*
364. deserved thus long,] *Q, F;* deserved, thus long *Barish.*   366.
Ambition],, Ambition *Q;* "Ambition *F.*   368. oft-times] *F;* oftimes *Q, which*
probably represents Jonson's pronunciation more closely.

355. *Aesculapius*] god of medicine.
359. *juleps*] sweet medicinal drink.
359. *apozems*] medicinal solutions.
360. *Magistral*] formula.
363–5.] Fortune, one notes, is Sejanus's 'one deity' (V.81). Briggs cites
Lucan, *The Civil War*, V.581–3: 'Fortune treats [Caesar] scurvily when she
comes merely in answer to his prayer'. Loeb ed., tr. J. D. Duff.
367–8.] Jonson cites Tacitus, *Annals*, IV.iii (again) on the pretext for
intimate discussions afforded physicians; and Pliny, *Natural History*, XXIX.i
(XXIX.viii is more to the point) on charges of doctors' criminal practices.
368. *still*] always.
373. *Pallas ... wit*] As goddess of wisdom, her aid can be sought to 'better'
one's 'wit'.

For Venus hath the smallest share in it.

[*Enter*] TIBERIUS [*and*] DRUSUS [*attended by* HATERIUS,
LATIARIS, SATRIUS, NATTA, *etc.*].

Tiberius. (*One kneels to him.*) We not endure these flatteries.
Let him stand.   375
Our Empire, ensigns, axes, rods, and state
Take not away our human nature from us:
Look up, on us, and fall before the gods.
Sejanus. How like a god speaks Caesar!
Arruntius.   There, observe!
He can endure that second, that's no flattery.   380
O, what is it proud slime will not believe
Of his own worth, to hear it equal praised
Thus with the gods?
Cordus.   He did not hear it, sir.
Arruntius. He did not? Tut, he must not, we think meanly.
'Tis your most courtly, known confederacy,   385
To have your private parasite redeem
What he, in public subtlety, will lose

374.1–2. [*Enter*] ... *etc.*] TIBERIVS. SEIANVS. DRVSVS. *Q;* TIBERIVS,
SEIANVS, DRVSVS. *F.*   375. *Tiberius.*] TIB. *Q; not in F.*   375. (*One kneels to
him,*)] *Marginal s.d. in F; not in Q.*   375. stand.] stand *Q;* stand; *F.*
377. human] humane *Q, F.*   387. lose] *F;* loose *Q.*

375.] On Tiberius's hatred of flattery, Jonson cites Tacitus, *Annals*, I. lxxii
('Tiberius rejected the title *Father of his Country*', and 'refused to allow the
taking of an oath to obey his enactments', though 'he failed to inspire the belief
that his sentiments were not monarchical'); *Annals*, IV.vi (senators' 'lapses
into subserviency' were 'checked by the sovereign himself'); Suetonius, *Lives*,
III.xxvii ('He so loathed flattery that he would not allow any senator to
approach his litter, either to pay his respects or on business, and when an ex-
consul in apologizing to him attempted to embrace his knees, he drew back in
such haste that he fell over backward ... Being once called 'Lord,' he warned
the speaker not to address him again in an insulting fashion'); and *Annals*,
I.xiii, which names Haterius as the embracer of knees.
    376. *axes, rods*] the *fasces*, consisting of an axe surrounded with rods, with
the blade protruding, carried by lictors (freeborn attendants) as symbols of
authority before the highest magistrates.
    379.] Arruntius and the other Germanicans are obviously not heard by
Tiberius, but they are not strictly speaking in asides; they occupy a distinct
area of the stage.
    380. *second*] second of flattery.
    385–8.] It is the sycophant's role to compensate a prince for the flatteries he
must publicly reject.

To making him a name.
Haterius.   Right mighty lord—
                                   [*Gives him letters.*]
Tiberius. We must make up our ears 'gainst these assaults
        Of charming tongues; we pray you use no more   390
        These contumelies to us: style not us
        Or lord, or mighty, who profess our self
        The servant of the Senate, and are proud
        T'enjoy them our good, just, and favouring lords.
Cordus. Rarely dissembled!
Arruntius.   Princelike, to the life.   395
Sabinus. When power, that may command, so much descends,
        Their bondage, whom it stoops to, it intends.
Tiberius. Whence are these letters?
Haterius.   From the Senate.
Tiberius.   So.
                                   [*Latiaris gives him letters.*]
        Whence these?
Latiaris.   From thence too.
Tiberius.   Are they sitting now?
Latiaris. They stay thy answer, Caesar.
Silius.   If this man   400
        Had but a mind allied unto his words,
        How blest a fate were it to us, and Rome!

396–7.] *Each line preceded by gnomic pointing, Q, F.*   401. words,] *F;*
wordes. *Q.*   402. blest] *F;* blist *Q.*   402. were] *F;* where *Q.*

389–94.] Jonson echoes the sources he cites: Tacitus, *Annals*, II.lxxxvii,
'he administered a severe reprimand to those who had termed his occupa-
tions "divine," and himself "Lord" '; and Suetonius, *Lives*, III.xxvii (see 375n.
above), and III.xxix, where Tiberius tells the Senate that a prince 'ought to be
the servant of the senate .... I have looked upon you as kind, just, and
indulgent masters.'
    389. *make up*] stop up (*O.E.D.*, *make*, *v.*, 96d, citing this line).
    391. *contumelies*] Jonson is aware that the L. *contumelia* carries the sense of
'assault'—thus the 'assaults of charming tongues', an antithesis elaborated
upon below, ll. 412ff.
    394. *enjoy*] have the benefit or advantage of.
    395.] Jonson quotes Tacitus, *Annals*, IV.lxxi, 'Of all his virtues, as he
regarded them, there was none which Tiberius held in such esteem as his
power of dissimulation.'
    396–7.] As Briggs notes, the idea is repeated in *Disc.*, 1110–15.
    400. *stay*] await.

We could not think that state for which to change,
Although the aim were our old liberty:
The ghosts of those that fell for that would grieve   405
Their bodies lived not now, again to serve.
Men are deceived who think there can be thrall
Beneath a virtuous prince. Wished liberty
Ne'er lovelier looks than under such a crown.
But when his grace is merely but lip-good,   410
And that, no longer than he airs himself
Abroad in public, there to seem to shun
The strokes and stripes of flatterers, which within
Are lechery unto him, and so feed
His brutish sense with their afflicting sound,   415
As (dead to virtue) he permits himself
Be carried like a pitcher, by the ears,
To every act of vice: this is a case
Deserves our fear, and doth presage the nigh
And close approach of blood and tyranny.   420
Flattery is midwife unto princes' rage;
And nothing sooner doth help forth a tyrant
Than that, and whisperers' grace, who have the time,
The place, the power to make all men offenders.

407–9.] *Each line preceded by gnomic pointing, Q, F.*   421–4.] *Each line
preceded by gnomic pointing, Q, F.*

---

403. *think*] imagine.
405. *those . . . for that*] Brutus, Cassius, Cato, etc.—as Jonson notes in the
margin.
407–9.] From Claudian, *On Stilicho's Consulship*, III.113–15, as Gifford
noted: 'He errs who thinks that submission to a noble prince is slavery; never
does liberty show more fair than beneath a good king.' The contradictions
here—Jonson having just invoked the heroes of republicanism—might seem
astute rather than naïve, in view of the trouble with the Privy Council.
410.] On Tiberius's hypocrisy Jonson cites Dio, *Roman History*, LVII.1.1:
'his words indicated the exact opposite of his real purpose'.
413–14. *The strokes . . . him*] The antithesis of ll. 389–90 is here given a
masochistic aspect.
416–17. *he . . . ears*] Cf. Melbanke, *Philotimus* (1583), N3ᵛ, 'Great men of
the world are like great pottes (quoth Diogines) which be they neuer so great,
you may carrie them about by the eares.' *H.&S.* cite Plutarch, *On Compliancy*,
18 (the source) to the same effect.
421–4.] For l. 421 Jonson cites Aristotle, *Politics*, V.ix.6, on the connection
between flattery and tyranny. On the influence of informers he refers the
reader to Tacitus, Dio, and Suetonius, '*per totum*', quotes Suetonius, *Lives*,

Arruntius. He should be told this; and be bid dissemble   425
    With fools, and blind men. We that know the evil
    Should hunt the palace-rats, or give them bane;
    Fright hence these worse than ravens, that devour
    The quick, where they but prey upon the dead.
    He shall be told it.
Sabinus.   Stay, Arruntius,   430
    We must abide our opportunity,
    And practise what is fit, as what is needful.
    It is not safe t'enforce a sovereign's ear:
    Princes hear well, if they at all will hear.
Arruntius. Ha? Say you so? Well. In the meantime, Jove   435
    (Say not, but I do call upon thee now),
    Of all wild beasts, preserve me from a tyrant;
    And of all tame, a flatterer.
Silius.   'Tis well prayed.
Tiberius. Return the lords this voice: we are their creature;
    And it is fit a good and honest prince,   440

---

425. He] *F;* Hc *Q.*   433–4.] *Each line preceded by gnomic pointing, Q, F.*
436. now),] now.) *Q.*   439. voice:] *Barish;* voice, *Q;* voyce, *F.*

III.lxi, 'Special rewards were voted the accusers' under Tiberius, and cites
Seneca, *On Benefits,* III.xxvi (see I.28n. above).
   427. *palace-rats*] '*Tineas, Soricesque Palatii vocat istos* Sext. Aurel. Victor'
(Sextus Aurelius Victor called them moths (or grubs) and rats (or shrews,
mice) of the Palatium, the hill on which most of the early Roman Emperors
had their residences), notes Jonson in the margin. *H.&S.* are incorrect in
claiming that 'Jonson's vague reference to Sextus Aurelius Victor cannot be
traced'. The phrase 'tineas soricesque palatii' is found in the *Epitome de
Caesaribus.* See *Sexti Avrelii Victoris Liber de Caesaribvs . . . et . . . Epitome de
Caesaribvs,* Lipsiae: Teubner (1966), ed. Fr. Pichlmayr, p. 167. Jonson also
quotes from Tacitus, *Histories,* I.lxiv: a military commander had been
'defamed . . . by secret charges of which [he] knew nothing' because the same
defamer had publicly praised him. This was later—A.D. 69. All refs. to the
Histories are to the Loeb ed., tr. J. Jackson (London, 1952).
   427. *bane*] poison.
   436. *Say not*] perhaps anticipating Jove's anger at Silius's irregular devotion
to him.
   437–8. *Of all . . . flatterer*] *H.&S.* note three different attributions of this
saying, all in Plutarch—to Bias ('How to Tell a Flatterer from a Friend', 19)
and to Thales and Pittacus ('*The Dinner of the Seven Wise Men*', 2).
   440–6.] Jonson cites Suetonius, *Lives,* III.xxix, 'in addressing and in paying
his respects to the senators . . . he himself almost exceeded the requirements of
courtesy'. Tiberius told them that a prince 'ought to be the servant of the

Whom they, out of their bounty, have instructed
With so dilate and absolute a power,
Should owe the office of it to their service,
And good of all and every citizen.
Nor shall it e'er repent us to have wished   445
The Senate just and fav'ring lords unto us,
Since their free loves do yield no less defence
To'a prince's state than his own innocence.
Say then, there can be nothing in their thought
Shall want to please us, that hath pleasèd them;   450
Our suffrage rather shall prevent than stay
Behind their wills: 'tis empire to obey
Where such, so great, so grave, so good, determine.
Yet, for the suit of Spain, t'erect a temple
In honour of our mother and our self,   455
We must (with pardon of the Senate) not

---

446. fav'ring] *F; fauo'ring Q*.   447–8.] *Each line preceded by gnomic pointing,*
Q, F.   448. To'a] *Q; T'a F*.

---

senate'. Jonson also cites Dio, *Roman History*, LVII.7.1–6, where Tiberius's
deference to the Senate is acknowledged.
      441. *instructed*] provided—the sense of the Latin *instructum*, but not re-
corded in *O.E.D.* Jonson may have wanted the ordinary sense of *instruct* to be
in mind also, since Tiberius is stressing the Senate's power.
      442. *dilate*] extended—the sense of the L. *dilatum*.
      443. *office*] duty, service (Latin *officium*).
      450. *want*] fail.
      451. *prevent*] anticipate.
      454–502.] Jonson cites Tacitus, *Annals*, IV.xxxvii, xxxviii: 'About the same
time, Further Spain sent a deputation to the senate, asking leave to follow the
example of Asia by erecting a shrine to Tiberius and his mother. On this
occasion, the Caesar, sturdily disdainful of compliments at any time, and now
convinced that an answer was due to the gossip charging him with a declension
into vanity, began his speech in the following vein:- "I know, Conscript
Fathers, that many deplored my want of consistency because, when a little
while ago the cities of Asia made this identical request, I offered no opposition.
I shall therefore state both the case for my previous silence and the rule I have
settled upon for the future. Since the deified Augustus had not forbidden the
construction of a temple at Pergamum to himself and the City of Rome,
observing as I do his every action and word as law, I followed the precedent
already sealed by his approval, with all the more readiness that with worship of
myself was associated veneration of the senate. But, though once to have
accepted may be pardonable, yet to be consecrated in the image of deity
through all the provinces would be vanity and arrogance, and the honour
paid to Augustus will soon be a mockery, if it is vulgarized by promiscuous
experiments in flattery.

Assent thereto. Their lordships may object
Our not denying the same late request
Unto the Asian cities; we desire
That our defence, for suffering that, be known   460
In these brief reasons, with our after-purpose.
Since deified Augustus hindered not
A temple to be built, at Pergamum,
In honour of himself and sacred Rome,
We, that have all his deeds and words observed   465
Ever, in place of laws, the rather followed
That pleasing precedent, because, with ours,
The Senate's reverence also, there, was joined.
But as t'have once received it may deserve
The gain of pardon, so, to be adored   470
With the continued style and note of gods,
Through all the provinces, were wild ambition,
And no less pride: yea, ev'n Augustus' name
Would early vanish, should it be prophaned
With such promiscuous flatteries. For our part,   475

---

468. also, there, was] Q, F; also there was *Barish.*   470. so, to be] Q, F; so
to be *Barish.*

'As for myself, Conscript Fathers, that I am mortal, that my functions are
the functions of men, and that I hold it enough if I fill the foremost place
among them—this I call upon you to witness, and I desire those who shall
follow us to bear it in mind. For they will do justice, and more, to my memory,
if they pronounce me worthy of my ancestry, provident of your interests, firm
in dangers, not fearful of offences in the cause of the national welfare. These
are my temples in your breasts, these my fairest and abiding effigies: for those
that are reared of stone, should the judgement of the future turn to hatred, are
scorned as sepulchres! And so my prayer to allies and citizens and to Heaven
itself is this: to Heaven, that to the end of my life it may endow me with a quiet
mind, gifted with understanding of law human and divine; and to my fel-
lowmen, that, whenever I shall depart, their praise and kindly thoughts may
still attend my deeds and the memories attached to my name.'
Tacitus adds that it was commonly thought that 'To princes all other
gratifications came instantly: for one they must toil and never know satiety—
the favourable opinion of the future. For in the scorn of fame was implied the
scorn of virtue!'
   460. *suffering*] allowing.
   461. *after-purpose*] intention for the future.
   465.] Jonson cites Strabo, *Geography*, VI.iv.2, 'Tiberius ... is making
Augustus the model of his administration and decrees.' Loeb ed., tr. H. L.
Jones, III (London, 1967).
   470. *gain*] winning.
   471. *note*] importance, reputation.

We here protest it, and are covetous
Posterity should know it, we are mortal,
And can but deeds of men: 'twere glory'enough,
Could we be truly a prince. And they shall add
Abounding grace unto our memory   480
That shall report us worthy our forefathers,
Careful of your affairs, constant in dangers,
And not afraid of any private frown
For public good. These things shall be to us
Temples and statues, rearèd in your minds,   485
The fairest and most during imag'ry;
For those of stone or brass, if they become
Odious in judgement of posterity,
Are more contemned as dying sepulchres
Than ta'en for living monuments. We then   490
Make here our suit, alike to gods and men,
The one, until the period of our race,
T'inspire us with a free and quiet mind,
Discerning both divine and human laws;
The other, to vouchsafe us after death   495
An honourable mention, and fair praise,
T'accompany our actions, and our name.
The rest of greatness princes may command,
And (therefore) may neglect; only a long,
A lasting, high, and happy memory   500
They should, without being satisfied, pursue.
Contempt of fame begets contempt of virtue.
Natta. Rare!
Satrius.   Most divine!
Sejanus.   The oracles are ceased,

---

494. human] humane *Q, F.*   498–502.] *Each line preceded by gnomic
pointing, Q.*   499. neglect;] *Q;* neglect, *F.*   503. Most divine!] most
diuine. *Q.*

---

478. *can*] can perform.
482. *constant*] standing firm.
486. *during*] enduring.
489. *dying sepulchres*] a witty inversion of the 'living monuments' of the
following line.
492. *period . . . race*] end of our life.
503. *The oracles are ceased*] According to tradition, the oracles ceased after
the birth of Christ. Prudentius, *Apotheosis*, 438–43, talks about the Priest at

That only Caesar, with their tongue, might speak.
Arruntius. Let me be gone; most felt and open, this!   505
Cordus. Stay.
Arruntius.   What? To hear more cunning, and fine
            words,
    With their sound flattered, ere their sense be meant?
Tiberius. Their choice of Antium, there to place the gift
    Vowed to the goddess for our mother's health,
    We will the Senate know we fairly like;   510
    As also of their grant to Lepidus,
    For his repairing the Aemilian place,
    And restoration of those monuments;
    Their grace too in confining of Silanus
    To th'other isle Cythera, at the suit   515
    Of his religious sister, much commends
    Their policy, so tempered with their mercy.
    But, for the honours which they have decreed

---

505. gone;] gone, *Q, F.*   505. felt and open,] felt, & open *Q;* felt and open
F.   510.] *Marginal note in F: Fortuna equestris. Not in Q.*   515. Cythera,
at] *F (subst.); Cithera.* at *Q.*

Delphos struck dumb, and Hammon also in Libya, at the moment of Christ's
birth. There is a deliberate blasphemy, for just as Christ replaced the pagan
oracles, so Tiberius is said to do so here.
    505. *felt*] perceived.
    508–9.] The Roman equestrian order donated the statue of Equestrian
Fortune ('*Fortuna equestris*', as per Jonson's marginal note) at Antium (Anzio).
Jonson cites Tacitus, *Annals*, III.lxxi (on the choice of Antium).
    511–13.] Jonson cites Tacitus, *Annals*, III.lxxii, 'Nearly at the same time,
Marcus Lepidus asked permission from the senate to strengthen and decorate
the Basilica of Paulus, a monument of the Aemilian house, at his own expense.'
    511. *grant*] permission.
    514–17.] Jonson cites Tacitus, *Annals*, III.lxix: Tiberius told the senate
that, as 'Gyarus was a bleak and uninhabited island, ... they might allow
[Silanus] to retire to Cythnus instead. This was also the desire of Silanus' sister
Torquata, a Vestal of old-world saintliness.'
    515. *Cythera*] Jonson adopts an old mis-correction of the erroneous 'Cythe-
num' in the Tacitus ms., which should read 'Cythnus'.
    516. *his ... sister*] Jonson acknowledges Lipsius's note that there was
later preserved at Rome a statue of Silanus's sister, the Vestal Torquata (see
I.514–17n.).
    518ff.] Jonson cites Tacitus, *Annals*, III.lxxii: Tiberius 'gave high praise to
Sejanus, "through whose energy and watchfulness so grave an outbreak had
stopped at one catastrophe". The Fathers voted a statue to Sejanus, to be
placed in the Theatre of Pompey'.

To our Sejanus, to advance his statue
In Pompey's theatre (whose ruining fire   520
His vigilance and labour kept restrained
In that one loss), they have therein outgone
Their own great wisdoms by their skilful choice,
And placing of their bounties on a man
Whose merit more adorns the dignity   525
Than that can him—and gives a benefit
In taking, greater than it can receive.
Blush not, Sejanus, thou great aid of Rome,
Associate of our labours, our chief helper,
Let us not force thy simple modesty   530
With off'ring at thy praise, for more we cannot,
Since there's no voice can take it. No man, here,
Receive our speeches as hyperboles;
For we are far from flattering our friend
(Let envy know) as from the need to flatter.   535
Nor let them ask the causes of our praise;
Princes have still their grounds reared with themselves,
Above the poor low flats of common men,
And who will search the reasons of their acts
Must stand on equal bases. Lead, away.   540
Our loves unto the Senate.
            [*Exeunt* TIBERIUS, SEJANUS, HATERIUS, LATIARIS,
                                SATRIUS, NATTA, *etc.*]
Arruntius.   Caesar!
Sabinus.   Peace.

---

534. flattering] *H.&S.* flat'ring *Q;* flatt'ring *F.*   537–40.] *Each line preceded
by gnomic pointing, Q.*

---

519. *advance*] raise up.
528–9.] Jonson cites Tacitus, *Annals*, IV.ii and vii—Tiberius called Sejanus
'the partner of his toils' and 'coadjutor in the empire'.
530. *force*] violate, do offence to.
532. *take*] undertake.
537–40.] *H.&S.* point out that these lines are echoed by Thomas Fuller,
The Holy State (1642), IV.i, maxim 6.
537. *grounds*] i.e. the 'bases' on which they 'stand' (l. 540). There is also a
pun here—princes have their own 'grounds', i.e. 'causes' (l. 536) and 'reasons'
(l. 539).
542–5.] Jonson cites Seneca, *To Marcia on Consolation*, XXII.iv–v: 'Cordus
exclaimed: "Now the theatre is ruined indeed!" What! Was it not to burst with
rage—to think of Sejanus planted upon the ashes of Gnaeus Pompeius, a

Cordus. Great Pompey's theatre was never ruined
    Till now, that proud Sejanus hath a statue
    Reared on his ashes.
Arruntius.   Place the shame of soldiers
    Above the best of generals? Crack the world!   545
    And bruise the name of Romans into dust,
    Ere we behold it!
Silius.   Check your passion;
    Lord Drusus tarries.
Drusus.   Is my father mad?
    Weary of life and rule, lords? Thus to heave
    An idol up with praise? Make him his mate?   550
    His rival in the Empire?
Arruntius.   O good prince!
Drusus. Allow him statues? Titles? Honours? Such
    As he himself refuseth?
Arruntius.   Brave, brave Drusus!
Drusus. The first ascents to sovereignty are hard
    But, entered once, there never wants or means,   555
    Or ministers, to help th'aspirer on.
Arruntius. True, gallant Drusus.
Drusus.   We must shortly pray
    To Modesty that he will rest contented—
Arruntius. Ay, where he is, and not write emperor.

        [*Enter*] SEJANUS, [LATIARIS, *and clients*].

---

550. praise? ... mate?] *Q;* praise! ... mate! *F.*   551. Empire?] *Q;* empire!
F.   554–6.] *Each line preceded by gnomic pointing, Q.*   559. emperor]
H.&S.; Emp'rour *Q;* emp'rour *F.*   559.1. [*Enter*] ... *clients.*]] SEIANVS,
DRVSVS, ARRVNTIVS, &c. *F; He enters, followed with clients. marginal s.d. in F.*

---

disloyal soldier hallowed by a statue in a memorial to one of the greatest
generals?'
    548–59.] Jonson cites Tacitus, *Annals*, IV.iii (Drusus's enmity towards
Sejanus) and IV.vii: Drusus often publicly remarked 'how short a step till the
coadjutor was termed a colleague! The first designs upon a throne were beset
with difficulty; but, the first step made, a faction and helpers were not far to
seek ... his effigy was visible in the monuments of Gnaeus Pompeius; ...
they could only pray that he might be endowed with moderation, and rest
content.'
    551. *rival*] partner.

Sejanus. There is your bill, and yours. Bring you your man.   560
    I'have moved for you too, Latiaris.
Drusus.   What?
    Is your vast greatness grown so blindly bold,
    That you will over us?
Sejanus.   Why, then give way.
Drusus. Give way, Colossus? Do you lift? Advance you?
    Take that!

                Drusus strikes him.

Arruntius.   Good! Brave! Excellent brave prince!   565
Drusus. Nay, come, approach. [*Draws his sword.*] What? Stand
    you off? At gaze?
    It looks too full of death, for thy cold spirits.
    Avoid mine eye, dull camel, or my sword
    Shall make thy brav'ry fitter for a grave
    Than for a triumph. I'll advance a statue   570
    O' your own bulk; but't shall be on the cross,
    Where I will nail your pride, at breadth, and length,
    And crack those sinews, which are yet but stretched
    With your swoll'n fortune's rage.
Arruntius.   A noble prince!

---

560. *Sejanus.*] SEI. *Q; not in F.*   565. *Drusus . . . him.*] *Marginal s.d. in F; not
in Q.*   566. [*Draws his sword.*]] *Gifford.*   567. spirits] *F;* spirit *Q.*   568.
dull camel] *F;* dull, Camell *Q, corr. in MS. in Wise Q.*

---

561. *moved*] interceded.

563. *over*] walk over ('blindly')—a sense not recorded in *O.E.D.* Sejanus is
behaving like a great blind statue, the 'Colossus' of the next line.

564. *lift*] raise the hand in a threatening motion. This sense not in *O.E.D.*
In Tacitus, *Annals*, IV.iii Drusus and Sejanus both make such a gesture before
Drusus slaps Sejanus in the face (see next note). This puts *O.E.D. lift,* v.3
and 3e, cited by *H.&S.* and other modern editors ('Used of a ship riding the
waves or of a horse rearing'), out of court.

565. *Take that*] Jonson cites Tacitus, *Annals,* IV.iii, 'Drusus, impatient of a
rival, and quick-tempered to a fault, had in a casual altercation raised his hand
against the favourite, and, upon a counter-demonstration, had struck him in
the face'. Jonson's marginal note points out that he follows Tacitus, not Dio,
who claims it was Sejanus who struck Drusus (*Roman History,* LVII.22.1).

566. *at gaze*] in an attitude of wonder.

569. *brav'ry*] finery, with a punning reference to proud demeanour.

571. *the cross*] as Jonson notes in the margin (citing various classical
sources, which he has silently taken over from Lipsius's notes), a particularly
ignominious death.

All. A Castor, a Castor, a Castor, a Castor!   575
                    [*Exeunt all but Sejanus.*]
Sejanus. He that, with such wrong moved, can bear it through
        With patience, and an even mind, knows how
        To turn it back. Wrath, covered, carries fate:
        Revenge is lost, if I profess my hate.
        What was my practice late I'll now pursue   580
        As my fell justice. This hath styled it new.
                                    [*Exit* SEJANUS.]

                Chorus of musicians.

575. a Castor!] *F; &c. Q.*   575.1. [*Exeunt ... Sejanus.*]] SEIANVS. *Q, F.*
576. *Sejanus.*] SEI. *Q; not in F.*   578. Wrath] *F; "Wrath Q.*   579.
Revenge] *F;* "Reuenge *Q.*   581.2. *Chorus of musicians.*] *F;* MV. CHORVS. *Q.*

575.] Jonson cites Dio, *Roman History*, LVII.14.9: 'he was so given to
violent anger that he inflicted blows upon a distinguished knight, and for this
exploit received the nickname of Castor' (after a famous gladiator of the time).
H.&S. repeat Whalley's error in ascribing this to Xiphilinus—an eleventh-
century monk of Constantinople who abridged Books XXXVI–LXXX of Dio
into an 'Epitome' and is our chief source for the contents of the lost Books
LXI–LXXX.
    576–9.] As Briggs points out, Jonson echoes Seneca, *Medea*, 150–4:
'Whoe'er has dumbly borne hard blows with patient and calm soul, has been
able to repay them; it is hidden wrath that harms; hatred proclaimed loses its
chance for vengeance'. Loeb ed., tr. F. J. Miller (London, 1961), to which
subsequent quotations from the tragedies refer.
    580. *practice*] machination.

Actus Secundus

[*Enter*] SEJANUS, LIVIA, [*and*] EUDEMUS.

Sejanus. Physician, thou art worthy of a province
    For the great favours done unto our loves;
    And, but that greatest Livia bears a part
    In the requital of thy services,
    I should alone despair of aught like means   5
    To give them worthy satisfaction.
Livia. Eudemus (I will see it) shall receive
    A fit and full reward for his large merit.
    But for this potion we intend to Drusus
    (No more our husband now), whom shall we choose   10
    As the most apt and abled instrument
    To minister it to him?
Eudemus.   I say Lygdus.
Sejanus. Lygdus? What's he?
Livia.   An eunuch Drusus loves.
Eudemus. Ay, and his cup-bearer.
Sejanus.   Name not a second.
    If Drusus love him, and he have that place,   15
    We cannot think a fitter.
Eudemus.   True, my lord,
    For free access and trust are two main aids.

ACTUS SECUNDUS] *Q; Act.* II. *F;* ACT II. SCENE I. *Gifford;* Act II, [Scene i]
Bolton; Act II *Barish.*   0.1. [*Enter*] ... EUDEMUS] *This ed.;* The Garden of
Eudemus. / Enter Sejanus, Livia, and Eudemus. *Gifford, and subst. Barish;*
[*Eudemus' garden. Enter*] SEJANUS, LIVIA, EUDEMUS *Bolton.*   1. *Sejanus.*]
SEI. *Q; not in F.*

---

   5. *aught like*] any similar, sufficient.
   9. *this potion*] Jonson cites Tacitus, *Annals*, IV.iii, 'he moved her to dream of
... the murder of her husband'; and IV.viii, 'Sejanus ... chose a poison so
gradual ... as to counterfeit the progress of a natural ailment'.
   11. *abled*] capable.
   12–14. *Lygdus ... cup-bearer*] Jonson cites Tacitus, *Annals*, IV.viii: the
poison 'was administered to Drusus by help of the eunuch Lygdus'. Tacitus
does not mention that he was a cup-bearer. A 'Ganymede' or cup-bearer was a
euphemism for a catamite.

Sejanus. Skilful physician!
Livia.   But he must be wrought
   To th'undertaking with some laboured art.
Sejanus. Is he ambitious?
Livia.   No.
Sejanus.   Or covetous?   20
Livia. Neither.
Eudemus.   Yet gold is a good general charm.
Sejanus. What is he then?
Livia.   Faith, only wanton, light.
Sejanus. How! Is he young? And fair?
Eudemus.   A delicate youth.
Sejanus. Send him to me, I'll work him. Royal lady,
   Though I have loved you long, and with that height   25
   Of zeal and duty (like the fire, which more
   It mounts, it trembles), thinking nought could add
   Unto the fervour which your eye had kindled,
   Yet, now I see your wisdom, judgement, strength,
   Quickness, and will to apprehend the means   30
   To your own good and greatness, I protest
   Myself through-rarefied, and turned all flame
   In your affection. Such a spirit as yours
   Was not created for the idle second
   To a poor flash as Drusus; but to shine   35
   Bright, as the moon, among the lesser lights,
   And share the sov'reignty of all the world.
   Then Livia triumphs in her proper sphere,
   When she and her Sejanus shall divide

---

21. gold] *F;* Gold *Q.*

---

   24. *Send . . . work him*] Jonson cites Tacitus, *Annals*, IV.x, 'Sejanus, by an indecent connection, also attached to himself the eunuch Lygdus'.

   32. *through-rarefied*] thoroughly purified.

   33. *In your affection*] in my affection to you.

   34–5. *second . . . flash*] assistant to a fop (*O.E.D. second, sb.*, B.II.8; and *flash, sb.*, 5).

   36, 40–1.] Cf. Shakespeare, *LLL*, IV.iii.227–8, 'My love, her mistress, is a gracious moon; / She an attending star, scarce seen a light'. *H.&S.* compare Horace, *Odes*, I.xii.46–8: 'As the moon among the lesser lights, so shines the Julian constellation amid all others'. Loeb ed., tr. C. E. Bennett (London, 1964).

   37. *sov'reignty*] Diana (Cynthia) was the queen of the heavens.

The name of Caesar, and Augusta's star   40
Be dimmed with glory of a brighter beam;
When Agrippina's fires are quite extinct,
And the scarce-seen Tiberius borrows all
His little light from us, whose folded arms
Shall make one perfect orb. Who's that? Eudemus,   45
Look, 'tis not Drusus?   [*Exit* EUDEMUS.]
                         Lady, do not fear.
Livia. Not I, my lord. My fear and love of him
  Left me at once.
Sejanus.   Illustrous lady! Stay—
                              [*Enter* EUDEMUS.]
Eudemus. I'll tell his lordship.
Sejanus.   Who is't, Eudemus?
Eudemus. One of your lordship's servants, brings you word   50
  The emp'ror hath sent for you.
Sejanus.   O! Where is he?
  With your fair leave, dear princess. I'll but ask
  A question, and return.   *He goes out.*
Eudemus.   Fortunate princess!
  How are you blest in the fruition
  Of this unequalled man, this Soul of Rome,   55
  The Empire's life, and voice of Caesar's world!
Livia. So blessèd, my Eudemus, as to know
  The bliss I have, with what I ought to owe
  The means that wrought it. How do'I look today?
Eudemus. Excellent clear, believe it. This same fucus   60

46. Look ... Lady,] *Bolton;* Look. [*Exit Eudemus.*] 'Tis not Drusus, lady,
Gifford, Barish.   47. fear and love] feare, and loue *Q, F.*   53. *He goes out.*]
F; not in Q.   55. unequalled] *F;* vnaequald *Q.*

---

40. *Augusta's star*] as Jonson notes, the 'Augusta' of the time was the mother
of Tiberius. In the Imperial period of Roman history 'Augusta' was used as the
title of the most influential or senior female relative (mother, wife, daughter,
sister) of the Emperor. Sejanus is playing to Livia's female vanity.
  42. *Agrippina's fires*] Agrippina was the wife of Germanicus (marginal note).
  44. *folded arms*] the phrase refers to a mutual embrace.
  48. *Illustrous*] illustrious, carrying on the imagery of gleaming and brilliance
(Latin *illustris*, 'clear' or 'bright', was used of stars in addition to its sense of
'famous', 'distinguished')'.
  54. *fruition*] possession.
  59. *The means ... it*] i.e. Eudemus.
  60. *fucus*] a wash or colouring for the face.

    Was well laid on.
Livia.   Methinks 'tis here not white.
Eudemus. Lend me your scarlet, lady. 'Tis the sun
    Hath giv'n some little taint unto the ceruse;
                          [Paints her cheeks.]
    You should have used of the white oil I gave you.
    Sejanus, for your love! His very name   65
    Commandeth above Cupid, or his shafts—
Livia. Nay, now you'have made it worse.
Eudemus.   I'll help it straight—
    And, but pronounced, is a sufficient charm
    Against all rumour; and of absolute power
    To satisfy for any lady's honour.   70
Livia. What do you now, Eudemus?
Eudemus.   Make a light fucus,
    To touch you o'er withal.—Honoured Sejanus!
    What act (though ne'er so strange, and insolent)
    But that addition will at least bear out,
    If't do not expiate?
Livia.   Here, good physician.   75
Eudemus. I like this study to preserve the love
    Of such a man, that comes not every hour
    To greet the world—'Tis now well, lady, you should
    Use of the dentifrice I prescribed you, too,
    To clear your teeth, and the prepared pomatum,   80
    To smooth the skin.—A lady cannot be
    Too curious of her form, that still would hold
    The heart of such a person, made her captive,
    As you have his: who, to endear him more

---

63. *[Paints her cheeks.]* Gifford, after l. 66.   65. love!] F; loue? Q.   81.
smooth] F; smoth Q.

---

   63. *ceruse*] white lead (cosmetic). Jonson notes its sensitivity to heat, quoting
Martial, *Epigrams*, II.xli.11–12: 'pearl-powdered Fabulla dreads a shower,
white-leaded Sabella dreads the sun'. Loeb ed., tr. W. C. A. Ker (London,
1947).
   72. *touch you o'er*] colour lightly over your face.
   73. *strange, and insolent*] abnormal and immoderate.
   74–5. *that . . . expiate*] that title will at least carry off if not atone for.
   80. *pomatum*] scented ointment for application to the skin.
   82. *curious*] careful.
   82. *form*] shape, image; and probably beauty (Latin *forma*, beauty).

In your clear eye, hath put away his wife,   85
The trouble of his bed and your delights,
Fair Apicata, and made spacious room
To your new pleasures.
Livia.   Have not we returned
That, with our hate of Drusus, and discovery
Of all his counsels?
Eudemus.   Yes, and wisely, lady.   90
The ages that succeed, and stand far off
To gaze at your high prudence, shall admire
And reckon it an act without your sex,
It hath that rare appearance. Some will think
Your fortune could not yield a deeper sound   95
Than mixed with Drusus; but when they shall hear
That, and the thunder of Sejanus meet,
Sejanus, whose high name doth strike the stars,
And rings about the concave, great Sejanus,

---

90. lady.] *Barish;* lady, *Q, F.*   91. off] *F;* of *Q.*   96. Drusus] *Q, F;*
Drusus' *Bolton.*

85–8. *hath . . . pleasures*] Jonson quotes Tacitus, *Annals*, IV.iii, 'Sejanus, to
forestall the suspicions of his mistress, closed his doors on Apicata, the wife
who had borne him three children'.

86. *trouble*] vexation.

89–90. *discovery . . . counsels*] Jonson cites Tacitus, *Annals*, IV.vii, 'Since
the seduction of his wife, his very confidences were betrayed'.

91–103.] This passage is interesting in the light of Renaissance astrological
theories of fortune, especially those of the distinguished fifteenth-century
Italian astrologer, Giovanni Pontano. Pontano thought fortune was connected
with prudence, but not with virtue. He developed a theory of the fortunate,
who are outside the moral law. See D. C. Allen, *The Star-Crossed Renaissance*
(London, 1966), pp. 40–2. Eudemus praises an amoral 'prudence' in Livia
(II.92) which will enhance her 'fortune' (II.95) through her alliance with 'the
thunder of Sejanus' (II.97). Sejanus is imaged in Jovian terms (Jupiter is
the 'thunderer'), and one notes that in astrological parlance, Jupiter was the
greater of the two 'good Planets and Fortunes', Jupiter and Venus ('A Planet is
said to be a Fortune when he is conjoyned to the Fortunes')—William Salmon,
Synopsis Medicinae (1671), I.viii, pp. 12, 22.

93. *without*] beyond the capacity or comprehension of. Cf. *C.R.*, I.iv.55,
'O, now I apprehend you; your phrase was without me, before'. The only
examples of this sense in *O.E.D.*

95. *sound*] sounding, a measure of depth by means of line and lead—with an
equivocation on the primary sense that the following lines assume.

98. *strike the stars*] as *H.&S.* note, a common classical hyperbole.

99. *concave*] vault of heaven. The earliest example given by *O.E.D.* is
1635.

Whose glories, style, and titles are himself,   100
The often iterating of Sejanus—
They then will lose their thoughts, and be ashamed
To take acquaintance of them.

[*Enter* SEJANUS.]

Sejanus.   I must make
A rude departure, lady. Caesar sends
With all his haste both of command and prayer.   105
Be resolute in our plot; you have my soul,
As certain yours as it is my body's.
And wise physician, so prepare the poison
As you may lay the subtle operation
Upon some natural disease of his.   110
Your eunuch send to me. I kiss your hands,
Glory of ladies, and commend my love
To your best faith and memory.
Livia.   My lord,
I shall but change your words. Farewell. Yet, this
Remember for your heed: he loves you not.   115
You know what I have told you: his designs
Are full of grudge and danger. We must use
More than a common speed.
Sejanus.   Excellent lady,
How you do fire my blood!
Livia.   Well, you must go?

---

102. lose] *F;* loose *Q.*   116. you:] *F;* you? *Q.*   120. The] *F;* "The *Q.*

100. *Whose ... himself*] whose honours, appellations and titles are appropriate or fitted to him.

103–5.] There is a comic effect in these lines, where the hyperbole of the previous lines is undercut by Sejanus's abject and instant obedience to Tiberius's 'command and prayer'. The phrase 'and prayer' sounds like Sejanus's attempt to save face.

108–10.] Jonson cites Tacitus, *Annals*, IV.viii, 'Sejanus ... chose a poison so gradual in its inroads as to counterfeit the progress of a natural ailment'; and Dio, *Roman History*, LVII.22.2, 'Drusus ... perished by poison ... administered ... through the agency of those in attendance upon him'.

109. *lay*] blame.

109. *subtle*] fine, delicate (the sense of Latin *subtilis*).

114. *change*] return.

The thoughts be best are least set forth to show.   120

                              [*Exit* SEJANUS.]

Eudemus. When will you take some physic, lady?

Livia.   When

    I shall, Eudemus; but let Drusus' drug

    Be first prepared.

Eudemus.   Were Lygdus made, that's done;

    I have it ready. And tomorrow morning

    I'll send you a perfume, first to resolve   125

    And procure sweat, and then prepare a bath

    To cleanse and clear the cutis; against when,

    I'll have an excellent new fucus made,

    Resistive 'gainst the sun, the rain, or wind,

    Which you shall lay on with a breath, or oil,   130

    As you best like, and last some fourteen hours.

    This change came timely, lady, for your health,

    And the restoring your complexion,

    Which Drusus' choler had almost burnt up;

    Wherein your fortune hath prescribed you better   135

    Than art could do.

Livia.   Thanks, good physician,

    I'll use my fortune (you shall see) with reverence.

---

124. tomorrow morning] *F;* to morrow e morning *Q.*   131. hours.] *F;*
hours, *Q.*   135. prescribed] praescrib'd *Q;* prescrib'd *F.*

120.] Cf. *Ham.*, I.iii.59, 'Give thy thoughts no tongue', and the proverbial
'Your thoughts close and your countenance loose' (Tilley, T 248).

123. *made*] initiated (into the conspiracy). *O.E.D.* quotes this example,
and, as its earliest, *E.M.I.*, IV.xi.46—in the Folio text: 'Come, let's before,
and make the Iustice, Captain'.

125. *resolve*] melt. Cf. *Cat.*, III.739–40, 'May my braine / Resolue to water,
and my bloud turne phlegme'.

127. *cutis*] skin—the earliest example in *O.E.D.* It is an anatomical term
for the derma or true skin beneath the epidermis. Here it is less a self-
conscious latinism than an appropriate term for Eudemus, a physician, to use.

130. *with a breath*] perhaps 'after gently warming with the breath' (to
soften).

134. *choler*] one of the humours and associated with heat and dryness—in
contrast to the cosmetics which are associated with moistening.

137.] This line, as *H.&S.* point out, derives from Ausonius, *Epigrams*,
II.7–8, 'Bear good fortune modestly [*reverenter*], whoe'er thou art who from a
lowly place shall rise suddenly to riches'. Loeb ed., tr. H. G. Evelyn White
(London, 1961). The idea recurs in *Volp.*, III.vii.88–9, *N.I.*, V.ii.58,
P.Hen.Barriers, 405–6, and *Und.*, xxvi.23.

Is my coach ready?

Eudemus.   It attends your highness.

                    [*Exeunt* LIVIA *and* EUDEMUS.]

                    [*Enter*] SEJANUS.

Sejanus. If this be not revenge, when I have done
        And made it perfect, let Egyptian slaves,   140
        Parthians, and barefoot Hebrews brand my face,
        And print my body full of injuries.
        Thou lost thyself, child Drusus, when thou thoughtst
        Thou couldst outskip my vengeance, or outstand
        The power I had to crush thee into air: 145
        Thy follies now shall taste what kind of man
        They have provoked, and this thy father's house
        Crack in the flame of my incensèd rage
        Whose fury shall admit no shame or mean.
        Adultery? It is the lightest ill   150
        I will commit. A race of wicked acts
        Shall flow out of my anger, and o'erspread
        The world's wide face, which no posterity
        Shall e'er approve, nor yet keep silent: things
        That for their cunning, close and cruel mark,   155
        Thy father would wish his—and shall, perhaps,

138.2. [*Enter*] SEJANUS] *This ed.*; SCENE II. / An Apartment in the Palace. /
Enter Sejanus. *Gifford;* [Act II, Scene ii] / [*An apartment in the palace.*
Enter] SEJANUS *Bolton;* [*An apartment in the palace. Enter*] *Sejanus. Barish.*
139. *Sejanus.*] SEI. *Q; not in* F.   140. Egyptian] Ægyptian Q, F.

140–1. *let ... face*] Jonson notes the very low esteem in which Egyptians
were held in Rome, giving, without specific references, Juvenal and Martial as
his sources. See, esp., Juvenal, *Satires*, xv. Juvenal also mentions that at
Jerusalem 'kings celebrate festal sabbaths with bare feet' (*Satires*, vi.159).
Subservience was a noted feature of orientals.

143. *child*] youth of noble birth, with a contemptuous play on the usual
sense of 'simple, unpractised', in contrast to the 'man' of p. 146.

149. *mean*] moderation.

150–6.] Briggs points out the Senecan source here—*Thyestes*, 25–7, 44–7,
192–5: 'let their passions know no bounds, no shame; let blind fury prick on
their souls; ... let shameful defilement be a trivial thing; let fraternal sanctity
and faith and every right be trampled under foot'; 'Up! my soul, do what no
coming age shall approve, but none forget. I must dare some crime, atrocious,
bloody, such as my brother would more wish were his'.

Carry the empty name, but we the prize.
On then, my soul, and start not in thy course.
Though heav'n drop sulphur, and hell belch out fire,
Laugh at the idle terrors. Tell proud Jove,   160
Between his power, and thine, there is no odds.
'Twas only fear first in the world made gods.

[*Enter*] TIBERIUS [*attended*].

Tiberius. Is yet Sejanus come?
Sejanus.   He's here, dread Caesar.
Tiberius. Let all depart that chamber, and the next.

[*Exeunt* ATTENDANTS.]

Sit down, my comfort. When the master prince   165
Of all the world, Sejanus, saith he fears,
Is it not fatal?
Sejanus.   Yes, to those are feared.
Tiberius. And not to him?
Sejanus.   Not if he wisely turn
That part of fate he holdeth, first on them.
Tiberius. That nature, blood, and laws of kind forbid.   170

162.1. [*Enter*] TIBERIUS [*attended*].] TIBERIVS. SEIANVS. *Q;* TIBERIVS,
SEIANVS. *F.*   163. *Tiberius.*] TIB. *Q; not in F.*   163. He's] *F;* H'is *Q.*

---

157. *Carry ... name*] have the reputation. Jonson has in mind the rumour that Tiberius was misled by Sejanus into believing that Drusus had poisoned his cup at a banquet, and, without checking any fact of the matter, passed it to his son to drink, who in ignorance drained it, and died. Thus Tiberius received the opprobrium due to Sejanus. Tacitus reports and refutes the rumour in *Annals*, IV.x-xi.

158. *start*] flinch, recoil (from danger).

159. *sulphur*] lightning—a Latin poetic usage. *O.E.D.*'s earliest citation is 1607.

162.] Jonson cites the classical sources: Petronius, *Poems*, 3; and Statius, *Thebaid*, III.661. According to the ed. of the Loeb *Statius* (London, 1961), tr. J. H. Mozley, it was a 'commonplace of the rhetoricians'.

165ff.] Jonson's note states that this interview is given authority by Suetonius's statement that Tiberius had promoted Sejanus 'to the highest power, not so much from regard for him, as that he might through his services and wiles destroy the children of Germanicus and secure the succession of his own grandson, the child of his son Drusus'.

170-2.] Briggs points out the indebtedness here and in the following lines to Seneca. Here the source is *Thyestes*, 215-18: 'ATTENDANT. Where is no shame, no care for right, no honour, virtue, faith, sovereignty is insecure. ATREUS. Honour, virtue, faith are the goods of common men; let kings go

Sejanus. Do policy and state forbid it?
Tiberius.   No.
Sejanus. The rest of poor respects, then, let go by;
    State is enough to make th'act just, them guilty.
Tiberius. Long hate pursues such acts.
Sejanus.   Whom hatred frights,
    Let him not dream on sov'reignty.
Tiberius.   Are rites   175
    Of faith, love, piety, to be trod down?
    Forgotten? And made vain?
Sejanus.   All for a crown.
    The prince, who shames a tyrant's name to bear,
    Shall never dare do anything but fear.
    All the command of sceptres quite doth perish   180
    If it begin religious thoughts to cherish:
    Whole empires fall, swayed by those nice respects.
    It is the licence of dark deeds protects
    Ev'n states most hated, when no laws resist
    The sword, but that it acteth what it list.   185

173–87.] *Each line preceded by gnomic pointing, Q.*

---

where they please'. A nearer source of the idea is Machiavelli as popularly understood.

170. *kind*] kinship.

171. *policy and state*] political expediency and state concerns.

172ff.] So much of the following dialogue is in rhyme not only to give the sense of strong emotion (as *H.&S.* state) but because the high proportion of maxims demands it.

172. *respects*] considerations.

174–5. *Whom . . . sov'reignty*] From Seneca, *Oedipus*, 703–4, 'He who fears hatred overmuch, knows not to rule; fear is the guard of kingdoms'; and *Phoenissae*, 654, 'To reign he hath no will who feareth to be hated'.

178–87.] For a first draft of these lines, discovered by W. D. Briggs— *Anglia*, XXXIX, 247–8—see *U. V.*, L.9–20. They are a loose translation of Lucan, *The Civil War (Pharsalia)*, VIII.489–95: 'The power of kings is utterly destroyed, once they begin to weigh considerations of justice; and regard for virtue levels the strongholds of tyrants. It is boundless wickedness and unlimited slaughter that protect the unpopularity of a sovereign. If all your deeds are cruel, you will suffer for it the moment you cease from cruelty. If a man would be righteous, let him depart from a court. Virtue is incompatible with absolute power. He who is ashamed to commit cruelty must always fear it.'

182. *nice*] fine, delicate.

183. *licence*] lack of restraint; lawlessness.

Tiberius. Yet so we may do all things cruelly,
   Not safely.
Sejanus.   Yes, and do them thoroughly.
Tiberius. Knows yet Sejanus whom we point at?
Sejanus.   Ay,
   Or else my thought, my sense, or both do err:
   'Tis Agrippina?
Tiberius.   She, and her proud race.   190
Sejanus. Proud? Dangerous, Caesar. For in them apace
   The father's spirit shoots up. Germanicus
   Lives in their looks, their gait, their form, t'upbraid us
   With his close death, if not revenge the same.
Tiberius. The act's not known.
Sejanus.   Not proved. But whisp'ring fame 195
   Knowledge and proof doth to the jealous give,
   Who, than to fail, would their own thought believe.
   It is not safe the children draw long breath,

---

187. thoroughly] *F;* throughly *Q.* 195. But] *F;* "But *Q.*
196–201.] *Each line preceded by gnomic pointing, Q.*

---

  187. *and*] if.
  189. *sense*] *i.e.,* observation.
  190. *Agrippina*] Jonson's note refers the reader to Dio, *Roman History*, LVII.5.6, 'Agrippina [Germanicus's wife] was the daughter of Agrippa and Julia, Augustus' daughter'.
  191. *Dangerous*] Jonson cites Tacitus, *Annals*, I.lxix, 'Sejanus inflamed and exacerbated has jealousies' in regard to Agrippina; and, to the same effect, IV.xii and IV.xvii. On Tiberius's envy of her popularity he cites III.iv, 'Nothing ... sank deeper into Tiberius' breast than the kindling of men's enthusiasm for Agrippina'.
  193–4. *t'upbraid ... death*] Jonson quotes Tacitus, *Annals*, III.ii, 'all men knew that Tiberius was with difficulty dissembling his joy at the death of Germanicus', cites III.xvi on the suspicion that Tiberius had ordered Piso to poison Germanicus, and quotes IV.i, 'he counted the death of Germanicus among his blessings'.
  194. *close*] secretly arranged.
  195–6. *fame ... give*] Cf. the prov. 'Jealousy is no judge—nor suspicion proof' (Tilley, S 1019).
  195. *fame*] rumour.
  196. *jealous*] suspicious.
  197. *than to fail*] rather than admit ignorance.
  197. *thought*] imagination.
  198–9.] Briggs compares the quotation in Aristotle, *Rhetoric*, I.xv.14, tr. H. Rackham, 'Foolish is he who, having killed the father, suffers the children to live'.
  198. *draw long breath*] live for long.

That are provokèd by a parent's death.
Tiberius. It is as dangerous to make them hence,   200
  If nothing but their birth be their offence.
Sejanus. Stay, till they strike at Caesar: then their crime
    Will be enough, but late, and out of time
    For him to punish.
Tiberius.   Do they purpose it?
Sejanus. You know, sir, thunder speaks not till it hit.   205
    Be not secure: none swiftlier are oppressed
    Than they whom confidence betrays to rest.
    Let not your daring make your danger such.
    All power's to be feared, where 'tis too much.
    The youths are, of themselves, hot, violent,   210
    Full of great thought; and that male-spirited dame,
    Their mother, slacks no means to put them on,
    By large allowance, popular presentings,
    Increase of train, and state, suing for titles;
    Hath them commended with like prayers, like vows,   215

---

205. sir,] *F;* sir. *Q.*   205. thunder] *F;* "Thunder *Q.* 206-9.] *Each line preceded by gnomic pointing, Q.*

---

205. Strange meteorology — presumably what is meant is that thunder is not heard until after the lightning strikes.

206. *secure*] free from anxiety (Latin *securus*).

206-7. *none . . . rest*] As Briggs points out, from Velleius Paterculus, *History of Rome*, II.cxviii.2, 'no one could be more quickly overpowered than the man who feared nothing, and . . . the most common beginning of disaster was a sense of security'. Loeb ed., tr. F. W. Shipley (London, 1967). Cf. Livy, XXV.28, 'Men are least safe from what success induces them not to fear'. Loeb ed., tr. F. G. Moore (London, 1951).

209.] Perhaps, as Briggs claims, from Tacitus, *Histories*, II.xcii, 'when a man has excessive power, he never can have complete trust'. Loeb ed., tr. C. H. Moore (London, 1968).

211. *great*] ambitious—a sense not recorded in *O.E.D.* The 'great thought' is thought of greatness.

211. *male-spirited*] Jonson cites Tacitus, *Annals*, on her 'rebellious spirit' (I.xxxiii), her saving of the Vetera bridge on the Rhine (I.lxix), and Germanicus's death-bed advice to her to temper her proud, ambitious nature (II.lxxii).

212. *slacks*] neglects.

213. *large allowance*] generous sums of money (an alternative sense, 'great tolerance', is less appropriate to the context).

213. *popular presentings*] appearances in public.

215-16. *Hath . . . Caesar*] Jonson cites Tacitus, *Annals*, IV.xvii: 'the pontiffs . . . while offering the vows for the life of the emperor, went further and commended Nero and Drusus to the same divinities'. Tiberius rebuked them

To the same gods, with Caesar. Days and nights
She spends in banquets, and ambitious feasts
For the nobility, where Caius Silius,
Titius Sabinus, old Arruntius,
Asinius Gallus, Furnius, Regulus,   220
And others of that discontented list
Are the prime guests. There, and to these, she tells
Whose niece she was, whose daughter, and whose wife;
And then must they compare her with Augusta,
Ay, and prefer her too, commend her form,   225
Extol her fruitfulness; at which a show'r
Falls for the memory of Germanicus,
Which they blow over straight with windy praise,
And puffing hopes of her aspiring sons;
Who, with these hourly ticklings, grow so pleased,   230

---

and warned, in the senate, against exciting 'to arrogance the impressionable
minds of the youths by such precocious distinctions'.

220. *Asinius Gallus*] He gave early offence to Tiberius in the senate (*Annals*,
I.xii; see also II.xxxvi), but was not consistently of Agrippina's party. At
III.356–8 Jonson, following Tacitus, has him moving the exiling of her friend,
Sosia Galla, wife of Caius Silius. He had married the first wife of Tiberius,
Vipsania. Imprisoned in A.D. 30, he died of starvation in 33.

220. *Furnius*] condemned in A.D. 26 for adultery with Claudia Pulchra,
Agrippina's second cousin.

220. *Regulus*] Publius Memmius Regulus, *consul suffectus* in A.D. 31.
Briggs, and *H.&S.*, are puzzled by the connection with Agrippina's party,
but Jonson obviously makes the connection in virtue of Regulus's independence
from all emperors. His 'authority, firmness, and character had earned him the
maximum of glory possible in the shadows cast by imperial greatness', and he
'survived . . . shielded by his quietude of life; . . . his modest fortune aroused
no envy' (Tacitus, *Annals*, XIV.xlvii).

222.] '*Neptis*' (granddaughter), notes Jonson, of Augustus, daughter of
Julia (Augustus's daughter), wife of Germanicus.

226. *her fruitfulness*] Jonson cites Tacitus, *Annals*, II.xliii and IV.xii regarding her '*fecunditas*'. Besides the three sons Nero, Drusus (junior) and Caius
(Caligula), she had three daughters.

226–9. *a show'r . . . hopes*] The metaphors of rain (tears) and wind (praise)
are commonplace, but their combination is very finely wrought.

230. *ticklings*] gratifications. 'Tickling' is also a method of catching trout—
'tracing it to the stone it lies under, then rubbing it gently beneath, which
causes the fish to gradually move backwards into the hand, till the fingers
suddenly close in the gills'. Richard Jefferies, *Red Deer* (1884), ix.174, quoted
in *O.E.D.*, *Tickling*, 3c, which also cites Beaumont and Fletcher, *The
Scornful Lady*, III.ii, 'Leave off your tickling of your heirs like trouts', a line
that compares interestingly with Jonson's usage.

    And wantonly conceited of themselves,
    As now they stick not to believe they'are such
    As these do give 'em out; and would be thought
    (More than competitors) immediate heirs;
    Whilst to their thirst of rule they win the rout,   235
    That's still the friend of novelty, with hope
    Of future freedom, which on every change,
    That greedily, though emptily, expects.
    Caesar, 'tis age in all things breeds neglects,
    And princes that will keep old dignity   240
    Must not admit too youthful heirs stand by—
    Not their own issue, but so darkly set
    As shadows are in picture, to give height
    And lustre to themselves.
Tiberius.   We will command
    Their rank thoughts down, and with a stricter hand   245
    Than we have yet put forth, their trains must bate,
    Their titles, feasts, and factions.
Sejanus.   Or your state.
    But how, sir, will you work?
Tiberius.   Confine 'em.
Sejanus.   No.

239–44.] *Each line preceded by gnomic pointing, Q.*

   235. *rout*] rabble.
   236. *novelty*] change, with strong political connotations in the seventeenth century.
   236–7. *with ... freedom*] Jonson quotes Tacitus, *Annals*, II.lxxxii: it was popularly claimed that 'sons with democratic tempers were not pleasing to fathers on a throne; and both [Nero Drusus, stepson of Augustus, and Germanicus] had been cut off for no other reason than because they designed to restore the age of freedom and take the Roman people into a partnership of equal rights'. To Sejanus (and Jonson), however, the 'freedom' demanded by the 'rout' is mere licence.
   242. *darkly*] humbly, not in public notice.
   244–7. *We will ... factions*] Jonson cites Suetonius, *Lives*, III.liv: Tiberius initially commended Germanicus's sons to the care of the senate, but, alarmed at their rising popularity and the honours being showered on them, he began to speak against them, and engineered their downfall.
   245. *rank*] haughty. (O. *E. D. rank, a.*, A. I. 1—a late example).
   246. *trains*] stratagems (*O.E.D. train sb.* ^{2}*Obs.*1b). Cf. *Mac.*, IV.iii.117–19, 'Devilish Macbeth / By many of these trains hath sought to win me / Into his power'.
   246. *bate*] put an end to (*O.E.D. bate, v*^{2}, 1).

They are too great, and that too faint a blow
To give them now. It would have served at first,   250
When, with the weakest touch, their knot had burst.
But now your care must be not to detect
The smallest cord or line of your suspect;
For such, who know the weight of princes' fear,
Will, when they find themselves discovered, rear   255
Their forces, like seen snakes, that else would lie
Rolled in their circles, close. Nought is more high,
Daring, or desperate, than offenders found;
Where guilt is, rage and courage both abound.
The course must be to let 'em still swell up,   260
Riot, and surfeit on blind Fortune's cup;
Give 'em more place, more dignities, more style,
Call 'em to court, to Senate; in the while,
Take from their strength some one or twain, or more
Of the main fautors—it will fright the store—   265

---

253. cord] *F*; *chord Q.*   257. Nought] *F*; "Nought *Q.*   258–9.] *Both lines
preceded by gnomic pointing, Q.*   259. both] *Q*; *doth F.*   266. sleight]
Barish; slight *Q, F, Bolton.*

---

251. *knot*] group, cluster (of snakes—II.256).
252. *detect*] reveal.
253. *cord or line*] the image presumably relates to snaring devices.
253. *suspect*] suspicion.
257–9.] Gifford claimed this was adapted from Juvenal, *Satires*, VI.284–5:
'There's no effrontery like that of a woman caught in the act; her very guilt
inspires her with wrath and insolence'. However, while Sejanus may have
Agrippina in mind here, there is no allusion in Jonson's lines to the adulterous
woman.
257. *high*] wrathful.
261. *blind Fortune's cup*] Fortuna was usually represented as blindfolded and
holding one or two *cornucopiae*. Given the insistent reference to snakes in
preceding lines, one is reminded that the Whore of Babylon was represented
in iconography holding a cup filled with serpents in allusion to Revelations
xvii.4 and Deuteronomy xxxii.33.
262–5. *Give ... fautors*] Jonson cites Tacitus, *Annals*, IV.viii (Tiberius's
commending of the sons of Germanicus to the care of the senate—'cherish
them, build up their fortunes, ... adopt them, train them'); and IV.xvii–
xviii, 'the only cure [argued Sejanus] for the growing disunion was to strike
down one or two of the most active malcontents'.
262. *place*] standing.
265. *fautors*] partisans (L. *fautor*, promoter).
265. *store*] rest.

And by some by-occasion. Thus, with sleight
You shall disarm them first, and they, in night
Of their ambition, not perceive the train
Till, in the engine, they are caught, and slain.
Tiberius. We would not kill, if we knew how to save;   270
Yet, than a throne, 'tis cheaper give a grave.
Is there no way to bind them by deserts?
Sejanus. Sir, wolves do change their hair, but not their hearts.
While thus your thought unto a mean is tied,
You neither dare enough, nor do provide.   275
All modesty is fond; and chiefly where
The subject is no less compelled to bear
Than praise his sov'reign's acts.
Tiberius.   We can no longer
Keep on our mask to thee, our dear Sejanus;

---

267. them] *Q; not in F.*   271. Yet] *F;* "Yet *Q.*   273–8.] *Each line preceded
by gnomic pointing, Q.*

---

266. *by-occasion*] separate or side issue.
266. *sleight*] with a play on 'slight', small scale.
267–8. *in . . . ambition*] blinded by ambition. The (partly nocturnal) activities described above, II.211–38, are practically *ambitio* in its primary sense
for the republican period, 'the going about of candidates for office in Rome,
and the soliciting of individual citizens for their vote, a canvassing, suing for
office' (*L.&S.*, *ambitio*, I).
268. *train*] lure, bait.
269. *engine*] trap.
272. *bind . . . deserts*] win them over by deserving their gratitude.
273. *wolves . . . hearts*] Tilley, W 616. Greek proverb, ascr. to Arsenius in
Corpus Paroemiographorum Graecorum, ed. E. L. Leutsch and F. G. Schneide-
win (Hildesheim, 1958; orig. publ. 1839, 1851), II, 558, item 66. Ascr. to
Apostolius, *Paroemiae*, XII, 66, in *Dictionary of Quotations (Classical)*, ed. T.
B. Harbottle, 2nd ed. (London, 1902), p. 430.
274–5.] From Tacitus, *Histories*, III.xl (Briggs): 'in following a middle
course—the worst of all policies in times of doubt—[Fabius Valens] showed
neither adequate courage nor foresight'.
275. *provide*] display forsight, literally 'look forward' in Latin (*providit* in
the Tacitus passage).
276. *modesty is fond*] moderation is foolish.
277–8. *The . . . acts*] From Seneca, *Thyestes*, 205–7 (Briggs): 'The greatest
advantage this of royal power, that their master's deeds the people are compelled as well to bear as praise'.
278–9. *We . . . Sejanus*] Jonson quotes Tacitus, *Annals*, IV.i, 'by his multi-
farious arts, [Sejanus] bound Tiberius fast: so much so that a man inscrutable

Thy thoughts are ours, in all, and we but proved   280
Their voice, in our designs, which by assenting
Hath more confirmed us than if heart'ning Jove
Had, from his hundred statues, bid us strike,
And at the stroke clicked all his marble thumbs.
But who shall first be struck?
Sejanus.   First, Caius Silius.   285
He is the most of mark, and most of danger:
In power and reputation equal strong,
Having commanded an imperial army
Seven years together, vanquished Sacrovir
In Germany, and thence obtained to wear   290
The ornaments triumphal. His steep fall,
By how much it doth give the weightier crack,
Will send more wounding terror to the rest,
Command them stand aloof, and give more way
To our surprising of the principal.   295
Tiberius. But what Sabinus?
Sejanus.   Let him grow a while,

---

285. struck] strooke *Q, F.*

---

to others became to Sejanus alone unguarded and unreserved'; and cites Dio,
Roman History, LVII.19.7—Tiberius 'made him his adviser and assistant in all
matters'.

280. *proved*] tested.

281. *Their voice*] presumably the consent of Sejanus's 'thoughts' to Tiberius's
designs.

284. *clicked ... thumbs*] turned all his thumbs down. Jonson cites various
sources on the meaning of the gesture, used by spectators at gladiatorial
contests. 'Clicked', presumably, is the sound Jonson associates with marble
thumbs being turned down.

285-93. *First ... the rest*] Jonson cites Tacitus, *Annals*, III. xlv–xlvi, which
describe Silius's victory over the Aedui, led by Sacrovir, in eastern Gaul,
A.D. 21. He also cites *Annals*, IV.xviii: Tiberius 'attacked Gaius Silius and
Titius Sabinus. The friendship of Germanicus was fatal to both; but in the case
of Silius there was the further point that, as he had commanded a great army
for seven years, had earned the emblems of triumph in Germany, and was the
victor of the war with Sacrovir, the greater ruin of his fall must spread a wider
alarm among others'.

286. *most of mark*] most outstanding or notable.

291. *ornaments triumphal*] Only the emperor, holder of the *imperium*, could
enjoy a triumph, but the *triumphalia ornamenta* or *insignia* conferred the same
honour.

296-7. *Sabinus ... ripe*] Jonson cites Tacitus, *Annals*, IV.xix, 'Sabinus
could be postponed awhile'.

His fate is not yet ripe. We must not pluck
At all together, lest we catch ourselves.
And there's Arruntius too, he only talks.
But Sosia, Silius' wife, would be wound in   300
Now, for she hath a fury in her breast
More, than hell ever knew; and would be sent
Thither in time. Then is there one Cremutius
Cordus, a writing fellow they have got
To gather notes of the precedent times,   305
And make them into annals—a most tart
And bitter spirit, I hear, who, under colour
Of praising those, doth tax the present state,
Censures the men, the actions, leaves no trick,
No practice unexamined, parallels   310
The times, the governments; a pròfessed champion
For the old liberty—

Tiberius.   A perishing wretch!
As if there were that chaos bred in things,
That laws and liberty would not rather choose
To be quite broken, and ta'en hence by us,   315
Than have the stain to be preserved by such.
Have we the means to make these guilty first?

Sejanus. Trust that to me. Let Caesar, by his power,
But cause a formal meeting of the Senate,

302. More,] *Q, F;* More *Barish.* 305. precedent] *F;* praecedent *Q.*
306. annals] Annal's *Q, F (where Jonson presumably meant* Annales *abbreviated).*
311. pròfessed] *Barish;* profest *Q, F.*

---

300. *Sosia . . . wife*] Jonson cites Tacitus, *Annals,* IV.xix, 'Silius had a wife,
Sosia Galla, who by her affection for Agrippina had incurred the detestation of
the emperor. On these two, it was decided, the blow should fall'.

300, 302. *would*] should.

301–2. *a fury . . . More,*] i.e. one fury more. The comma after *More*
emphasises this sense.

303. *in time*] sooner or later.

303–4. *Cremutius Cordus*] Jonson cites the sources (apart from Suetonius) he
cited at I.73. See note to that line.

309. *Censures*] criticises.

313–16.] Tiberius echoes the famous words of Caesar to the tribune Metellus: 'The course of time has not wrought such confusion that the laws would
not rather be trampled on by Caesar than saved by Metellus'. Lucan, *The
Civil War,* III.138–40. As Briggs notes, there is a similar passage in *Cat.,*
IV.480–8.

316. *stain*] disgrace.

I will have matter and accusers ready.   320
Tiberius. But how? Let us consult.
Sejanus.   We shall misspend
    The time of action. Counsels are unfit
    In business, where all rest is more pernicious
    Than rashness can be. Acts of this close kind
    Thrive more by execution than advice: 325
    There is no ling'ring in that work begun,
    Which cannot praisèd be, until through done.
Tiberius. Our edict shall forthwith command a court.
    While I can live, I will prevent earth's fury;
    Ἐμοῦ θανόντος γαῖα μιχθήτω πυρί.   330

                                                    [*Exit* TIBERIUS.]

                        [*Enter*] POSTUMUS.

Postumus. My lord Sejanus—
Sejanus.   Julius Postumus,
    Come with my wish! What news from Agrippina's?
Postumus. Faith, none. They all lock up themselves a'late,
    Or talk in character. I have not seen

322. Counsels] *F;* "Councells *Q.*   323–7.] *Each line preceded by gnomic
pointing, Q.*   329. prevent] *F;* praevent *Q.*   330. Ἐμοῦ] Ε'μοῦ *Q, F.*
330. γαῖα] γᾶια *Q, F.*   330.2. [*Enter*] POSTUMUS.] POSTVMVS. SEIANVS.
Q; POSTHVMVS, SEIANVS *F.*   331. *Postumus.*] POS. *Q; not in F.*
331. Sejanus—] *F;* Seianus? *Q.*

322–3. *Counsels . . . business*] Cf. the proverbial 'Take not counsel in the
combat' (Tilley, C 698).
    323–4. *where . . . can be*] As Briggs notes, from Tacitus, *Histories*, I.xxi, 'a
man must not delay when inactivity is more ruinous than rash action'.
    325. *advice*] consultation.
    328.] Jonson cites Tacitus, *Annals*, I.vii, where there is reference to 'his
edict, convening the Fathers to the senate-house . . . issued . . . beneath the
tribunician title'.
    330.] Jonson cites Dio, *Roman History*, LVIII.23.4, 'he is said to have
uttered frequently that old sentiment: "When I am dead, let fire o'erwhelm
the earth"'. Milton translated the anonymous line in *Reason of Church
Government*, I.v.
    331. *Julius Postumus*] Jonson cites Tacitus, *Annals*, IV.xii: this character
was employed because he was an intimate of the Augusta 'owing to his
adulterous connection with Mutilia Prisca', who had a great influence on the
old lady. The Augusta was 'by nature anxious to maintain her power', and
together, Postumus and Prisca worked to estrange her from Agrippina.
    334. *character*] cryptology, code for oral (as distinct from written) communi-
cation—a sense not recorded in *O.E.D.*

    A company so changed. Except they had   335
    Intelligence by augury'of our practice.
Sejanus. When were you there?
Postumus.   Last night.
Sejanus.   And what guests found you?
Postumus. Sabinus, Silius—the old list—Arruntius,
    Furnius, and Gallus.
Sejanus.   Would not these talk?
Postumus.   Little.
    And yet we offered choice of argument.   340
    Satrius was with me.
Sejanus.   Well, 'tis guilt enough
    Their often meeting. You forgot t'extol
    The hospitable lady?
Postumus.   No, that trick
    Was well put home, and had succeeded too,
    But that Sabinus coughed a caution out,   345
    For she began to swell.
Sejanus.   And may she burst!
    Julius, I would have you go instantly
    Unto the palace of the great Augusta,
    And, by your kindest friend, get swift access.
    Acquaint her with these meetings. Tell the words   350
    You brought me, th'other day, of Silius,
    Add somewhat to 'em. Make her understand
    The danger of Sabinus, and the times,
    Out of his closeness. Give Arruntius words

---

345. *coughed*] cought *Q, F, H.&S., Barish;* caught *F2, Bolton.*   349.] *Side-note in F: Mutilia Prisca.; not in Q.*

340. *argument*] topic.

342–3. *t'extol . . . lady*] Jonson quotes Tacitus, *Annals*, IV.xii, 'Even Agrip-pina's nearest friends were suborned to infuriate her haughty temper by their pernicious gossip'.

342. *extol*] 'lift up' with pride—presumably by retailing pernicious gossip (see I.342–3n. above).

346. *swell*] presumably with pride and anger.

349. *your . . . friend*] Mutilia Prisca, as Jonson's marginal note, citing Tacitus, makes clear. See II.331n.

350–1. *the words . . . Silius*] See below, III.272–82 (from Tacitus, *Annals*, IV.xviii, which Jonson here cites).

354. *Out of his closeness*] resulting from his secretiveness.

354. *Give*] attribute to.

Of malice against Caesar; so, to Gallus;   355
But, above all, to Agrippina. Say,
As you may truly, that her infinite pride,
Propped with the hopes of her too-fruitful womb,
With popular studies gapes for sov'reignty,
And threatens Caesar. Pray Augusta, then,   360
That for her own, great Caesar's, and the pub-
lic safety, she be pleased to urge these dangers.
Caesar is too secure, he must be told,
And best he'll take it from a mother's tongue.
Alas! What is't for us to sound, t'explore,   365
To watch, oppose, plot, practise, or prevent,
If he, for whom it is so strongly laboured,
Shall, out of greatness and free spirit, be
Supinely negligent? Our city's now
Divided, as in time o'th'civil war,   370
And men forbear not to declare themselves
Of Agrippina's party. Every day
The faction multiplies; and will do more
If not resisted. You can best enlarge it
As you find audience. Noble Postumus,   375
Commend me to your Prisca; and pray her

---

358. too-fruitful] *This ed.;* too-fruictfull *Q;* too fruitfull *F.*   359. sov'reignty]
Q, Barish; soueraigntie *F, Bolton.*

356–60. *Say ... Caesar*] Jonson cites Tacitus, *Annals*, IV.xii: Sejanus
caused word to come to Caesar that, 'proud of her fruitfulness and confident in
the favour of the populace, she was turning a covetous eye to the throne'.

359. *popular studies*] favour, devotion of the people [*popularibus studiis* in
Tacitus). Latin *studium*, zeal, eagerness.

359. *sov'reignty*] After Germanicus's death, Agrippina had annoyed Tiberius
with various complaints. 'Do you think a wrong is done you, dear daughter, if
you are not empress?', he asked her. Suetonius, *Lives*, III.liii.

361–2. *pub-/lic*] Not, as Briggs and *H.&S.* think, a modish 'ugly enjamb-
ment', but a classicism. Bolton cites, e.g., Horace, *Odes*, I.ii.19–20, I. xxv.
11–12, and others.

363. *secure*] careless, over-confident.

364.] Suetonius claims that Tiberius wanted 'to avoid the appearance of
being guided by her advice; though in point of fact he was wont every now and
then to need and follow it'. Gradually distancing himself from her, he later
'reached the point of open enmity'. *Lives*, III.l-li.

369–72. *Our ... party*] Jonson cites Tacitus, *Annals*, IV.xvii. See I.8on.

374. *enlarge*] embroider.

She will solicit this great business
To earnest and most present execution,
With all her utmost credit with Augusta.
Postumus. I shall not fail in my instructions.   [*Exit.*]   380
Sejanus. This second, from his mother, will well urge
   Our late design, and spur on Caesar's rage,
   Which else might grow remiss. The way to put
   A prince in blood is to present the shapes
   Of dangers greater than they are, like late   385
   Or early shadows, and, sometimes, to feign
   Where there are none, only to make him fear;
   His fear will make him cruel; and once entered,
   He doth not easily learn to stop, or spare
   Where he may doubt. This have I made my rule,   390
   To thrust Tiberius into tyranny,
   And make him toil to turn aside those blocks
   Which I, alone, could not remove with safety.
   Drusus once gone, Germanicus' three sons
   Would clog my way, whose guards have too much faith   395
   To be corrupted, and their mother known
   Of too too unreproved a chastity
   To be attempted, as light Livia was.

---

383. The] *F;* "The *Q.*   384-90.] *Each line preceded by gnomic pointing, Q.*
393. I, alone,] *This ed.;* I alone, *Q, F, Bolton;* I alone *Barish.*

---

377. *business*] tri-syllabic.
381. *second*] assistance.
383. *remiss*] slack (Latin *remissus*, relaxed, slack).
384. *in blood*] in a state of full vigour—*O.E.D. blood, sb.,* 7 (hunting phrase)—in contrast to the lethargy glanced at in the previous line. Tiberius's customary heaviness was remarked by Augustus (see III.486–7n.).
387–8. *to make ... cruel*] The sense and construction (effectively *anadiplosis*) recall Ennius, *Unassigned Fragments*, 410, 'Whom men fear they hate; whom anyone hates he desires to be dead'. Loeb ed., tr. E. H. Warmington (London, 1967). Quoted by Cicero, *de Officiis*, II.vii.23. Cf. also Ovid, *Amores*, II.ii.10, 'whom each man fears, he longs to see destroyed'. Loeb ed., tr. G. Showerman (London, 1971).
394–8. *Germanicus' ... was*] Jonson quotes in part Tacitus, *Annals,* IV.xii: their 'succession was a thing undoubted. To distribute poison among the three was impossible; for their custodians were patterns of fidelity, Agrippina's chastity impenetrable'.
397. *too too*] Cf. *Ham.*, I.ii.129, 'O, that this too too solid flesh would melt, / Thaw, and resolve itself into a dew!'

Work then, my art, on Caesar's fears, as they
On those they fear, till all my lets be cleared,   400
And he in ruins of his house, and hate
Of all his subjects, bury his own state;
When, with my peace and safety, I will rise,
By making him the public sacrifice.   [*Exit.*]

[*Enter*] SATRIUS [*and*] NATTA.

Satrius. They'are grown exceeding circumspect, and wary.   405
Natta. They have us in the wind. And yet Arruntius
     Cannot contain himself.
Satrius.   Tut, he's not yet
     Looked after; there are others more desired,
     That are more silent.
Natta.   Here he comes. Away.   [*Exeunt.*]

[*Enter*] SABINUS, ARRUNTIUS, [*and*] CORDUS.

Sabinus. How is it that these beagles haunt the house   410
     Of Agrippina?
Arruntius.   O, they hunt, they hunt.
     There is some game here lodged, which they must rouse,
     To make the great ones sport.
Cordus.   Did you observe
     How they inveighed 'gainst Caesar?
Arruntius.   Ay, baits, baits,

---

399. then, my art,] *F;* then my Art *Q.*   400. lets] *Q;* betts *F.*   403. safety]
corr. Q, F; saftly *uncorr. Q.*   404.1. [*Enter*] SATRIUS [*and*] NATTA] *This ed.;*
SCENE III. / A room in Agrippina's House. / Enter Satrius and Natta. *Gifford;*
[Act II, Scene iii] / [*Agrippina's house. Enter*] SATRIUS, NATTA *Bolton, and subst.
Barish.*   405. *Satrius.*] SAT. *Q; not in F.*   405. They'are] *Q;* They're *F.*
410. *Sabinus.*] SAB. *Q; not in F.*   413. great ones] *Q;* great-ones *F;* great one's
Bolton.

---

   400. *lets*] obstacles.
   406. *They ... wind*] They smell us—Jonson's phrase is proverbial, the
metaphor derived from a hunting expression. Tilley, W 434, gives many
examples, including *E.M.I.*, II.iii.54, 'shee has me i' the wind'.
   407. *contain himself*] restrain his tongue.
   408. *Looked*] sought.
   408. *there ... desired*] Silius and Sabinus (marginal note).
   411. *they hunt, they hunt*] As his source for the metaphor Jonson quotes
Tacitus, *Annals*, IV.xxx, 'the informers, a breed invented for the national ruin
..., were now lured into the field with rewards'.

For us to bite at. Would I have my flesh   415
Torn by the public hook, these qualified hangmen
Should be my company.   *Afer passeth by.*
Cordus.   Here comes another.
Arruntius. Ay, there's a man, Afer the orator!
One that hath phrases, figures, and fine flowers
To strew his rhetoric with, and doth make haste   420
To get him note, or name, by any offer
Where blood or gain be objects; steeps his words,
When he would kill, in artificial tears—
The crocodile of Tiber! Him I love,
That man is mine. He hath my heart, and voice,   425
When I would curse, he, he!
Sabinus.   Contemn the slaves;
Their present lives will be their future graves.   [*Exeunt.*]

[*Enter*] SILIUS, AGRIPPINA, NERO, [*and*] SOSIA.

Silius. May't please your highness not forget yourself,
I dare not, with my manners, to attempt

---

417. *Afer passeth by.*] *Marginal s.d. in F; not in Q.*   419. flowers] *Q;* flowres *F;*
flow'rs *Barish.*   426. would] *F;* could *Q.*   427. Their] *F;* "Their *Q.*
427.1. [*Enter*] . . . SOSIA.] SCENE IV. / Another Apartment in the same. / Enter
Silius, Agrippina, Nero, and Sosia. *Gifford.*   428. *Silius.*] SIL. *Q; not in F.*
428. yourself,] *Q, F;* yourself. *Barish.*

---

416. *public hook*] The *uncus*, with which executed criminals were dragged to
the Gemonian steps and, three days later, to the Tiber.
418–23.] In his two notes to these lines, Jonson cites and in part quotes
Tacitus, *Annals*, IV.lii and lxvi: Domitius Afer, accuser of Claudia Pulchra
(see II.220n.), was 'hurrying towards a reputation by way of any crime' and
'enjoyed a fame which stood higher for eloquence than for virtue'. Later,
'girding himself to fresh enormities', he accused Quintilius Varus, Claudia
Pulchra's son.
419. *figures . . . flowers*] devices of rhetoric.
421. *offer*] proposal.
424. *crocodile of Tiber*] since crocodiles come from Africa, and since 'Afer'
means African, this is a particularly apt pun. Crocodiles, of course, also have a
reputation for false tears.
427.] In the sense that 'The life of the dead is set in the memory of the
living'. Cicero, *Philippics*, IX.v.10. Loeb ed., tr. W. C. A. Ker (London,
1957).
429. *with my manners*] within the bounds of mannerly behaviour.
429–30. *attempt . . . trouble*] try to trouble you.

Your trouble farther.

Agrippina.   Farewell, noble Silius.   430
Silius. Most royal princess.
Agrippina.   Sosia stays with us?
Silius. She is your servant, and doth owe your grace
    An honest but unprofitable love.
Agrippina. How can that be, when there's no gain but virtue's?
Silius. You take the moral, not the politic sense.   435
    I meant, as she is bold, and free of speech,
    Earnest to utter what her zealous thought
    Travails withal, in honour of your house;
    Which act, as it is simply borne in her,
    Partakes of love and honesty, but may,   440
    By th'over-often and unseasoned use,
    Turn to your loss and danger—for your state
    Is waited on by envies, as by eyes;
    And every second guest your tables take
    Is a fee'd spy, t'observe who goes, who comes,   445
    What conference you have, with whom, where, when;
    What the discourse is, what the looks, the thoughts
    Of every person there, they do extract,
    And make into a substance.
Agrippina.   Hear me, Silius,
    Were all Tiberius' body stuck with eyes,   450
    And every wall and hanging in my house

---

430. farther] farder *Q, F.*   434. virtue's] *Q, Gifford, Barish, Bolton;* vertuous
F.   436. bold,] *Q, F;* bold *Barish.*   439. borne] *Q, F, Barish;* born *Bolton.*
440. Partakes] Pertakes *Q, F.*   446. when;] *Barish;* when, *Q, F.*
449. *Agrippina.*] *F2;* ARR. *Q, F.*

437–8.] Jonson cites Tacitus, *Annals*, IV.xix: Silius's wife, Sosia Galla, 'by
her affection for Agrippina had incurred the detestation of the emperor'.
438. *Travails withal*] labours with.
439. *simply borne*] done without calculation.
441. *unseasoned*] untimely, inopportune.
442–8.] Jonson cites Tacitus, *Annals*, IV.xii. See II.342–3n.
443. *by envies . . . eyes*] The connection between envy (which included the
sense 'ill will') and eyes was commonplace. *H.&S.* cite Jonson's 'as many
enuies, there, as eyes' in *Pan.*, 83–4, and Spenser's Envy, 'ypainted full of
eyes', in *The Faerie Queene*, I.iv.31. One might also note the etymology of
envy / *invidia* / *invideo* (to look spitefully at).
448–9. *extract . . . substance*] take out of context and make something of it.

Transparent, as this lawn I wear, or air;
Yea, had Sejanus both his ears as long
As to my inmost closet, I would hate
To whisper any thought, or change an act,   455
To be made Juno's rival. Virtue's forces
Show ever noblest in conspicuous courses.
Silius. 'Tis great, and bravely spoken, like the spirit
Of Agrippina; yet your highness knows
There is nor loss nor shame in providence: 460
Few can, what all should do, beware enough.
You may perceive with what officious face
Satrius and Natta, Afer and the rest
Visit your house, of late, t'enquire the secrets;
And with what bold and privileged art they rail   465
Against Augusta, yea, and at Tiberius,
Tell tricks of Livia, and Sejanus, all
T'excite and call your indignation on,
That they might hear it at more liberty.
Agrippina. You'are too suspicious, Silius.
Silius.   Pray the gods   470
I be so, Agrippina; but I fear
Some subtle practice. They, that durst to strike
At so exampless and unblamed a life
As that of the renowned Germanicus,
Will not sit down with that exploit alone.   475

---

456. Virtue's] *F;* "Vertues *Q.*   457. Show] *F;* "Shew *Q.*   460–1.] *Both
lines preceded by gnomic pointing,* Q.   470. You'are] *This ed.;* Yo'are *Q, F.*

---

452. *lawn*] fine linen.
456. *Juno's rival*] Juno was the wife of Jupiter, the chief Roman god.
457. *conspicuous courses*] open ways of acting.
460. *providence*] foresight.
462–69.] Jonson again cites Tacitus, *Annals*, IV.xii, and also IV.liv and lix,
which refer to the penetration of Agrippina's home by agents of Sejanus.
462. *officious*] eagerly attentive.
472. *practice*] intrigue, plot.
472–4. *They ... Germanicus*] Jonson cites Suetonius, *Lives*, III.lii, 'As to
Germanicus, [Tiberius] was so far from appreciating him, that he made light of
his illustrious deeds as unimportant, and railed at his brilliant victories as
ruinous to his country'; and Dio, *Roman History*, LVII.18.6, 'At the death of
Germanicus Tiberius and Livia were thoroughly pleased'.
473. *exampless*] unparalleled.

He threatens many, that hath injured one.
Nero. 'Twere best rip forth their tongues, sear out their eyes,
    When next they come.
Sosia.   A fit reward for spies.

           [*Enter*] DRUSUS JUNIOR.

Drusus Junior. Hear you the rumour?
Agrippina.   What?
Drusus Junior.   Drusus is dying.
Agrippina. Dying?
Nero.   That's strange!
Agrippina.   You'were with him yesternight.   480
Drusus Junior. One met Eudemus the physician,
    Sent for but now, who thinks he cannot live.
Silius. Thinks? If't be arrived at that, he knows,
    Or none.
Agrippina.   This's quick! What should be his disease?
Silius. Poison. Poison—
Agrippina.   How, Silius!
Nero.   What's that?   485
Silius. Nay, nothing. There was, late, a certain blow
    Giv'n o'the face.
Nero.   Ay, to Sejanus?
Silius.   True.
Drusus Junior. And what of that?
Silius.   I'am glad I gave it not.
Nero. But there is somewhat else?
Silius.   Yes, private meetings,

---

476. He] "He *Q, F.*   476. threatens] *F;* threatents *Q.*   478.1. [*Enter*] ...
JUNIOR.] DRVSVS *iu:* AGRIPPINA, &c. *Q;* DRVSVS *iu:* AGRIPPINA, NERO,
SILIVS. *F.* 479. *Drusus Junior.*] DRV. *Q, here and henceforth; not in F.*
480. You'were] *This ed.;* yo'were *Q;* Yo'were *F.*   485. Poison. Poison—] *F;*
Poison. poyson. *Q.*

---

   476. Proverbial (maxim 302 of Publius Syrus). English sources, apart from
Jonson, include Gabriel Harvey and Thomas Fuller (Tilley, T 255), as well as
Bacon.
   479. *Drusus is dying*] Jonson cites Tacitus, *Annals*, IV.iii–xii, which includes
(IV.viii) the death of Drusus. This citation seems rather superfluous—the rest
of IV.iii–xii has already been cited.
   484. *should be*] is said to be.
   485. *Poison*] Jonson (again superfluously) cites Tacitus, *Annals*, IV.iii–xii.

With a great lady, at a physician's,   490
And a wife turned away—
Nero.   Ha!
Silius.   Toys, mere toys.
What wisdom's now i'th'streets? I'th'common mouth?
Drusus Junior. Fears, whisp'rings, tumults, noise, I know not what.
They say the Senate sit.
Silius.   I'll thither, straight,
And see what's in the forge.
Agrippina.   Good Silius, do.   495
Sosia and I will in.
Silius.   Haste you, my lords,
To visit the sick prince. Tender your loves
And sorrows to the people. This Sejanus,
Trust my divining soul, hath plots on all;
No tree, that stops his prospect, but must fall. [*Exeunt.*]   500
                    Chorus of musicians.

---

491. away—] *F;* away. *Q.*   494. thither] *F;* thether *Q.*   500. No] *F;* "No
Q.   500.1. *Chorus of musicians.*] *F;* MV. CHORVS. *Q.*

---

491. *toys*] trifles.
494. *the Senate sit*] Jonson cites Tacitus, *Annals*, IV.viii, 'Tiberius ...
through all the days of his son's illness, ... continued to visit the senate, doing
so even after his death, while he was still unburied. The consuls were seated on
the ordinary benches as a sign of mourning'.
500. *prospect*] view; prospects.

Actus Tertius

THE SENATE.

[*Enter*] PRAECONES, LICTORES, VARRO, SEJANUS, LATIARIS,
COTTA, [*and*] AFER.

Sejanus. 'Tis only you must urge against him, Varro.
    Nor I nor Caesar may appear therein,
    Except in your defence, who are the consul,
    And under colour of late enmity
    Between your father and his, may better do it,   5
    As free from all suspicion of a practice.
    Here be your notes, what points to touch at. Read;
    Be cunning in them. Afer has them too.
Varro. But is he summoned?
Sejanus.   No. It was debated

ACTUS TERTIUS.] *Q;* Act. III. *F;* Act III. SCENE I *Gifford;* [Act III, Scene i]
Bolton; Act III *Barish.*   0.1–2. [*Enter*] ... AFER.] *subst. Gifford and Barish;*
SABINUS *added, Briggs;* PRAECONES. LICTORES. / VARRO. SEIANVS. LATIARIS.
/ COTTA. AFER. / GALLVS. LEPIDVS. ARRVNTIVS.*Q;* SEIANVS, VARRO,
LATIARIS. / COTTA, AFER. / GALLVS, LEPIDVS, ARRVNTIVS. / PRAECONES,
LICTORES. *F.*   1. *Sejanus.*] SEI. *Q; not in F.*

0.1–3.] The order of entry here, as in Q, seems formally more correct than
that in F. The consul precedes Sejanus, and is himself preceded by the
Praecones and *Lictores.* The Senate sits as a court, and the consul presides.
Three meetings of the Senate are here conflated: one after the death of Drusus
(A.D. 23); one for the trial of Silius (A.D. 24); one for the trial of Cordus
(A.D. 25).

    1–6.] Jonson cites Tacitus, *Annals*, IV.xix: 'Varro, the consul [in 24], was
unleashed, and, under the pretext of continuing his father's feud, gratified the
animosities of Sejanus at the price of his own degradation'. In *Annals*, III.xliii,
Tacitus had related how 'relations were strained between the Roman generals
[Varro's father and Silius] ... over the conduct of the campaign [against
Sacrovir], which was claimed by each as his own prerogative. Finally, Varro,
now old and weakly, withdrew in favour of Silius, who was still in the prime of
life'.

    4–6.] As *H.&S.* point out, animus on the prosecutor's part was seen in
Rome as a proof of his honest motives. There was no class of professional
advocates.

    5. *his*] Jonson should have written *him*—i.e. Silius, not Silius's father.
    6. *practice*] machination.

By Caesar, and concluded as most fit   10
  To take him unprepared.
Afer.   And prosecute
  All under name of treason.
Varro.   I conceive.

  [*Enter* SABINUS, GALLUS, LEPIDUS, *and* ARRUNTIUS.]

Sabinus. Drusus being dead, Caesar will not be here.
Gallus. What should the business of this Senate be?
Arruntius. That can my subtle whisperers tell you. We,   15
  That are the good-dull-noble lookers-on,
  Are only called to keep the marble warm.
  What should we do with those deep mysteries,
  Proper to these fine heads? Let them alone.
  Our ignorance may, perchance, help us be saved   20
  From whips and furies.
Gallus.   See, see, see, their action!
Arruntius. Ay, now their heads do travail, now they work;
  Their faces run like shuttles; they are weaving
  Some curious cobweb to catch flies.
Sabinus.   Observe,
  They take their places.
Arruntius.   What, so low?
Gallus.   O yes,   25
  They must be seen to flatter Caesar's grief,
  Though but in sitting.
Varro.   Bid us silence.
Praeco.   Silence!

---

11. take him] *Q;* him take *F.*   12.1. [*Enter* ... ARRUNTIUS.]] *Gifford,*
Barish.   23. shuttles] shittles *Q, F.*

11–12. *And ... treason*] Jonson quotes Tacitus, *Annals*, IV.xix: although
Silius and his wife had been 'inextricably involved' in extortion during the war
against Sacrovir, 'the entire case was handled as an impeachment for treason'.
  20–21. *Our ignorance ... whips and furies*] i.e., our not being party to state
crime may save us from punishment after death. The Furies were normally
depicted as holding a whip of scorpions in one hand, a flaming torch in the
other. With the whips they visited the vengeance of the gods upon the guilty in
hell.
  21. *action*] operation.
  24. *curious*] skilfully spun.
  25. *so low?*] Jonson quotes Tacitus, *Annals*, IV.viii, 'The consuls were
seated on the ordinary benches as a sign of mourning'.

Varro. Fathers conscript, may this our present meeting
Turn fair and fortunate to the commonwealth.

[*Enter*] SILIUS [*and other* SENATORS].

Sejanus. See, Silius enters.
Silius.   Hail, grave fathers!
Lictor.   Stand.   30
Silius, forbear thy place.
Senators.   How!
Praeco.   Silius, stand forth,
The consul hath to charge thee.
Lictor.   Room for Caesar!
Arruntius. Is he come too? Nay then, expect a trick.
Sabinus. Silius accused? Sure he will answer nobly.

[*Enter*] TIBERIUS, [*attended*].

Tiberius. We stand amazèd, fathers, to behold   35
This general dejection. Wherefore sit

28–9. Fathers ... commonwealth.] *Italics, Q, F.*   29.1. [*Enter*] ...
SENATORS].] SILIVS, &c. *Q;* SILIVS, SENATE *F.*   30. *Sejanus.*] SEI. *Q; not in
F. Briggs assigns the words to Varro, adding 'Speaks to Lictors'.*   34.1. [*Enter*]
... [*attended*].] TIBERVS. &c. *Q;* TIBERIVS, SENATE. *F.*   35. *Tiberius.*] TIB.
Q; not in F.

28–9.] For this formula Jonson cites Barnabé Brisson, *De Formulis et
Sollemnibus Populi Romani Verbis* (Paris, 1583), Book II. See F. F. Abbott, *A
History and Description of Roman Political Institutions,* 3rd edn. (Boston, 1911),
p. 227: 'the presiding officer ... began with the formula: *quod bonum felixque
sit populo Romano Quiritium, referimus ad vos, patres conscripti*'—'may this
a good and happy matter for the Roman people which we lay before you,
senators'. 'Fathers conscript' was the formal title for senators.
35–81.] Jonson cites Tacitus, *Annals,* IV.viii: 'The consuls were seated on
the ordinary benches as a sign of mourning: he reminded them of their dignity
and their place. The members broke into tears: he repressed their lamentation,
and at the same time revived their spirits in a formal speech:- "He was not,
indeed, unaware that he might be criticized for appearing before the eyes of
the senate while his grief was still fresh. Mourners in general could hardly
support the condolences of their own kindred—hardly tolerate the light of
day. Nor were they to be condemned as weaklings; but personally he had
sought a manlier consolation by taking the commonwealth to his heart." After
deploring the extreme old age of his august mother, the still tender years of his
grandsons, and his own declining days, he asked for Germanicus' sons, their
sole comfort in the present affliction, to be introduced. The consuls went out,
and, after reassuring the boys, brought them in and set them before the
emperor. "Conscript Fathers," he said, "when these children lost their parent,

Rome's consuls thus dissolved, as they had lost
All the remembrance both of style and place?
It not becomes. No woes are of fit weight
To make the honour of the Empire stoop;   40
Though I, in my peculiar self, may meet
Just reprehension, that so suddenly,
And in so fresh a grief, would greet the Senate,
When private tongues of kinsmen and allies,
Inspired with comforts, loathly are endured,   45
The face of men not seen, and scarce the day,
To thousands that communicate our loss.
Nor can I argue these of weakness, since
They take but natural ways; yet I must seek
For stronger aids, and those fair helps draw out   50
From warm embraces of the commonwealth.
Our mother, great Augusta,'is struck with time,
Ourself impressed with agèd characters;
Drusus is gone, his children young, and babes.

43. Senate,] *F; Senate. Q.*   52. struck] strooke *Q, F.*   54. babes.] *Edd.;*
babes, *Q, F.*

I gave them to their uncle, and begged him, though he had issue of his own, to
use them as if they were blood of his blood—to cherish them, build up their
fortunes, form them after his own image and for the welfare of posterity. With
Drusus gone, I turn my prayers to you; I conjure you in the sight of Heaven
and of your country:- These are the great-grandchildren of Augustus, scions of
a glorious ancestry; adopt them, train them, do your part—and do mine! Nero
and Drusus, these shall be your father and your mother: it is the penalty of
your birth that your good and your evil are the good and the evil of the
commonwealth"'.

37. *dissolved*] discomposed. Tiberius is referring to their vacating of their
normal places of honour, in sign of mourning, thus leaving the Senate
leaderless.

41. *peculiar*] private.

47. *To ... loss*] In the case of thousands who share our loss. The construction seems awkward, but the sense is perhaps 'To thousands who mourn,
the faces of men and the light of day are anathema.'

48. *argue*] accuse, convict (*O.E.D. argue, v.,* 1).

51. *commonwealth*] *i.e.* the Roman people.

52. *struck with time*] as *H.&S.* point out, 'an incorrect variant of "stricken
[advanced] in years"'. The Augusta was eighty years old at this time (23).

53.] Tiberius was sixty-five in 23; 'impressed with agèd characters' means
'marked with the features of old age'. 'Impressed' carries on the image latent
in 'struck'.

54. *his children*] Tiberius Gemellus and Livia Julia.

Our aims must now reflect on those, that may   55
Give timely succour to these present ills,
And are our only glad-surviving hopes,
The noble issue of Germanicus,
Nero and Drusus. Might it please the consul
Honour them in—they both attend without—   60
I would present them to the Senate's care,
And raise those suns of joy, that should drink up
These floods of sorrow in your drownèd eyes.
Arruntius. By Jove, I am not Oedipus enough
To understand this Sphinx.
Sabinus.   The princes come.   65

[*Enter*] NERO [*and*] DRUSUS JUNIOR.

Tiberius. Approach you, noble Nero, noble Drusus.
These princes, fathers, when their parent died,
I gave unto their uncle, with this prayer:
That, though h'had proper issue of his own,
He would no less bring up and foster these   70
Than that self-blood; and by that act confirm
Their worths to him, and to posterity.
Drusus ta'en hence, I turn my prayers to you,
And, 'fore our country, and our gods, beseech
You take, and rule, Augustus' nephew's sons,   75
Sprung of the noblest ancestors; and so
Accomplish both my duty and your own.
Nero, and Drusus, these shall be to you
In place of parents, these your fathers, these,
And not unfitly: for you are so born   80
As all your good or ill's the commonwealth's.

___

62. suns] *F;* springs *Q.*   62. drink up] *F;* exhaust *Q.*   65.1. [*Enter*] ...
JUNIOR.] NERO. DRVSVS. *iu. Q;* TIBERIVS, NERO, DRVSVS *iunior. F.*
66. *Tiberius.*] TIB *Q; not in F.*   66. you,] you *Q, F.*   66. Drusus.] *Drusus,*
Q; DRVSVS, *F.*   67. princes,] princes *Q, F. Comma added in MS. in Wise Q.*
69. h'had] *F;* he had *Q.*   80. born] *Edd.;* borne *Q, F.*

___

55. *reflect on*] consider, take account of.
62. *suns*] with the obvious pun on 'sons'.
64–5. *I ... Sphinx*] By answering the Sphinx's riddle, Oedipus caused its
death and gained the throne of Thebes.
69. *proper*] excellent, admirable.
77. *Accomplish*] fulfil (Latin *compleo,* to fill).

Receive them, you strong guardians; and, blest gods,
Make all their actions answer to their bloods.
Let their great titles find increase by them,
Not they by titles. Set them, as in place,   85
So in example, above all the Romans;
And may they know no rivals but themselves.
Let Fortune give them nothing; but attend
Upon their virtue—and that still come forth
Greater than hope, and better than their fame.   90
Relieve me, fathers, with your general voice.
Senators. May all the gods consent to Caesar's wish,
And add to any honours that may crown
The hopeful issue of Germanicus.
Tiberius. We thank you, reverend fathers, in their right.   95
Arruntius. [*Aside.*] If this were true now! But the space, the space
Between the breast and lips—Tiberius' heart
Lies a thought farther than another man's.
Tiberius. My comforts are so flowing in my joys
As, in them, all my streams of grief are lost,   100
No less than are land waters in the sea,
Or show'rs in rivers; though their cause was such

92–4. May ... Germanicus] *Italics, Q; italics, except* CAESAR'S *and* GERMAN-
ICVS, *F.*   93–4. *Marginal note in F: A forme of speaking they had. Not in Q.*
96. now!] *corr. Q;* now? *uncorr. Q.*   98. farther] farder *Q, F.*

84–5. *Let ... by titles*] As *H.&S.* point out, Jonson quotes the source of
this expression—Claudian, *On Stilicho's Consulship*, II.317–18—in *Hadd.M.*,
229.
85. *place*] rank.
87. *no ... themselves*] As Briggs, 'Source-Material', p. 329, points out, from
Seneca, *Hercules Furens*, 84–5, 'Dost then seek Alcides' match? None is there
save himself'. Tr. F. J. Miller, Loeb ed. of *Senecan Tragedies*, I, 11.
91. *Relieve*] support—and, perhaps, succour.
91. *general*] collective.
92–4.] In *F* Jonson notes this as a 'form of speaking' in the Senate. His
source would have been Brisson, *De formulis* (III.28–9n).
95. *right*] behalf—a sense not recorded in *O.E.D.*
96–7. *the space ... lips*] Proverbial. Cf. Florio, *First Fruits*, XIX, 'Betwene
doing and saying ther is great space' (Tilley, W 802, with further examples)
and Jonson, *N.I.*, I.vi.63, 'Their tongues and thoughts, oft times lie far
asunder'.
97. *breast*] private feelings or thoughts; heart.
99–105.] Tiberius's rhetorical extravagances here are meant to seem pain-
fully contrived—more evidence of 'the space / Between the breast, and lips'.

As might have sprinkled ev'n the gods with tears.
Yet since the greater doth embrace the less,
We covetously obey.

Arruntius. [*Aside.*]   Well acted, Caesar.   105

Tiberius. And now I am the happy witness made
    Of your so much desired affections
    To this great issue, I could wish the fates
    Would here set peaceful period to my days;
    However, to my labours, I entreat,   110
    And beg it of this Senate, some fit ease.

Arruntius. [*Aside.*] Laugh, fathers, laugh! Ha' you no spleens
     about you?

Tiberius. The burden is too heavy I sustain
    On my unwilling shoulders; and I pray
    It may be taken off, and reconferred   115
    Upon the consuls, or some other Roman,
    More able, and more worthy.

Arruntius. [*Aside.*]   Laugh on, still.

Sabinus. Why, this doth render all the rest suspected!

Gallus. It poisons all.

Arruntius.   O, do'you taste it then?

Sabinus. It takes away my faith to anything   120
    He shall hereafter speak.

Arruntius.   Ay, to pray that
    Which would be to his head as hot as thunder—
    'Gainst which he wears that charm—should but the court

---

105. covetously] *F*; coueteously *Q*.   115. off] *F*; of *Q*.   123. *Marginal note in F: A wreath of laurell. Not in Q.*

---

   104. *the greater . . . less*] Proverbial. Tilley, G 437.

   105. *covetously obey*] eagerly act in accordance [with the relief from grief brought by the 'comforts' and 'joys']. I.e., we do not weep. *O.E.D.*, *Covetous, a.*, 1.

   112–27.] Jonson quotes in part Tacitus, *Annals*, IV.ix: 'All this was listened to amid general tears, then with prayers for a happy issue; and, had he only set a limit to his speech, he must have left the minds of his hearers full of compassion for himself, and of pride: instead, by reverting to those vain and oft-derided themes, the restoration of the republic and his wish that the consuls or others would take the reins of government, he destroyed the credibility even of the true and honourable part of his statement'.

   112. *spleens*] The spleen was regarded as the seat of laughter (and of melancholy!).

   123. *that charm*] Jonson quotes in part Suetonius, *Lives* III.lxix: 'Although

    Receive him at his word.
Gallus.   Hear!
Tiberius.   For myself,
    I know my weakness, and so little covet—   125
    Like some gone past—the weight that will oppress me,
    As my ambition is the counter-point.
Arruntius. [*Aside.*] Finely maintained; good still.
Sejanus.   But Rome, whose blood,
    Whose nerves, whose life, whose very frame relies
    On Caesar's strength, no less than heav'n on Atlas,   130
    Cannot admit it but with general ruin.
Arruntius. [*Aside.*] Ah! Are you there, to bring him off?
Sejanus.   Let Caesar
    No more, then, urge a point so contrary
    To Caesar's greatness, the grieved Senate's vows,
    Or Rome's necessity.
Gallus. [*Aside.*]   He comes about.   135
Arruntius. [*Aside.*] More nimbly than Vertumnus.
Tiberius.   For the public,
    I may be drawn to show I can neglect
    All private aims, though I affect my rest.
    But if the Senate still command me serve,
    I must be glad to practise my obedience.   140

---

132. off] of *Q, F.*   133. then] *Q, F, Barish;* than *Bolton.*

---

somewhat neglectful of the gods and of religious matters, being addicted to
astrology and firmly convinced that everything was in the hands of fate, he was
nevertheless immoderately afraid of thunder. Whenever the sky was lowering,
he always wore a laurel wreath, because it is said that that kind of leaf is not
blasted by lightning'. (Augustus had shared this fear, putting his faith in a seal-
skin!—*Lives,* II.xc.) Jonson also cites Pliny, *Natural History,* XV.xl: 'the
laurel alone . . . is never struck by lightning'. Pliny mentions Tiberius in this
connection. (Jonson incorrectly cites chapter xxx.)
    127. *counter-point*] opposite—i.e., seclusion.
    130. *Atlas*] a god supposed to hold up the pillars of the universe.
    132. *bring him off*] rescue him.
    133. *No more, then, urge*] it is possible to read this as 'no more than urge'—
i.e., not insist upon. *Q* and *F* print 'No more then vrge'.
    136. *Vertumnus*] god of the seasons, and a symbol of mutability.
    136. *For the public*] For the benefit of the people.
    137. *drawn*] persuaded.
    138. *affect*] aspire to (*O.E.D. affect, v.*1, 1).
    140.] On the 'gladly' reluctant Tiberius, Jonson cites Tacitus, *Annals,* I.xi:
'the diction of Tiberius, by habit or by nature, was always indirect and

Arruntius. [*Aside.*] You must, and will, sir. We do know it.
Senators.   Caesar,
    Live long, and happy, great and royal Caesar!
    The gods preserve thee, and thy modesty,
    Thy wisdom, and thy innocence.
Arruntius. [*Aside.*]   Where is't?
    The prayer's made before the subject.
Senators.   Guard   145
    His meekness, Jove, his piety, his care,
    His bounty—
Arruntius. [*Aside.*] And his subtlety, I'll put in—
    Yet he'll keep that himself, without the gods.
    All prayers are vain for him.
Tiberius.   We will not hold
    Your patience, fathers, with long answer; but   150
    Shall still contend to be what you desire,
    And work to satisfy so great a hope.
    Proceed to your affairs.
Arruntius. [*Aside.*]   Now, Silius, guard thee.
    The curtain's drawing. Afer advanceth.
Praeco.   Silence!
Afer. Cite Caius Silius.
Praeco.   Caius Silius!
Silius.   Here.   155
Afer. The triumph that thou hadst in Germany
    For thy late victory on Sacrovir,

141–4. Caesar ... innocence] *Italics, Q; italics, except* CAESAR *(twice),* F.
141. Caesar,] *F;* Caesar. *Q.*   142. *Marginal note in F: Another forme. Not in
Q.*   142. Caesar!] *Barish;* Caesar, *Q;* CAESAR, *F.*   145–7. Guard ...
bounty] *Italics, Q, F, except* Ioue *(Q),* IOVE *(F).*   149. prayers] prayer's *Q, F.*

obscure, even when he had no wish to conceal his thought'. The one fear of
the senators 'was that they might seem to comprehend him'!

   142–4. *Live ... innocence*] Jonson notes in *F*, 'Another form', his source
obviously Brisson (III.28–9n.).

   143. *modesty*] moderation.

   145. *the subject*] i.e. Caesar's possession of these qualities.

   154. *The curtain's drawing*] i.e. something is about to be revealed.

   154. *Afer advanceth*] There is no reference in Jonson's sources to any part
played by Afer in this trial.

   155.] Jonson quotes in Latin from Brisson, *De formulis,* V, who affirms that
the accused was called from the tribunal by the voice of the *praeco,* or herald.

   157. *Sacrovir*] Julius Sacrovir, who in A.D. 21 led a powerful revolt of the
Aedui, put down by Silius.

    Thou hast enjoyed so freely, Caius Silius,
    As no man it envied thee; nor would Caesar
    Or Rome admit that thou wert then defrauded   160
    Of any honours thy deserts could claim
    In the fair service of the commonwealth.
    But now, if after all their loves and graces,
    Thy actions and their courses being discovered,
    It shall appear to Caesar, and this Senate,   165
    Thou hast defiled those glories with thy crimes—
Silius. Crimes?
Afer.   Patience, Silius.
Silius.   Tell thy mule of patience,
    I'am a Roman. What are my crimes? Proclaim them.
    Am I too rich? Too honest for the times?
    Have I or treasure, jewels, land, or houses   170
    That some informer gapes for? Is my strength
    Too much to be admitted? Or my knowledge?
    These now are crimes.
Afer.   Nay, Silius, if the name
    Of crime so touch thee, with what impotence
    Wilt thou endure the matter to be searched?   175
Silius. I tell thee, Afer, with more scorn than fear:
    Employ your mercenary tongue and art.
    Where's my accuser?
Varro.   Here.
Arruntius. [*Aside.*]   Varro? The consul?
    Is he thrust in?
Varro.   'Tis I accuse thee, Silius.

---

167. mule] Moile *Q*, moile *F*.

   160. *admit*] permit.
   167. *of*] about.
   169–73. *Am I ... crimes*] On fortune-hunting through the bringing of charges, Jonson cites, without the specific references, Suetonius, *Lives*, (III.xlix, 'property confiscated on trivial and shameless charges'); Tacitus, *Annals* (various profitable charges—see, e.g., IV.xx); Dio, *Roman History* (LVII.19.2, 'Those who had accused or testified against persons divided by lot the property of the convicted and received in addition both offices and honours'); and Seneca, *On Benefits* (III.xxvi, the 'almost universal frenzy for bringing charges of treason' at this time).
   174. *touch*] affect, irritate.
   174. *impotence*] inability to defend yourself, helplessness.
   177. *mercenary*] open to hire.

Against the majesty of Rome and Caesar,   180
I do pronounce thee here a guilty cause,
First, of beginning and occasioning,
Next, drawing out the war in Gallia,
For which thou late triumphst; dissembling long
That Sacrovir to be an enemy,   185
Only to make thy entertainment more,
Whilst thou, and thy wife Sosia, polled the province;
Wherein, with sordid-base desire of gain,
Thou hast discredited thy actions' worth
And been a traitor to the state.
Silius.   Thou liest.   190
Arruntius. [*Aside.*] I thank thee, Silius, speak so still, and often.
Varro. If I not prove it, Caesar, but unjustly
Have called him into trial, here I bind
Myself to suffer what I claim 'gainst him,
And yield to have what I have spoke confirmed   195
By judgement of the court, and all good men.
Silius. Caesar, I crave to have my cause deferred
Till this man's consulship be out.
Tiberius.   We cannot,

---

189. actions'] *Edd.*; actions *Q, F.*   192. unjustly] iniustly *Q, F.*

181–90. *I do ... state*] Jonson cites and partly quotes Tacitus, *Annals*,
IV.xix: 'the indictment was presented: Sacrovir long screened through complicity in his revolt, a victory besmirched by rapine, a wife the partner of his
sins. Nor was there any doubt that, on the charges of extortion, the pair were
inextricably involved; but the entire case was handled as an impeachment for
treason'. Jonson, of course, quietly ignores Tacitus's point about the charge of
extortion.
    184. *For ... triumphst*] Jonson notes that the triumph was celebrated in
Germany. See II.285–93, note, above.
    184. *dissembling*] falsely pretending.
    186. *entertainment*] provisions, revenue from the state.
    187. *polled*] plundered.
    192–4.] Jonson cites as his source for this formula Brisson, *De formulis*, V.
    197–208.] Jonson cites and partly quotes Tacitus, *Annals*, IV.xix: 'The
defendant asked a short adjournment till the prosecutor could lay down his
consulate, but the Caesar opposed:- "It was quite usual for magistrates to take
legal action against private citizens, nor must there be any infraction of the
prerogatives of the consul, on whose vigilance it depended 'that the commonwealth take no harm'". It was a characteristic of Tiberius to shroud his latest
discoveries in crime under the phrases of an older world.' This particular
phrase originated in 121 B.C. when, during a virtual state of siege, the Senate

    Nor may we grant it.
Silius.   Why? Shall he design
    My day of trial? Is he my accuser?   200
    And must he be my judge?
Tiberius.   It hath been usual,
    And is a right that custom hath allowed
    The magistrate, to call forth private men,
    And to appoint their day; which privilege
    We may not in the consul see infringed,   205
    By whose deep watches and industrious care
    It is so laboured as the commonwealth
    Receive no loss, by any oblique course.
Silius. Caesar, thy fraud is worse than violence.
Tiberius. Silius, mistake us not, we dare not use   210
    The credit of the consul to thy wrong,
    But only do preserve his place and power
    So far as it concerns the dignity
    And honour of the state.
Arruntius.   Believe him, Silius.
Cotta. Why, so he may, Arruntius.
Arruntius.   I say so.   215
    And he may choose, too.
Tiberius.   By the Capitol,
    And all our gods, but that the dear Republic,
    Our sacred laws, and just authority

---

216. choose, too] *Barish;* choose too *Q, F;* choose to *Bolton.*

first passed the *senatus consultum ultimum* (final and most extreme decree of the senate), giving moral support to extraordinary consular action against the threat to the state posed by the demagogic Caius Sempronius Gracchus and his followers.

    199–200. *design . . . trial*] impeach me—see following note.

    204. *appoint their day*] The Latin phrase *dicere diem alicui*, to impeach or lay an accusation against a person, is here translated literally.

    207. *laboured*] painstakingly managed.

    208. *oblique*] evil, ill-intentioned.

    209.] The conditions for a *senatus consultum ultimum* hardly exist in this case (see III.197–208n.), hence Silius's remark.

    211. *credit*] status, authority.

    212. *preserve*] protect (Lat. *servo*).

    215. Cotta] Marcus Aurelius Cotta Maximus Messalinus, consul A.D. 20, is presented by Tacitus as the 'father of every barbarous proposal and therefore the object of inveterate dislike'. *Annals*, VI.v.

Are interested therein, I should be silent.

Afer. Please Caesar to give way unto his trial.   220
    He shall have justice.

Silius.   Nay, I shall have law;
    Shall I not, Afer? Speak.

Afer.   Would you have more?

Silius. No, my well-spoken man, I would no more;
    Nor less—might I enjoy it natural,
    Not taught to speak unto your present ends,   225
    Free from thine, his, and all your unkind handling,
    Furious enforcing, most unjust presuming,
    Malicious and manifold applying,
    Foul wresting, and impossible construction.

Afer. He raves, he raves.

Silius.   Thou durst not tell me so,   230
    Hadst thou not Caesar's warrant. I can see
    Whose power condemns me.

Varro.   This betrays his spirit.
    This doth enough declare him what he is.

Silius. What am I? Speak.

Varro.   An enemy to the state.

Silius. Because I am an enemy to thee,   235
    And such corrupted ministers o'the state,
    That here art made a present instrument
    To gratify it with thine own disgrace.

Sejanus. This, to the consul, is most insolent!
    And impious!

Silius.   Ay, take part. Reveal yourselves.   240

---

220. Please Casesar] Please' Caesar *Q;* Please' CAESAR *F.*   222. more?] *Q;* mo
(faulty impression), F.   236. o'the] *F;* of the *corr. Q;* of *uncorr. Q.*
240. *Silius.*] SIL. *F;* SEI. *Q, corr. in MS. in Wise Q.*

---

219. *interested*] involved.

223. *well-spoken*] gifted or ready in speech—Afer considering himself a
great orator.

224. *natural*] uncontrived.

226. *unkind*] unnatural—in contrast to 'natural', l. 224 above.

229. *construction*] interpretation put upon the law.

231–2. *I can ... me*] Tacitus, *Annals*, IV.xix: Silius made 'no secret of the
person under whose resentment he was sinking'—i.e., Sejanus. See III.242–3.

238.] Jonson cites and quotes the source in Tacitus that this line echoes:
Varro 'gratified the animosities of Sejanus at the price of his own degradation',
Annals, IV.xix.

240. *impious*] because the consul performed both civil and religious duties.

Alas, I scent not your confederacies?
Your plots and combinations? I not know
Minion Sejanus hates me, and that all
This boast of law, and law, is but a form,
A net of Vulcan's filing, a mere engine,   245
To take that life by a pretext of justice
Which you pursue in malice? I want brain
Or nostril to persuade me that your ends
And purposes are made to what they are,
Before my answer? O you equal gods,   250
Whose justice not a world of wolf-turned men
Shall make me to accuse, howe'er provoke,
Have I for this so oft engaged myself?
Stood in the heat and fervour of a fight,
When Phoebus sooner hath forsook the day   255
Than I the field? Against the blue-eyed Gauls?
And crispèd Germans? When our Roman eagles
Have fanned the fire, with their labouring wings,
And no blow dealt that left not death behind it?
When I have charged, alone, into the troops   260
Of curled Sicambrians, routed them, and came

252. provoke] *Q, F, Bolton*; provoked *other edd.*   259. it?] *F*; it: *Q.*

243. *Minion*] obsequious favourite.

245. *A net . . . filing*] The reference is to Vulcan's trapping of the adulterous Venus and Mars in a finely-wrought wire net. As Briggs points out, Massinger echoed the phrase in *The Roman Actor*, IV.ii.

245. *filing*] perfect elaboration.

245. *engine*] contrivance.

248. *nostril*] with which to smell a rat. Lat. *nares* (nostrils) could signify the nose 'as an organ expressive of sagacity' (*L.&S.*, *naris*, I.B.)

250. *equal*] impartial.

252. *howe'er provoke*] The sense is, 'however they provoke me', *provoke* having the same subject and object as *make*. Most previous editors, not seeing this, have unnecessarily 'amended' the word to *provoked*.

255. *When . . . day*] James A. Riddell, 'Seventeenth-Century Identifications of Jonson's Sources in the Classics', *Ren. Q.*, XXVIII (1975), 207, provides a possible source: Seneca, *Medea*, 768, 'the bright day has come back . . .'; Phoebus has halted in mid-heaven'. This seems a doubtful source to me.

257. *crispèd*] with closely and stiffly curled hair.

257. *eagles*] legionary standards, introduced by Marius, at first of silver, later of gold.

261. *curled Sicambrians*] Jonson cites and quotes Martial, *Epigrams*, 'On the Spectacles', iii, which describes them 'With hair twined in a knot'. They were defeated and resettled by Tiberius in 8 B.C., and, though Jonson seems well-

Not off with backward ensigns of a slave,
But forward marks, wounds on my breast, and face,
Were meant to thee, O Caesar, and thy Rome?
And have I this return? Did I, for this,   265
Perform so noble and so brave defeat
On Sacrovir? O Jove, let it become me
To boast my deeds, when he, whom they concern,
Shall thus forget them!
Afer.   Silius, Silius,
These are the common customs of thy blood,   270
When it is high with wine, as now with rage.
This well agrees with that intemperate vaunt
Thou lately mad'st at Agrippina's table,
That when all other of the troops were prone
To fall into rebellion, only yours   275
Remained in their obedience. You were he
That saved the Empire; which had then been lost,
Had but your legions, there, rebelled, or mutined.
Your virtue met and fronted every peril.
You gave to Caesar and to Rome their surety.   280

---

262. off] *F;* of *Q.*   267. Sacrovir?] *F; Sacrouir, Q.*   272. vaunt] *F;* vant *Q.*
275. yours] *F;* thine *Q.*   276. You were] *F;* Thou wert *Q.*   277. saved]
sau'd *F;* sau'dst *Q.*   278. your] *F;* thy *Q.*   279. Your] *F;* Thy *Q.*
280. You gave] *F;* Thou gau'st *Q.*

---

informed about them, there is no evidence that Silius ever had anything to do
with them. Jonson's note tells us that they exist 'today' as the 'Geldri' (of
Gelderland in Holland), living between the Meuse and the Rhine.
   262. *backward ensigns*] i.e. wounds on the back.
   264. *Were meant to thee*] which were intended for you—i.e. aimed at Rome.
   270. *common . . . blood*] familiar traits of your temper.
   272–8, 288–91, 305–8.] Jonson cites Tacitus, *Annals*, IV.xviii: 'Many
considered his offence to have been aggravated by his own discretion: he
boasted too loudly that "his troops had stood loyal while others were rushing
into mutiny; nor could Tiberius have retained the throne, if those legions too
had caught the passion for revolution". Such claims, the Caesar thought, were
destructive of his position, and left it inadequate to cope with such high
deserts. For services are welcome exactly so long as it seems possible to requite
them: when that stage is left far behind, the return is hatred instead of
gratitude.'
   275–82.] The Folio changed the Quarto's 'thou', 'thy', and 'thine' to 'you',
'your', 'yours', perhaps because Afer is in effect quoting Silius in these lines
rather than addressing him. Barish accepts this explanation.
   278. *mutined*] mutinied.

  Their name, their strength, their spirit, and their state,
  Their being was a donative from you.
Arruntius. [*Aside.*] Well worded, and most like an orator.
Tiberius. Is this true, Silius?
Silius.   Save thy question, Caesar.
  Thy spy, of famous credit, hath affirmed it.   285
Arruntius. [*Aside.*] Excellent Roman!
Sabinus. [*Aside.*]   He doth answer stoutly.
Sejanus. If this be so, there needs no farther cause
  Of crime against him.
Varro.   What can more impeach
  The royal dignity and state of Caesar
  Than to be urgèd with a benefit   290
  He cannot pay?
Cotta.   In this, all Caesar's fortune
  Is made unequal to the courtesy.
Latiaris. His means are clean destroyed, that should requite.
Gallus. Nothing is great enough for Silius' merit.
Arruntius. [*Aside.*] Gallus o' that side too?
Silius.   Come, do not hunt 295
  And labour so about for circumstance,
  To make him guilty whom you have foredoomed.
  Take shorter ways; I'll meet your purposes.
  The words were mine; and more I now will say:
  Since I have done thee that great service, Caesar,   300
  Thou still hast feared me; and, in place of grace,
  Returned me hatred. So soon, all best turns,

---

282. you] *F;* thee *Q.* 287. farther] farder *Q, F.* 295. o'] *Q;* on *F.*
297. foredoomed] *F;* fore-dom'd *Q.*

---

 282. *donative*] The *donativum* was a largess given on special occasions by an emperor to his soldiers. An irony: Silius reverses the process.
 285. *Thy spy*] Afer, with Satrius Secundus and Pinnarius Natta, is identified as a spy in Agrippina's household at II.417–18.
 285. *famous credit*] notorious repute (*O.E.D. credit, sb.,* 5b).
 285. *affirmed*] confirmed.
 287–8. *cause . . . crime*] ground for charges.
 290. *be urgèd with*] have pressed upon his attention.
 295. *Gallus . . . too*] Gallus was an independent! See II.220n.
 302–5.] Briggs compares Bacon, *History of King Henry VII,* on one of Sir William Stanley's handicaps: 'First, an over-merit; for convenient merit, unto which reward may easily reach, doth best with Kings'. See the edn by F. J. Levy (New York, 1972), p. 166. Also rather apt is Seneca, *On Benefits,*

With princes, do convert to injuries
In estimation, when they greater rise
Than can be answered. Benefits, with you,   305
Are of no longer pleasure than you can
With ease restore them; that transcended once,
Your studies are not how to thank, but kill.
It is your nature to have all men slaves
To you, but you acknowledging to none.   310
The means that makes your greatness must not come
In mention of it. If it do, it takes
So much away, you think; and that which helped
Shall soonest perish, if it stand in eye,
Where it may front, or but upbraid the high.   315

Cotta. Suffer him speak no more.
Varro.   Note but his spirit.
Afer. This shows him in the rest.
Latiaris.   Let him be censured.
Sejanus. He'hath spoke enough to prove him Caesar's foe.
Cotta. His thoughts look through his words.
Sejanus.   A censure.
Silius.   Stay,
Stay, most officious Senate, I shall straight   320
Delude thy fury. Silius hath not placed
His guards within him, against Fortune's spite,
So weakly but he can escape your gripe

---

303. With . . . to] Q; With doubtful Princes, turne deepe F.   311. makes] F;
make Q.

II.xxiv.1, 'It is safer to offend some men than to have done them a service; for,
in order to prove that they owe nothing, they have recourse to hatred'.
    303.] See Introduction, p. 7.
    305. *answered*] repaid.
    307. *restore*] return.
    312. *in mention of it*] into any discussion of your greatness.
    314. *stand in eye*] be seen, perhaps on a similarly high level.
    315. *front*] present a bold front to. There may be a pun on Latin *frons*,
forehead, suggesting a confronting of Tiberius on his own supreme plane. See
previous note.
    317. *shows . . . rest*] reveals (and, in effect, convicts) him in regard to the rest
of the charges.
    317. *censured*] judged.
    321. *Delude*] mock.
    323. *gripe*] grasp.

That are but hands of Fortune. She herself,
When virtue doth oppose, must lose her threats.   325
All that can happen in humanity,
The frown of Caesar, proud Sejanus' hatred,
Base Varro's spleen, and Afer's bloodying tongue,
The Senate's servile flattery, and these
Mustered to kill, I'am fortified against,   330
And can look down upon: they are beneath me.
It is not life whereof I stand enamoured;
Nor shall my end make me accuse my fate.
The coward and the valiant man must fall;
Only the cause, and manner how, discerns them,   335
Which then are gladdest, when they cost us dearest.
Romans, if any here be in this Senate,
Would know to mock Tiberius' tyranny,
Look upon Silius, and so learn to die.   [*Stabs himself.*]
Varro. O desperate act!
Arruntius. [*Aside.*]   An honourable hand!   340
Tiberius. Look, is he dead?
Sabinus. [*Aside.*]   'Twas nobly struck, and home.

---

325. lose] *F;* loose *Q.*   341. struck] strooke *Q, F.*

324. *That are*] with ref. to the senators, not to *gripe.*
324–5. *She ... threats*] Briggs cites Lucan, *The Civil War*, IX.569–70,
'Fortune threatens in vain when Virtue is her antagonist', also used in *N.I.*,
IV.iv.154–6.
326–31.] Briggs, 'Source-Material', p. 330, compares Cicero, *Tusculan
Disputations*, V.i.4: 'virtue ... keeps beneath its own level all the issues that
can fall to man's lot, and looking down upon them despises the chances of
mortal life'. Loeb ed., tr. J. E. King (London, 1960).
326. *humanity*] human life.
334.] Lucan, *The Civil War*, IX.583, 'The timid and the brave must fall
alike' (Briggs).
335. *discerns*] distinguishes.
336. *Which ... dearest*] Lucan, *The Civil War*, IX.404, 'virtue rejoices when
it pays dear for its existence'. Identified by Riddell, 'Seventeenth-Century
Identifications', p. 207.
336. *gladdest*] most welcome.
338. *mock ... tyranny*] Briggs compares *Nero* (1624), IV.vii, 'Nero, my end
shall mock thy tyranny'.
339–40.] Jonson cites Tacitus, *Annals*, IV.xix: 'Silius anticipated the im-
pending condemnation by a voluntary end'. Tacitus does not say that the
suicide was in the Senate.

Arruntius. [*Aside.*] My thought did prompt him to it.

Farewell, Silius!

Be famous ever for thy great example.

Tiberius. We are not pleased in this sad accident,

That thus hath stallèd and abused our mercy,   345

Intended to preserve thee, noble Roman,

And to prevent thy hopes.

Arruntius. [*Aside.*]   Excellent wolf!

Now he is full, he howls.

Sejanus.   Caesar doth wrong

His dignity and safety, thus to mourn

The deservèd end of so professed a traitor,   350

And doth, by this his lenity, instruct

Others as factious to the like offence.

Tiberius. The confiscation merely of his state

Had been enough.

Arruntius. [*Aside.*]   O, that was gaped for, then?

Varro. Remove the body.

Sejanus.   Let citation   355

Go out for Sosia.

Gallus.   Let her be proscribed.

And for the goods, I think it fit that half

Go to the treasure, half unto the children.

Lepidus. With leave of Caesar, I would think that fourth

Part, which the law doth cast on the informers,   360

---

360. Part, which] *F; The which Q.*

---

342. *My thought . . . to it*] *i.e.*, 'I thought of that—he read my mind'.

345. *stallèd*] rendered unable to proceed. Tacitus mentions no such regrets over Silius, but compare Tiberius's reaction to Libo's suicide, *Annals*, II.xxxi: 'he would have interceded for his life, had he not laid an over-hasty hand upon himself'; and III.1, where there is reference to the frequency with which Tiberius would 'express his regret when anyone by taking his own life had forestalled his clemency'.

347. *prevent*] anticipate.

348. *Now . . . howls*] an original variation of the myth that crocodiles weep false tears.

353. *state*] estate.

356–69. *Let . . . better*] Jonson cites Tacitus, *Annals*, IV.xx: 'Sosia was driven into exile on the motion of Asinius Gallus, who had proposed to confiscate one half of her estate, while leaving the other to her children. A counter-motion by [Marcus] Lepidus assigned a quarter, which was legally necessary, to the accusers, and the residue to the family. / This Lepidus, I

Should be enough; the rest go to the children—
Wherein the prince shall show humanity
And bounty, not to force them by their want,
Which in their parents' trespass they deserved,
To take ill courses.
Tiberius.   It shall please us.
Arruntius. [*Aside.*]   Ay,   365
Out of necessity. This Lepidus
Is grave and honest, and I have observed
A moderation still in all his censures.
Sabinus. And bending to the better—

    [*Enter*] CORDUS [*guarded*], SATRIUS [*and*] NATTA.

                                Stay, who's this?
Cremutius Cordus? What? Is he brought in?   370
Arruntius. More blood unto the banquet? Noble Cordus,

---

364. parents'] *Barish;* Parents *Q;* parents *F;* parent's *Bolton.*   369. [*Enter*]
... NATTA.] *Subst. Gifford, Barish; after 373:* CORDVS. SATRIVS. NATTA. *Q;*
PRAECO, CORDVS, SATRIVS, NATTA. *F, and subst. Bolton.*

---

gather, was, for his period, a man of principle and intelligence: for the number
of motions to which he gave a more equitable turn, in opposition to the
cringing brutality of others, is very considerable. Nor yet did he lack discretion, since with Tiberius he stood uniformly high in influence and in
favour.' See also note on Lepidus in 'Notes on the Characters'.

356. *Let ... proscribed*] Proscription entailed not only the outlawing, but
the confiscation of the property, of the proscribed. Silius had not been proscribed, and by taking his own life before being convicted, had legally avoided
the confiscation of his property (see Tacitus, *Annals,* VI.xxix, which refers to
the law on this matter)—thus the past tense of 'O, that was gaped for, then?',
l. 354. Tacitus, *Annals,* IV.xx, notes certain claims on and deductions from
Silius's estate, but there is no question of its confiscation. Only Sosia's estate
was open to confiscation, and on the grounds of her proscription.

358. *treasure*] treasury. 'Rare', acc. to *O.E.D.,* where the last instance is
from 1596; see *treasure,* sb., 3.

368. *censures*] expressed opinions.

369. *bending to the better*] tendency to the better [course of action].

370–406.] Jonson cites Tacitus, *Annals,* IV.xxxiv: the year 25 'opened with
the prosecution of Cremutius Cordus upon the novel and till then unheard-of-
charge of publishing a history, eulogizing Brutus, and styling Cassius the last
of the Romans. The accusers were Satrius Secundus and Pinnarius Natta,
clients of Sejanus. That circumstance sealed the defendant's fate—that and the
lowering brows of Caesar, as he bent his attention to the defence'. Jonson also
cites Dio, *Roman History,* LVII.24.2–4 (see I.73n.).

I wish thee good. Be as thy writings, free,
  And honest.
Tiberius.   What is he?
Sejanus.   For th'annals, Caesar.
Praeco. Cremutius Cordus!
Cordus.   Here.
Praeco.   Satrius Secundus,
  Pinnarius Natta, you are his accusers.   375
Arruntius. [*Aside.*] Two of Sejanus' bloodhounds, whom he
      breeds
  With human flesh, to bay at citizens.
Afer. Stand forth before the Senate, and confront him.
Satrius. I do accuse thee here, Cremutius Cordus,
  To be a man factious and dangerous,   380
  A sower of sedition in the state,
  A turbulent and discontented spirit,
  Which I will prove from thine own writings, here,
  The annals thou hast published; where thou bit'st
  The present age, and with a viper's tooth,   385
  Being a member of it, dar'st that ill
  Which never yet degenerous bastard did
  Upon his parent.
Natta.   To this I subscribe;
  And, forth a world of more particulars,
  Instance in only one: comparing men   390
  And times, thou praisest Brutus, and affirmst

---

374. *Praeco.* Cremutius Cordus!] PRAE. *Cremutius Cordus. Q;* CREMVTIVS
CORD'. *F.*   377. human] humane *Q, F.*   384. hast] *F;* last *Q.*   385. with]
F; wtih *Q.*

---

372. *free*] open, candid.
    376–7.] The imagery, as Briggs points out, is Seneca's: 'and those fiercest of
dogs, which, savage toward all others, he kept friendly only to himself by
feeding them on human blood, began to bark around that great man [Cordus],
who was already caught in a trap'. *To Marcia on Consolation,* XXII.v.
    384–8. *here ... parent*] The fond idea, still current in Jonson's day, that
the female viper was killed by impatient unborn young eating their way out
derives from Pliny, *Natural History,* X.lxxxii.170. Shakespeare employs it in
Per., I.i.64–5. See also *Poet.,* V.iii.327.
    387. *degenerous*] degenerate—and in this case heavily influenced by the
Latin sense of *gens* (race, stock): untrue to one's ancestry.
    389. *forth*] out of.

That 'Cassius was the last of all the Romans.'
Cotta. How! What are we then?
Varro.   What is Caesar? Nothing?
Afer. My lords, this strikes at every Roman's private,
    In whom reigns gentry and estate of spirit,   395
    To have a Brutus brought in parallel,
    A parricide, an enemy of his country,
    Ranked and preferred to any real worth
    That Rome now holds. This is most strangely invective;
    Most full of spite, and insolent upbraiding.   400
    Nor is't the time alone is here disprized,
    But the whole man of time, yea, Caesar's self
    Brought in disvalue; and he aimed at most
    By oblique glance of his licentious pen.
    Caesar, if Cassius were the last of Romans,   405
    Thou hast no name.
Tiberius.   Let's hear him answer. Silence.
Cordus. So innocent I am of fact, my lords,

---

392. 'Cassius ... Romans.'] *Quotation marks, this edn.; words in italics, Q.*
394. *Afer.*] AFE. *F;* ARR. *Q, corr. in MS. in Wise Q.*   404. pen.] *F;* pen? *Q.*

392.] See I.73n.
394. *private*] personal interest.
395. *gentry*] rank, nobility. Cf. V.570–1, 'we have raised Sejanus, from obscure and almost unknown gentry'.
395. *estate*] grandeur.
397. *parricide*] Lat. *parricida* (*L.&S.*, II.B.), lit., murderer of one's father or parents, but also specifically used of the murderer of the chief magistrate, and in particular of the murderers of Julius Caesar, especially Brutus, '*patriae parentis parricida*' (Valerius Maximus, *Factorum et dictorum memorabilium libri novem* (Stuttgart, 1888), 6.4.5.).
399. *invective*] abusive.
401. *disprized*] held in contempt.
402. *the ... time*] Barish glosses this as 'the greatest man of the present day', i.e. Tiberius, the 'perfected product of time', as it were. However, the following phrase, 'yea Caesar's self', sounds more like a new (or after-) thought than a definition of 'the whole man of time', a rather odd way to describe Tiberius. It seems to me more likely that Jonson is referring to the processes of (personified) Time ('the *whole* man of time' as distinct from '*the* time' of the previous line), controller of events, the father of truth (Aulus Gellius, *Attic Nights*, XII.xi.7), 'the king of men ... [who] gives them what he will, not what they crave' (*Per.*, II.iii.45–7).
404. *oblique glance*] covert allusion.
407–60.] The entire speech is from Tacitus, *Annals*, IV.xxxiv-xxxv, repro-

As but my words are argued; yet those words
Not reaching either prince or prince's parent,
The which your law of treason comprehends.   410
Brutus and Cassius I am charged t'have praised;
Whose deeds, when many more, besides myself,
Have writ, not one hath mentioned without honour.
Great Titus Livius, great for eloquence
And faith amongst us, in his history,   415
With so great praises Pompey did extol,
As oft Augustus called him a Pompeian—
Yet this not hurt their friendship. In his book
He often names Scipio, Afranius,
Yea, the same Cassius, and this Brutus too,   420
As worthi'st men; not thieves and parricides,
Which notes upon their fames are now imposed.
Asinius Pollio's writings quite throughout
Give them a noble memory; so Messalla
Renowned his general Cassius—yet both these   425
Lived with Augustus, full of wealth and honours.

421. worthi'st] *Q, F, Bolton;* worthi'⟨e⟩st *H.&S.; worthiest Barish.*
425. Renowned] Renown'd *F;* Renowm'd *Q.*

---

duced in Appendix A.
   407. *fact*] evil deed, crime.
   409. *reaching*] affecting.
   409. *parent*] i.e. Augustus, Tiberius's step-father.
   410. *comprehends*] embraces.
   414. *Titus Livius*] Roman historian. Those books of his *From the Founding of the City* that deal with the Civil Wars are lost.
   415. *faith*] convincing authority (*O.E.D., faith, sb.,* 6–a slightly earlier example than those cited).
   419. *Scipio*] Metellus Scipio, consul 52 B.C., father-in-law of Pompey, fought at Pharsalia, and was defeated by Caesar at Thapsus.
   419. *Afranius*] Lucius Afranius, consul 60 B.C., joint commander of the Pompeian forces in Spain, where he was defeated by Caesar.
   422. *notes*] marks of infamy—not recorded in *O.E.D.,* this is the transf. sense of Lat. *nota* (*censoria*), the mark affixed by the censors to the names of those censured for immorality or lack of patriotism. *L.&S., nota,* II.B.2.b.
   423. *Asinius Pollio's writings*] a history of seventeen books, as Jonson notes, on the Civil Wars, now lost. Caius Asinius Pollio, consul 40 B.C., became a friend of Augustus after Actium, and founded the first public library in Rome. Suetonius quotes him, *Lives,* I.xxx.4.
   424. *Messalla*] Marcus Valerius Messalla Corvinus fought with Cassius and Brutus at Philippi and later wrote a history of the Civil Wars. He was consul 31 B.C., and later became a patron of various poets, including Tibullus and Ovid.

To Cicero's book, where Cato was heaved up
Equal with heav'n, what else did Caesar answer,
Being then dictator, but with a penned oration,
As if before the judges? Do but see   430
Antonius' letters; read but Brutus' pleadings,
What vile reproach they hold against Augustus—
False, I confess, but with much bitterness.
The epigrams of Bibaculus and Catullus
Are read, full stuffed with spite of both the Caesars;   435
Yet deifiéd Julius, and no less Augustus,
Both bore them and contemned them—I not know
Promptly to speak it, whether done with more
Temper or wisdom; for such obloquies,
If they despiséd be, they die suppressed,   440
But if with rage acknowledged, they are confessed.
The Greeks I slip, whose licence not alone,
But also lust did scape unpunishéd;
Or where some one, by chance, exception took,
He words with words revenged. But in my work,   445
What could be aimed more free, or farther off
From the time's scandal, than to write of those
Whom death from grace or hatred had exempted?
Did I, with Brutus and with Cassius,

---

431. pleadings,] *Q*; pleadings: *F.*   428. Equal] *F*; Æquall *Q.*
436. Augustus,] *Q*; AVGVSTVS! *F.*   439. for] *F*; "For *Q.*   440–1.] *Both*
lines preceded by gnomic pointing, Q.   446. farther off] farder of *Q, F.*

427–9.] Caesar's lost *Anticato*, in two volumes, was a reply to Cicero's lost
Cato. See Suetonius, *Lives*, I. lvi.5.

431. *Antonius' . . . pleadings*] lost. When Suetonius, *Lives*, quotes Antony,
he may be using the 'letters'.

434.] Marcus Furius Bibaculus wrote epigrams and an epic on Caesar's
Gallic wars. He was called 'the pompous poet of the Alps', 'stuffed with rich
tripe', by Horace (*Satires*, I.x.36, II.v.41). Quintilian (*Institutio Oratoria*,
VIII.vi.17) also mocks him, quoting this example of inept metaphor from his
poetry: 'Jove with white snow the wintry Alps bespewed'. Catullus, d. 54 B.C.,
attacks Julius Caesar in Poems 11, 54, 57, and 93.

438. *Promptly*] readily, *i.e.* without thinking much about the matter.

439. *Temper*] equanimity.

440–1.] Briggs cites Seneca, *On Anger*, III.v.8, 'no injury whatever can
cause a truly great mind to be aware of it, since the injury is more fragile than
that at which it is aimed . . . . Revenge is the confession of a hurt'.

442. *slip*] pass by.

Armed, and possessed of the Philippi fields,   450
Incense the people in the civil cause
With dangerous speeches? Or do they, being slain
Seventy years since, as by their images—
Which not the conqueror hath defaced—appears,
Retain that guilty memory with writers?   455
Posterity pays every man his honour.
Nor shall there want, though I condemnèd am,
That will not only Cassius well approve,
And of great Brutus' honour mindful be,
But that will, also, mention make of me.   460
Arruntius. Freely and nobly spoken.
Sabinus.   With good temper.
I like him, that he is not moved with passion.
Arruntius. He puts 'em to their whisper.
Tiberius.   Take him hence,
We shall determine of him at next sitting.
                    [*Exeunt* GUARDS *with* CORDUS.]
Cotta. Meantime, give order that his books be burnt,   465

---

456. Posterity] *F;* "Posterity *Q.*   457. there] *F;* their *Q.*   461. temper.]
Barish; temper, *Q, F, other edd.*   464.1. [*Exeunt* ... CORDUS.]] *Subst.*
Gifford, Barish.   465. burnt] *F;* burn'd *Q.*

451. *the civil cause*] the cause of the state.
453–4. *their* ... *defaced*] Plutarch, *Dion and Brutus*, V, relates how
Augustus, travelling through Mediolanum in Cisalpine Gaul, came across a
statue of Brutus, made a jest of the town's harbouring of his 'enemy', and
ordered that it be left in place.
457–60.] Briggs thinks these lines are imitated in the anon. *Nero* (1624),
IV.v, but an imitation of Tacitus is likelier.
463. *puts* ... *whisper*] Imitated twice by Massinger—in *The Roman Actor*
(1626), I.iii (as *H.&S.* point out), and also in *The Parliament of Love* (1624),
V.i, 'She has put the judges to their whisper'.
463–80.] Jonson cites and partly quotes Tacitus, *Annals*, IV.xxxv: 'He then
left the senate, and closed his life by self-starvation. The fathers ordered his
books to be burned by the aediles; but copies remained, hidden and afterwards
published: a fact which moves us the more to deride the folly of those who
believe that by an act of despotism in the present there can be extinguished also
the memory of a succeeding age. On the contrary, genius chastened grows in
authority; nor have alien kings or the imitators of their cruelty effected more
than to crown themselves with ignominy and their victims with renown'. He
also cites Seneca, *To Marcia on Consolation*, XXII (on Cordus's suicide). It was
only in an expurgated edition that Cordus's books were later published. See
Quintilian, *Institutio Oratoria*, X.i.104. See also III.480n.

To the'aediles.
Sejanus.   You have well advised.
Afer. It fits not such licentious things should live
     T'upbraid the age.
Arruntius. [*Aside.*]   If th'age were good, they might.
Latiaris. Let 'em be burnt.
Gallus.   All sought, and burnt, today.
Praeco. The court is up. Lictors, resume the fasces.   470
     [*Exeunt all but*] ARRUNTIUS, SABINUS, [*and*] LEPIDUS.
Arruntius. Let 'em be burnt! O how ridiculous
     Appears the Senate's brainless diligence,
     Who think they can, with present power, extinguish
     The memory of all succeeding times!
Sabinus. 'Tis true, when, contrary, the punishment   475
     Of wit doth make th'authority increase.
     Nor do they aught, that use this cruelty
     Of interdiction, and this rage of burning,
     But purchase to themselves rebuke and shame,
     And to the writers an eternal name.   480
Lepidus. It is an argument the times are sore,
     When virtue cannot safely be advanced,
     Nor vice reproved.
Arruntius.   Ay, noble Lepidus.
     Augustus well foresaw what we should suffer
     Under Tiberius, when he did pronounce   485
     The Roman race most wretched that should live

469. burnt, today] *F;* burnt. Today. *Q.*   470. up.] *Barish;* up, *Q, F, other edd.*   470.1. SABINUS] *F;* SABINNS *Q.*   471. *Arruntius.*] ARR. *Q; not in F.*
471. burnt!] *F;* burnt? *Q.*   485. pronounce] *Q;* pronouuce *F.*

466. *aediles*] perhaps trisyllabic. See *H.&S.*, IV, 341. The *aediles plebeii* were entrusted with preservation of senatorial decrees.
470. *Lictors ... fasces*] See I.376n.
476. *wit*] genius.
477. *use*] practise.
480. *an eternal name*] Jonson notes that although Cordus's accounts of the civil wars, and of Augustus, are lost, a fragment of his writing survives in the elder Seneca's *Suasoriae*, VI.xix.
481. *sore*] distressed.
482. *advanced*] promoted.
486–7.] Jonson cites the source, Suetonius, *Lives*, III.xxi: after Tiberius had spent an entire day with the dying Augustus, 'Augustus was overheard by

Between so slow jaws, and so long a-bruising.

[*Exeunt.*]

[*Enter*] TIBERIUS [*and*] SEJANUS.

Tiberius. This business hath succeeded well, Sejanus—
  And quite removed all jealousy of practice
  'Gainst Agrippina and our nephews. Now   490
  We must bethink us how to plant our engines
  For th'other pair, Sabinus and Arruntius;
  And Gallus too—howe'er he flatter us,
  His heart we know.
Sejanus.   Give it some respite, Caesar.
  Time shall mature, and bring to perfect crown,   495
  What we with so good vultures have begun.
  Sabinus shall be next.
Tiberius.   Rather Arruntius.
Sejanus. By any means, preserve him. His frank tongue
  Being lent the reins, will take away all thought
  Of malice in your course against the rest.   500
  We must keep him to stalk with.
Tiberius.   Dearest head,

---

487. a-bruising] *Bolton;* a bruising *Q, F, Barish.*   487.2. [*Enter*] . . .
SEJANUS.] *This ed.;* SCENE II. / A Room in the Palace. / Enter Tiberius and
Sejanus. *Gifford, and subst. Bolton;* [*The imperial palace. Enter*] *Tiberius* [*and*]
Sejanus. Barish.   488. *Tiberius.*] TIB. *Q; not in F.*

---

his chamberlains to say: "Alas for the Roman people, to be ground by jaws that
crunch so slowly!'".

   487. *a-bruising*] i.e. by the effects of being chewed up by Tiberius.
   489. *jealousy of practice*] suspicion of a conspiracy.
   491. *engines*] traps.
   493. *Gallus ... us*] Jonson cites Tacitus, *Annals*, I.xiii, where the
independence of Gallus is demonstrated, and II.xxxv, where Tacitus reaffirms
it despite a piece of flattery on Gallus's part.
   496. *so good vultures*] As *H.&S.* point out, only secondarily a reference to
Afer and Varro, and primarily a reference to augury. To Remus six, to
Romulus twelve vultures appeared in the sky at the founding of Rome. See
Livy, *From the Founding of the City*, I.vii.1, and cf. V.604. This sense of
vultures is not in *O.E.D.* The effect here is ironic: Sejanus and Tiberius are
founding a new and very different Rome.
   501. *to stalk with*] to pursue our game by use of him as a stalking horse,
concealing ourselves from view.
   501. *head*] person, esp. in ref. to the mind or disposition. *O.E.D., head, sb.,*
I, 7.a ('a merrie head', 'learned heads', 'young heads', etc.).

To thy most fortunate design I yield it.

Sejanus. Sir—I'have been so long trained up in grace,
First with your father, great Augustus, since
With your most happy bounties so familiar,   505
As I not sooner would commit my hopes
Or wishes to the gods than to your ears.
Nor have I ever, yet, been covetous
Of overbright and dazzling honours; rather
To watch and travail in great Caesar's safety,   510
With the most common soldier.

Tiberius.   'Tis confessed.

Sejanus. The only gain, and which I count most fair
Of all my fortunes, is that mighty Caesar
Hath thought me worthy his alliance. Hence
Begin my hopes.

Tiberius.   H'mh?

Sejanus.   I have heard, Augustus,   515
In the bestowing of his daughter, thought
But even of gentlemen of Rome. If so—
I know not how to hope so great a favour—
But if a husband should be sought for Livia,
And I be had in mind, as Caesar's friend,   520
I would but use the glory of the kindred.
It should not make me slothful, or less caring
For Caesar's state; it were enough to me

---

502. fortunate] *Q;* forunate *F.*   503. I'have] *F;* I haue *Q.*   505. With . . .
familiar]   *F;*   To . . . inur'd   *Q.*   510. travail]   *F;*   trauell   *Q.*
513–6.] *Marginal note in F: His daughter was betroth'd to Claudius, his sonne.
Not in Q.*   521. kindred.] *F;* Kindred, *Q.*

---

502. *fortunate*] auspicious.
503–29.] Jonson cites Tacitus, *Annals,* IV.xxxix, reproduced in Appendix
A.
510. *travail in*] work for.
514. *worthy his alliance*] In his Latin note Jonson reminds us that Sejanus's
daughter had been betrothed to the future emperor Claudius's son, Drusus
(days before the latter's death, 'strangled by a pear which he had thrown in the
air in play and caught in his open mouth'—Suetonius, *Lives,* V.xxvii).
517. *But even*] equally, without prejudice.
517. *gentlemen*] citizens of the equestrian order (below the nobility), to
which Sejanus belonged.
521. *use*] profit from.
521. *kindred*] connection.

It did confirm and strengthen my weak house
Against the now unequal opposition   525
Of Agrippina; and for dear regard
Unto my children, this I wish. Myself
Have no ambition farther than to end
My days in service of so dear a master.
Tiberius. We cannot but commend thy piety,   530
Most loved Sejanus, in acknowledging
Those 'bounties', which we, faintly, such remember.
But to thy suit. The rest of mortal men,
In all their drifts and counsels, pursue profit;
Princes, alone, are of a different sort,   535
Directing their main actions still to fame.
We therefore will take time to think, and answer.
For Livia, she can best, herself, resolve
If she will marry after Drusus, or
Continue in the family; besides,   540
She hath a mother, and a grandam yet,
Whose nearer counsels she may guide her by—
But I will simply deal. That enmity
Thou fearst in Agrippina would burn more
If Livia's marriage should, as 'twere in parts,   545
Divide th'imperial house. An emulation

---

525. unequal] *F;* vnaequall *Q.*   526. Agrippina; and] *H.&S.; Agrippina;*
'And *Q;* AGRIPPINA; 'and *F.*   528. farther] farder *Q, F.*   529. master]
F; Prince *Q.*   530. piety] *F;* pitty *Q, corr. in MS. in Wise Q.*   532. Those
'bounties'] *This ed.;* Those, bounties *Q;* Those bounties *F.*   532. we, faintly,
such] *corr. F;* we faintly, such, *Q, uncorr. F.*   546. emulation] *F;* Æmulation
Q.

---

524. *confirm*] establish firmly.
530–76.] Jonson cites Tacitus, *Annals,* IV.xl, reproduced in Appendix A.
530. *piety*] more than dutiful conduct: grateful devotion. *L.&S., pietas,* I.B.
Sense not recorded in *O.E.D.*
532. *Those 'bounties'*] See textual note on *Q* reading. *H.&S.*'s note to the line
reads 'Tiberius hesitates as if trying to find a simpler word'. But there is
another explanation: since Sejanus himself has just used the word twenty-
seven lines earlier, surely Tiberius pauses before the word not out of modesty
but to indicate that he is quoting Sejanus.
534. *drifts*] designs.
535. *sort*] destiny—Latin *sors.*
541. *a mother . . . yet*] Antonia (daughter of Marc Antony and Octavia), and
Livia (the Augusta).
543. *simply deal*] speak plainly on the matter.
546. *emulation*] jealousy—Tacitus's *aemulatio.*

Between the women might break forth—and discord
Ruin the sons and nephews on both hands.
What if it cause some present difference?
Thou art not safe, Sejanus, if thou prove it.   550
Canst thou believe that Livia, first the wife
To Caius Caesar, then my Drusus, now
Will be contented to grow old with thee,
Born but a private gentleman of Rome?
And raise thee with her loss, if not her shame?   555
Or say that I should wish it, canst thou think
The Senate, or the people, who have seen
Her brother, father, and our ancestors
In highest place of empire, will endure it?
The state thou holdst already is in talk;   560
Men murmur at thy greatness; and the nobles
Stick not, in public, to upbraid thy climbing
Above our father's favours, or thy scale—
And dare accuse me, from their hate to thee.
Be wise, dear friend. We would not hide these things   565
For friendship's dear respect. Nor will we stand
Adverse to thine or Livia's designments.
What we had purposed to thee, in our thought,
And with what near degrees of love to bind thee,
And make thee equal to us, for the present   570
We will forbear to speak. Only, thus much
Believe, our loved Sejanus, we not know
That height in blood, or honour, which thy virtue,
And mind to us, may not aspire with merit.

---

551. first the wife] *corr. F;* who was wife *Q, uncorr. F.*   552. my] *F;* to *Q.*
570. equal] *F;* aequall *Q.*   571. Only,] *corr. F;* Only *Q, uncorr. F.*

549. *present*] immediate.
550. *prove*] try.
552. *Caius Caesar*] As Jonson notes, grandson of Augustus and son of his d.
Julia and Marcus Agrippa.
554. *private gentleman*] Sejanus was born of an equestrian family, but see
comment on his mother's family in the note on him in Notes on the Characters.
560. *state*] rank.
560. *in talk*] gossiped about.
561. *murmur at*] are discontented by.
563. *scale*] appropriate stature.
574. *mind to us*] thoughtfulness towards us.

And this we'll publish, on all watched occasion   575
The Senate or the people shall present.
Sejanus. I am restored, and to my sense again,
    Which I had lost in this so blinding suit.
    Caesar hath taught me better to refuse
    Than I knew how to ask. How pleaseth Caesar   580
    T'embrace my late advice for leaving Rome?
Tiberius. We are resolved.
Sejanus. [*Gives him a paper.*] Here are some motives more,
    Which I have thought on since, may more confirm.
Tiberius. Careful Sejanus! We will straight peruse them.
    Go forward in our main design, and prosper.   [*Exit.*] 585
Sejanus. If those but take, I shall—dull, heavy Caesar!
    Wouldst thou tell me thy favours were made crimes?
    And that my fortunes were esteemed thy faults?
    That thou, for me, wert hated? And not think
    I would with wingèd haste prevent that change,   590
    When thou mightst win all to thyself again
    By forfeiture of me? Did those fond words
    Fly swifter from thy lips than this my brain,

---

582. [*Gives ... paper.*]] *Gifford, Barish.*   before 586] SEIANVS. *Q, F.*
586. *Sejanus.*] SEI. *Q; not in F.*   586. shall—dull] shall. Dull *Q, uncorr. F;*
shall: dull *corr. F.*

---

575. *all watched occasion*] every watched-for opportunity.
580–1. *How ... Rome*] Jonson cites Tacitus, *Annals*, IV. xli: 'unwilling
either to enfeeble his influence by prohibiting the throngs which besieged his
doors or to give a handle to his detractors by receiving them, he turned to the
idea of inducing Tiberius to spend his days in some pleasant retreat at a
distance from Rome'. Also (superfluously) cited is Dio, *Roman History*,
opening of LVIII: 'Tiberius left Rome at this time [A.D. 26] and never
again returned'.
584. *Careful*] solicitous.
586. *If ... take*] if the 'motives' motivate.
590. *prevent*] anticipate and forestall.
591–2. *When ... me*] Briggs compares *Disc.*, ll. 1158–61, 'A Prince should
exercise his cruelty, not by himselfe, but by his Ministers: so hee may save
himselfe, and his dignity with his people, by sacrificing those, when he list,
saith the great *Doctor of State, Macchiavell*'.
592. *forfeiture*] sacrifice.
592. *fond*] foolish.
593–4. *this ... forge*] Cf. *H5*, V.pr.23, 'In the quick forge and working-
house of thought'. *O.E.D.*, *forge, sb.*, 2 quotes Jeremy Collier, *Essays upon
Several Moral Subjects*, II (1703), 78, 'The brain ... is the forge in which all

This sparkling forge, created me an armour
T'encounter chance, and thee? Well, read my charms,   595
And may they lay that hold upon thy senses
As thou hadst snuffed up hemlock, or ta'en down
The juice of poppy and of mandrakes. Sleep,
Voluptuous Caesar, and security
Seize on thy stupid powers, and leave them dead   600
To public cares, awake but to thy lusts—
The strength of which makes thy libidinous soul
Itch to leave Rome; and I have thrust it on,
With blaming of the city business,
The multitude of suits, the confluence   605
Of suitors, then their importunacies,
The manifold distractions he must suffer,
Besides ill rumours, envies, and reproaches—
All which, a quiet and retirèd life,
Larded with ease and pleasure, did avoid;   610
And yet, for any weighty'and great affair,
The fittest place to give the soundest counsels.
By this shall I remove him both from thought
And knowledge of his own most dear affairs,

---

the speculations of the understanding . . . are hammered out'. Thought was
commonly associated with air and fire.

595. *charms*] the seductive 'motives' for leaving Rome.

597–8. *hemlock . . . mandrakes*] potent narcotics. Jonson seems to have in
mind a powdered form of the hemlock plant, as distinct from the liquid form
taken as a poison by Socrates.

599. *security*] carelessness. Cf. *Macb.*, III.v.32–3, 'And you all know
security / Is mortals' chiefest enemy'. In both cases the 'carelessness' is
described as the effect of a narcotic.

603–12. *and . . . counsels*] Jonson cites Tacitus, *Annals*, IV.xli: 'Little by
little, therefore, he began to denounce the drudgeries of the capital, its jostling
crowds, the endless stream of suitors, and to give his eulogies to quiet and
solitude, where tedium and bickering were unknown and a man's chief
attention could be centred on affairs of first importance'.

606. *importunacies*] troublesome pressing solicitations.

610. *Larded*] garnished. *O.E.D. lard, v.*, 4 should thus apply to a state of
life as well as to 'speech or writing'.

610. *did*] would.

613–20.] From Tacitus, *Annals*, IV.xli, cited by Jonson, the passage
preceding that quoted in III.603–12n.: 'The advantages, he foresaw, were
numerous. Interviews would lie in his own bestowal; letters he could largely
supervise, as they were transmitted by soldiers: before long, the Caesar, who

Draw all dispatches through my private hands,   615
Know his designments, and pursue mine own,
Make mine own strengths, by giving suits and places,
Conferring dignities and offices;
And these that hate me now, wanting access
To him, will make their envy none, or less.   620
For when they see me arbiter of all,
They must observe—or else, with Caesar, fall.   [*Exit.*]

                    [*Enter*] TIBERIUS.

Tiberius. To marry Livia? Will no less, Sejanus,
          Content thy aims? No lower object? Well!
          Thou knowst how thou art wrought into our trust,   625
          Woven in our design; and thinkst we must
          Now use thee, whatsoe'er thy projects are.
          'Tis true. But yet with caution, and fit care.
          And, now we better think—Who's there, within?

                    [*Enter* SERVUS.]

Servus. Caesar?
Tiberius.   To leave our journey off were sin   630
          'Gainst our decreed delights; and would appear
          Doubt—or, what less becomes a prince, low fear.

622.1. [*Enter*] TIBERIUS.] TIBERIVS. SERVVS. *Q;* TIBERIVS, SERVUS. *F;*
SCENE III. / Another Room in the same. / Enter Tiberius. *Gifford.*
623. *Tiberius.*] TIB. *Q; not in F.*   624. Well!] *F;* well? *Q.*

---

was already in the decline of life and would be rendered laxer by seclusion,
would be readier to transfer the functions of sovereignty; while his own
unpopularity would diminish with the abolition of his great levées, and the
realities of his power be increased by the removal of its vanities'. In other
words, Sejanus will need to entertain far less, thus exciting less envy; but in his
translation at III.619–20, Jonson has misread this as a restriction of access to
Tiberius. In this, he follows Greneway's translation of the *Annals* (1598),
p. 104. See Introduction, pp. 14–15.
    614. *dear*] important.
    615.] Since mounted *speculatores* of the praetorian guard would carry these
dispatches, Sejanus, as prefect of the guard, would have power to intercept all
communication with Tiberius.
    619–20.] See introduction, pp. 14–15.
    622. *observe*] show respect.
    629.1. *SERVUS*] servant.

Yet, doubt hath law, and fears have their excuse,
Where princes' states plead necessary use,
As ours doth now—more in Sejanus' pride   635
Than all fell Agrippina's hates beside.
Those are the dreadful enemies we raise
With favours, and make dangerous with praise.
The injured by us may have will alike,
But 'tis the favourite hath the power to strike;   640
And fury ever boils more high and strong,
Heat'with ambition, than revenge of wrong.
'Tis then a part of supreme skill to grace
No man too much, but hold a certain space
Between th'ascender's rise and thine own flat,   645
Lest, when all rounds be reached, his aim be that.

---

637. Those] *F;* "They *Q.*   638–46.] *Each line preceded by gnomic pointing,*
Q.   642. Heat'with] *F;* Heat with *Q.*   646. Lest] *F;* Least *Q.*
647. thought—Is] *F;* thought. Is *Q.*

---

634. *necessary use*] vital advantage, benefit. Cf. John Manwood, *Lawes of the*
Forest (1598), 'To the Reader': 'The necessarie use and common good, that
may arise ... by the publishing of this Treatise'.

635. *in*] because of.

636. *fell*] fierce.

637–42.] As Briggs points out, from Machiavelli, *Discourses*, III.vi: 'A
prince, then, who wishes to guard against conspiracies should fear those on
whom he has heaped benefits quite as much, and even more, than those whom
he has wronged; for the latter lack the convenient opportunities which the
former have in abundance. The intention of both is the same, for the thirst of
dominion is as great as that of revenge, and even greater. A prince, therefore,
should never bestow so much authority upon his friends but that there should
always by a certain distance between them and himself, and that there should
always be something left for them to desire; otherwise they will almost in-
variably become victims of their own imprudence, as happened to those whom
we have mentioned above.' One of these was Sejanus. See *The Prince and the*
Discourses, ed. Max Lerner (New York, 1950), p. 415; and cf. *Disc.*, 1224–9,
cited in *H.&S.*

637. *dreadful*] to be feared.

642. *Heat*] heated. Cf. *John*, IV.i.61–3, 'The iron of itself, though heat red-
hot, / Approaching near these eyes would drink my tears, / And quench his
fiery indignation.'

645. *flat*] level, elevation.

646. *rounds*] rungs (of the ladder). *O.E.D., round, sb.,* I.3.b., cites
Marston, *Jacke Drums Entertainment* (1600), in the edn. of R. Simpson, *The*
School of Shakespeare (1878), I.127, 'Let who will climbe ambitions glibbery
rounds'.

'Tis thought—Is Macro in the palace? See.
If not, go seek him, to come to us.   [*Exit* SERVUS.]
                         He
Must be the organ we must work by now,
Though none less apt for trust. Need doth allow   650
What choice would not. I'have heard that aconite,
Being timely taken, hath a healing might
Against the scorpion's stroke. The proof we'll give—
That, while two poisons wrestle, we may live.
He hath a spirit too working to be used   655
But to th'encounter of his like. Excused
Are wiser sov'reigns then, that raise one ill
Against another, and both safely kill.
The prince that feeds great natures, they will sway him;
Who nourisheth a lion must obey him.   660

        [*Enter*] MACRO [*and* SERVUS].

650. Need] *F;* "Neede *Q.*   651. What] *F;* "What *Q.*   659–60.] *Both lines
preceded by gnomic pointing, Q.*   660.1 [*Enter*] ... SERVUS].] TIBERIVS.
MACRO. *Q;* TIBERIVS, MACRO. *F.*

647. *Macro*] On Naevius Sertorius Macro, Jonson cites the sources—Dio,
Roman History, LVIII.9, which, however, relates nothing about Macro prior
to his secret appointment by Tiberius as commander of the praetorian guard;
and sections of Tacitus, *Annals*, VI, which cover the period following Sejanus's
fall, and present Macro (who had been 'chosen as the worse villain of the pair,
to crush Sejanus') as the author of 'crimes more numerous' than his prede-
cessor (IV.xlviii). Suetonius, *Lives*, III.lxxiii, is sceptical of the popular
notion that Macro suffocated Tiberius in his sickbed. Macro was forced into
suicide by Caligula, A.D. 38.
651–4. *I'have ... live*] As *H.&S.* point out, this derives from Pliny,
Natural History, XXVII.ii: 'Yet even aconite [a poisonous herb] the ancients
have turned to the benefit of human health, by finding out by experience that
administered in warm wine it neutralizes the stings of scorpions.... What a
marvel! Although by themselves both are deadly, yet the two poisons in a
human being perish together so that the human survives'. The passage was
well-known in Jonson's day; cf. the proverb 'One poison expels another',
Tilley, P. 457.
653. *the ... give*] we'll test it.
655. *working*] energetic.
656. *But*] except.
660.] Briggs, 'Source-Material', p. 330, cites Aristophanes, *The Frogs*,
1431–2: ''Twere best to rear no lion in the state: / But having reared, 'tis best
to humour him'. Loeb ed., tr. B. B. Rogers (London, 1968). Aristophanes
gives it to Aeschylus.

Tiberius. Macro, we sent for you.
Macro.   I heard so, Caesar.
Tiberius. [*To Servus.*] Leave us awhile.   [*Exit* SERVUS.]
                    When you shall know, good Macro,
  The causes of our sending, and the ends,
  You then will hearken nearer—and be pleased
  You stand so high, both in our choice and trust.   665
Macro. The humblest place in Caesar's choice or trust
  May make glad Macro proud, without ambition—
  Save to do Caesar service.
Tiberius.   Leave our courtings.
  We are in purpose, Macro, to depart
  The city for a time, and see Campania—   670
  Not for our pleasures, but to dedicate
  A pair of temples, one to Jupiter
  At Capua, th'other at Nola, to Augustus;
  In which great work, perhaps, our stay will be
  Beyond our will produced. Now, since we are   675
  Not ignorant what danger may be born
  Out of our shortest absence in a state
  So subject unto envy, and embroiled
  With hate and faction, we have thought on thee,
  Amongst a field of Romans, worthiest Macro,   680
  To be our eye and ear; to keep strict watch
  On Agrippina, Nero, Drusus—ay,
  And on Sejanus. Not that we distrust

---

661. *Tiberius.*] TIB. *Q; not in F.*   663. our] *Q, corr. F;* your *uncorr. F.*

664. *hearken nearer*] listen more closely.
668. *our courtings*] courting of us.
669–75.] Jonson's two notes to these lines cite Suetonius, *Lives*, III.xl and Tacitus, *Annals*, IV. lvii: both comment that the dedication of these temples was but the pretext for a journey whose destination was, from the first, Capri. Jonson also, superfluously, cites Dio, *Roman History*, LVIII.1 (see III.580–1n.).
670. *Campania*] area to the south of Rome, including the cities of Pompeii, Capua, Nola, and Misenum.
675. *produced*] extended—the first usage cited in *O.E.D.*, *produce, v.*, 2.c (from *produco*, II.C in *L.&S.*).
680. *field*] large number (Macro being the one chosen stalk out of a whole crop).

His loyalty, or do repent one grace
Of all that heap we have conferred on him—   685
For that were to disparage our election,
And call that judgement now in doubt, which then
Seemed as unquestioned as an oracle.
But greatness hath his cankers. Worms and moths
Breed out of too fit matter in the things   690
Which after they consume, transferring quite
The substance of their makers int' themselves.
Macro is sharp, and apprehends. Besides,
I know him subtle, close, wise, and well-read
In man and his large nature. He hath studied   695
Affections, passions, knows their springs, their ends,
Which way, and whether they will work. 'Tis proof
Enough of his great merit that we trust him.
Then to a point—because our conference
Cannot be long without suspicion: 700
Here, Macro, we assign thee, both to spy,
Inform, and chastise. Think, and use thy means,
Thy ministers, what, where, on whom thou wilt.
Explore, plot, practise: all thou dost in this
Shall be as if the Senate or the laws   705
Had giv'n it privilege, and thou thence styled
The saviour both of Caesar and of Rome.

689–92.] *Each line preceded by gnomic pointing, Q.*   690. fit matter] *corr. F;*
much humor *Q;* much humour *uncorr. F.*   707. saviour] *Q;* sauier *F;* saver
edd. conj.

---

686. *election*] choice.
689. *cankers*] sores, ulcers. The metaphor changes from the body to cloth.
689–92.] Sejanus is the worm, or moth (cf. I.427n.), growing out of and
feeding upon the 'greatness' of Tiberius, transferring the latter's 'substance'
(power) to himself.
696. *Affections*] feelings.
697. *whether*] whither.
699. *to a point*] to a conclusion—*O.E.D.*, *point*, sb. 1, 29—rather than 'to
come to the point' (Barish). *O.E.D.* cites *MND*, I.ii.7–9, 'say what the play
treats on; then read the names of the actors; and so grow to a point'.
701–4. *to spy ... practise*] Jonson cites Suetonius, *Lives*, III.lxv, 'yet it was
with difficulty that he at last overthrew [Sejanus], rather by craft and deceit
than by his imperial authority'; and Dio, *Roman History*, LVIII.4ff., on
various underhand tactics used against Sejanus.
704. *practise*] lay schemes for an evil purpose, conspire.

We will not take thy answer, but in act—
Whereto, as thou proceedst, we hope to hear
By trusted messengers. If't be enquired   710
Wherefore we called you, say you have in charge
To see our chariots ready, and our horse.
Be still our loved and (shortly) honoured Macro. [*Exit.*]
Macro. I will not ask why Caesar bids do this,
But joy that he bids me. It is the bliss   715
Of courts to be employed, no matter how:
A prince's power makes all his actions virtue.
We, whom he works by, are dumb instruments,
To do, but not enquire: his great intents
Are to be served, not searched. Yet, as that bow   720
Is most in hand whose owner best doth know
T'affect his aims, so let that statesman hope
Most use, most price, can hit his prince's scope.
Nor must he look at what or whom to strike,
But loose at all; each mark must be alike.   725
Were it to plot against the fame, the life
Of one with whom I twinned; remove a wife
From my warm side, as loved as is the air;
Practise away each parent; draw mine heir
In compass, though but one; work all my kin   730
To swift perdition; leave no untrained engine,
For friendship or for innocence; nay, make
The gods all guilty: I would undertake

---

preceding 714.] MACRO. *Q, F.*   714. *Macro.*] MAC. *Q; not in F.*   715. It]
F; "It *Q.*   716. Of] *F;* "Of *Q.*   723. price] *F;* prise *Q.*   725. loose] *Q;*
lose *F.*

714–49.] Jonson cites Tacitus, *Annals*, VI.xlv-l on Macro's character—
his excessive influence by the end of Tiberius's reign (xlv), his opportunism
(xlvi) and involvement in fabricating evidence of treason (xlvii), and the
report of his murdering Tiberius (see also III.647n.).
    720. *searched*] enquired into.
    720–3. *Yet ... scope*] Yet as that bow is most used whose owner is most
skilled, so that statesman can expect most employment and reward who gives
best effect to his prince's aims.
    725.] But let fly at all targets without discrimination.
    727. *one ... twinned*] my own twin.
    729. *Practise away*] plot the death of.
    730. *In compass*] within the scope of my plots.
    731. *untrained engine*] trap unset.

This, being imposed me, both with gain and ease.
The way to rise is to obey and please.   735
He that will thrive in state, he must neglect
The trodden paths that truth and right respect,
And prove new, wilder ways; for virtue, there,
Is not that narrow thing she is elsewhere.
Men's fortune there is virtue; reason, their will;   740
Their licence, law; and their observance, skill.
Occasion is their foil; conscience, their stain;
Profit, their lustre; and what else is, vain.
If then it be the lust of Caesar's power
T'have raised Sejanus up, and in an hour   745
O'erturn him, tumbling down from height of all,
We are his ready engine; and his fall
May be our rise. It is no uncouth thing
To see fresh buildings from old ruins spring.   [*Exit.*]

Chorus of musicians.

735–43.] *Each line preceded by gnomic pointing, Q.*   748. It] *F;* "It *Q.*
749. To] *F;* "To *Q.*   749.1. *Chorus of Musicians.*] *F;* MV. CHORVS. *Q.*

736–8.] Cf. Lucan, *The Civil War* (*Pharsalia*), VIII.489–91: 'The power of kings is utterly destroyed, once they begin to weigh considerations of justice; and regard for virtue levels the strongholds of tyrants'. Jonson has Macro rephrase the maxims of Sejanus at II.178–87, to underline their identical Machiavellian natures.

737. *respect*] have regard to.

738. *prove*] test.

740–41.] *i.e.*, the reverse of conventional values.

741. *observance*] deference, obsequiousness.

742. *Occasion . . . foil*] opportunism is their adornment.

742. *stain*] disgrace.

744–7. *If then . . . engine*] Jonson cites Dio, *Roman History*, LVIII.9–10: Sejanus was told by Macro that he was to be 'raised up' with the tribunician power, and, put off guard, entered the Senate where he was denounced through the medium of a letter from Tiberius—all within the space of an hour.

744. *lust*] pleasure.

747. *engine*] instrument.

747–8. *his fall . . . rise*] Proverbial—Tilley, R 136. Cf. Marston, *Malcontent*, ed. M. L. Wine (London, 1965), V.ii.40–1, 'the falling of the one is the rising of the other'; and Tourneur, *Revenger's Tragedy*, ed. R. A. Foakes (London, 1966), III.i.28, 'The falling of one head lifts up another'. See also I.17–18n.

748. *uncouth*] unfamiliar.

Actus Quartus

[*Enter*] GALLUS [*and*] AGRIPPINA.

Gallus. You must have patience, royal Agrippina.
Agrippina. I must have vengeance first—and that were nectar
    Unto my famished spirits. O my fortune,
    Let it be sudden thou prepar'st against me.
    Strike all my powers of understanding blind,   5
    And ignorant of destiny to come.
    Let me not fear, that cannot hope.
Gallus.   Dear princess,
    These tyrannies on yourself are worse than Caesar's.
Agrippina. Is this the happiness of being born great?
    Still to be aimed at? Still to be suspected?   10
    To live the subject of all jealousies?
    At least the colour made, if not the ground

ACTUS QUARTUS] *Q;* Act IIII. *F;* ACT IV. SCENE I. *Gifford;* [Act IV, Scene i]
Bolton; Act IV *Barish.*   0.1. [*Enter*] . . . AGRIPPINA.] An Apartment
in Agrippina's House. / Enter Gallus and Agrippina. *Gifford;* GALLVS. AGRIP-
PINA. NERO. / DRVSVS. CALIGVIA. *Q;* GALLVS, AGRIPPINA, NERO, DRUSUS, /
CALIGVLA. *F;* [*Agrippina's house. Enter*] GALLUS, AGRIPPINA *Bolton, subst.*
Barish.   1. *Gallus.*] GAL. *Q; not in F.*   12. At least the] *Q, F;* At the least
H.&S., in error, followed by Bolton, Barish.

   1.] Jonson cites and quotes from Tacitus, *Annals* IV.lii, 'Agrippina, fierce-
tempered always and now inflamed by the danger of her kinswoman [Claudia
Pulchra]'.
   1–2. *You . . . first*] *H.&S.* compare Webster, *The White Devil*—III.ii.270 in
the Revels edn.: '*Fran.* You must have patience. *Vit.* I must first have
vengeance.'
   3–7. *O . . . hope*] As Briggs points out, adapted from Lucan, *The Civil War*,
II.14–15, 'let thy purpose, whatever it be, be sudden; let the mind of
man be blind to coming doom; he fears, but leave him hope'. For l. 7,
which is almost the antithesis of Lucan, Riddell, 'Seventeenth-Century Identifications', p. 208, provides another source: Seneca, *Medea*, 163, 'Whoso
has naught to hope, let him despair of naught'.
   10. *Still . . . aimed at*] always to be the target of enemies.
   12–13. *At . . . danger*] made the pretext at least, if not the source or reason,
for every pretended danger. There is an intricate pun on 'colour' as opposed to
'ground', a technical term in painting.

To every painted danger? Who would not
Choose once to fall, than thus to hang forever?
Gallus. You might be safe, if you would—
Agrippina.   What, my Gallus?   15
    Be lewd Sejanus' strumpet? Or the bawd
    To Caesar's lusts he now is gone to practise?
    Not these are safe, where nothing is. Yourself,
    While thus you stand but by me, are not safe.
    Was Silius safe? Or the good Sosia safe?   20
    Or was my niece, dear Claudia Pulchra, safe?
    Or innocent Furnius? They that latest have,
    By being made guilty, added reputation
    To Afer's eloquence? O foolish friends,
    Could not so fresh example warn your loves,   25
    But you must buy my favours with that loss
    Unto yourselves—and when you might perceive
    That Caesar's cause of raging must forsake him
    Before his will? Away, good Gallus, leave me.
    Here to be seen is danger; to speak, treason;   30
    To do me least observance is called faction.
    You are unhappy'in me, and I in all.
    Where are my sons? Nero? And Drusus? We
    Are they be shot at. Let us fall apart;

---

18. Not] *F;* "Not *Q.*   21. niece] Neiee *Q.*   32. unhappy'in] *Q, H.&S.;*
vnhappy in *F.*

13–14. *Who ... forever*] Clearly, as Briggs suggests, from Seneca, *On
Benefits*, II.v.1, 'Nothing is so bitter as long suspense; some can endure more
calmly to have their expectation cut off than deferred'. The contexts are
dissimilar.

21–4. *Or was ... eloquence*] In two notes on these lines Jonson quotes
Tacitus, *Annals*, IV.lii. 'Pulchra and Furnius were condemned. Afer took
rank with the great advocates: his genius had found publicity, and there had
followed a pronouncement from the Caesar, styling him "an orator by natural
right"'. See also II.220n. and II.418–23n.

28–9. *That ... will*] This echoes Seneca, *On Mercy*, I.viii.7 (Briggs): 'The
inclination [*voluntas*] to vent one's rage should be less strong than the
provocation [*causa*] for it'. Argippina is saying that Tiberius's will to vent his
rage will only disappear ('forsake him') when those he perceives as his enemies
(the 'cause' of his rage) have all disappeared.

31. *do ... observance*] pay ... deference.

33–4. *We ... shot at*] i.e. we are being attacked through them.

34. *apart*] alone.

Not, in our ruins, sepulchre our friends.   35
Or shall we do some action, like offence,
To mock their studies, that would make us faulty?
And frustrate practice by preventing it?
The danger's like—for what they can contrive,
They will make good. No innocence is safe   40
When power contests. Nor can they trespass more,
Whose only being was all crime before.

[*Enter* NERO, DRUSUS JUNIOR, *and* CALIGULA.]

Nero. You hear Sejanus is come back from Caesar?
Gallus. No. How? Disgraced?
Drusus Junior.   More gracèd now than ever.
Gallus. By what mischance?
Caligula.   A fortune, like enough   45
Once to be bad.
Drusus Junior.   But turned too good, to both.
Gallus. What was't?
Nero.   Tiberius sitting at his meat,
In a farmhouse they call Spelunca, sited

---

40. No] *F;* "No *Q.*   41-2.] *Both lines preceded by gnomic pointing, Q.*

___

36-8.] The sense is, shall we take some action like the offence they charge
us with, treating lightly their design to make us guilty, upsetting their plot by
forestalling it?
39. *like*] equal.
41. *contests*] challenges that innocence.
42. *only*] very.
46. *Once*] at some moment.
47-60.] Jonson cites Tacitus, *Annals*, IV.lix: 'a serious accident which
occurred to the Caesar ... [gave him] a reason for greater faith in the
friendship and firmness of Sejanus. They were at table in a villa known as the
Grotto [*cui vocabulum speluncae*], built in a natural cavern between the Gulf of
Amyclae and the mountains of Fundi. A sudden fall of rock at the mouth
buried a number of servants, the consequence being a general panic and the
flight of the guests present. Sejanus alone hung over the Caesar with knee, face
and hands, and opposed himself to the falling stones—an attitude in which he
was found by the soldiers who had come to their assistance. This brought an
accession of greatness, and, fatal though his advice might be, yet, as a man
whose thoughts were not for himself, he found a confiding listener.'
47. *meat*] meal.
48. *Spelunca*] now Sperlongo, between Terracina and Gaeta. Jonson notes
that Suetonius, *Lives*, III.xxxix, refers to it as Tiberius's country seat.

By the seaside, among the Fundane Hills,
Within a natural cave, part of the grot   50
About the entry fell, and overwhelmed
Some of the waiters; others ran away.
Only Sejanus, with his knees, hands, face,
O'erhanging Caesar, did oppose himself
To the remaining ruins, and was found   55
In that so labouring posture by the soldiers
That came to succour him. With which adventure
He hath so fixed himself in Caesar's trust
As thunder cannot move him, and is come,
With all the height of Caesar's praise, to Rome.   60
Agrippina. And power, to turn those ruins all on us,
And bury whole posterities beneath them.
Nero, and Drusus, and Caligula,
Your places are the next, and therefore most
In their offence. Think on your birth and blood,   65
Awake your spirits, meet their violence;
'Tis princely when a tyrant doth oppose,
And is a fortune sent to exercise
Your virtue, as the wind doth try strong trees,
Who by vexation grow more sound and firm.   70
After your father's fall, and uncle's fate,
What can you hope, but all the change of stroke

67–70.] *Each line preceded by gnomic pointing, Q.*   67. tyrant] *Tyranne Q;*
tyran *F.*   73. sleight] *Barish;* Slight *Q, F, Bolton.*

58.] Jonson quotes the second part of the first sentence of Tacitus, *Annals,*
IV.lix (see IV.47–60n.).

63–7.] Adapted from Tacitus, *Annals,* IV.lix, 'Nero . . . stood next in the
line of succession, and . . . his freedmen and clients, bent on the rapid acquisi-
tion of power, urged him to a display of spirit and confidence. . . . Sejanus . . .
would not risk a counter-stroke.' Instead of the advice to turn the attack upon
Sejanus, Jonson has Agrippina deliver a counsel of stoical fortitude.

65. *In their offence*] resented by them.

67. *oppose*] set himself against or oppress you.

68–70.] As Briggs points out, from Seneca, *On Providence,* iv.15–16: 'Why
then do you wonder that good men are shaken in order that they may grow
strong? No tree becomes rooted and sturdy unless many a wind assails it. For
by its very tossing it tightens its grip and plants its roots more securely.'

71. *uncle's fate*] i.e. the poisoning of Drusus.

72. *change of stroke*] variety of blows.

That force or sleight can give? Then stand upright;
And though you do not act, yet suffer nobly.
Be worthy of my womb, and take strong cheer.   75
What we do know will come, we should not fear.

[*Exeunt.*]

[*Enter*] MACRO.

Macro. Returned so soon? Renewed in trust and grace?
Is Caesar then so weak? Or hath the place
But wrought this alteration with the air,
And he, on next remove, will all repair?   80
Macro, thou art engaged; and what before
Was public, now must be thy private, more.
The weal of Caesar fitness did imply,
But thine own fate confers necessity
On thy employment; and the thoughts borne nearest   85
Unto ourselves move swiftest still, and dearest.
If he recover, thou art lost—yea, all
The weight of preparation to his fall
Will turn on thee, and crush thee. Therefore, strike
Before he settle, to prevent the like   90
Upon thyself. He doth his vantage know

---

76. What] *F;* "What *Q.*   76.1. [*Enter*] MACRO.] *This ed.;* SCENE II. / The
Street. / Enter Macro. *Gifford, and subst. Bolton;* [*The street. Enter*] *Macro.*
Barish.   77. *Macro*]. MAC. *Q; not in F.*   82. must] *corr. Q, F; most uncorr.*
Q.   85. and] *F;* "And *Q.*   85. borne] *Q, F, Barish;* born *Bolton.*
86. Unto] *F;* "Vnto *Q.*   91. He] *F;* "He *Q.*

76.] Cf. Seneca, *On Firmness,* xix.3, 'all misfortune will fall more lightly on
those who expect it'.
80. *on next remove*] on the next stage of his journey.
81. *engaged*] vitally involved.
81–2. *and what ... more*] explained in the following couplet.
83.] The sense is, The welfare of Caesar justified my employment (or,
perhaps, fitted it for self-aggrandisement). The 'fitness' of this line and the
'necessity' of the following present contrasting kinds of obligation.
85–6. *borne ... Unto*] most concerning.
86. *dearest*] in the most heartfelt manner. *O.E.D.* does not include this sense
under *dear, adv.,* but see the *adj.,* 7.a.
87. *if he recover*] if Sejanus regains favour.
88. *weight*] imputed guilt.

That makes it home, and gives the foremost blow.

[Exit.]

[Enter] LATIARIS, RUFUS, [*and*] OPSIUS.

Latiaris. It is a service great Sejanus will
    See well requited, and accept of nobly.
    Here place yourselves, between the roof and ceiling,   95
    And when I bring him to his words of danger,
    Reveal yourselves, and take him.
Rufus.   Is he come?
Latiaris. I'll now go fetch him.   *[Exit.]*
Opsius.   With good speed. I long
    To merit from the state in such an action.
Rufus. I hope it will obtain the consulship   100
    For one of us.
Opsius.   We cannot think of less,
    To bring in one so dangerous as Sabinus.
Rufus. He was a follower of Germanicus,
    And still is an observer of his wife

92. That] *F;* "That *Q.*   92.1. [*Enter*] ... OPSIUS.] *This ed.;* SCENE III. / An
upper Room of Agrippina's House. / Enter Latiaris, Rufus, and Opsius.
Gifford; [Act IV, Scene iii] / [*Agrippina's house. Enter*] LATIARIS, RUFUS,
OPSIUS *Bolton;* [*An upper room of Agrippina's house. Enter*] *Latiaris, Rufus,*
[*and*] *Opsius. Barish.*   93. *Latiaris.*] LAT *Q; not in F.*   93. great] *F;* Lord
Q.

---

    92. makes] presses.
    92.1. *LATIARIS, RUFUS ... OPSIUS*] Tacitus, in the passage quoted
below, tells all that is known of Rufus and Opsius. Latiaris was later
denounced by Tiberius—*Annals,* VI.iv.
    93–232.] Adapted from Tacitus, *Annals,* IV.lxviii–lxx, which Jonson in
several notes cites. See Appendix A.
    93–5.] As well as Tacitus, Jonson cites Dio, *Roman History,* LVIII.1.1.,
'Latiaris ... [wished] to do Sejanus a favour'.
    95. *between ... ceiling*] Considering the staging of this scene, *H.&S.*
suppose that 'At line 114 the spies mount a rope ladder into the "hut" above
and draw it up after them; they drop it again at line 217 and descend'. More
probably, as William A. Armstrong argues, 'Latiaris and his spies were on the
balcony when he gave them the order ..., the spies concealed themselves by
lying behind the balcony rails while Latiaris and Sabinus talked below, and
... they jumped to the platform when the time came for them to arrest
Sabinus'. See 'Ben Jonson and Jacobean Stagecraft', *Jacobean Theatre,* Strat-
ford-upon-Avon Studies I (London, 1960), 53.
    104. *an observer of*] one who shows dutiful attention to.

And children, though they be declined in grace—   105
A daily visitant, keeps them company
In private, and in public; and is noted
To be the only client of the house.
Pray Jove he will be free to Latiaris.
Opsius. He'is allied to him, and doth trust him well.   110
Rufus. And he'll requite his trust?
Opsius.   To do an office
So grateful to the state, I know no man
But would strain nearer bands than kindred—
Rufus.   List,
I hear them come.
Opsius.   Shift to our holes, with silence.
                                          [*They retire.*]

                    [*Enter*] LATIARIS [*and*] SABINUS.

Latiaris. It is a noble constancy you show   115
To this afflicted house—that not like others,
The friends of season, you do follow fortune,
And in the winter of their fate forsake
The place whose glories warmed you. You are just,
And worthy such a princely patron's love,   120
As was the world's renowned Germanicus;
Whose ample merit when I call to thought,
And see his wife and issue objects made
To so much envy, jealousy, and hate,
It makes me ready to accuse the gods   125
Of negligence, as men of tyranny.
Sabinus. They must be patient, so must we.
Latiaris.   O Jove!
What will become of us, or of the times,

110. He'is] *Q;* H'is *F.*   115. *Latiaris.*] LAT. *Q; not in F.*

___

105. *grace*] favour.
108. *client*] favourite follower. There was a rather formal relationship of *cliens* to *patronus* in ancient Rome.
109. *free*] frank.
110. *He'is allied to him*] See Introduction, pp. 14–15.
111. *requite*] return (ironic).
117. *friends of season*] 'fair weather friends'.
127. *They ... we*] Contrast this with Tacitus, where Sabinus, anything but stoical, 'broke into tears coupled with complaints'.

When to be high, or noble, are made crimes?
When land and treasure are most dangerous faults?   130
Sabinus. Nay, when our table, yea our bed, assaults
Our peace and safety? When our writings are,
By any envious instruments, that dare
Apply them to the guilty, made to speak
What they will have, to fit their tyrannous wreak?   135
When ignorance is scarcely innocence,
And knowledge made a capital offence?
When not so much but the bare empty shade
Of liberty is reft us? And we made
The prey to greedy vultures and vile spies   140
That first transfix us with their murdering eyes?
Latiaris. Methinks the genius of the Roman race
Should not be so extinct, but that bright flame
Of liberty might be revived again,
Which no good man but with his life should lose,   145
And we not sit like spent and patient fools,
Still puffing in the dark at one poor coal,
Held on by hope, till the last spark is out.
The cause is public, and the honour, name,
The immortality of every soul   150
That is not bastard or a slave in Rome,
Therein concerned. Whereto, if men would change
The wearied arm, and for the weighty shield
So long sustained, employ the ready sword,
We might have some assurance of our vows.   155

---

145. lose] *F;* loose *Q.*   154. ready] *corr. F;* facile *Q, uncorr. F.*

131–2. *yea . . . safety*] Jonson cites and quotes Tacitus, *Annals*, IV. lx,
'Even night itself was not secure, since [Nero's] . . . slumbers, his sighs, were
communicated by his wife [Livia Julia] to her mother Livia, and by Livia
to Sejanus'.

133. *envious instruments*] agents full of ill-will.

135. *wreak*] vengeance.

139. *reft*] taken from.

139–41. *and . . . eyes*] Barish notes the irony here—Sabinus, 'a victim of the
thing he is describing, in the very moment in which he describes it. As he
talks, he is being transfixed by Latiaris' murdering eye'. One may add, and by
the 'vultures' crouched above, ready to fall upon their 'prey'.

145. *with his life*] i.e., at his death.

147. *coal*] ember.

155. *vows*] wishes, desires.

    This ass's fortitude doth tire us all.
    It must be active valour must redeem
    Our loss, or none. The rock and our hard steel
    Should meet, t'enforce those glorious fires again
    Whose splendour cheered the world, and heat gave life   160
    No less than doth the sun's.
Sabinus.   'Twere better stay
    In lasting darkness, and despair of day.
    No ill should force the subject undertake
    Against the sovereign, more than hell should make
    The gods do wrong. A good man should and must   165
    Sit rather down with loss, than rise unjust—
    Though, when the Romans first did yield themselves
    To one man's power, they did not mean their lives,
    Their fortunes, and their liberties should be
    His absolute spoil, as purchased by the sword.   170
Latiaris. Why, we are worse, if to be slaves, and bond
    To Caesar's slave, be such, the proud Sejanus!
    He that is all, does all, gives Caesar leave
    To hide his ulcerous and anointed face,
    With his bald crown, at Rhodes, while he here stalks   175
    Upon the heads of Romans and their princes,
    Familiarly to empire.
Sabinus.   Now you touch

163–6.] *Each line preceded by gnomic pointing,* Q.   172. Sejanus!]
corr. F; *Seianus?* Q, *uncorr.* F.

---

   156. *ass's fortitude*] As a beast of burden, the ass was an emblem of patient
endurance.
   158. *The rock . . . steel*] 'Flint and steel' was a term for an apparatus
consisting of a piece of each. When the steel struck the flint, the flash produced
was used to ignite tinder or touchwood. In the context of Latiaris's speech, the
'hard steel' is the sword.
   163–70.] Cf. I.244–50 and n. These lines, as editors have pointed out, seem
anachronistic—perhaps a sop to Jonson's critics on the Privy Council.
   166. *rise unjust*] unjustly start into rebellion.
   174. *his . . . face*] Jonson cites and quotes Tacitus, *Annals*, IV. lvii, 'he
possessed . . . an ulcerous face generally variegated with plasters'.
   174. *anointed*] covered with ointment.
   175. *at Rhodes*] A major error in Jonson. See Introduction, pp. 14–15.
   175–6. *he . . . Romans*] As Briggs points out, from Seneca, *To Marcia on
Consolation*, XXII.iv: Cremutius Cordus could not endure 'that a Sejanus
should be set upon our necks, much less climb there'.
   177. *Familiarly to empire*] freely to rule absolutely as an emperor.

A point, indeed, wherein he shows his art
As well as power.
Latiaris.   And villainy in both.
　　Do you observe where Livia lodges? How   180
　　Drusus came dead? What men have been cut off?
Sabinus. Yes, those are things removed. I nearer looked,
　　Into his later practice, where he stands
　　Declared a master in his mystery.
　　First, ere Tiberius went, he wrought his fear   185
　　To think that Agrippina sought his death;
　　Then put those doubts in her; sent her oft word,
　　Under the show of friendship, to beware
　　Of Caesar, for he laid to poison her;
　　Drave them to frowns, to mutual jealousies,   190
　　Which now in visible hatred are burst out.
　　Since, he hath had his hirèd instruments
　　To work on Nero, and to heave him up;
　　To tell him Caesar's old; that all the people,
　　Yea, all the army have their eyes on him;   195
　　That both do long to have him undertake
　　Something of worth, to give the world a hope;
　　Bids him to court their grace. The easy youth
　　Perhaps gives ear, which straight he writes to Caesar,

---

191. burst] *corr Q*; bursl *uncorr. Q.*

　　182. *removed*] distant in time.
　　184. *mystery*] profession. The phrase 'master in his mystery' related to the apprenticeship system.
　　187–9. *sent ... her*] Jonson cites Tacitus, *Annals*, IV.liv: to Agrippina Sejanus sent 'agents to warn her, under the colour of friendship, that poison was ready for her: she would do well to avoid the dinners of her father-in-law' (Germanicus had been the adopted son of Tiberius). This led to an embarrassing scene when, during a subsequent dinner, she passed some fruit he had handed her to her slaves.
　　189. *laid*] plotted.
　　190. *Drave*] drove.
　　190. *jealousies*] suspicions.
　　193–9. *To work ... ear*] Jonson cites Tacitus, *Annals*, IV.lix-lx: Sejanus, through his agents, incited Nero to ambitious thoughts and 'a display of spirit and confidence:- "It was this the nation desired and the armies yearned for, and Sejanus ... would not risk a counter-stroke!"' Hence 'at intervals there fell from him defiant and unconsidered phrases'. His reputation as a malcontent quickly established, public ostracism followed as a matter of course.
　　193. *heave him up*] exalt him.

And with this comment: 'See yon dangerous boy;   200
Note but the practice of the mother, there;
She's tying him, for purposes at hand,
With men of sword.' Here's Caesar put in fright
'Gainst son and mother. Yet he leaves not thus.
The second brother, Drusus—a fierce nature,   205
And fitter for his snares, because ambitious
And full of envy—him he clasps and hugs,
Poisons with praise, tells him what hearts he wears,
How bright he stands in popular expectance;
That Rome doth suffer with him in the wrong   210
His mother does him by preferring Nero.
Thus sets he them asunder, each 'gainst other,
Projects the course that serves him to condemn,
Keeps in opinion of a friend to all,
And all drives on to ruin.
Latiaris.   Caesar sleeps,   215
And nods at this?
Sabinus.   Would he might ever sleep,
Bogged in his filthy lusts.

[OPSIUS *and* RUFUS *rush in.*]

---

200. yon] yon'd *Q;* yond' *F.*   207. clasps] *corr. Q;* clings *uncorr. Q.*
217. [OPSIUS ... *in.*]] *Gifford, Barish.*

---

199. *he*] Sejanus.
202. *tying*] linking, associating.
202. *at hand*] soon to be revealed.
205–15. *The second ... ruin*] Jonson cites Tacitus, *Annals*, IV.lx: Sejanus
'had actually made a convert of ... Drusus by holding before his eyes the
prospect of supremacy, once he should have ousted his senior from his already
precarious position. Over and above the lust of power and the hatred habitual
to brothers, the savage temper of Drusus was inflamed by envy, as the
preferences of his mother Agrippina were for Nero. None the less, Sejanus'
solicitude for Drusus was not so great but that, even against him, he was
pondering the measures which should ripen to his destruction: for he knew the
rash hardihood which laid him peculiarly open to treachery'.
208. *what ... wears*] whose devotion he has.
209. *expectance*] expectation.
211. *preferring*] promoting.
213. *Projects ... condemn*] devises the proceedings which enable him to
condemn them.
217. *Bogged ... lusts*] H.&S. compare *Und.*, xv.30, 'bogg'd in vices'. Cf.
also *Ado*, IV.i.133, 'mir'd with infamy'.

Opsius.   Treason to Caesar!
Rufus. Lay hands upon the traitor, Latiaris,
      Or take the name thyself.
Latiaris.   I am for Caesar.
Sabinus. Am I then catched?
Rufus.   How think you, sir? You are.   220
Sabinus. Spies of this head! So white! So full of years!
      Well, my most reverend monsters, you may live
      To see yourselves thus snared.
Opsius.   Away with him!
Latiaris. Hale him away.
Rufus.   To be a spy for traitors
      Is honourable vigilance
Sabinus.   You do well,   225
      My most officious instruments of state,
      Men of all uses. Drag me hence, away.
      The year is well begun, and I fall fit
      To be an off'ring to Sejanus. Go.
Opsius. Cover him with his garments, hide his face.   230
Sabinus. It shall not need. Forbear your rude assault;
      The fault's not shameful villainy makes a fault.   [*Exeunt.*]

                [*Enter*] MACRO [*and*] CALIGULA.

232. The] *F;* "The *Q.*   232.1. [*Enter*] . . . CALIGULA.] *This ed.;* SCENE IV./
The Street before Agrippina's House. / Enter Macro and Caligula. *Gifford, and
subst. Bolton;* [*The street. Enter*] Macro [*and*] Caligula. Barish.   233. Macro.]
MAC *Q; not in F.*

---

221. *head*] category—with a pun.
    222. *reverend*] Jonson equivocates between the senses 'fear-inspiring' and
'venerable' or aged, both given by the Lat. *reverendus.*
    224–9.] Jonson cites Tacitus, *Annals*, IV.lxx. See IV.93–232n., final
paragraph.
    228. *The year . . . begun*] The Kalends of January was considered a
particularly fortunate festival day. Good wishes were exchanged, and on this
day executions would not normally take place. But Sabinus sees himself as a
sacrificial offering to Sejanus, so that his arrest is 'fit'! Prayers and sacrifices
were being offered to Sejanus at this time—see Dio, *Roman History*,
LVIII.ii.8.
    230.] Acc. to Cicero, 'those phrases . . . "Lictor, go bind his hands", . . .
"Veil his head" . . . have long since disappeared from our state, overwhelmed
not only by the shadows of antiquity but by the light of Liberty'. *In Defence of
Rabirius*, IV.xiii. Loeb ed., tr. H. Grose Hodge (London, 1959). Jonson is
aware of the irony.

Macro. Sir, but observe how thick your dangers meet
        In his clear drifts! Your mother and your brothers
        Now cited to the Senate! Their friend Gallus,   235
        Feasted today by Caesar, since committed!
        Sabinus here we met, hurried to fetters!
        The senators all struck with fear and silence,
        Save those whose hopes depend not on good means,
        But force their private prey from public spoil!   240
        And you must know, if here you stay, your state
        Is sure to be the subject of his hate,
        As now the object.
Caligula.   What would you advise me?
Macro. To go for Capreae presently—and there
        Give up yourself, entirely, to your uncle.   245
        Tell Caesar, since your mother is accused
        To fly for succours to Augustus' statue,
        And to the army, with your brethren, you
        Have rather chose to place your aids in him
        Than live suspected, or in hourly fear   250
        To be thrust out by bold Sejanus' plots—
        Which you shall confidently urge to be

---

238. struck] strooke *Q, F.*

234. *clear drifts*] obvious schemes.
234–5. *Your ... Senate*] Jonson cites Tacitus, *Annals*, V.iii: the Augusta
having died, Tiberius felt less restraint, and 'a letter denouncing Agrippina
and Nero was forwarded to Rome', imputing to Nero the offence of 'unnatural
love and moral depravity' and upbraiding Agrippina's 'haughty language and
refractory spirit'. The Senate took no action, unsure and fearful of Tiberius's
intentions.
235–6. *Gallus ... committed*] Jonson quotes Dio, *Roman History*, LVIII.3.3,
'this man had a most remarkable experience, one that never happened to
anyone else: on one and the same day he was banqueted at the house of
Tiberius, ... and was condemned in the senate'.
240. *force ... spoil*] wrest their private plunder from the public purse.
241. *state*] property, possessions.
242–3. *the subject ... object*] the actual victim of his hatred, as it is now the
thing that excites that hatred.
244. *presently*] at once.
245. *uncle*] great-uncle.
246–8. *since ... army*] Jonson cites Tacitus, *Annals*, IV.lxx—apparently in
error, intending V.iii (see IV.234–5n.); and Suetonius, *Lives*, III.liii: Tiberius
finally resorted to 'falsely charging [Agrippina] with a desire to take refuge,
now at the statue of Augustus and now with the armies'.

Most full of peril to the state and Caesar,
As being laid to his peculiar ends,
And not to be let run with common safety.   255
All which, upon the second, I'll make plain,
So both shall love and trust with Caesar gain.
Caligula. Away then, let's prepare us for our journey.

[*Exeunt.*]

[*Enter*] ARRUNTIUS.

Arruntius. Still dost thou suffer, heav'n? Will no flame,
No heat of sin make thy just wrath to boil   260
In thy distempered bosom, and o'erflow
The pitchy blazes of impiety
Kindled beneath thy throne? Still canst thou sleep,
Patient, while vice doth make an antic face
At thy dread power, and blow dust and smoke   265
Into thy nostrils? Jove, will nothing wake thee?
Must vile Sejanus pull thee by the beard
Ere thou wilt open thy black-lidded eye,
And look him dead? Well! Snore on, dreaming gods—
And let this last of that proud giant race   270
Heave mountain upon mountain 'gainst your state.
Be good unto me, Fortune, and you powers
Whom I, expostulating, have profaned.

---

255. common] *F;* commune *Q.*   257. So] *F;* And *Q.*   258.1. [*Enter*
ARRUNTIUS.] SCENE V./ Another Part of the Street. / Enter Arruntius. *Gifford.*
259. *Arruntius.*] ARR. *Q; not in F.*   265. dread] drâd *Q;* drad *F.*

---

254. *to . . . ends*] for his private aims.
256. *upon the second*] in the support (of you).
259–63. *Still . . . throne*] Cf. Kyd, *Spanish Tragedy*, III.vii.10–18, Tourneur, *Revenger's Tragedy*, IV.ii.158–9, as well as *Cat.*, III.235–7—all inspired
by Seneca, *Hippolytus* (*Phaedra*), 671–4.
264. *antic*] grinning.
267. *pull . . . beard*] Whalley cites Persius, *Satires*, II.28–9, 'will Jupiter
therefore offer you his foolish beard to pluck?'
268. *thy . . . eye*] Cf. Dryden, *Hind & Panther*, III.1144, 'Black-brow'd, and
bluff, like Homer's Jupiter'. Briggs points out that Spenser uses the phrase
'black-lidded eye' in *Mother Hubberds Tale*, 1228.
270. *this . . . giant race*] Sejanus is imagined as the last of the Titans, whose
attempt to scale heaven by piling mountain upon mountain was defeated by
Jupiter.
273. *expostulating*] complaining of. Cf. Marston, *Ant.&Mell.*, ed. G. K.
Hunter (London, 1965), IV.i.124, 'Do not expostulate the heavens' will'.

I see (what's equal with a prodigy)
A great, a noble Roman, and an honest,   275
Live an old man!

[*Enter* LEPIDUS.]

O, Marcus Lepidus,
When is our turn to bleed? Thyself and I,
Without our boast, are almost all the few
Left to be honest in these impious times.
Lepidus. What we are left to be, we will be, Lucius,   280
Though tyranny did stare as wide as death
To fright us from it.
Arruntius.   'T hath so, on Sabinus!
Lepidus. I saw him now drawn from the Gemonies,
And, what increased the direness of the fact,
His faithful dog, upbraiding all us Romans,   285
Never forsook the corpse, but, seeing it thrown
Into the stream, leaped in, and drowned with it.
Arruntius. O act, to be envied him of us men!
We are the next the hook lays hold on, Marcus.
What are thy arts—good patriot, teach them me—   290

---

274. equal] *F;* aequall *Q.*   278. almost] *Edd.;* a'most *Q, F.*   before
280] LEPIDVS. ARRVNTIVS. *Q;* LEPIDVS, ARRVNTIVS. *F.*   280. *Lepidus.*]
LEP. *Q; not in F.*

274-6. *what's ... man*] This refers to Lepidus. As Briggs points out,
Jonson borrows from Juvenal, *Satires*, IV.96-7, 'But to be both old and noble
has long since become as good as a prodigy'.
276. *Marcus Lepidus*] See note on him in 'Notes on Characters'. Jonson cites
Tacitus, *Annals*, I.xiii. (Augustus saw him as capable, but disdainful, of being
emperor); III.xxxv (declines proconsulate of Africa); III.l (pleads for leniency
towards an accused knight); and IV.xx (see III.356-69n.).
283. *Gemonies*] see IV.309n.
284. *fact*] crime.
285-7. Jonson cites Dio, *Roman History*, LVIII.1.3.: Sabinus's death 'was
rendered still more tragic by the behaviour of a dog belonging to Sabinus that
went with him to prison, remained beside him at his death, and finally leaped
into the river with his body'. Oddly he also cites Tacitus, *Annals*, IV.
lxx—which does not mention the dog.
288. *of*] by.
289. *the hook*] See II.416n.
290. *patriot*] *O.E.D., sb.* 2, the modern sense, where the first occurrence is
given as 1605, *Volp.*, IV.i.95-6, 'knowne patriots, / Sound louers of their
country'.

That have preserved thy hairs to this white dye,
And kept so reverend and so dear a head
Safe on his comely shoulders?
Lepidus.   Arts, Arruntius?
None, but the plain and passive fortitude
To suffer, and be silent; never stretch   295
These arms against the torrent; live at home,
With my own thoughts, and innocence about me,
Not tempting the wolves' jaws: these are my arts.
Arruntius. I would begin to study 'em, if I thought
They would secure me. May I pray to Jove   300
In secret, and be safe? Ay, or aloud?
With open wishes? So I do not mention
Tiberius, or Sejanus? Yes, I must,
If I speak out. 'Tis hard, that. May I think,
And not be racked? What danger is't to dream?   305
Talk in one's sleep? Or cough? Who knows the law?
May'I shake my head, without a comment? Say
It rains, or it holds up, and not be thrown
Upon the Gemonies? These now are things
Whereon men's fortune, yea their fate depends.   310

---

298. wolves'] *Bolton;* Wolues *Q;* wolues *F;* wolf's *Barish.*   307. May'I] *Q,*
H.&S.; May I *F.*

294–8.] Jonson cites Tacitus, *Annals*, IV.xx: Lepidus was 'a man of principle and intelligence.... Nor yet did he lack discretion, since with Tiberius he stood uniformly high in influence and in favour'—which suggests that perhaps 'we are free, between the extremes of bluff contumacy and repellent servility, to walk a straight road, clear of intrigues and perils'. There is also a debt to Juvenal, *Satires*, IV.86–93 (*H.&S.*): since a tyrant's ear turns all to treason, 'Crispus never struck out those arms of his against the torrent, nor was he one to speak freely the thoughts of his heart, and stake his life upon the truth'. Thus he lived over eighty years.

298. *wolves' jaws*] i.e., the enmity of detractors. Cf. 'Ode to Himself', *Und.* xxiii, 'Safe from the wolves black jaw, and the dull Asses hoofe'.

300–2. *May ... wishes*] Briggs compares Persius, *Satires*, II.5–7, 'Most of our great men offer their libations from censers that divulge no secrets'; few 'offer prayers such as all men may hear'.

307. *without a comment*] i.e. without it being commented upon.

308. *it holds up*] the fine weather holds out.

309. *the Gemonies*] Jonson's note, in which he cites various authorities—Rhodiginus Caelius (*Lectiones antiquae*, 1517), Tacitus, Suetonius, Dio, Seneca, and Juvenal—points out that upon the Gemonian steps on the Aventine hill were thrown the bodies of the condemned.

Nothing hath privilege 'gainst the violent ear.
No place, no day, no hour, we see, is free—
Not our religious and most sacred times—
From some one kind of cruelty. All matter,
Nay all occasion pleaseth. Madmen's rage,   315
The idleness of drunkards, women's nothing,
Jesters' simplicity—all, all is good
That can be catched at. Nor is now th'event
Of any person, or for any crime,
To be expected; for 'tis always one: 320
Death, with some little difference of place,
Or time—what's this? Prince Nero? Guarded?

        [Enter] LACO *[and*] NERO *[with* LICTORES].

Laco. On, lictors, keep your way. My lords, forbear.
    On pain of Caesar's wrath, no man attempt
    Speech with the prisoner.
Nero.   Noble friends, be safe.   325
    To lose yourselves for words were as vain hazard
    As unto me small comfort. Fare you well.
    Would all Rome's suff'rings in my fate did dwell.
Laco. Lictors, away.
Lepidus.   Where goes he, Laco?
Laco.   Sir,

322.1. *[Enter]* . . . LICTORES]] LACO. NERO. LEPIDVS. ARRVNTIVS. *Q;* LACO,
NERO, LEPIDVS, ARRVNTIVS. *F.*   323. *Laco.*] LAC. *Q; not in F.*   326. lose]
loose *Q, F.*

311. *violent*] 'Tending to wrest or pervert the meaning'—*O.E.D.*, *violent,
a.*, 4.c., but antedating the *O.E.D.* example by 117 years.
    313. *most sacred times*] Sabinus was put to death on the New Year, a sacred
day.
    315. *all occasion pleaseth*] any pretext serves.
    315–18. *Madmen's . . . at*] See the quotation from Seneca, I.67–8n.
    316. *idleness*] delirium.
    316. *nothing*] trivial remarks.
    317. *simplicity*] rude directness of speech.
    318. *catched at*] seized upon.
    318. *event*] fate.
    320. *expected*] waited for, wondered about—literal translation from Latin
exspectare, to wait to see.
    322.1. *LACO*] Jonson cites Dio, *Roman History*, LVIII.9.3–6: Graecinus
Laco was commander of the night-watch. He was loyal to Macro on the day
Sejanus was overthrown.

He'is banished into Pontia, by the Senate.   330
Arruntius. Do'I see? And hear? And feel? May I trust sense?
    Or doth my fant'sy form it?
Lepidus.   Where's his brother?
Laco. Drusus is prisoner in the palace.
Arruntius.   Ha?
    I smell it now: 'tis rank. Where's Agrippina?
Laco. The princess is confined, to Pandataria.   335
Arruntius. Bolts, Vulcan; bolts for Jove! Phoebus, thy bow;
    Stern Mars, thy sword; and blue-eyed maid, thy spear;
    Thy club, Alcides—all the armoury
    Of heaven is too little!—Ha? To guard
    The gods, I meant. Fine, rare dispatch! This same   340
    Was swiftly borne! Confined? Imprisoned? Banished?
    Most tripartite! The cause, sir?
Laco.   Treason.
Arruntius.   O?
    The complement of all accusings? That
    Will hit, when all else fails.
Lepidus.   This turn is strange!

---

330. He'is] *This ed.;* H'is *Q, F.*   332. fant'sy] *Bolton;* Phant'sy *Q;* phant'sie
F; fancy *Barish.*   343. accusings?] *Q, F;* accusings! *Barish.*

330, 333.] Jonson's notes to these lines cite Suetonius, *Lives*, III.liv: after
bringing charges against them, resulting in them being 'pronounced public
enemies, he starved them to death, Nero on the island of Pontia [Ponza, west
of Naples] and Drusus in a lower room of the palace'.
    331. *sense*] my senses.
    332. *fant'sy*] i.e. fantasy, imagination. Cf. V.89.
    334. *I . . . rank*] referring back to l. 331: the sense of smell is so affected
that he cannot be dreaming! The sense is the commonplace 'smell it out',
understand it.
    335.] Jonson cites Suetonius, *Lives*, III.liii, 'he exiled her to Pandataria'
(Ventotene, west of Naples).
    336. *Bolts*] thunderbolts.
    336–9. *Bolts . . . little*] Briggs compares Juvenal, *Satires*, XIII.78–83, which
gives these and other examples of swearing by 'all the weapons contained in
all the armouries of Heaven'.
    337. *blue-eyed maid*] Pallas Athena, sometimes called Glaucopis from the
Greek meaning 'blue-eyed'.
    338. *Alcides*] Hercules.
    343. *The . . . accusings*] Jonson cites Tacitus, *Annals*, III.xxxviii: against
Caesius Cordus was brought a charge of malversation; 'a charge of treason, the
complement now of all arraignments, was appended'.

But yesterday, the people would not hear   345
Far less objected, but cried, Caesar's letters
Were false, and forged; that all these plots were malice;
And that the ruin of the prince's house
Was practised 'gainst his knowledge. Where are now
Their voices? Now, that they behold his heirs   350
Locked up, disgraced, led into exile?
Arruntius.   Hushed.
Drowned in their bellies. Wild Sejanus' breath
Hath, like a whirlwind, scattered that poor dust
With this rude blast.
                    He turns to Laco and the rest.
                  We'll talk no treason, sir,
If that be it you stand for. Fare you well.   355
We have no need of horse-leeches. Good spy,
Now you are spied, begone.

              [*Exeunt* LACO, NERO, *and* LICTORES.]

Lepidus.   I fear you wrong him.
He has the voice to be an honest Roman.
Arruntius. And trusted to this office? Lepidus,
I'd sooner trust Greek Sinon than a man   360

---

348. prince's] *Edd;* Princes *Q, F.*   354. *He . . . rest.*] *Marginal s.d. in F; not
in Q.*   360. I'd] I'ld *Q, F.*

345–9. *But . . . knowledge*] Jonson cites Tacitus, *Annals*, V.iv: there being
some doubt about the genuineness of Tiberius's accusatory letter (see IV.234–
5n), 'the people, carrying effigies of Agrippina and Nero, surrounded the
curia, and, cheering for the Caesar, clamoured that the letter was spurious and
that it was contrary to the Emperor's wish that destruction was plotted against
his house'.
    348. *prince's*] Germanicus's.
    352. *Drowned . . . bellies*] Cf. Lyly, *Campaspe* (1584), I.ii.78, 'An old saw of
abstinence, Socrates: "The belly is the heads graue"'. Quoted in Tilley, B 293.
Lyly and Jonson seem to have greed in mind here—conscience is 'drowned'
in the juices of the belly, whose demands are more insistent than those of
the 'head'.
    353. *poor dust*] in reference to the human frailty of Sejanus's enemies (and to
Genesis, where man is described as dust).
    356. *horse-leeches*] lit. large leeches, fig. rapacious persons, here those who
would suck dry the Germanicans.
    360. *Greek Sinon*] By his cunning, Sinon persuaded the Trojans to admit the
wooden horse into the city. Graecinus Laco's name gives him away as one of
Sinon's compatriots.

Our state employs. He's gone—and being gone,
I dare tell you, whom I dare better trust,
That our night-eyed Tiberius doth not see
His minion's drifts; or if he do, he'is not
So errant subtle as we fools do take him,   365
To breed a mongrel up, in his own house,
With his own blood, and, if the good gods please,
At his own throat flesh him to take a leap.
I do not beg it, heav'n; but if the fates
Grant it these eyes, they must not wink.
Lepidus.   They must   370
      Not see it, Lucius.
Arruntius.   Who should let 'em?
Lepidus.   Zeal,
      And duty; with the thought he is our prince.
Arruntius. He is our monster: forfeited to vice
      So far, as no racked virtue can redeem him,
      His loathèd person fouler than all crimes—   375
      An emp'ror only in his lusts; retired,
      From all regard of his own fame, or Rome's,

---

364. he'is] *This ed.;* H'is *Q;* h'is *F.*   368. flesh] *F;* traine *Q.*   374. him,]
This ed.; him. *Q, F, Bolton, Barish.*

---

363. *night-eyed*] Jonson cites Dio, *Roman History*, LVII.2.4, 'although he
saw extremely well in the dark, his sight was very poor in the daytime'; and
Pliny, *Natural History*, XI.liv.143: 'It is stated that . . . if [Tiberius] woke up
in the night for a short time he could see everything just as in bright daylight,
although darkness gradually closed over him'. Jonson seems unaware that the
earliest source of this information is Suetonius, *Lives*, III.lxviii.
    365. *errant subtle*] thoroughly cunning ('errant' here having the sense of
'arrant').
    368. *flesh . . . leap*] (unwittingly) encourage him with the sight and smell of
flesh to leap for the throat instead.
    370. *wink*] close.
    371. *let*] prevent.
    373–4. *our monster . . . him*] Briggs cites Juvenal, *Satires*, IV.2–4, which is
the source of Jonson's phrases here ('monstrum nulla virtute redemptum /
a vitiis, aegrae solaque libidine fortes deliciae'—the Loeb tr. is less literal
than Jonson).
    374. *racked*] forced, wrung out of him.
    375.] Jonson cites Tacitus, *Annals*, IV.lvii—the ref. to Tiberius's ugliness
(IV.174n.). *H.&S.* compare Juvenal, *Satires*, IV.14–15, 'What can you do
when the man himself is more foul and monstrous than any charge you can
bring against him?'

Into an obscure island, where he lives,
Acting his tragedies with a comic face,
Amidst his rout of Chaldees; spending hours,   380
Days, weeks, and months in the unkind abuse
Of grave astrology, to the bane of men,
Casting the scope of men's nativities,
And having found aught worthy in their fortune,
Kill, or precipitate them in the sea,   385
And boast he can mock fate! Nay, muse not: these
Are far from ends of evil, scarce degrees.
He hath his slaughterhouse at Capreae,
Where he doth study murder as an art;
And they are dearest in his grace that can   390
Devise the deepest tortures. Thither, too,
He hath his boys and beauteous girls ta'en up
Out of our noblest houses, the best formed,

378–80. *Into ... Chaldees*] Jonson cites various accounts of the emperor's
activities on Capreae: Suetonius, *Lives*, III.xliiiff.; Dio, *Roman History*,
LVIII. 5.1; Juvenal, *Satires*, X.91–4 ('a Prince seated on the narrow ledge of
Capri with his herd of Chaldaean astrologers').

379. *comic face*] the mask appropriate to comedy.

380–6. *spending ... fate*] Jonson cites Tacitus, *Annals*, VI.xxi: Tiberius
walked with each astrologer by the edges of cliffs, and, 'had any suspicion
arisen of incompetence or of fraud, hurled him into the sea below'; Dio,
Roman History, LVII.57.3–4 (the emperor's skill in astrology); and Suetonius,
Lives, III.lxii (executions on Capreae).

381. *unkind*] unnatural.

387. *ends ... degrees*] limits ... stages on the way.

388–91. *He ... tortures*] Jonson cites Suetonius, *Lives*, III.lxii, on the
torments which Tiberius engaged in while on Capri.

391–401. *Thither ... name*] In two notes to these lines, Jonson cites
Suetonius, *Lives*, III.xliv, 'Imagine training little boys, whom he called his
"minnows", to chase him while he went swimming and get between his legs to
lick and nibble him'; III.xliii, 'a private sporting house, where sexual
extravagances were practised for his secret pleasure ... girls and young
men ... known as *spintriae*, would copulate before him in groups of three, to
excite his waning passions' (from *The Twelve Caesars*, ed. Robert Graves, rev.
Michael Grant, Harmondsworth, 1981. Loeb edn. leaves untranslated); and,
most relevantly, Tacitus, *Annals*, VI.i, 'Nor were beauty and physical charm
his only incitements to lasciviousness, but sometimes a boyish modesty and
sometimes a noble lineage. And now were coined the names, hitherto
unknown, of *sellarii* and *spintriae*, ... while slaves, commissioned to seek and
fetch, plied the willing with gratuities, the reluctant with threats, and, if a
kinsman or parent refused compliance, resorted to force, abduction, and the
slaking of their own desires as if in a captured city'.

Best nurtured, and most modest. What's their good
Serves to provoke his bad. Some are allured,   395
Some threatened; others, by their friends detained,
Are ravished hence like captives, and, in sight
Of their most grievèd parents, dealt away
Unto his spintries, sellaries, and slaves,
Masters of strange and new-commented lusts,   400
For which wise nature hath not left a name.
To this (what most strikes us, and bleeding Rome)
He is, with all his craft, become the ward
To his own vassal, a stale catamite—
Whom he, upon our low and suffering necks,   405
Hath raised from excrement to side the gods,
And have his proper sacrifice in Rome;
Which Jove beholds, and yet will sooner rive
A senseless oak with thunder than his trunk.

[*Enter*] LACO, POMPONIUS, [*and*] MINUTIUS.

409.1. [*Enter*] ... MINUTIUS.] LACO. POMPONIVS. MINVTIVS. &c. *Q;* LACO,
POMPONIVS, MINVTIVS, TERENTIVS. *F.*   before 410] *Marginal s.d. in F: To
them.*

396. *detained*] kept back (presumably from a protective instinct).
397. *ravished*] carried away by force.
399. *spintries, sellaries*] See second quotation in IV.391–401 n. The English
words are taken from Richard Greneway's tr. of Tacitus (1598), to which
Jonson was more indebted than he acknowledged (Introduction, pp. 14–16.)
400. *commented*] devised, invented (from Lat. *commentus*) *O.E.D.*, *comment*,
v., I.l, gives no example later than 1596.
401.] Briggs identifies the source: Juvenal, *Satires*, XIII.28–30, 'an age ...
for whose wickedness Nature herself can find no name'.
402. *strikes*] pierces to the heart.
403–7.] Jonson cites Dio, *Roman History*, LVIII.4. 2–4: Sejanus was better
informed about Tiberius than *vice-versa*, and at Rome 'they sacrificed to the
images of Sejanus as they did to those of Tiberius'. Juvenal, *Satires*, X.92–3
refers to Sejanus as 'tutor ... principis'.
404. *catamite*] *Catamitus* was the Lat. form of Ganymede, Jupiter's cup-
bearer. The insult is that Sejanus is the catamite (i.e. the boy used for sexual
purposes), not the sodomite or user.
406. *side*] rival.
407. *proper*] distinctive.
408–9. *will ... trunk*] Briggs cites Persius, *Satires*, II.24–5: that 'the sacred
fire rends an oak-tree in twain sooner than you and your house' does not mean
Jupiter has condoned all.
409. *trunk*] body.
409.1. *POMPONIUS ... MINUTIUS*] Jonson cites Tacitus, *Annals*, VI:

Laco. These letters make men doubtful what t'expect,   410
  Whether his coming, or his death.
Pomponius.   Troth, both—
  And which comes soonest, thank the gods for.
Arruntius. [*To Lepidus.*]   List,
  Their talk is Caesar, I would hear all voices.
Minutius. One day, he's well, and will return to Rome;
  The next day, sick, and knows not when to hope it.   415
Laco. True, and today, one of Sejanus' friends
  Honoured by special writ; and on the morrow
  Another punished—
Pomponius.   By more special writ.
Minutius. This man receives his praises of Sejanus;
  A second, but slight mention; a third, none;   420
  A fourth, rebukes. And thus he leaves the Senate
  Divided and suspended, all uncertain.
Laco. These forkèd tricks, I understand 'em not.
  Would he would tell us whom he loves or hates,
  That we might follow, without fear or doubt.   425
Arruntius. [*Aside.*] Good heliotrope! Is this your honest man?
  Let him be yours so still. He is my knave.
Pomponius. I cannot tell; Sejanus still goes on,

---

410. *Laco.*] LAC. *Q; not in* F.   after 413] *Arruntius and Lepidus stand aside.*
Gifford, Barish.   414. *Minutius.*] MIN. *corr.* Q, *corr.* F; MAR. *uncorr.* Q,
uncorr. F.

Quintus Pomponius was 'a restless character' who curried favour with
Tiberius, chiefly by being an accuser (VI.xviii); Minucius [*sic*] Thermus was a
friend of Sejanus, later condemned on that account; on being found guilty, he
'joined the informers' (VI.vii).

  410–22.] In three notes to these lines Jonson cites Dio, *Roman History*,
LVIII.6.3–5: Tiberius 'kept sending despatches of all kinds regarding himself
both to Sejanus and to the senate, now saying that he was in a bad state of
health and almost at the point of death, and now that he was exceedingly well
and would arrive in Rome directly. At one moment he would heartily praise
Sejanus, and again would as heartily denounce him; and, while honouring
some of Sejanus' friends out of regard for him, he would be disgracing others'.
Thus both Sejanus and the senate were kept insecure.

  415. *it*] his return.

  426. *heliotrope*] Pliny, *Natural History*, II.xli.109: 'one plant, called heliotrope, always looks towards the sun as it passes and at every hour of the day
turns with it, even when it is obscured by a cloud'. Cf. *K.Ent.*, 168–73,
'AGRYPNIA, or *Vigilance*, . . . her chaplet of *Heliotropium*, or turnesole . . . .
The *Heliotropium* [signifying] care and respecting her object'. *Sejanus* presents
the first figurative usage of the word, which literally means 'sun-turning'.

And mounts, we see. New statues are advanced,
Fresh leaves of titles, large inscriptions read,   430
His fortune sworn by, himself new gone out
Caesar's colleague in the fifth consulship.
More altars smoke to him than all the gods.
What would we more?
Arruntius. [*Aside.*]   That the dear smoke would choke him,
That would I more.
Lepidus. [*Aside.*]   Peace, good Arruntius.   435
Laco. But there are letters come they say, ev'n now,
Which do forbid that last.
Minutius.   Do you hear so?
Laco.   Yes.
Pomponius. By Pollux, that's the worst.
Arruntius. [*Aside.*]   By Hercules, best!
Minutius. I did not like the sign, when Regulus,
Whom all we know no friend unto Sejanus,   440
Did, by Tiberius' so precise command,

---

435. That ... Arruntius.] *corr. F; not in Q, uncorr. F.*   438. Pollux] *corr. F;*
Castor Q; CASTOR *uncorr. F.*   438. Hercules] *corr. F; Pollux Q;* POLLVX
uncorr. F.

---

429. *New ... advanced*] Jonson cites Tacitus, *Annals*, IV.lxxiv: the senate
'voted an altar of Mercy and an altar of Friendship with statues of the Caesar
and Sejanus on either hand'.

431–2.] In two notes, Jonson quotes Dio, *Roman History*, LVIII.6.2, 'they
swore by his Fortune interminably'; cites LVIII.4.4, 'Finally it was voted that
they should be made consuls together every five years'; and cites Suetonius,
Lives, III.lxv, 'to remove [Sejanus] from his person ... [Tiberius] chose him
as his colleague in a fifth consulship'. Cf. V.43n.

436–7. *But ... last*] Jonson cites Dio, *Roman History*, LVIII.8.4, 'because
sacrifices were being offered to Sejanus, he forbade such offerings to be made
to any human being'.

438. *Pollux ... Hercules*] 'Castor' and 'Pollux', which appear in *Q* and the
first state of *F*, were replaced at the press by Jonson, because (as Briggs
pointed out) he only realized at the last moment that Aulus Gellius, in his *Attic
Nights*, XI.vi.1, had stated that 'In our early writings neither do Roman
women swear by Hercules nor the men by Castor', adding that 'why the men
did not name Castor in oaths is not easy to say' (XI.vi.3). The original version
sounds better. *L.&S.*, 2. Castor, II.A, deny that the oath *ecastor* (or *mecastor*)
was exclusively used by women, but all their examples are spoken by women.

439–44. *Regulus*] In two notes Jonson cites Dio, *Roman History*, LVIII.9.3:
Macro had the consul Memmius Regulus on his side; 'his colleague sided with
Sejanus'. See next note.

Succeed a fellow in the consulship.
It boded somewhat.
Pomponius.   Not a mote. His partner,
Fulcinius Trio, is his own, and sure.
Here comes Terentius.

[*Enter* TERENTIUS.]

He can give us more.   445
They whisper with Terentius.
Lepidus. I'll ne'er believe but Caesar hath some scent
Of bold Sejanus' footing. These cross-points
Of varying letters and opposing consuls,
Mingling his honours and his punishments,
Feigning now ill, now well, raising Sejanus   450
And then depressing him, as now of late
In all reports we have it, cannot be
Empty of practice. 'Tis Tiberius' art.
For, having found his favourite grown too great,
And, with his greatness, strong; that all the soldiers   455
Are, with their leaders, made at his devotion;
That almost all the Senate are his creatures,

445.1. *They ... Terentius.*] *Marginal s.d. in corr. F; not in Q, uncorr. F.*
449. Mingling] *corr. F; Mixing Q, uncorr. F.*

---

442. *a fellow ... consulship*] Memmius Regulus and Fulcinius Trio were *consules suffecti*, holding office in the second half of A.D. 31. As Jonson has already pointed out through Pomponius (l. 432), Tiberius and Sejanus were the *consules ordinarii*, appointed at the beginning of the year. See also V.515n.

444. *his own*] Sejanus's own follower.

447. *footing*] dancing.

447. *cross-points*] particular steps in dancing, an espec. appropriate metaphor. See Robert Greene, *James the Fourth*, ed. Norman Sanders, Revels edn. (London, 1970), IV.iii.105–7, 'Nay, but my friends, one hornpipe further, a refluence back and two doubles forward. What, not one cross-point against Sundays?' The cross-point involved crossing the feet—in the air as well as on the floor.

447–51. *These ... him*] In two notes Jonson cites Suetonius, *Lives*, III.lxv—how Tiberius overthrew Sejanus 'by craft and deceit'—and, more relevantly, Dio, *Roman History*, LVIII.6.3–5 (see IV.410–22n.).

453. *practice*] scheming.

455–6. *all ... devotion*] Jonson cites Dio, *Roman History*, LVIII.4.2, 'Sejanus had completely won over the entire Pretorian guard'.

456. *made ... devotion*] secured as devotees.

Or hold on him their main dependences,
Either for benefit, or hope, or fear;
And that himself hath lost much of his own,   460
By parting unto him, and by th'increase
Of his rank lusts and rages, quite disarmed
Himself of love, or other public means
To dare an open contestation—
His subtlety hath chose this doubling line,   465
To hold him even in; not so to fear him
As wholly put him out, and yet give check
Unto his farther boldness. In meantime,
By his employments, makes him odious
Unto the staggering rout, whose aid (in fine)   470
He hopes to use, as sure, who, when they sway,
Bear down, o'erturn all objects in their way.

Arruntius. You may be a Lynceus, Lepidus, yet I
See no such cause but that a politic tyrant,
Who can so well disguise it, should have ta'en   475
A nearer way: feigned honest, and come home
To cut his throat, by law.

Lepidus.   Ay, but his fear

---

468. farther] farder Q, F.   474. tyrant] Tyranne Q; tyranne F.   477. but]
F; "but Q.

---

458. *hold ... dependences*] depend mainly upon him.
459. *for*] by reason of.
461. *parting unto*] sharing with.
465. *doubling line*] presumably in reference to the management of a horse.
466–8. *To ... boldness*] Jonson cites Dio, *Roman History*, LVIII.6.4, 'Thus
Sejanus ... was in constant suspense; for it never occurred to him, on the one
hand, to be afraid and so attempt a revolution, inasmuch as he was still held in
honour, nor, on the other hand, to be bold and attempt some desperate
venture, inasmuch as he was frequently abased'.
466. *even in*] in check.
466. *fear*] frighten.
470. *staggering rout*] fickle, unsteady crowd. Cf. Marston, *Malcontent*, ed.
G. K. Hunter (London, 1975), III.iii.6, 'staggering multitude'.
470. *in fine*] eventually (Latin *in fine*, in the end).
471. *sure*] dependable.
471. *sway*] hold sway, with a play on the sense 'to incline, lean, swerve',
continuing the 'staggering' image of the previous line.
473. *Lynceus*] one of the Argonauts, renowned for his sharp sight.
474. *See ... that*] cannot see why not.

Would ne'er be masked, albe his vices were.
Pomponius. His lordship then is still in grace?
Terentius.   Assure you,
Never in more, either of grace or power.   480
Pomponius. The gods are wise and just.
Arruntius. [*Aside.*]   The fiends they are,
To suffer thee belie 'em!
Terentius.   I have here
His last and present letters, where he writes him
The 'partner of his cares' and 'his Sejanus'—
Laco. But is that true, it is prohibited   485
To sacrifice unto him?
Terentius.   Some such thing
Caesar makes scruple of, but forbids it not,
No more than to himself; says he could wish
It were forborne to all.
Laco.   Is it no other?
Terentius. No other, on my trust. For your more surety,   490
Here is that letter too.
Arruntius. [*Aside.*]   How easily
Do wretched men believe what they would have!
Looks this like plot?
Lepidus. [*Aside.*]   Noble Arruntius, stay.
Laco. He names him here without his titles.
Lepidus. [*Aside.*]   Note.

---

478. Would] *F;* "Would *Q.*   478. ne'er] neere *Q;* ne're *F.*   481. are,]
Most edd.; are. *Q, F, Bolton.*   482. 'em!] 'hem *Q, F.*   485. it is] *Edd.;* it
'tis *Q, F.*

---

478. *albe*] albeit.
481–2. *The fiends . . . belie 'em*] *i.e.* the gods are wicked for not striking you
down when you belie them by calling them 'wise and just'.
483–4.] Dio, *Roman History*, LVIII.4.3: Tiberius 'termed him Sharer of his
Cares, often repeated the phrase "My Sejanus," . . . using it in letters
addressed to the senate and to the people'.
485–9. *it . . . all*] Jonson cites Dio, *Roman History*, LVIII.8.4: 'because
sacrifices were being offered to Sejanus, he forbade such offerings to be made
to any human being'.
491–2. *How . . . have*] Briggs cites Seneca, *Hercules Furens*, 313–4: 'What
the wretched overmuch desire, they easily believe'.
494. *He . . . titles*] Jonson cites Dio, *Roman History*, LVIII.8.4: 'in a letter to
the senate . . . he referred to Sejanus by that name simply, without the
addition of the customary titles'.

Arruntius. [*Aside.*] Yes, and come off your notable fool. I will.   495
Laco. No other than Sejanus.
Pomponius.   That's but haste
   In him that writes. Here he gives large amends.
Minutius. And with his own hand written?
Pomponius.   Yes.
Laco.   Indeed?
Terentius. Believe it, gentlemen, Sejanus' breast
   Never received more full contentments in   500
   Than at this present.
Pomponius.   Takes he well th'escape
   Of young Caligula with Macro?
Terentius.   Faith,
   At the first air, it somewhat troubled him.
Lepidus. [*Aside.*] Observe you?
Arruntius. [*Aside.*]   Nothing. Riddles. Till I see
   Sejanus struck, no sound thereof strikes me.   505
           [*Exeunt* ARRUNTIUS *and* LEPIDUS.]
Pomponius. I like it not. I muse h'would not attempt
   Somewhat against him in the consulship,
   Seeing the people 'gin to favour him.
Terentius. He doth repent it now, but h'has employed
   Pagonianus after him; and he holds   510

---

495. off] of *Q, F.*   498. Minutius.] *Edd.;* MAR. *Q, F.*   503. troubled] *F;*
mated *Q.*   505. struck] strooke *Q, F.*   505.1. [*Exeunt* ... LEPIDUS.]
Gifford, Barish; Bolton has them exeunt with the others at the end of the act.

  495. *come off*] turn out to be.
  501–2. *th'escape ... Caligula*] Jonson cites Dio, *Roman History*, LVIII.8,
which concerns the jealousy felt by Sejanus towards Caligula, but not his
concern over Caligula's presence on Capri.
  503. *air*] publication of the fact.
  505. *sound ... strikes*] rumour ... affects.
  506–9. *I muse ... now*] Jonson cites Dio, *Roman History*, LVIII.8.2: 'and
now, finding [the populace] earnest supporters of Gaius, [Sejanus] became
dejected, and regretted that he had not begun a rebellion during his
consulship'.
  506. *muse*] wonder.
  510. *Pagonianus*] Jonson cites Tacitus, *Annals*, VI.iii: 'Sextius Paconia-
nus—fearless, mischievous, a searcher into all men's secrets, and the chosen
helper of Sejanus in the laying of his plot against Gaius Caesar'. Later strangled
in prison (*Annals*, VI.xxxix).
  510. *after him*] to follow him.

That correspondence there with all that are
Near about Caesar, as no thought can pass
Without his knowledge thence in act to front him.
Pomponius. I gratulate the news.
Laco.   But how comes Macro
So'in trust and favour with Caligula?   515
Pomponius. O, sir, he has a wife, and the young prince
An appetite. He can look up, and spy
Flies in the roof when there are fleas i'bed,
And hath a learnèd nose to'assure his sleeps.
Who, to be favoured of the rising sun,   520
Would not lend little of his waning moon?
'Tis the saf'st ambition. Noble Terentius!
Terentius. The night grows fast upon us. At your service.

[Exeunt.]

Chorus of musicians.

---

514. Laco.] *Edd.*; MAC. *Q, F.*   515. So'in]*Q, H.&S.*; So in *F.*   516. has]
F; ha's *Q.*   522. 'Tis] *Q, F;* It is *Gifford.*   522.2. *Chorus of musicians.*] *F;*
MV. CHORVS *Q.*

511. *correspondence*] communication—*O.E.D.*'s first instance of the word in
this sense.

512–13. *no thought ... him*] no scheme can, without his knowledge, emerge
from there to become an active threat to him.

514. *gratulate*] am joyed at.

516–21.] Jonson cites Tacitus, *Annals*, VI.xlv: Macro, 'Never careless of
the good graces of Gaius Caesar, ... had induced his wife Ennia to captivate
the youth by a mockery of love and to bind him by a promise of marriage'. In
Tacitus this comes after the fall of Sejanus. Dio, *Roman History*, LVIII. 38.4,
is the source of IV.520–1: suspecting the liaison, Tiberius told Macro, 'You do
well, indeed, to abandon the setting and hasten to the rising sun'. Historically,
after the fall of Sejanus.

517–18. *He ... i'bed*] *i.e.*, he has his priorities in a peculiar order.

519. *a learnèd nose*] Briggs cites Juvenal, *Satires*, I.57, 'to snore with wakeful
nose'.

520–1. Caligula is the 'rising sun', Macro's wife the 'waning moon'.

Actus Quintus

[*Enter*] SEJANUS.

Sejanus. Swell, swell, my joys, and faint not to declare
    Yourselves as ample as your causes are.
    I did not live till now, this my first hour,
    Wherein I see my thoughts reached by my power.
    But this, and gripe my wishes. Great, and high,   5
    The world knows only two, that's Rome, and I.
    My roof receives me not; 'tis air I tread—
    And, at each step, I feel my'advancèd head
    Knock out a star in heav'n! Reared to this height,

ACTUS QUINTUS] *Q;* Act V. *F;* ACT V. SCENE I. *Gifford;* [Act V, Scene i]
Bolton; Act V *Barish.*   0.1. [*Enter*] SEJANUS.] An apartment in Sejanus's
House. / Enter Sejanus. *Gifford;* [*Sejanus' house. Enter*] SEJANUS *Bolton, subst.*
Barish.   1. *Sejanus.*] SEI. *Q; not in F.*   3. now,] now; *Q, F.*   5. gripe]
Q, F, Barish; grip *Bolton.*   9. height,] *F;* height. *Q.*

   1. *faint*] fear (*O.E.D. faint,* v., 1).
   3.] Briggs, 'Source-Material', p. 331, cites Statius, *Silvae,* IV.ii.12–13, 'I
have lived barren years, but this is my natal day, this day is the threshold of
my life'. Loeb ed., tr. J. H. Mozley (London, 1961).
   5. *But ... wishes*] Only this last step, and my wishes are realized.
   5. *gripe*] seize.
   5. *Great, and high*] Jonson cites, as evidence of the prideful arrogance of
Sejanus, Dio, *Roman History,* LVIII.5.1 ('excessive haughtiness') and Tacitus,
Annals, IV.lxxiv ('His arrogance was increased by the sight of this repulsive
servility so openly exhibited').
   6. *that's Rome*] 'Great' and 'high' were commonly appended to the city's
name. For 'great' see examples quoted by *O.E.D.*, *great,* adj., 11d; for 'high',
cf. Ovid, *Tristia,* I.iii.33.
   7. *My ... not*] This image was probably suggested by Statius, *Silvae,*
IV.ii.18ff. (following the lines that suggested V.3 above): 'An edifice august,
huge, magnificent ...; he fills the house, and gladdens it with his mighty
spirit'.
   7–9. *tis ... heav'n*] Briggs cites Seneca, *Thyestes,* 885–8, 'Peer of the stars
I move, and, towering over all, touch with proud head the lofty heavens ....
the utmost of my prayers have I attained'; and Horace, *Odes,* I.i.35 'I shall
touch the stars with my exalted head'. 'Knock out' is a superb twist to the
Latin source.

All my desires seem modest, poor, and slight,   10
That did before sound impudent. 'Tis place,
Not blood, discerns the noble and the base.
Is there not something more than to be Caesar?
Must we rest there? It irks t'have come so far,
To be so near a stay. Caligula,   15
Would thou stoodst stiff, and many, in our way!
Winds lose their strength when they do empty fly,
Unmet of woods or buildings; great fires die
That want their matter to withstand them. So
It is our grief, and will be'our loss, to know   20
Our power shall want opposites; unless
The gods, by mixing in the cause, would bless
Our fortune with their conquest. That were worth
Sejanus' strife—durst fates but bring it forth.

> [*Enter*] TERENTIUS [*and* SERVUS].

Terentius. Safety to great Sejanus!
Sejanus.   Now, Terentius?   25
Terentius. Hears not my lord the wonder?
Sejanus.   Speak it, no.
Terentius. I meet it violent in the people's mouths,
    Who run, in routs, to Pompey's theatre

---

11. 'Tis] *F;* "Tis *Q.*   12. Not] *F;* "Not *Q.*   16. many,] *F;* many *Q,*
Barish.   17. lose] *F;* loose *Q.*   24. strife—] *This ed.;* strife: *corr. F;* strife,
Q, uncorr. F.   24.1. [*Enter*] ... SERVUS.] TERENTIVS. SEIANVS. *Q;* TEREN-
TIVS, SEIANVS. *F; Gifford, Barish omit Servus.*   25. Terentius.] TER. *Q; not in*
F.   26. no] *corr. F;* No *Q, uncorr. F.*

10–11. *All ... impudent*] Briggs cites Seneca, *On Benefits*, II.xxvii.4, 'And
just as little does ambition suffer any man to rest content with the measure of
public honours that was once his shameless prayer'.

11–12. *'Tis ... base*] Cf. Tilley, C 586, 'He is noble who hath noble
conditions'.

12. *discerns*] distinguishes (*O.E.D. discern, v.,* 1).

15. *stay*] standstill.

16. *stiff, and many*] steadfast, and many of you.

17–21.] Briggs cites Lucan, *The Civil War*, III.362–6: 'As a gale, unless it
meets with thick-timbered forests, loses strength and is scattered through
empty space, and as a great fire sinks when there is nothing in its way —so the
absence of a foe is destructive to me, and I think my arms wasted if those who
might have been conquered fail to fight against me'.

23. *their conquest*] our conquering them.

28. *routs*] tumultuous mobs.

To view your statue, which, they say, sends forth
A smoke as from a furnace, black and dreadful.   30
Sejanus. Some traitor hath put fire in. You, go see.
    And let the head be taken off, to look
    What 'tis—   [*Exit* SERVUS.]
            Some slave hath practised an imposture
    To stir the people.

            [*Enter*] SATRIUS, NATTA, [*with* SERVUS].

                    How now? Why return you?
Satrius. The head, my lord, already is ta'en off,   35
    I saw it; and, at op'ning, there leapt out
    A great and monstrous serpent!
Sejanus.   Monstrous! Why?
    Had it a beard? And horns? No heart? A tongue
    Forkèd as flattery? Looked it of the hue
    To such as live in great men's bosoms? Was   40
    The spirit of it Macro's?
Natta.   May it please
    The most divine Sejanus, in my days—
    And by his sacred fortune I affirm it—
    I have not seen a more extended, grown,
    Foul, spotted, venomous, ugly—
Sejanus.   O, the fates!   45
    What a wild muster's here of attributes,
    T'express a worm, a snake!
Terentius.   But how that should

33. [*Exit* SERVUS.] *Briggs, Barish, Bolton; Exit Terentius. Gifford.*   34. [*Enter*]
... SERVUS.] *Subst. Briggs, Barish, Bolton; Re-enter Terentius, with Satrius and
Natta. Gifford. Following 34:* SATRIVS. NATTA. *Q;* SATRIVS, NATTA. *F; corr. F
adds in margin To them.*   35. *Satrius.*] SAT. *Q; not in F.*   37. Monstrous!]
Q, F; Monstrous? *Barish.*   45. ugly] *F;* ougly *Q.*   47. snake!] *Barish;*
snake? *Q, F.*

29–37. *your ... serpent*] In two notes, Jonson cites Dio, *Roman History*,
LVIII.7.1, 'Sejanus was ... much more disturbed when from one of his
statues there at first burst forth smoke, and then, when the head was removed
so that the trouble might be investigated, a huge serpent leapt up'.
    39–40. *the hue ... bosoms*] the colour (presumably pale) appropriate to such
men who live under the protection of the great.
    43. *by ... fortune*] Fortuna was worshipped under various aspects and cult-
titles which linked her powers with individuals, groups, and classes.
    44. *extended*] Latin *extendere*, to stretch out.

Come there, my lord!
Sejanus.   What! And you too, Terentius?
I think you mean to make't a prodigy
In your reporting.
Terentius.   Can the wise Sejanus   50
Think heav'n hath meant it less?
Sejanus.   O superstition!
Why, then the falling of our bed, that brake
This morning, burdened with the populous weight
Of our expecting clients to salute us,
Or running of the cat betwixt our legs,   55
As we set forth unto the Capitol,
Were prodigies.
Terentius.   I think them ominous—
And would they had not happened, as today
The fate of some your servants, who, declining
Their way, not able, for the throng, to follow,   60
Slipped down the Gemonies, and brake their necks.
Besides, in taking your last augury,
No prosperous bird appeared, but croaking ravens

---

48. lord!] *corr. F;* Lord? *Q, uncorr. F.*   50. reporting.] reporting? *Q, F.*
50. *Terentius.*] TFR. *Q;* TER. *F.*   59. declining] *F;* diuerting *Q.*

---

49. *prodigy*] ill omen.

52–7.] In two notes Jonson cites Dio, *Roman History*, LVIII.5.5, 'Now on a New Year's day, when all were assembling at Sejanus's house, the couch that stood in the reception room utterly collapsed under the weight of the throng seated upon it; and, as he was leaving the house, a weasel darted through the midst of the crowd'.

54. *expecting*] awaiting.

59–66.] Jonson's two notes to these lines cite Dio, *Roman History*, LVIII.5.6–7: 'After he had sacrificed on the Capitol and was now descending to the Forum, the servants who were acting as his body-guard turned aside along the road leading to the prison, being unable by reason of the crowd to keep up with him, and while they were descending the steps down which condemned criminals were cast, they slipped and fell. Later, as he was taking the auspices, not one bird of good omen appeared, but many crows flew round him and cawed, then all flew off together to the jail and perched there'. Note Jonson's addition, 'and brake their necks.' Jonson's characterisation of Terentius here flies in the face of Dio's statement following the above passage, 'Neither Sejanus nor anyone else took these omens to heart'.

59. *declining*] diverting (thus *Q*)—O.E.D. *decline, v.,* 11b. Jonson's alteration from *Q* may have been a learned pun meant to incorporate both senses.

63. *ravens*] birds of ill omen, forboding death and bringing bad luck.

Flagged up and down, and from the sacrifice
Flew to the prison, where they sat, all night,   65
Beating the air with their obstreperous beaks.
I dare not counsel, but I could entreat
That great Sejanus would attempt the gods,
Once more, with sacrifice.
Sejanus.   What excellent fools
Religion makes of men! Believes Terentius,   70
If these were dangers, as I shame to think them,
The gods could change the certain course of fate?
Or, if they could, they would—now, in a moment—
For a beef's fat, or less, be bribed t'invert
Those long decrees? Then think the gods, like flies,   75
Are to be taken with the steam of flesh
Or blood diffused about their altars; think
Their power as cheap as I esteem it small.
Of all the throng that fill th'Olympian hall,
And, without pity, lade poor Atlas' back,   80
I know not that one deity, but Fortune,
To whom I would throw up, in begging smoke,
One grain of incense, or whose ear I'd buy

---

65. sat] sate *Q, F.*   70. men!] *Barish;* men? *Q, F.*   74. beef's] *Edd.;*
beiues *Q;* beeues *F.*   83. I'd] I'ld *Q, F.*

64. *Flagged*] flapped feebly (*O.E.D. flag, v*I., 3).
65. *the prison*] probably the Tullianum, where state criminals were executed.
66. *Beating*] *O.E.D.*, beat, v., 7, 'Said of the impact of sounds. *arch.* or
Obs.', cites *2H4*, I.iii.91–2, 'with what loud applause / Didst thou beat heaven
with blessing Bolingbroke'.
66. *obstreperous*] clamorous, noisy.
68. *attempt*] try to move.
74. *a beef's fat*] *O.E.D.*, beef, sb., 3b, 'An ox; ... *esp.* a fattened beast, or
its carcase', claims the word is unusual in the singular.
76. *taken with*] captivated, won over by.
79. *Olympian*] of Mount Olympus, where the gods resided in the court of
Jupiter. The earliest example cited in *O.E.D.*, from Philemon Holland,
Plutarch's Morals, is also 1603.
80. *lade ... back*] Riddell, 'Seventeenth-Century Identifications', p. 208,
provides an unconvincing source in Juvenal, *Satires*, XIII.48–9, 'the stars ...
pressed with a lighter load upon the hapless Atlas'. Atlas, of course, was fabled
to hold up the world.
83. *grain of incense*] Jonson cites Plautus, *Poenulus*, II.451 (Jonson quotes I.i
in error) as an example of the phrase '*turis granum*', 'a single grain of incense',
used in a similar tone; and Ovid, *Fasti*, IV, where use of incense in offerings is
frequently mentioned.

With thus much oil. Her I indeed adore,
And keep her grateful image in my house,   85
Sometimes belonging to a Roman king,
But now called mine, as by the better style.
To her I care not if, for satisfying
Your scrupu'lous fant'sies, I go offer. Bid
Our priest prepare us honey, milk, and poppy,   90
His masculine odours and night vestments. Say
Our rites are instant, which performed, you'll see
How vain, and worthy laughter, your fears be. [*Exeunt.*]

       [*Enter*] COTTA [*and*] POMPONIUS.

Cotta. Pomponius! Whither in such speed?
Pomponius.   I go
    To give my lord Sejanus notice—
Cotta.   What?   95

---

89. scrupu'lous] *Q;* scrupulous *F.*   89. fant'sies] *Bolton;* phant'sies *Q, F;*
fancies *Barish.*   93.1. [*Enter*] ... POMPONIUS.] SCENE II./ Another Room
in the same. / Enter Cotta and Pomponius. *Gifford.*   94. *Cotta.*] COT. *Q; not
in F.*   94. Whither] *F;* whether *Q.*

---

83. *whose ear I'd buy*] Riddell, p. 208, offers Persius, *Satires*, II.29–30,
'deorum emeris auriculas'—an identical metaphor.
85–7.] Jonson cites Dio, *Roman History*, LVIII.7.2: '... a statue of Fortune, which had belonged, they say, to Tullius, one of the former kings of
Rome, but was at this time kept by Sejanus at his house and was a source of
great pride to him: he himself saw this statue turn its back to him while he was
sacrificing'. The translation here is perhaps misleading: Dio says only that the
statue turned away—and Jonson's image at V.197–8 below implies that only
her head is turned away.
85. *grateful*] pleasing, welcome (Latin *gratus*, pleasing).
86. *Sometimes*] once.
86. *a Roman king*] Servius Tullius, sixth king of Rome.
89. *scrupu'lous*] distrustful, doubtful (Latin *scrupulus*, anxiety, doubt).
90. *honey, milk, and poppy*] Jonson cites sixteenth-century authorities: Lilius
Gregorius Giraldus, *De Deis Gentium* (Basel, 1548), Syntagma XVII; and
Johann Wilhelm Stuck, *Sacrorum, Sacrificiorumque Gentilium* (Tiguri, 1598).
91. *masculine odours*] *O.E.D.*, *male*, a., 6, quotes W. Phillip, tr., *Linschoten
his ... Voyages* (1598), I.lxxii.119, 'Frankinsence is of two sorts, one white,
that is round and like vnto drops, which is the best, and called the masle; the
other blacke'. See also Jonson's note to *K.Ent.*, 616, which quotes Virgil and
Pliny. Sejanus, of course, is speaking ironically.
91. *night vestments*] Again ironical. Sejanus's contempt for the priest extends
to his vestments, which to Sejanus's mind resemble night attire.
92. *instant*] to be performed immediately (Latin *instans*, pressing, urgent).

Pomponius. Of Macro.

Cotta.   Is he come?

Pomponius.   Entered but now
The house of Regulus.

Cotta.   The opposite consul?

Pomponius. Some half hour since.

Cotta.   And by night too! Stay, sir.
I'll bear you company.

Pomponius.   Along, then—   [*Exeunt.*]

[*Enter*] MACRO, REGULUS [*and* SERVUS.]

Macro. 'Tis Caesar's will to have a frequent Senate,   100
And therefore must your edict lay deep mulct
On such as shall be absent.

Regulus.   So it doth.
Bear it my fellow consul to adscribe.

Macro. And tell him it must early be proclaimed;
The place, Apollo's temple.   [*Exit* SERVUS.]

Regulus.   That's remembered.   105

---

97. consul?] *Q, F;* consul! *Barish.*   98. too!] *F;* too? *Q.*   99.1. [*Enter*] ...
SERVUS.] *This ed.;* MACRO. REGVLVS. LACO. *Q;* MACRO, REGVLVS, LACO.
F; SCENE III. / A Room in Regulus's House. / Enter Macro, Regulus, and
Attendant. *Gifford;* [Act V, Scene ii] / [*Regulus' house. Enter*] MACRO,
REGULUS, [SERVUS] *Bolton;* [*Regulus's house. Enter*] Macro, Regulus, [*and
attendant.*] *Barish.*   100. *Macro.*] MAC. *Q; not in F.*   100. Senate,] Senate.
Q, F.   102. doth.] *F;* doth, *Q.*   103. adscribe] *F;* ascribe *Q.*

96–7. *Entered ... Regulus*] Jonson cites Dio, *Roman History*, LVIII.9.3,
'Macro entered Rome by night ... and communicated his [Tiberius's] instructions to Memmius Regulus, then consul (his colleague [i.e. Fulcinius Trio]
sided with Sejanus), and to Graecinius Laco, commander of the night-watch'.

97. *opposite*] see prev. note (Latin *oppositus*, opposing, set against).

100. *frequent*] fully attended (*L.&S.*, *frequens*, II; *senatus frequens* is the
usual expression).

101. *your edict*] Jonson cites, as sources of examples of such edicts, Tacitus,
Annals, I; Livy, Book II; Sextus Pompeius Festus, *De Verborum Significatione*,
Book XV; Brisson, *De formulis*, Book I; and Justus Lipsius, *Satyra Menippaea*.

101. *mulct*] fine.

103. *adscribe*] add his name to it, sign—the first example in this sense cited
in *O.E.D.* The latinised spelling is uncommon.

105. *The ... temple*] Jonson cites as his authority Dio, *Roman History*,
LVIII.9.4, 'the senate was to sit in the temple of Apollo'. This temple, on
the Palatine hill, had been repaired by Augustus, who endowed it with an
important library.

Macro. And at what hour.
Regulus.   Yes.
Macro.   You do forget
    To send one for the provost of the watch?
Regulus. I have not: here he comes.

                    [*Enter* LACO.]

Macro.   Gracinus Laco,
    You'are a friend most welcome. By and by
    I'll speak with you. [*To Regulus.*] You must procure
        this list   110
    Of the praetorian cohorts, with the names
    Of the centurions, and their tribunes.
Regulus.   Ay.
Macro. I bring you letters and a health from Caesar.
Laco. Sir, both come well.
Macro. [*To Regulus.*]   And hear you—with your note,
    Which are the eminent men, and most of action.   115
Regulus. That shall be done you too.
Macro.   Most worthy Laco,
    Caesar salutes you.   *The consul goes out.*
                    Consul! Death and furies!
    Gone now? The argument will please you, sir.
    Ho! Regulus? The anger of the gods
    Follow his diligent legs, and overtake 'em,   120
    In likeness of the gout.
                              [*The consul*] *returns.*
                    O, good my lord,
    We lacked you present. I would pray you send
    Another to Fulcinius Trio straight,

---

106. hour.] *F; howre? Q.*   109. You'are] *Q, F;* You are *Q, H.&S.*
114. you—] *This ed.;* you, *Q, F;* you? *Barish.*   117. *The . . . out.*] *Marginal
s.d. in F; not in Q.*   119. Regulus?] *Q, F;* Regulus! *Barish.*   120. his] *F;*
your *Q.*   120. overtake] ouer'take *Q;* ouer-take *F.*   121. *returns.*] *Marginal
s.d. in F; not in Q.*

---

    107. *provost . . . watch*] Jonson cites the passage quoted at v.96–7n.
    111–12. *praetorian . . . tribunes*] At this time there were nine praetorian
cohorts, each with up to 1000 men and under the command of its military
tribune, and subdivided into *centuriae* commanded by centurions.
    113. *letters . . . Caesar*] Jonson cites the same passage—see v.96–7n.

To tell him you will come and speak with him—
The matter we'll devise—to stay him there,   125
While I, with Laco, do survey the watch.
                       [The consul] goes out again.
What are your strengths, Gracinus?
Laco.   Seven cohorts.
Macro. You see what Caesar writes; and—gone again?
H'has sure a vein of Mercury in his feet.
Know you what store of the praetorian soldiers   130
Sejanus holds about him for his guard?
Laco. I cannot the just number—but I think
Three centuries.
Macro.   Three? Good.
Laco.   At most, not four.
Macro. And who be those centurions?
Laco.   That the consul
Can best deliver you.
Macro.   When h'is away—   135
Spite on his nimble industry. Gracinus,
You find what place you hold there in the trust
Of royal Caesar?
Laco.   Ay, and I am—
Macro.   Sir,
The honours there proposed are but beginnings
Of his great favours.
Laco.   They are more—
Macro.   I heard him   140

126.1. *goes out again.*] *Marginal s.d. in* F; *not in* Q.   129. Mercury] Q, *Bolton;* mercury F, *Barish.*   130. Know] *Barish;* Knew Q, F.   135. away—] *This ed.;* away, Q; away F; away? *Barish.*

127. *Seven cohorts*] Jonson cites his authorities: Joannes Rosinus, *Antiquitatum Romanarum* (Basel, 1583), Book VII, and the direct source, Dio, *Roman History*, LV.26.4–5: 'When many parts of the city were at this time [A.D. 6] destroyed by fire, [Augustus] organized a company of freedmen, in seven divisions, to render assistance on such occasions, and appointed a knight in command over them.... They have barracks in the city and draw pay from the public treasury.'
129. *a vein ... feet*] A punning allusion to Mercury, messenger of the gods.
132. *cannot*] do not know (*to can* = to know. *Obs.*).
132. *just*] precise.
133. *centuries*] See V.111–12n.

When he did study what to add—
Laco.   My life,
And all I hold—
Macro.   You were his own first choice,
Which doth confirm as much as you can speak;
And will, if we succeed, make more—Your guards
Are seven cohorts, you say?
Laco.   Yes.
Macro.   Those we must   145
Hold still in readiness, and undischarged.
Laco. I understand so much. But how it can—
Macro. Be done without suspicion, you'll object?
                                    [*The consul*] *returns.*
Regulus. What's that?
Laco.   The keeping of the watch in arms
When morning comes.
Macro.   The Senate shall be met, and set   150
So early in the temple, as all mark
Of that will be avoided.
Regulus.   If we need,
We have commission to possess the palace,
Enlarge Prince Drusus, and make him our chief.
Macro. [*Aside.*] That secret would have burnt his reverend
       mouth,   155
Had he not spit it out now. [*To Regulus.*] By the gods,
You carry things too—Let me borrow'a man
Or two, to bear these—   [*Exit* REGULUS.]
       [*To Laco.*] That of freeing Drusus

148.1. *returns.*] *Marginal s.d. in corr. F; not in Q, uncorr. F.*   158. [*Exit*
REGULUS.] *This ed. (also his re-entry at 160).*   158. [*To Laco.*] *This ed.*

145–52. *Those ... avoided*] Jonson cites Dio, *Roman History*, LVIII.9.5–
6: Macro's 'stationing the night-watch about the temple' occurred after the
sitting of the senate had begun.
   151. *mark*] notice.
   153–4.] Jonson cites Tacitus, *Annals*, VI.xxiii: 'Macro's orders were, if
Sejanus appealed to arms, to withdraw the youth from custody (he was
confined in the Palace) and to place him at the head of the people'; and
Suetonius, *Lives*, III.lxv—the same information.
   154. *Enlarge*] free.
   155. *his ... mouth*] alluding to the religious functions of the consulship.
Latin *os*, the mouth, was used to express character, *e.g. os durum*, brazen
face, or *os molle*, a bashful fellow. Jonson is being learned (and punning) again.

Caesar projected as the last, and utmost;
Not else to be remembered.

[*Enter* REGULUS *with* SERVI.]

Regulus.   Here are servants.   160
Macro. [*Giving letters.*] These to Arruntius, these to Lepidus,
    This bear to Cotta, this to Latiaris.
    If they demand you'of me, say I have ta'en
    Fresh horse, and am departed.   [*Exeunt* SERVI.]
                You, my lord,
    To your colleague; and be you sure to hold him   165
    With long narration of the new fresh favours
    Meant to Sejanus, his great partron. I,
    With trusted Laco here, are for the guards—
    Then, to divide. For night hath many eyes,
    Whereof, though most do sleep, yet some are spies.
                      [*Exeunt.*]   170

[*Enter*] TUBICINES, TIBICINES, PRAECONES, FLAMEN, MINISTRI,
    SEJANUS, TERENTIUS, SATRIUS, [NATTA,] *etc.*

Praeco. Be all profane far hence. Fly, fly far off.

169. For] *F;* "For *Q.*   170. Whereof] *F;* "Whereof *Q.*   170.1–2. [*Enter*]
... &c.] *This ed.;* TVBICINES. TIBICINES. / PRAECONES. / FLAMEN.
MINISTRI. / SEIANVS. TERENTIVS. SATRIVS. &c. *Q*; PRAECONES, / FLAMEN,
MINISTRI, / SEIANVS, TERENTIVS, SATRIVS, &c. *F; Scene IV in Gifford, iii in
Bolton. Location given by Barish, Bolton: Sejanus's house; by Gifford: A Sacellum
(or Chapel) in Sejanus's House. These edd. add Tubicines, Tibicines, Natta to F
list.*   171. *Praeco.*] PRAE. *Q; not in F.*   171–2. Be ... profane.] *Caps. in
Q, except* Fly, fly far off. / Be absent far. *in italics; all in italics, F.*   171. off]
F; of *Q.*

159. *last, and utmost*] final resort.
163. *demand ... me*] ask you about me.
169. *night ... eyes*] Proverbial (though not in Tilley).
170.1. [*TUBICINES, TIBICINES*]] Trumpeters and flautists. Jonson
notes that these were a part of every sacrifice, citing secondary sources:
Rosinus, *Antiquitatum Romanarum*, Book III, and Stuck, *Sacrorum, Sacrificiorumque Gentilium*, p. 72.
170.1. *FLAMEN*] a priest, generally of a particular deity. On the *flamines
curiales* (priests of the districts of Rome) Jonson refers his readers to Lilius
Gregorius Giraldus, *De Deis Gentium*, XVII, and to Onofrio Panvinio, *Rei-
publicae Romanae*, commentary II.
171. *Be all profane far hence*] Glancing at Brisson, Rosinus, Stuck and
Giraldus, Jonson notes that the heralds always preceded the priest, prevent-

Be absent far. Far hence be all profane.
Tubicines, tibicines sound while the flamen washeth.
Flamen. We have been faulty, but repent us now,
And bring pure hands, pure vestments, and pure minds.
[*1*] *Minister.* Pure vessels.
[*2*] *Minister.*   And pure off'rings.
[*3*] *Minister.*   Garlands pure.   175
Flamen. Bestow your garlands; and, with reverence, place
The vervin on the altar.
Praeco.   Favour your tongues.
Flamen. Great mother Fortune, queen of human state,

172.1. *Tubicines . . . washeth.*] *Marginal s.d. in corr.* F; TVB. TIB. These sound, while the *Flamen* washeth. *Q, uncorr,* F.   174. pure hands . . . minds] *Italics except* and, *Q,* F.   175.] *italics except* And, *Q,* F.   175. Garlands] *F;* Ghyrlonds *Q. So 176.*   177. Favour . . . tongues.] *Caps., Q; italics,* F. 178. human] humane *Q,* F.   178–81.] *Italics, except* FORTVNE, *Q,* F.

ing the presence of any profane thing. The standard beginning of sacred ceremonies, *Procul o, procul este, profani*, is quoted in transtation by Jonson exactly in this line. For a concise modern treatment of this and other topics relevant to this scene, see William W. Fowler, *The Religious Experience of the Roman People* (London, 1911), esp. Lecture VIII, 'The Ritual of the *Ius Divinum*'.
    172.1. while the flamen washeth] Referring to Giraldus, *De Deis Gentium*, XVII, Jonson notes that the ritual demanded that the priest first wash himself and repent of any faults or offences.
    175.] Naming Virgil, Martial, Tibullus, and Ovid as authorities, Jonson notes the ancient insistence that everything connected with the sacrifice—the hands, the clothes, the vessels—be pure.
    176–7. *Bestow . . . altar*] Jonson notes that it was customary to furnish the altar with flowers and to place *verbenae* (vervin)—branches of laurel, olive, myrtle, cypress, etc.—upon it.
    177, 182. *Favour your tongues* and *Favour . . . tongues*] Jonson notes that the phrase *favete linguis*, originally a call to utter *bona verba*, good words, became in the ritual of sacrifice a call to keep silent. Seneca discusses it in *On the Happy Life*, XXVI.vii, which Jonson cites. Latin *faveo* is followed by a direct object in the dative. However, in the Latin phrase, *linguis* is ablative, not dative (since it is not the direct object and means 'with your tongues'). Jonson equivocates: at 177 he takes it as dative, at 182, correctly, as ablative. On the interpretation of the phrase, he cites, besides Seneca, Servius Honoratus and Aelius Donatus, who wrote commentaries on Virgil in the late fourth century, specifically their comments on *Aeneid*, V.71; Brisson, *De formulis*, Book I; Ovid, *Fasti*, I.71; and *Metamorphoses*, XV.681–2. Herrick borrowed this and other of Jonson's phrases from this passage for his *The Faerie Temple: or, Oberon's Chapell*. See the *Works*, ed. L. C. Martin (Oxford, 1956), pp. 91, 520.
    178–81.] An established formula, Jonson notes, used in sacred rites.

> Rectress of action, arbitress of fate,
> To whom all sway, all power, all empire bows,   180
> Be present, and propitious to our vows.

Praeco. Favour it with your tongues.

Minister. Be present, and propitious to our vows.

> *Tubicines, tibicines [sound again].*
>
> *While they sound again, the flamen takes of the honey with his finger,
> and tastes, then ministers to all the rest; so of the milk, in an earthen
> vessel, he deals about. Which done, he sprinkleth upon the altar milk,
> then imposeth the honey, and kindleth his gums, and after censing about
> the altar, placeth his censer thereon, into which they put several branches
> of poppy, and the music ceasing, say all,*

All. Accept our off'ring, and be pleased, great goddess.

Terentius. See, see, the image stirs!

Satrius.   And turns away!   185

Natta. Fortune averts her face!

Flamen.   Avert, you gods,

---

182. Favour ... tongues] *Caps., Q; italics, F.*   183. Be ... vows] *Italics, Q,
F.*   183.1. *Tubicines ... again*].] *This ed.;* TVBICINES. TIBICINES. *Q; not in
F.*   183.1–183.7.] *Q, in text as here; in margin beginning alongside 184, F.
H.&S. incorrectly begin it alongside 177. Barish, Bolton, following H.&S. rather
than F, incorrectly place the s.d. between 177 and 178.*   183.7. *say all*] *Q;
proceed F, where Q reading would be inappropriate at end of F's long marginal
s.d. terminating alongside 205.*   184. *All.*] *This ed.; implied in s.d., Q; not in F.
Omnes. Gifford.*   184. Accept ... goddess] *Italics except* Goddesse, *Q; italics,
F.*

---

179. *Rectress*] governor.

183.2–7. takes ... poppy] Jonson's note informs us that this was called
the libation rite. He cites Rosinus, Book III; Brisson, Book I; Stuck; and
Giraldus, XVII.

183.3. the milk] Citing the same authorities, Jonson notes that milk, not
wine, was used in the libation rite in (non-intoxicating) sacrifices to Fortuna.

183.5. kindleth] inflames.

183.6–7. into ... poppy] Citing the third-century grammarian Nonius
Marcellus and Macrobius's *Saturnalia* (as well as 'Plaut. Suet. Senec. &c' for
good measure!) Jonson points out that this offering, at the end of the sacrifice,
was intended to propitiate the goddess and to have one's prayers answered.

184.] A solemn formula, Jonson notes, used in making offerings to
Fortuna.

186. *Fortune ... face*] See V.85–7n. The statue does not simply swivel
around, but—more effective theatrically—turns only its head, neck, and
torso away, so that Sejanus can mock it with its 'neck / Writhed to [its] tail,
like a ridiculous cat' at ll. 197–8. Thus in a performance it must be represented by an actor—a stage statue will not do. For this reason, Gifford's s.d. at

The prodigy. Still! Still! Some pious rite
We have neglected. Yet! Heav'n, be appeased.
And be all tokens false, or void, that speak
Thy present wrath.
Sejanus.   Be thou dumb, scrupu'lous priest;   190
And gather up thyself, with these thy wares,
Which I, in spite of thy blind mistress, or
Thy juggling mystery, religion, throw
Thus, scornèd, on the earth.

>   [*Sweeps the altar clean.*]
>   Nay, hold thy look
Averted, till I woo thee turn again;   195
And thou shalt stand to all posterity
Th'eternal game and laughter, with thy neck
Writhed to thy tail, like a ridiculous cat.
Avoid these fumes, these superstitious lights,
And all these coz'ning ceremonies—you,   200
Your pure and spicèd conscience!

>   [*Exeunt all but Sejanus, Terentius, Satrius, and Natta.*]
>   I, the slave

---

190. scrupu'lous] *Q;* scrupulous *F.*   194. Thus, scornèd,] *This ed.;* Thus,
scorned *Q, F;* Thus scornèd *Barish.*   194. [*Sweeps . . . clean.*] *This ed.;*
[*Overturns the statue and the altar.*] *Gifford, Barish.*   195. woo] *F;* woe *Q.*
195. thee] *Q;* thee, *F;* thee; *Barish.*   200. ceremonies—] *This ed.;* Ceremonies; *Q;* ceremonies: *F.*   200. you,] *F;* You. *Q.*   201. [*Exeunt . . .
Natta.*] *Gifford.*

194, *Overturns the statue and the altar,* cannot be what Jonson intended, since
no actor could stiffly maintain the required posture during and after falling.
    186. *averts . . . Avert*] Jonson puns on the meanings of the word (Latin
averto allows a similar ambiguity).
    187. *prodigy*] portent, ill omen.
    187. *Still!*] even yet!
    189. *tokens*] divine signs.
    190. *scrupu'lous*] punctiliously careful and exact—*O.E.D.*, *scrupulous*, 5,
gives the first instance of this sense as 1638, but it fits better than the other
senses the context here. However, the word may carry for the learned Jonson
the secondary sense of Latin *scrupulus*, uneasiness, anxiety, doubt.
    193. *juggling mystery*] deceiving trade.
    195. *woo thee turn again*] 'to' is understood after 'thee'.
    197. *game*] mockery.
    197–8. *with . . . tail*] See V.85–7n.
    199. *Avoid*] clear away.
    200. *coz'ning*] fraudulent.
    201. *spicèd*] precise, over-scrupulous (*O.E.D. spiced, ppl. a.,* 2).

And mock of fools, scorn on my worthy head,
That have been titled and adored a god,
Yea, sacrificed unto, myself, in Rome,
No less than Jove—and I be brought to do   205
A peevish giglot rites? Perhaps the thought
And shame of that made Fortune turn her face,
Knowing herself the lesser deity,
And but my servant. Bashful queen, if so,
Sejanus thanks thy modesty. Who's that?   210

                   [*Enter*] POMPONIUS [*and*] MINUTIUS.

Pomponius. His fortune suffers, till he hears my news.
        I'have waited here too long. Macro, my lord—
Sejanus. Speak lower, and withdraw.   [*Takes him aside.*]
Terentius.   Are these things true?
Minutius. Thousands are gazing at it, in the streets.
Sejanus. What's that?
Terentius.   Minutius tells us here, my lord,   215
        That, a new head being set upon your statue,
        A rope is since found weathed about it; and,
        But now, a fiery meteor, in the form

202. fools,] *Q, F*; fools? *Barish.*   202. head,] *Q*; head *F*; head! *Barish.*
210.1. [*Enter*] . . . MINUTIUS.] POMPONIVS. MINVTIVS. &c. *Q*; POMPONIVS,
SEIANVS, MINVTIVS, &c. *F.*   211. *Pomponius.*] POM. *Q*; *not in F.*
212. I'have] *Q, H.&S.*; I haue *F.*   213. [*Takes him aside.*]] *Gifford.*
216. statue,] *F*; Statue. *Q.*

203–4. *That . . . unto*] In two notes to these lines, Jonson cites Tacitus,
Annals, IV.lxxiv: the senate 'voted an altar of Mercy and an altar of Friend
ship with statues of the Caesar and Sejanus on either hand, and with reiterated
petitions conjured the pair to vouchsafe themselves to sight' (neither, however, had returned to Rome at that time); and Dio, *Roman History*, LVIII.4.4:
'And in the end they sacrificed to the images of Sejanus as they did to those of
Tiberius'.
206. *giglot*] at this time, a wanton woman. Shakespeare uses it in three
plays, *1H6*, IV.vii.41; *M.M.*, V.i.345; and *Cym.*, III.i.31, the last in reference
to Fortune ('O, giglot fortune!').
210.1. *MINUTIUS*] Jonson cites Tacitus, *Annals*, VI.vii—see IV.409.1n.
211.] As *H.&S.* observe, a nice ironic touch.
217. *A rope . . . it*] Jonson cites Dio, *Roman History*, LVIII.7.2: when the
head was replaced on Sejanus's statue, 'a rope was discovered coiled about
the neck of the statue'.
218–21. *a fiery . . . multitude*] Jonson cites Seneca, *Natural Questions*, I.i.3:
'we have more than once seen a flaming light in the shape of a huge ball

Of a great ball, was seen to roll along
The troubled air, where yet it hangs, unperfect,   220
The'amazing wonder of the multitude!
Sejanus. No more. That Macro's come is more than all!
Terentius. Is Macro come?
Pomponius.   I saw him.
Terentius.   Where? With whom?
Pomponius. With Regulus.
Sejanus.   Terentius—
Terentius.   My lord?
Sejanus. Send for the tribunes, we will straight have up   225
More of the soldiers for our guard. [*Exit* TERENTIUS.]
                                    Minutius,
We pray you, go for Cotta, Latiaris,
Trio the consul, or what senators
You know are sure, and ours.   [*Exit* MINUTIUS.]
                                    You, my good Natta,
For Laco, provost of the watch.   [*Exit* NATTA.]
                                    Now, Satrius,   230
The time of proof comes on. Arm all our servants,
And without tumult.   [*Exit* SATRIUS.]
                                    You, Pomponius,
Hold some good correspondence with the consul;
Attempt him, noble friend.   [*Exit* POMPONIUS.]
                                    These things begin

---

221. The'amazing] *Q, H.&S.;* The amazing *F.*

which was then dissipated in mid-flight'; one was seen 'at the time when
Sejanus was condemned'. Loeb ed., tr. T. H. Corcoran (London, 1971).
    220. *unperfect*] its flight unfinished.
    221. *amazing*] striking with amazement.
    225. *the tribunes*] i.e. the military tribunes commanding the praetorian
cohorts. Jonson cites Dio, *Roman History*, LVIII.9.5, which makes it clear
that Sejanus, before entering the senate-chamber, had been guarded by a
praetorian detachment.
    231. *proof*] testing—perhaps referring to the loyalty of the servants, which
will be tested when they are armed.
    233. *correspondence*] communication. Cf. IV.511 and n.
    233. *the consul*] i.e. Regulus; Trio (228-9) is 'sure'.
    234. *Attempt*] attempt to influence.
    234-8. *These ... still*] As Briggs points out, from Lucan, *The Civil War*,
V.653-4, 'Caesar considers at last that the danger is on a scale to match his
destiny'; and IX.581-3, 'Men who doubt and are ever uncertain of future

To look like dangers, now, worthy my fates.   235
Fortune, I see thy worst. Let doubtful states
And things uncertain hang upon thy will;
Me surest death shall render certain still.
Yet why is now my thought turned toward death,
Whom fates have let go on so far in breath,   240
Unchecked or unreproved? I, that did help
To fell the lofty cedar of the world,
Germanicus; that, at one stroke, cut down
Drusus, that upright elm; withered his vine;
Laid Silius and Sabinus, two strong oaks,   245
Flat on the earth; besides those other shrubs,
Cordus and Sosia, Claudia Pulchra,
Furnius and Gallus, which I have grubbed up;
And since, have set my axe so strong and deep
Into the root of spreading Agrippine;   250
Lopped off and scattered her proud branches, Nero,
Drusus, and Caius too, although replanted—
If you will, destinies, that, after all,

---

236. Let] *F;* "Let *Q.*   237–8.] *Both lines preceded by gnomic pointing, Q.*
239. turned] turn'd *Q, F; turnèd Barish.*

---

events—let *them* cry out for prophets: I draw my assurance from no oracle
but from the sureness of death'.
   241–3. *I ... Germanicus*] Jonson cites Tacitus, *Annals*, I.lxix: Sejanus had
been 'sowing the seed of future hatreds' between Germanicus and Tiberius
since the time of the former's campaigns in Germany. The imagery here and
in the following lines, *H.&S.* point out, was imitated by Fletcher in *The
False One* (c. 1620), IV.iii, 'I cut the Cedar *Pompey*, and I'le fell / This huge
Oake *Caesar* too'. However, the cedar image was not uncommonly applied to
great men at the time, particularly James I.
   243–52.] In six short notes on the characters mentioned here, Jonson cites
passages in Tacitus, Dio and Suetonius he has already cited earlier and which
have been reproduced above at the relevant points.
   244. *his vine*] i.e. Livia. The vine trained upon the elm was a common
image for marriage in Latin literature, and popular with the Elizabethans:
Shakespeare, *C.E.*, II.ii.173, 'Thou art an elm, my husband, I a vine';
M.N.D., IV.i.40–1, 'The female ivy so / Enrings the barky fingers of the elm'.
   253–64. *If ... second*] This, as Briggs points out, echoes Lucan, *The Civil
War*, V.659–60, 'Although the date, hastened on by destiny, cuts short a
great career, my achievements are sufficient'; III.108–12, 'Caesar was all in
all, and the Senate met to register the utterance of a private man. Should he
demand kingly power and divine honours for himself, or execution and exile
for the Senate, the assembled Fathers were ready to give their sanction.

I faint now, ere I touch my period,
You are but cruel; and I already'have done   255
Things great enough. All Rome hath been my slave.
The Senate sat an idle looker-on
And witness of my power, when I have blushed
More to command, than it to suffer. All
The fathers have sat ready and prepared   260
To give me empire, temples, or their throats,
When I would ask 'em. And, what crowns the top,
Rome, Senate, people, all the world have seen
Jove but my equal, Caesar but my second.
'Tis then your malice, fates, who, but your own,   265
Envy and fear t'have any power long known.   [Exit.]

          [Enter] TERENTIUS [and] TRIBUNI.

Terentius. Stay here. I'll give his lordship you are come.

          [Enter] MINUTIUS, COTTA, [and] LATIARIS.

Minutius. Marcus Terentius, pray you tell my lord
     Here's Cotta and Latiaris.
Terentius.   Sir, I shall.   [Exit.]
          [Cotta and Latiaris] confer their letters.

---

255. already'have] Q, H.&S.; already haue F.   257. sat] sate Q, F.
260. sat] sate Q, F.   264. equal] F; aequall Q.   265–6.] Both lines preceded
by gnomic pointing, Q.   266.1. [Enter] . . . TRIBUNI] TERENTIVS. TRIBVNES.
Q; TERENTIUS, TRIBUNES. F; SCENE V. / A Room in the same. / Enter
Terentius and Tribunes. Gifford.   267. Terentius.] TER. Q; not in F.
267.1. [Enter] . . . LATIARIS.] MINVTIVS. COTTA. LATIARIS. &c. Q; MINV-
TIVS, COTTA, LATIARIS. F.
268. Minutius.] MIN. Q; not in F.   269. [Exit.] Bolton omits.   269.1. [Cotta
. . . letters.] Marginal s.d. in F at 268: They confer their letters. Not in Q.

Fortunately, there were more things that he was ashamed to decree than
Romans were ashamed to allow'; and V.662, 'Rome has seen me take
precedence of Magnus [Magnum mihi . . . secundum]'.
     253. destinies] the three Fates or Parcae which, according to Greek and
Roman mythology, determined one's course of life. Traditionally represented
as jealous (265–6 below).
     254. period] goal. As the sentence is long, there may be a pun intended
here (Latin periodus, a complete sentence, a period). See Arthur F. Marotti,
'The Self-Reflexive Art of Ben Jonson's Sejanus, T.S.L.L., XII (1970), 201.
     258. blushed] been ashamed.
     267. give] inform.
     269.1. confer] compare (O.E.D. confer, v., 4).

Cotta. My letter is the very same with yours;   270
　　Only requires me to be present there,
　　And give my voice, to strengthen his design.
Latiaris. Names he not what it is?
Cotta.   No, nor to you.
Latiaris. 'Tis strange, and singular doubtful!
Cotta.   So it is!
　　It may be all is left to lord Sejanus.   275

　　　　　　[*Enter*] NATTA [*and*] LACO.

Natta. Gentlemen, where's my lord?
Tribunus.   We wait him here.
Cotta. The provost Laco? What's the news?
Latiaris.   My lord—

　　　　[*Enter*] SEJANUS [*and*] TERENTIUS.

Sejanus. Now, my right dear, noble, and trusted friends.
　　How much I am a captive to your kindness!
　　Most worthy Cotta, Latiaris; Laco,   280
　　Your valiant hand; and gentlemen, your loves.
　　I wish I could divide myself unto you;
　　Or that it lay within our narrow powers
　　To satisfy for so enlargèd bounty.
　　Gracinus, we much pray you, hold your guards   285
　　Unquit when morning comes. Saw you the consul?
Minutius. Trio will presently be here, my lord.
Cotta. They are but giving order for the edict,

---

270. yours;] *Q, F;* yours, *Barish.*   272. voice,] *Q, F;* voice *Barish.*
274. is!] *Q;* is? *F.*   275.1. [*Enter*] . . . LACO.] NATTA. LACO. &c *Q;* NATTA,
LACO. *F.*   275.1.] *Marginal s.d. in F: To them.; not in Q.*   276. *Natta.*]
NAT. *Q; not in F.*   277. Laco?] *Q, F;* Laco! *Barish.*   277.1. [*Enter*] . . .
TERENTIUS.] *This ed.;* SEIANVS. TERENTIVS. &c. *Q;* SEIANVS. *F; Barish*
leaves Terentius off.   277.1.] *Marginal s.d. in F: To them.; not in Q.*
278. *Sejanus.*] SEI *Q; not in F.*   278. friends.] *This ed.;* Friends; *Q;* friends;
F; friends, *Barish.*   280. Latiaris;] *F;* Latiaris, *Q.*

---

　274. *singular doubtful*] strangely ambiguous.
　286. *Unquit*] undischarged. This is the only example in *O.E.D.*
　288–90. *They . . . temple*] Jonson cites Dio, *Roman History,* LVIII.9.4: 'the
senate was to sit in the temple of Apollo'. Trio and Regulus, as consuls,
would have called the senators together although Dio does not actually say
this. See V.103 above.

    To warn the Senate.
Sejanus.   How! The Senate?
Latiaris.   Yes.
    This morning, in Apollo's temple.
Cotta.   We   290
    Are charged by letter to be there, my lord.
Sejanus. By letter? Pray you let's see.
Latiaris.   Knows not his lordship?
Cotta. It seems so!
Sejanus.   A Senate warned? Without my knowledge?
    And on this sudden? Senators by letters
    Requirèd to be there! Who brought these?
Cotta.   Macro.   295
Sejanus. Mine enemy! And when?
Cotta.   This midnight.
Sejanus.   Time,
    With every other circumstance, doth give
    It hath some strain of engine in't!—How now?

           [*Enter*] SATRIUS.

Satrius. My lord, Sertorius Macro is without,
    Alone, and prays t'have private conference   300
    In business of high nature with your lordship,
    He says to me, and which regards you much.

---

292. lordship?] Lorsh? *Q;* lordship! *F.*   294. sudden] sodaine *Q, F.*
295. there!] *F;* there? *Q.*   297. every] eu'ry *Q, F.*   298.1. [*Enter*]
SATRIUS.] SATRIVS, &c. *Q;* SATRIVS, SEIANVS, &c. *F.*   299. *Satrius.*] SAT.
Q; not in F.   303. withdraw.] withdraw, *Q, F.*

   293. *warned*] officially summoned.
   296. *Mine enemy*] Jonson cites 'Dio. *ibid.*' superfluously—it is obvious
from previous citations that Macro is Sejanus's enemy!
   297. *give*] show.
   298. *engine*] machination.
   299. *Macro is without*] Jonson cites Dio, *Roman History*, LVIII.9.4: 'Macro
ascended the Palatine (for the senate was to sit in the temple of Apollo), and
encountering Sejanus, who had not yet gone in, and perceiving that he was
troubled because Tiberius had sent him no message, he encouraged him,
telling him aside and in confidence that he was bringing him the tribunician
power'.
   299. *without*] outside.
   302. *regards*] affects.

Sejanus. Let him come here.
Satrius.   Better, my lord, withdraw.
        You will betray what store and strength of friends
        Are now about you, which he comes to spy.   305
Sejanus. Is he not armed?
Satrius.   We'll search him.
Sejanus.   No, but take
        And lead him to some room where you, concealed,
        May keep a guard upon us.   [*Exit* SATRIUS.]
                                  Noble Laco,
        You are our trust—and, till our own cohorts
        Can be brought up, your strengths must be our guard.   310
                                  He salutes them humbly.
        Now, good Minutius, honoured Latiaris,
        Most worthy, and my most unwearied friends,
        I return instantly.   [*Exit.*]
Latiaris.   Most worthy lord!
Cotta. His lordship is turned instant kind, methinks.
        I'have not observed it in him heretofore.   315
1 Tribunus. 'Tis true, and it becomes him nobly.
Minutius.   I
        Am rapt withal.
2 Tribunus.   By Mars, he has my lives,
        Were they a million, for this only grace.
Laco. Ay, and to name a man!
Latiaris.   As he did me!
Minutius. And me!
Latiaris.   Who would not spend his life and fortunes   320
        To purchase but the look of such a lord?

310. guard.] *F*; Guard, *Q*.   310.1. *He ... humbly.*] *Marginal s.d. in F; not in*
Q.   314. methinks.] me thinks, *Q*; me thinkes, *F*.   319. man!] *F*; man?
Q.

---

    304. *store*] number.
    307. *some room*] probably represented by the upper stage or gallery.
    313. *instantly*] in a moment.
    314. *instant*] suddenly.
    317. *rapt withal*] enraptured likewise.
    317–18. *my ... million*] Cf. *E.M.I.*, III.i.131–2, 'I had beene slaine, if I
had had a million of liues'.
    318. *only*] single.
    319. *name*] call by some title ('Noble Laco ... good Minutius, honoured
Latiaris'). Cf. v.504–5, 543.

Laco. [*Aside.*] He that would nor be lord's fool, nor the
world's.
[*Exeunt.*]

[*Enter*] SEJANUS, MACRO, [*and* SATRIUS].

Sejanus. Macro! Most welcome, as most coveted friend!
Let me enjoy my longings. When arrived you?
Macro. About the noon of night.
Sejanus.   Satrius, give leave.   325
[*Exit* SATRIUS.]
Macro. I have been, since I came, with both the consuls,
On a particular design from Caesar.
Sejanus. How fares it with our great and royal master?
Macro. Right plentifully well, as with a prince
That still holds out the great proportion   330
Of his large favours, where his judgement hath
Made once divine election—like the god,
That wants not, nor is wearied to bestow
Where merit meets his bounty, as it doth

322.1. [*Exeunt.*]] *Barish omits.*   322.2. [*Enter*] ... SATRIUS.]] *Barish;*
SCENE VI. / Another Room in the same. / *Enter Sejanus, Macro, and Satrius.*
Gifford; Curtain drawn, disclosing another room. Briggs; [Act V, Scene iv] /
[*Another room in Sejanus' house. Enter*] SEJANUS, MACRO, / SATRIUS. *Bolton.*
323. *Sejanus.*] SEI. *Q; not in F.*   323. friend!] *F;* friend, *Q.*   332. god,] *Q,*
F; god *Barish.*

323–99.] Barish, p. 201, suggests the gallery for this interview.
323. *Macro* ... *welcome*] Jonson again cites Dio, *Roman History,*
LVIII.9.4; see V.299 n. above.
323. *coveted*] desired, wished-for.
325. *the noon of night*] Jonson cites Nonius Marcellus's quoting of the
phrase *noctis circiter meridiem* from Varro's *Marcipor. H.&S.,* following
Whalley and Gifford, quote Jacobean and later examples of the phrase, which
they assume Jonson first used in English. However, Jonson was anticipated by
Alexander Scott who, in his *Poems* of *c.* 1560 (Scottish Text Society, 1896;
Early English Text Society, 1902), iv. 66, uses the phrase 'At nonetyd of the
nicht'.
325. *give leave*] either 'give us leave to speak alone', or 'give yourself
leave'—neither sense in *O.E.D.*
327. *design*] mission.
330–1. *That – favours*] Jonson again cites Dio, *Roman History,* LVIII.9.4
('he encouraged him').
330. *great proportion*] large bounty.
333. *wants*] fails.

In you, already the most happy,'and ere   335
The sun shall climb the south, most high Sejanus.
Let not my lord be'amused. For to this end
Was I by Caesar sent for, to the isle,
With special caution to conceal my journey;
And thence had my dispatch as privately   340
Again to Rome; charged to come here by night;
And only to the consuls make narration
Of his great purpose—that the benefit
Might come more full and striking, by how much
It was less looked for or aspired by you,   345
Or least informèd to the common thought.
Sejanus. What may this be? Part of myself, dear Macro!
    If good, speak out, and share with your Sejanus.
Macro. If bad, I should forever loathe myself
    To be the messenger to so good a lord.   350
    I do exceed m'instructions, to acquaint
    Your lordship with thus much; but 'tis my venture
    On your retentive wisdom—and because
    I would no jealous scruple should molest
    Or rack your peace of thought. For I assure   355
    My noble lord, no senator yet knows
    The business meant; though all, by several letters,
    Are warnèd to be there, and give their voices,
    Only to add unto the state and grace

---

335. happy,'and] *Q, H.&S.;* happy, and *F.*   339. With] *corr. F;* Which *Q,*
uncorr. F.   347. Macro!] *corr. F; Macro, Q;* MACRO, *uncorr. F.*

336. *high*] a pun on the idea of execution.
337. *amused*] puzzled. This antedates *O.E.D.*'s first citation, Chapman's
Monsieur d'Olive, by three years.
338. *the isle*] of Caesar's self-exile.
341. *charged ... night*] Jonson cites Dio, *Roman History,* LVIII.9.3, 'Macro
entered Rome by night'.
346. *informèd ... thought*] publicized.
352. *venture*] stake, bet.
353. *retentive wisdom*] prudent silence.
354–5. *I ... thought*] Jonson again cites Dio, *Roman History,* LVIII.9.4
('perceiving that he was troubled ... he encouraged him').
354. *jealous scruple*] apprehensive doubt.
357. *several*] separate.
359. *state and grace*] dignity and favour.

Of what is purposed.

Sejanus.   You take pleasure, Macro,   360
   Like a coy wench, in torturing your lover.
   What can be worth this suffering?

Macro.   That which follows—
   The tribunicial dignity and power;
   Both which Sejanus is to have this day
   Conferred upon him, and by public Senate.   365

Sejanus. Fortune, be mine again. Thou'hast satisfied
   For thy suspected loyalty.

Macro.   My lord,
   I have no longer time, the day approacheth,
   And I must back to Caesar.

Sejanus.   Where's Caligula?

Macro. That I forgot to tell your lordship. Why,   370
   He lingers yonder, about Capreae,
   Disgraced. Tiberius hath not seen him yet.
   He needs would thrust himself to go with me,
   Against my wish or will, but I have quitted
   His forward trouble with as tardy note   375
   As my neglect or silence could afford him.
   Your lordship cannot now command me aught,
   Because I take no knowledge that I saw you,
   But I shall boast to live to serve your lordship—
   And so take leave.

Sejanus.   Honest and worthy Macro,   380

---

362. follows—] *This ed.;* follows, *Q, F.*   366. Thou'hast] *Q, H.&S.;* thou
hast *F.*   376. afford him.] *F;* bestow. *Q.*

---

363. *The tribunicial dignity*] Jonson cites Dio (see V.299n.) and Suetonius,
Lives, III.lxv: Tiberius, 'beguiling him with hope of … the tribunicial
power, … accused him when he least expected it'. The tribunicial power—
tribunicia potestas—was the most important constitutional form under which
Augustus, and subsequent emperors, exercised their authority. It gave its
holder, whose person was inviolable, the right of *intercessio*, or veto, over
Senatorial decrees, as well as the right to propose laws, and its conferral upon
Sejanus would mark him as heir to Tiberius, as it had marked out Tiberius
under the principate of Augustus.

367. *suspected loyalty*] *i.e.* imagined disloyalty.

374. *quitted*] requited.

375. *forward trouble*] presumptuous troubling of me.

375. *note*] notice.

Your love and friendship. Who's there?

[*Enter* SATRIUS.]

                    Satrius,

Attend my honourable friend forth.

            [*Exeunt* MACRO *and* SATRIUS.]

               O,

How vain and vile a passion is this fear!
What base, uncomely things it makes men do!
Suspect their noblest friends, as I did this,   385
Flatter poor enemies, entreat their servants,
Stoop, court, and catch at the benevolence
Of creatures unto whom, within this hour,
I would not have vouchsafed a quarter-look,
Or piece of face! By you, that fools call gods,   390
Hang all the sky with your prodigious signs,
Fill earth with monsters, drop the scorpion down
Out of the zodiac, or the fiercer lion,
Shake off the loosened globe from her long hinge,
Roll all the world in darkness, and let loose   395
Th'enragèd winds to turn up groves and towns!
When I do fear again, let me be struck
With forkèd fire, and unpitied die.
Who fears, is worthy of calamity.   [*Exit.*]

---

381. [*Enter* SATRIUS.]] *This ed. Unless he briefly appears, Sejanus's* Who's
there? *is nonsensical.*   382. [*Exeunt* ... SATRIUS.]] *This ed.; Exit Macro.
Gifford, subst. Barish, Bolton, all at 381.*   383. fear!] Feare? *Q;* feare? *F.*
384. do!] doe? *Q, F.*   390. face!] face? *Q, F.*   394. hinge] henge *Q, F.*
396. towns!] Townes; *Q;* townes *F.*   397. struck] strooke *Q, F.*
399. Who] *F;* "Who *Q.*   399.1–2. [*Enter* ... TRIO.] *This ed.;* POMPONIVS.

---

389. *quarter-look*] sidelong glance. Cf. Massinger, *Bashful Lover* (1636),
ed. F. Cunningham (Longon, 1870), I.i, 'Observe his posture, / But with a
quarter-look'; and Jonson, *For.*, xii. 28–9, 'and let them still, / Turne, vpon
scorned verse, their quarter-face'.

391–4.] Adapted, as *H.&S.* point out, from Seneca, *Thyestes*, 855–77:
'Alcides' Lion ... shall fall down from the sky; ... the fierce Scorpion
down.... Have we of all mankind been deemed deserving that heaven, its
poles uptorn [*everso cardine*], should overwhelm us?' *Cardo*, the word for a
hinge, was also used to refer to the poles, hence Jonson's image.

398. *forkèd fire*] lightning.

[*Enter* TERENTIUS, MINUTIUS, LACO, COTTA, LATIARIS, TRIBUNI,
    and others. To them] POMPONIUS, REGULUS, [*and*] TRIO.

Pomponius. Is not my lord here?
Terentius.   Sir, he will be straight.   400
Cotta. What news, Fulcinius Trio?
Trio.   Good, good tidings.
   But keep it to yourself. My lord Sejanus
   Is to receive this day, in open Senate,
   The tribunicial dignity.
Cotta.   Is't true?
Trio. No words—not to your thought—but sir, believe it.   405
Latiaris. What says the consul?
Cotta.   Speak it not again.
   He tells me that today my lord Sejanus—
Trio. I must entreat you, Cotta, on your honour
   Not to reveal it.
Cotta.   On my life, sir.
Latiaris.   Say.
Cotta. Is to receive the tribunicial power.   410
   But as you are an honourable man,
   Let me conjure you not to utter it—
   For it is trusted to me with that bond.
Latiaris. I am Harpocrates.
Terentius.   Can you assure it?
Pomponius. The consul told it me, but keep it close.   415
Minutius. Lord Latiaris, what's the news?
Latiaris.   I'll tell you,

REGVLVS. TRIO. &c. *Q*; POMPONIVS, REGVLVS, TRIO. *To the rest. F (last 3 words marginal);* SCENE VII. / Another Room in the same. / *Enter Terentius, Minutius, Laco, Cotta, Latiaris, and Pomponius; Regulus, Trio, and others on different sides. Gifford;* [Act V, Scene v] / [*Same as scene iii. Enter*] POMPONIUS, REGULUS, TRIO / *To the rest Bolton; Barish subst. as Gifford, but no scene div.; Briggs reverts to main stage.*   400. Pomponius.] POM. *Q; not in F.*

400.] Another citation of 'Dio. *ibid.*'
405. not ... thought] *i.e.*, do not give words to your thought.
413. *bond*] proviso.
414. *Harpocrates*] the god of silence, represented as holding a finger to his
lips. Cf. *S.W.*, II.ii.4, and *B.F.*, V.vi.48.
414. *assure*] guarantee.

But you must swear to keep it secret—

[*Enter*] SEJANUS.

Sejanus. I knew the fates had on their distaff left
    More of our thread, than so.
Regulus.   Hail, great Sejanus!
Trio. Hail, the most honoured!
Cotta.   Happy!
Latiaris.   High Sejanus!   420
Sejanus. Do you bring prodigies too?
Trio.   May all presage
    Turn to those fair effects, whereof we bring
    Your lordship news.
Regulus.   May't please my lord withdraw.
Sejanus. Yes.
    (*To some that stand by.*) I will speak with you anon.
Terentius   My lord,
    What is your pleasure for the tribunes?
Sejanus.   Why,   425
    Let 'em be thanked, and sent away.
Minutius.   My lord—
Laco. Will't please your lordship to command me—
Sejanus.   No.
    You'are troublesome.
Minutius.   The mood is changed.
[*1*] *Tribunus.*   Not speak?

417.1. [*Enter*] SEJANUS.] SEIANVS. &c. *Q*; SEIANVS. *F. Marginal s.d. in F:
To them.*   418. *Sejanus.*] SEI *Q; not in F.*   424. *To . . . by.*] *Marginal s.d. in
F; not in Q.*   428. You'are] *Q, H.&S.;* You are *F.*   428. [*1*] *Tribunus.*]
TRI. *Q, F.*

418–19. *I . . . so*] perhaps ironic. 'To have more tow on one's distaff than
one can spin' (Tilley, T 450), a sixteenth-century saying, meant to have
trouble in store. Although the fates have little of Sejanus's thread left to spin,
Sejanus himself has rather too much!

420.] Another superfluous citation of the same passage in Dio.

421. *presage*] omens.

428. *The mood is changed*] Jonson's note at this point embraces as well
Arruntius's and Lepidus's lines in the opening of the following scene. Dio,
Roman History, LVIII.5, 2–4, is cited: 'every word and every look, especially
in the case of the most prominent men, was carefully observed. Those now,
who hold a prominent position as the result of native worth are not much given
to seeking signs of friendship from others . . .; but those, on the other hand,

[2] *Tribunus.* Nor look?
Laco.   Ay. He is wise, will make him friends
    Of such, who never love but for their ends.   [*Exeunt.*]   430

   [*Enter*] ARRUNTIUS [*and*] LEPIDUS, *divers other* SENATORS
                     passing by them.

Arruntius. Ay, go, make haste. Take heed you be not last
    To tender your 'All hail!' in the wide hall
    Of huge Sejanus. Run a lictor's pace.
    Stay not to put your robes on, but away,
    With the pale troubled ensigns of great friendship   435
    Stamped i'your face! Now, Marcus Lepidus,
    You still believe your former augury?
    Sejanus must go downward? You perceive
    His wane approaching fast?
Lepidus.   Believe me, Lucius,
    I wonder at this rising!
Arruntius.   Ay, and that we   440

---

429. [2] *Tribunus.*] TRI. *Q, F.*   429. He] *F;* "He *Q.*   430. Of] *F;*
"Of *Q.*   430.1–2. [*Enter*] ... *them.*] Subst. *F. (last 6 words marginal);*
ARRVNTIVS. LEPIDVS. *Q;* SCENE VIII. / A space before the Temple of Apollo. /
Enter Arruntius and Lepidus, divers Senators passing by them. Gifford, subst.
Barish, but no scene div.; [Act V, Scene vi] / [*The temple of Apollo. Enter*]
ARRUNTIUS, LEPIDUS, *divers* / *other* SENATORS *passing by them Bolton.*
431. *Arruntius.*] ARR. *Q; not in F.*

who enjoy an adventitious splendour seek very eagerly all such attentions,
feeling them to be necessary to render their position complete, and if they fail
to obtain them, are as vexed as if they were being slandered and as angry as if
they were being insulted.... Consequently the world is more scrupulous in
the case of such persons than in the case of the emperors themselves'.
   429–30. *Ay ... ends*] Cf. Petronius, *Satyricon*, Loeb ed., tr. M. Heseltine
(London, 1956), lxxx, 'The name of friendship endures so long as there
is profit in it'; and Tacitus, *Histories*, III.lxxxvi, on Vitellius's view 'that
friendships are cemented by great gifts rather than by high character'.
   432. *All hail*] Jonson points out that this was used as a morning greeting. He
cites Brisson, *De formulis*, Book VIII.
   432. *wide hall*] where Sejanus's clients would await him.
   433. *a lictor's pace*] Since they had to maintain the pace of the magistrates
they preceded through the streets by clearing a path for them, lictors were
necessarily quick-footed.
   435–6.] Whalley quoted Juvenal, *Satires*, IV.74–5, on men 'on whose faces
sat the pallor of that great and perilous friendship'.
   435. *ensigns*] characteristic marks.

Must give our suffrage to it? You will say
It is to make his fall more steep and grievous?
It may be so. But think it they that can
With idle wishes 'say to bring back time.
In cases desperate, all hope is crime.   445
See, see! What troops of his officious friends
Flock to salute my lord! And start before
My great proud lord, to get a lord-like nod!
Attend my lord unto the Senate house!
Bring back my lord! Like servile ushers, make   450
Way for my lord! Proclaim his idol lordship,
More than ten criers, or six noise of trumpets!
Make legs, kiss hands, and take a scattered hair
From my lord's eminent shoulder! See Sanquinius!
With his slow belly, and his dropsy! Look   455
What toiling haste he makes! Yet here's another,
Retarded with the gout, will be afore him!
Get thee Liburnian porters, thou gross fool,

---

441. it?] *Q, F; it. Barish.*   442. grievous?] *Q, F;* grievous—*Barish.*
445. In] *F;* "In *Q.*   450. ushers] huishers *Q, F.*   454. eminent] *F;*
excellent *Q.*   454.] *After* shoulder: *Sanquinius and Haterius pass over the
stage. Gifford.*

---

441. *suffrage*] votes, support.
442. *his ... grievous*] Briggs gives Claudian, *Against Rufinus*, I.22–3 as the
source: 'He is raised aloft that he may be hurled down in more headlong ruin'.
444. *'say*] essay, try.
447. *start*] burst into view.
452. *noise*] bands. Cf. *S.W.*, III.iii.85–6, 'The smell of the venison, going
through the street, will inuite one noyse of fidlers, or other'.
453. *Make legs*] bow.
454. *eminent*] a pun on Latin *emineo*, to stand out, project.
454–5. *Sanquinius ... dropsy*] Jonson cites Tacitus, *Annals*, VI.vii, which
names him as an accuser of Arruntius (in 37, when the latter was one of
Macro's victims). Tacitus does not mention the 'slow belly'; the phrase is
Juvenal's: *abdomine tardus* ('unwieldy paunch', Loeb tr.), used in reference to
Montanus in *Satires*, IV.107, as Briggs points out.
456. *another*] Jonson's note identifies him as Haterius. His gout is mentioned again below, at V.633. Jonson cites Tacitus, *Annals*, VI.iv, but the
reference here is to Haterius Agrippa, son of Quintus Haterius the orator (i.e.
Jonson's Haterius) whose death Tacitus has recorded earlier, at IV.lxi. Jonson
has conflated the two, and inferred the gout from Tacitus's description of the
son 'amid his gluttony and lecheries'.
458. *Liburnian porters*] Jonson notes that the Liburnians in Rome were
of great stature, and quotes Juvenal, *Satires*, III.239–40: 'the mob makes

To bear thy'obsequious fatness, like thy peers.
They'are met! The gout returns, and his great carriage.   460
    LICTORS, CONSULS, SEJANUS, *etc. pass over the stage.*
Lictor. Give way! Make place! Room for the consul!
Sanquinius.   Hail,
    Hail, great Sejanus!
Haterius.   Hail, my honoured lord!
Arruntius. We shall be marked anon for our not-hail.
Lepidus. That is already done.
Arruntius.   It is a note
    Of upstart greatness to observe and watch   465
    For these poor trifles, which the noble mind
    Neglects and scorns.
Lepidus.   Ay, and they think themselves
    Deeply dishonoured where they are omitted,
    As if they were necessities that helped
    To the perfection of their dignities,   470
    And hate the men that but refrain 'em.
Arruntius.   O,
    There is a farther cause of hate. Their breasts
    Are guilty that we know their obscure springs
    And base beginnings. Thence the anger grows. On.
    Follow.
                                   [Exeunt.]

           [Enter] MACRO *[and]* LACO.

Macro. When all are entered, shut the temple doors,   475

459. thy'obsequious] *Q, H.&S.;* thy obsequious *F.*   460. They'are] *Q,*
H.&S.; They are *F.*   460.1. LICTORS ... *stage.*] *Subst. F (last 4 words*
marginal); LICTORS. CONSVLS. SEIANVS. &c. *Q.*   461. Lictor.] LIC. *Q; not in*
F.   472. farther] farder *Q, F.*   474.2. *[Enter]* ... LACO.] SCENE IX. /
Another Part of the same. / Enter Macro and Laco. *Gifford.*   475. Macro.]
MAC. *Q; not in F.*

---

way for him as he is borne swiftly over their heads in a huge Liburnian
car'. Liburnia, in Illyria, corresponds roughly with the modern Croatia.
    463. *marked*] noticed.
    464–71. *It is ... refrain 'em*] In two notes to these lines Jonson cites Dio,
Roman History, LVIII.5.2–4—quoted above, V.428n.
    473. *springs*] parentage, origins.
    475–6. *When ... gate*] Jonson cites Dio, *Roman History,* LVIII.9.6: Macro,
'after stationing the night-watch about the temple in [the Pretorians'] place,
... went in, delivered the letter to the consuls, and came out again before a

And bring your guards up to the gate.
Laco.   I will.
Macro. If you shall hear commotion in the Senate,
    Present yourself—and charge on any man
    Shall offer to come forth.
Laco.   I am instructed.   [*Exeunt.*]

THE SENATE.

[*Enter*] PRAECONES, LICTORES, REGULUS, SEJANUS, TRIO,
    HATERIUS, SANQUINIUS, COTTA, POMPONIUS,
    LATIARIS, LEPIDUS, ARRUNTIUS, [PRAETOR,
        and other SENATORS].

Haterius. How well his lordship looks today!
Trio.   As if   480
    He had been born or made for this hour's state.
Cotta. Your fellow consul's come about, methinks?
Trio. Ay, he'is wise.
Sanquinius.   Sejanus trusts him well.
Trio. Sejanus is a noble, bounteous lord.
Haterius. He is so, and most valiant.
Latiaris.   And most wise.   485
[*1*] *Senator.* He's everything.
Latiaris.   Worthy of all, and more

479.2–5. [*Enter*] ... SENATORS].] *This ed.;* PRAECONES. LICTORES. /
REGVLVS. SEIANVS. TRIO. / HATERIVS. SANQVINIVS. COTTA. / POMPONIVS.
LATIARIS. / LEPIDVS. ARRVNTIVS. *Q;* HATERIVS, TRIO, SANQVINIVS, /
COTTA, REGVLVS, SEIANVS, / POMPONIVS, LATIARIS, / LEPIDVS, ARRVNTIVS,
/ PRAECONES, LICTORES. *F; Gifford, Barish, Bolton follow F, but Gifford adds*
SCENE X. / The Temple of Apollo; *Barish gives locality, continues scene; Bolton
adds* PRAETORS.   479.3. SANQUINIUS] *corr. Q;* AANQVINIVS *uncorr. Q.*
480. *Haterius.*] HAT. *Q; not in F.*   483. he'is] *Q;* he is *F.*   486. [*1*]
Senator.] *Edd.;* SEN. *Q, F.*

word was read. He then instructed Laco to keep guard there and himself
hurried away to the [Pretorian] camp to prevent any uprising'.
    481. *state*] dignity.
    484ff.] Jonson's note here cites Dio, *Roman History*, LVIII.10.3: before the
letter was read, senators 'had been lauding Sejanus, thinking that he was about
to receive the tribunician power, and had kept cheering him, anticipating the
honours for which they hoped and making it clear to him that they would
concur in bestowing them'.

Than bounty can bestow.
Trio.   This dignity
　　Will make him worthy.
Pomponius.   Above Caesar.
Sanquinius.   Tut,
　　Caesar is but the rector of an isle,
　　He of the Empire.
Trio.   Now he will have power   490
　　More to reward than ever.
Cotta.   Let us look
　　We be not slack in giving him our voices.
Latiaris. Not I.
Sanquinius.   Nor I.
Cotta.   The readier we seem
　　To propagate his honours, will more bind
　　His thought to ours.
Haterius.   I think right with your lordship.   495
　　It is the way to have us hold our places.
Sanquinius. Ay, and get more.
Latiaris.   More office, and more titles.
Pomponius. I will not lose the part I hope to share
　　In these his fortunes, for my patrimony.

---

488. *Sanquinius.*] SAN. *corr. Q, F;* SAM. *uncorr. Q.*   489. isle] I'sle *Q, F.*
498. lose] *F;* loose *Q.*

487–8. *This ... worthy*] As Bolton observes, a pun: L. *dignus* = worthy.

489–90. *Caesar ... Empire*] Jonson cites Dio, *Roman History*, LVIII.5.1:
Sejanus, 'to put it briefly, ... seemed to be emperor and Tiberius a kind
of island potentate, inasmuch as the latter spent his time on the island of
Capreae'.

489. *rector*] controller.

491. *look*] ensure.

492.] Jonson again cites the Dio passage quoted above, n. to V.484ff.

493–504. *The ... favours*] The theme of sycophantic parasitism is reinforced by the imagery of woodbine or ivy, which seems to add to the glory of
the tree it eventually kills. Like creepers, which bind themselves to the tree,
these senators bind themselves to Sejanus and him to them. 'It is the way to
have us hold our places', as creepers are held in place by the tree; and like
creepers, they 'get more. More ... more'. Independently they are nothing:
'Men grow not in the State, but as they are planted / Warm in his favours'.

494. *propagate*] The technical Latin *propagare*, to set slips, or extend a plant
by layering. Cotta and the others, like creepers, only 'seem' to increase the
plant they feed on.

497.] Another citation of the Dio passage quoted above, n. to V.484ff.

Latiaris. See how Arruntius sits, and Lepidus.   500
Trio. Let 'em alone, they will be marked anon.
[*1*] *Senator.* I'll do with others.
[*2*] *Senator.*   So will I.
[*3*] *Senator.*   And I.
    Men grow not in the state, but as they are planted
    Warm in his favours.
Cotta.   Noble Sejanus!
Haterius. Honoured Sejanus!
Latiaris.   Worthy and great Sejanus!   505
Arruntius. Gods! How the sponges open, and take in!
    And shut again! Look, look! Is not he blest
    That gets a seat in eye-reach of him? More,
    That comes in ear- or tongue-reach? O, but most,
    Can claw his subtle elbow, or with a buzz   510
    Flyblow his ears.
Praetor.   Proclaim the Senate's peace,
    And give last summons by the edict.
Praeco.   Silence!
    In name of Caesar and the Senate, silence!
    MEMMIVS.REGVLVS.AND.FVLCINIVS.TRIO.CONSVLS.
    THESE.PRESENT.KALENDS.OF.IVNE.VVITH.THE.   515

502. [*1*] *Senator* ... [*2*] *Senator* ... [*3*] *Senator.*] Edd.; SEN ... SEN ...
SEN. *Q, F.*   509. most,] *Q, F;* most *Barish.*   511. Flyblow] *Q;* Fly-blow
F.   511. *Praetor.*] PRAET. *Q, F; Praeco. Barish.* 513. Senate,] SENATE. *Q,*
F.   514–23. MEMMIVS ... TAKEN.] *Q, F prints all in italics except*
MEMMIVS REGVLVS, FVLCINIVS TRIO, *and* APOLLO PALATINE.

    502. *do with*] deal with, have to do with. Cf. *Revenger's Tragedy*, ed. R. A.
Foakes (London, 1966), I.i.4, 'And thou his duchess, that will do with devil'
(where there is an additional sexual connotation probably not intended by
Jonson).
    510–11. *with ... ears*] The parasitical dependence of Sejanus's clients on
their patron is reinforced by this image. Cf. the relationship of Mosca ('the fly')
to Volpone in that play. Jonson's use of 'Fly-blow' as a verb is *O.E.D.*'s first
instance. Chapman wittily employs it against him in 'An Invective ... Against
Mr. Ben: Johnson', ll. 10–12. See *The Poems of George Chapman*, ed. Phyllis
Brooks Bartlett (New York, 1962; 1st ed. 1941), p. 374.
    511. *peace*] silence.
    512. *last summons*] referring to the passage about to be read.
    514–23.] Jonson cites as authorities for this formula (really a compound of
formulae) Brisson, *De formulis*, Book II; and Justus Lipsius, *Satyra Menippaea.*
    515. *KALENDS.OF.IVNE*] 1 June 31. Jonson is in error. In this period

FIRST.LIGHT.SHALL.HOLD.A.SENATE.IN.THE.TEMPLE.
OF.APOLLO.PALATINE.ALL.THAT.ARE.FATHERS.AND.
ARE.REGISTERED.FATHERS.THAT.HAVE.RIGHT.OF.
ENTERING.THE.SENATE.VVE.VVARN.OR.COMMAND.
YOV.BE.FREQUENTLY.PRESENT.TAKE.KNOVVLEDGE.   520
THE.BVSINESS.IS.THE.COMMON.VVEALTHS.
VVHOSOEVER.IS.ABSENT.HIS.FINE.OR.MVLCT.VVILL.BE
TAKEN.HIS.EXCVSE.VVILL.NOT.BE.TAKEN.

Trio. Note who are absent, and record their names.

Regulus. Fathers conscript, may what I am to utter   525
Turn good and happy for the commonwealth.
And thou, Apollo, in whose holy house
We here are met, inspire us all with truth,
And liberty of censure, to our thought.
The majesty of great Tiberius Caesar   530
Propounds to this grave Senate the bestowing
Upon the man he loves, honoured Sejanus,
The tribunicial dignity and power.

525–6. Fathers … commonwealth.] *Caps. (non-inscriptional form) in Q, italics
in F.*   525. conscript,] CONSCRIPT. *Q; Conscript. F.*   532. loves] *F; lones
Q.*

---

the Senate normally met on the kalends and on the ides, i.e. the first and
the thirteenth or fifteenth of the month. However, it is now known that
Sejanus was condemned on 18 October 31 (see *Inscriptiones Latinae Selectae*,
ed. H. Dessau, I (Berlin, 1962), 158), and even in Jonson's day this date
was commonly inferred from the known fact that Tiberius instituted a
special holiday, to celebrate the fall of Sejanus, on the fifteenth kalends of
November—i.e. 18 October. It is also now known that Fulcinius Trio became
consul suffectus on 1 July 31 and that Memmius Regulus became his partner on
1 October, only seventeen days before the events depicted here. See *Corpus
Inscriptionum Latinarum*, X (Berlin, 1883), 1233.
    516–17. *IN … PALATINE*] Jonson notes that the temple was so called
after the hill on which it was built. The senate assembled in consecrated
places—the temple of Concord (see V.787), of Apollo, Castor and Pollux,
Jupiter Capitolinus, etc., and the *Curiae* (specifically Senate-houses).
    518. *REGISTERED*] 'conscript' (l. 525 below).
    520. *FREQVENTLY*] in full number.
    522–3. *VVHOSOEVER … NOT BE TAKEN*] imitated, as Briggs points
out, by Shakerley Marmion, *Legend of Cupid and Psyche*, II.iii.266–7.
    525–6.] Jonson draws attention to the formula here. See III.28–9n. He
also cites Dio, *Roman History*, LVIII.9, rather unnecessarily.
    527–8.] Apollo was thought of as god of light and hence of truth.
    529. *censure*] judgement, opinion.
    533.] Jonson again cites Suetonius, *Lives*, III.lxv—see V.363n.

Here are his letters, signèd with his signet.
What pleaseth now the fathers to be done?   535
Senators. Read, read 'em, open, publicly, read 'em.
Cotta. Caesar hath honoured his own greatness much
        In thinking of this act.
Trio.   It was a thought
        Happy, and worthy Caesar.
Latiaris.   And the lord
        As worthy it, on whom it is directed!   540
Haterius. Most worthy!
Sanquinius.   Rome did never boast the virtue
        That could give envy bounds, but his: Sejanus—
[1] Senator. Honoured and noble!
[2] Senator.   Good and great Sejanus!
Arruntius. [*Aside.*] O, most tame slavery, and fierce flattery!
Praeco.   Silence!

                        The epistle is read.

                'TIBERIUS CAESAR   545
                TO THE SENATE,
                    GREETING.

        IF.YOV.CONSCRIPT.FATHERS.VVITH.YOVR.CHILDREN.
        BE.IN.HEALTH.IT.IS.ABUNDANTLY.VVELL.VVE.VVITH.

535. What ... done] *Caps. in Q, italics in* F.   536. *Senators.*] *Edd.;* SFN. *Q;*
SEN. *F.*   543. [*1*] *Senator.* ... [2] *Senator.*] *Edd.;* SEN. ... SEN. *Q, F.*
544.1. *The ... read.*] *Marginal s.d. in* F; *not in* Q.   545–7. TIBERIUS ...
GREETING.] *F;* TIBERIVS CAESAR TO THE SENATE / GREETING *Q.*

535.] Jonson notes this as a customary form used in the Senate, citing
Brisson, *De formulis*, Book II.
536–43.] Jonson again cites Dio, *Roman History*, LVIII.10.3—quoted
above, V.484ff.n.
541–42. the ... bounds] H.&S. cite the source: Claudian, *On Stilicho's
Consulship*, III.39: '*solus hic invidiae fines virtute reliquit*', 'Stilicho alone was
raised above the range of envy'.
544. *fierce*] furiously zealous, ardent. Cf. *Poet.*, V.iii.129–30, 'And LVPVS,
for your fierce credulitie, / One fit him with a paire of larger eares'.
545–659.] This superbly effective piece of studied equivocation and manipulation has been developed by Jonson from the following sketchy accounts of
it: Suetonius, *Lives*, III.lxv, 'a shameful and pitiable speech'; Juvenal, *Satires*,
X.71–2, 'a great and wordy letter came from Capri'; and, more importantly,
Dio, *Roman History*, LVIII.10.1–5. See Appendix A.

OVR.FRIENDS.HERE.ARE.SO. The care of the common-   550
wealth, howsoever we are removed in person, cannot be
absent to our thought; although, oftentimes, even to
princes most present, the truth of their own affairs is
hid—than which nothing falls out more miserable to a
state, or makes the art of governing more difficult. But   555
since it hath been our easeful happiness to enjoy both the
aids and industry of so vigilant a Senate, we profess to have
been the more indulgent to our pleasures, not as being
careless of our office, but rather secure of the necessity.
Neither do these common rumours of many and infamous   560
libels published against our retirement at all afflict us,
being born more out of men's ignorance than their
malice—and will, neglected, find their own grave quickly,
whereas too sensibly acknowledged, it would make their
obloquy ours. Nor do we desire their authors, though   565
found, be censured, since in a free state (as ours) all men
ought to enjoy both their minds and tongues free.'
Arruntius. [*Aside.*] The lapwing, the lapwing!
'Yet, in things which shall worthily and more near concern
the majesty of a prince, we shall fear to be so unnaturally   570
cruel to our own fame as to neglect them. True it is,
conscript fathers, that we have raised Sejanus, from
obscure and almost unknown gentry,—'
Senators. How! How!

548–50. IF. . . . SO.] *Q; italics in F.*   550–659. The care . . . exacts it.'] *Q, F*
print speech subst. in italics. No quotation marks in Q, F.   562. born] *H.&S.;*
borne Q, F.   567. both] *Q, F; H.&S., Barish, omit,*   569. things] *things:*
Q; things, F.   574. How! How!] *Q, F; How? How? Barish.*

548–50. *IF . . . SO*] For the formula here, Jonson cites Brisson, *De formulis*,
Book VIII.
559. *Secure of the necessity*] free of the anxiety of its being necessary (to
attend to aspects of government so well managed by the Senate).
564. *sensibly acknowledged*] feelingly reacted to.
566–7. *in . . . tongues free*] Jonson cites Suetonius, *Lives*, III.xxviii: 'he was
self-contained and patient in the face of abuse and slander, and of lampoons on
himself and his family, often asserting that in a free country there should be
free speech and free thought'.
568. *lapwing*] Tilley, L 68, 'The lapwing cries most when farthest from her
nest'. Cf. Shakespeare, *Err.*, IV.ii.27, 'Far from her nest the lapwing cries
away; / My heart prays for him, though my tongue do curse'; and *Poet.*,
IV.vii.53, 'their false lapwing-cries'.
573. *gentry*] rank by birth (*O.E.D. gentry*, 1). Latin *gens*, a clan.

'to the highest and most conspicuous point of greatness,   575
and, we hope, deservingly; yet not without danger—it
being a most bold hazard in that sovereign who, by his
particular love to one, dares adventure the hatred of all his
other subjects.'

Arruntius. [*Aside.*] This touches, the blood turns.   580

'But we affy in your loves and understandings, and do no
way suspect the merit of our Sejanus to make our favours
offensive to any.'

Senators. O! Good, good!

'Though we could have wished his zeal had run a calmer   585
course against Agrippina and our nephews, howsoever the
openness of their actions declared them delinquents; and
that he would have remembered no innocence is so safe,
but it rejoiceth to stand in the sight of mercy—the use of
which in us he hath so quite taken away toward them by   590
his loyal fury, as now our clemency would be thought but
wearied cruelty, if we should offer to exercise it.'

Arruntius. [*Aside.*] I thank him, there I looked for't. A good
        fox!

'Some there be that would interpret this his public severity
to be particular ambition; and that under a pretext of   595
service to us, he doth but remove his own lets; alleging
the strengths he hath made to himself by the praetorian
soldiers, by his faction in court and Senate, by the offices
he holds himself and confers on others, his popularity and

---

584. *Senators.*] SEN. *Q, F.*   595. pretext] *pretext F;* praetext *Q.*

---

578. *particular*] personal, private. Cf. V.589.
578. *adventure*] risk.
580. *blood turns*] mood changes.
581. *affy in*] have faith in.
588–9. *no ... mercy*] From Seneca, *On Mercy*, I.i.9, as Briggs points out:
'nor is there any man so wholly satisfied with his own innocence as not to
rejoice that mercy stands in sight, waiting for human errors'.
592. *wearied cruelty*] Ibid., I.xi.2, 'I, surely, do not call weariness of cruelty
mercy'.
593. *A good fox*] an ironical ref. to the proverbial 'The fox may grow grey
but never good' (Tilley, F 638).
594.] Jonson cites the Dio and Juvenal passage quoted at V.545–659n.
595. *particular*] personal.
596. *lets*] hindrances.
596. *alleging*] citing.

dependents, his urging (and almost driving) us to this our   600
unwilling retirement, and lastly, his aspiring to be our
son-in-law.'
Senators. This's strange!
Arruntius. [*Aside.*] I shall anon believe your vultures, Marcus.
'Your wisdoms, conscript fathers, are able to examine and   605
censure these suggestions. But, were they left to our
absolving voice, we durst pronounce them, as we think
them, most malicious.'
Senators. O, he has restored all, list.
'Yet are they offered to be averred, and on the lives of   610
the informers. What we should say, or rather what we
should not say, lords of the Senate, if this be true, our
gods and goddesses confound us if we know! Only, we
must think we have placed our benefits ill; and conclude
that in our choice, either we were wanting to the gods, or   615
the gods to us.'

The senators shift their places.

Arruntius. [*Aside.*] The place grows hot, they shift.
'We have not been covetous, honourable fathers, to
change; neither is it now any new lust that alters our   620
affection, or old loathing, but those needful jealousies of
state, that warn wiser princes, hourly, to provide their

---

603. *Senators.*] SEN. *Q, F.*   603. This's strange] *F;* 'This 'strange *Q.*
616.1. *The* ... *places.*] *Marginal s.d. in F; not in Q.*

---

604. *your vultures*] in ref. to Lepidus's earlier premonition regarding Sejanus
(IV.466ff.). The vulture was a bird of omen.
606. *censure*] judge.
607. *absolving voice*] acquitting verdict.
611–13. *What* ... *know*] This echoes a well-known opening sentence from
one of Tiberius's letters to the Senate. Both Tacitus (*Annals*, VI.vi) and
Suetonius (*Lives*, III.lxvii) quote it: 'If I know what to write to you, Conscript
Fathers, or how to write it, or what not to write at all at this time, may gods
and goddesses destroy me more wretchedly than I feel myself to be perishing
every day!' (Loeb Tacitus). Both Suetonius and Tacitus cite it as a product of a
tormented rather than a crafty mind. It postdates the fall of Sejanus.
618. *covetous*] eagerly desirous.
620. *jealousies*] worries, concerns.
621. *provide*] look to, the sense being that of *L.&S.*, *provideo*, B.2, rather
than of *O.E.D.*, *provide*, I.1 ('foresee'—the sense of the example *H.&S.* cite
from *Volp.*, Ded., 78).

safety; and do teach them how learnèd a thing it is to
beware of the humblest enemy—much more of those great
ones whom their own employed favours have made fit for
their fears.'   625

[*1*] *Senator.* Away!

[*2*] *Senator.*   Sit farther.

Cotta.   Let's remove—

Arruntius. [*Aside.*] Gods! How the leaves drop off, this little
     wind!

'We therefore desire that the offices he holds be first seized
by the Senate; and himself suspended from all exercise
of place or power—'   630

Senators. How!

Sanquinius. [*Thrusting by.*] By your leave.

Arruntius.   Come, porpoise.
                        [*Aside.*] Where's Haterius?

His gout keeps him most miserably constant.

Your dancing shows a tempest.

Sejanus.   Read no more.

Regulus. Lords of the Senate, hold your seats. Read on.

Sejanus. These letters, they are forged.

626. [*1*] *Senator* ... [*2*] *Senator.*] *Edd.;* SEN. ... SEN. *Q, F.*   626. farther]
farder *Q, F.*   627. off, ... wind!] *corr. Q;* off! ... winde. *uncorr. Q.*
631. *Senators.*] SEN. *F;* SE. *Q.*   631. [*Thrusting by.*] *Barish.*   631. por-
poise] *Porcpisce Q, F.*

622. *learnèd*] deeply-read—esp. in history.
623–5. *beware ... fears*] Cf. Machiavelli, *Discourses*, III.vi: 'A prince,
then, who wishes to guard against conspiracies should fear those on whom he
has heaped benefits quite as much, and even more, than those whom he has
wronged; for the latter lack the convenient opportunities which the former
have in abundance'. *The Prince and the Discourses*, ed. Max Lerner (New York,
1950), p. 415. Machiavelli has Sejanus in mind here.
628–30.] Jonson inserts another ref. to the same passage in Dio—V.
545–659n.
631. *porpoise*] Tilley, P 483, 'The porpoise plays before a storm'—i.e. its
appearance signals a storm. Elsewhere Jonson preferred the spelling 'porpuse'
or 'porpuis', but for *Sejanus* he tellingly chose the more latinate form 'porcpisce'. Cf. *E.M.I.*, Quarto, V.iii.240–1: 'well since there is such a tempest
towarde, ile be the porpuis, ile daunce'. Eric Partridge, *A Dictionary of Slang
and Unconventional English* (London, 1937; *ed. cit.* 1963), I, 650, has this
entry: '*porpoise.* A very stout man: late C. 19–20: coll., ca. 1905, S.E.'.
632. *constant*] unmoving, not changing places ('dancing') like the others.
633. *dancing ... tempest*] see 631n.

Regulus.   A guard, sit still.   635

            LACO *enters with the guards.*

Arruntius. [*Aside.*] Here's change.
Regulus.   Bid silence, and read forward.
Praeco. Silence!—'and himself suspended from all exercise of
   place or power, but till due and mature trial be made of
   his innocency, which yet we can faintly apprehend the
   necessity to doubt. If, conscript fathers, to your more   640
   searching wisdoms there shall appear farther cause—or of
   farther proceeding, either to seizure of lands, goods, or
   more—it is not our power that shall limit your authority,
   or our favour that must corrupt your justice. Either were
   dishonourable in you, and both uncharitable to ourself.   645
   We would willingly be present with your counsels in this
   business, but the danger of so potent a faction, if it should
   prove so, forbids our attempting it—except one of the
   consuls would be entreated for our safety to undertake the
   guard of us home; then we should most readily adventure.   650
   In the meantime, it shall not be fit for us to importune
   so judicious a Senate, who know how much they hurt the
   innocent that spare the guilty—and how grateful a sacrifice
   to the gods is the life of an ingrateful person. We reflect not
   in this on Sejanus—notwithstanding, if you keep an eye   655
   upon him—and there is Latiaris, a senator, and Pinnarius
   Natta, two of his most trusted ministers, and so professed,
   whom we desire not to have apprênded, but as the
   necessity of the cause exacts it.'
Regulus. A guard on Latiaris.
Arruntius.   O, the spy!   660

635.1. *Laco ... guards.*] *Marginal s.d. in F; not in Q.*   636. Here's] *corr. Q;*
There's *uncorr. Q, F, edd.*   642. farther] farder *Q, F.*   648. attempting
it] *attempting it F; attempt Q.*   658. apprênded *apprênded Q, F, Barish;*
apprehended *other edd.*

   646–50. *We ... adventure*] Jonson again cites the Dio passage quoted above
at V.545–659n.
   654–59. *We ... exacts it*] In *F* the parenthetical part of the sentence closes
with 'apprênded' (unclosed in *Q*), making for a curious equivocation within
the very grammar of Tiberius's letter.
   658. *apprênded*] a rare C16 and 17 form, from the Latin *apprendo,* a poetical
form of *apprehendo.*

The reverend spy is caught! Who pities him?
Reward, sir, for your service. Now you ha'done
Your property, you see what use is made?

                         [Exeunt LATIARIS *and* NATTA, *guarded.]*

Hang up the instrument.

Sejanus.   Give leave.

Laco.   Stand, stand.

He comes upon his death that doth advance   665
  An inch toward my point.

Sejanus.   Have we no friend here?

Arruntius. Hushed. Where   now   are   all   the   hails   and
    acclamations?

                    [Enter] MACRO.

Macro. Hail to the consuls, and this noble Senate!
Sejanus. *[Aside.]* Is Macro here? O, thou art lost, Sejanus.
Macro. Sit still, and unaffrighted, reverend fathers.   670
  Macro, by Caesar's grace the new-made provost,
  And now possessed of the praetorian bands,
  An honour late belonged to that proud man,
  Bids you be safe; and to your constant doom
  Of his deservings, offers you the surety   675
  Of all the soldiers, tribunes, and centurions
  Received in our command.

Regulus.   Sejanus, Sejanus!

  Stand forth, Sejanus!

Sejanus.   Am I called?

Macro.   Ay, thou,

---

661. caught!] *Barish;* caught, Q, F.   663.1. [*Exeunt . . . guarded.]*] *Gifford.*
666. friend] *corr.* Q; friends *uncorr.* Q, F, *edd.*   667.1. [*Enter]* MACRO.]
MACRO. &c. Q; MACRO, SENATE. F.   668. *Macro.*] MAC. Q; *not in* F.

---

    661. *reverend*] venerable—this spy is a senator! Jonson may intend an
ironical equivocation on the latinate meaning of 'awe-inspiring' or frightening.
    663. *property*] function. Not in *O.E.D.* in this sense.
    664. *instrument*] person made use of.
    668. Although Jonson's note here again cites the Dio passage quoted above
at V.545–659n., Macro's entry at this point, and his subsequent behaviour,
are Jonson's invention.
    674. *to . . . doom*] as a support for your resolute judgement.
    678–83. *Ay, thou . . . most*] To Sejanus it seems 'insolent' not so much that
Macro calls him 'insolent monster' as that he uses 'thou' twice, emphatically

Thou insolent monster, art bid stand.
Sejanus.   Why, Macro,
It hath been otherwise between you and I.   680
This court, that knows us both, hath seen a difference,
And can, if it be pleased to speak, confirm
Whose insolence is most.
Macro.   Come down, Typhoeus.
If mine be most, lo, thus I make it more;
Kick up thy heels in air, tear off thy robe,   685
Play with thy beard, and nostrils—thus 'tis fit
(And no man take compassion of thy state)
To use th'ingrateful viper, tread his brains
Into the earth.
Regulus.   Forbear.
Macro.   If I could lose
All my humanity now, 'twere well to torture   690
So meriting a traitor. Wherefore, fathers,
Sit you amazed and silent, and not censure
This wretch, who in the hour he first rebelled
'Gainst Caesar's bounty, did condemn himself?
Phlegra, the field where all the sons of earth   695
Mustered against the gods, did ne'er acknowledge
So proud and huge a monster.
Regulus.   Take him hence.

680. I.] I? *Q, F.*   683. Typhoeus] *Typhaeus Q;* Typhoeus *F.*
686. nostrils—] *This ed.;* nostrils: *second corr. state Q;* nostril: *first corr. state Q;*
nostrils. *uncorr. Q.*   689. lose] *F;* loose *Q.*   695. Phlegra] *Edd.;* P'hlegra
Q, F.

---

employing this personal pronoun 'familiarly, to an inferior, in contempt or
insult' (*O.E.D.*, *Thou, pers. pron.*, 1.b). Sejanus is more polite ('between you,
and I'). Cf. Coke at the trial of Ralegh, 1603: 'All that Cobham did was by thy
instigation, thou viper; for I *thou* thee, thou traitor!' *The Works of Sir Walter
Ralegh* (Oxford, 1829), I, 660. In the exchange between Macro and Sejanus
there may be a punning allusion to the root meaning of Latin *insolens,*
'unaccustomed'.
   683–9. *Come down ... earth*] In a production, Macro should clearly *do* all
these things to Sejanus.
   683. *Typhoeus*] A Titan who made war against the gods and frightened them
away—temporarily. Jupiter finally crushed him under Mount Etna. Typhoeus
had 100 serpent-like heads, adding force to 'viper' at V.688.
   688. *ingrateful*] This may carry a secondary, Latin root, meaning of 'un-
pleasant, ugly'.
   689–90. *If ... now*] Cf. *Epigrams*, xlv, 'On My First Sonne': 'O, could I
loose all father, now'.

And all the gods guard Caesar.

Trio.   Take him hence.

Haterius. Hence!

Cotta.   To the dungeon with him!

Sanquinius.   He deserves it.

[1] Senator. Crown all our doors with bays.

Sanquinius.   And let an ox   700
With gilded horns and garlands straight he led
Unto the Capitol.

Haterius.   And sacrificed
To Jove for Caesar's safety.

Trio.   All our gods
Be present still to Caesar!

Cotta.   Phoebus!

Sanquinius.   Mars!

Haterius. Diana!

Sanquinius.   Pallas!

[2] Senator.   Juno, Mercury,   705
All guard him!

Macro.   Forth, thou prodigy of men!

                              [*Exit* SEJANUS *guarded.*]

Cotta. Let all the traitor's titles be defaced.

Trio. His images and statues be pulled down.

Haterius. His chariot wheels be broken.

Arruntius.   And the legs
Of the poor horses, that deservèd naught,   710
Let them be broken too.

Lepidus.   O violent change,
And whirl of men's affections!

Arruntius.   Like as both
Their bulks and souls were bound on Fortune's wheel,

---

700. [*1*] *Senator.*] SEN. *Q, F.*   701. garlands] *F;* Gyrlonds *Q.*   705. [*2*]
Senator.] SEN. *Q, F.*   706.1. [*Exit . . . guarded.*]] *Gifford.*

---

695. *Phlegra*] in Macedonia, where Zeus defeated the Titans.
    696. *acknowledge*] own the knowledge of (Latin *agnosco*, know, recognise).
    700–711.] Jonson cites Juvenal, *Satires*, X.58–66: 'down come their
statues, obedient to the rope; the axe hews in pieces their chariot wheels and
the legs of the unoffending nags .... Up with the laurel-wreaths over your
doors! Lead forth a grand chalked bull to the Capitol!'
    700. *bays*] laurel wreaths, used as a sign of victory.

And must act only with her motion.
[*Exeunt all but*] Lepidus, Arruntius, [*and a few senators*].
Lepidus. Who would depend upon the popular air,   715
    Or voice of men, that have today beheld
    That which if all the gods had foredeclared,
    Would not have been believed, Sejanus' fall?
    He, that this morn rose proudly as the sun,
    And, breaking through a mist of clients' breath,   720
    Came on as gazed at and admired as he
    When superstitious Moors salute his light!
    That had our servile nobles waiting him
    As common grooms, and hanging on his look,
    No less than human life on destiny!   725
    That had men's knees as frequent as the gods,
    And sacrifices more than Rome had altars—
    And this man fall! Fall? Ay, without a look
    That durst appear his friend, or lend so much
    Of vain relief to his changed state as pity!   730

714.1. [*Exeunt . . . senators.*]] *Subst. Gifford.*   715. *Lepidus.*] LEP. *Q; not in*
F.   725. human] humane *Q, F.*

---

715. *popular air*] *aura popularis*, popular favour, was a common Latin
phrase: *L.&S.* cite examples in Cicero, Livy, Horace, and Quintilian. It was
also used of a shifting wind, and Jonson may have had this is mind.

717–8.] Jonson's note at V.728 refers to this passage as well as to V.
728–39. For this passage he cites Dio, *Roman History*, LVIII.6.1, 'not even if
some god had plainly foretold that so great a change would take place in a short
time, would anyone have believed it'.

721–22. *as he . . . light*] Briggs cites Herodotus, IV.clxxxviii: the nomadic
Lybians 'sacrifice to no gods save the sun and moon'. Loeb ed., tr. A. D.
Godley (London, 1950).

723. *waiting*] waiting upon, attending.

728–39.] Jonson cites Dio, *Roman History*, LVIII.11.1–3: 'Thereupon one
might have witnessed such a surpassing proof of human frailty as to prevent
one's ever again being puffed up with conceit. For the man whom at dawn they
had escorted to the senate-hall as a superior being, they were now dragging to
prison as if no better than the worst; on him whom they had previously
thought worthy of many crowns, they now laid bonds; him whom they were
wont to protect as a master, they now guarded like a run-away slave, un-
covering his head when he would fain cover it; him whom they had adorned
with the purple-bordered toga, they struck in the face; and him whom they
were wont to adore and worship with sacrifices as a god, they were now leading
to execution. The populace also assailed him, shouting many reproaches at
him for the lives he had taken and many jeers for the hopes he had cherished.'

Arruntius. They that before, like gnats, played in his beams,
　　　　And thronged to circumscribe him, now not seen!
　　　　Nor deign to hold a common seat with him!
　　　　Others, that waited him unto the Senate,
　　　　Now inhumanely ravish him to prison!　　　　　　　735
　　　　Whom, but this morn, they followed as their lord,
　　　　Guard through the streets, bound like a fugitive!
　　　　Instead of wreaths, give fetters; strokes for stoops;
　　　　Blind shame for honours; and black taunts for titles!
　　　　Who could trust slippery chance?
Lepidus.　　　　　　　　　　They that would make　740
　　　　Themselves her spoil, and foolishly forget,
　　　　When she doth flatter, that she comes to prey.
　　　　Fortune, thou hadst no deity if men
　　　　Had wisdom. We have placèd thee so high
　　　　By fond belief in thy felicity.　　　　　　　　　745
　　　　　　　　　　　Shout within.
Senators. [*Within.*] The gods guard Caesar! All the gods guard
　　　　Caesar!

　　　　　　[*Enter*] MACRO, REGULUS, [*and* SENATORS].

Macro. Now, great Sejanus, you that awed the state,

---

735. inhumanely] *Q, F, Barish;* inhumanly *Bolton.*　　735. prison!] *Q, F,
Bolton;* prison, *H.&S., Barish.*　　736. lord,] *Q, F, Bolton;* lord! *Q, H.&S.,
Barish.*　　737. fugitive!] *Q, F, Bolton;* fugitive; *Barish.*　　743–5.] *Each line
preceded by gnomic pointing, Q.*　　745.1. *Shout within.*] *Q; in margin, F.*
746. *Senators.*] SEN. *F; not in Q.*　　746.1. [*Enter*] ... SENATORS].] MACRO.
LACO. SENATE. *Q;* MACRO, REGVLVS, SENATORS. *F.*　　747. *Macro.*] MAC. *Q;
not in F.*

---

732. *circumscribe*] encircle—*O.E.D.*'s first example of this sense.

735. *ravish*] seize and carry off, take by violence (as in 'the rape of the
Sabine women').

733. *common*] shared.

737. *fugitive*] *fugitivus,* a runaway slave—the only meaning of the *sb.* in
Latin—gives the most appropriate sense.

738. *stoops*] bows.

741. *spoil*] booty, plunder.

743–5.] Another passage from Juvenal: *Satires,* X.365–6, 'Thou wouldst
have no divinity, O Fortune, if we had but wisdom; it is we that make a
goddess of thee, and place thee in the skies'.

745. *fond*] foolish.

747.] At this point Jonson cites Dio, *Roman History,* LVIII.11.ff. Specific
debts are quoted below.

And sought to bring the nobles to your whip;
That would be Caesar's tutor, and dispose
Of dignities and offices; that had   750
The public head still bare to your designs,
And made the general voice to echo yours;
That looked for salutations twelve score off,
And would have pyramids, yea temples reared
To your huge greatness—now you lie as flat   755
As was your pride advanced.
Regulus.   Thanks to the gods.
Senators. And praise to Macro, that hath savèd Rome!
    Liberty, liberty, liberty! Lead on!
    And praise to Macro, that hath savèd Rome!
            [*Exeunt all but Arruntius and Lepidus.*]
Arruntius. I prophesy, out of this Senate's flattery,   760
    That this new fellow, Macro, will become
    A greater prodigy in Rome than he
    That now is fall'n.

            [*Enter* TERENTIUS.]

Terentius.   O you whose minds are good,
    And have not forced all mankind from your breasts,
    That yet have so much stock of virtue left   765

757. *Senators.*] SEN. *Q, F.*   759.1. [*Exeunt* ... *Lepidus.*]] *Gifford;*
ARRVNTIVS. LEPIDVS. TERENTIVS. *Q;* ARRVNTIVS, LEPIDVS, TERENTIVS. *F.*
760. *Arruntius.*] ARR. *Q; not in F.*

---

751. *The ... designs*] the crowd respectfully attendant upon your plans and projects.

753. *twelve score*] 240 paces—often, but not exclusively, used in reference to a shooting distance in archery. See examples quoted by *O.E.D.*, *score, sb.*, 18.

754–6. *And ... advanced*] From Claudian, *Against Rufinus*, II.447–9, 'trodden under foot at the cross-roads him who built pyramids for himself and a tomb, large as a temple, to the glory of his own ghost'.

754. *pyramids*] not necessarily of the Egyptian kind; pyramidal monuments. Cf. the 'pyramid' of Caius Cestius, a contemporary of Augustus, in Rome. It stands 36.40 metres high, and its inscriptions record Cestius's titles and the circumstances of its erection. Its shape reflects a fashion for Egyptian styles consequent upon the victory at Actium. See J. M. C. Toynbee, *Death and Burial in the Roman World* (London, 1971), p. 33, 127–8.

760–3. *I ... fall'n*] Arruntius, acc. to Tacitus, saw Macro as having 'been chosen, the worse villain of the pair, to crush Sejanus'. *Annals*, VI.xlviii.

760. *out of*] due to.

764. *mankind*] humanity.

To pity guilty states, when they are wretched;
Lend your soft ears to hear, and eyes to weep
Deeds done by men, beyond the acts of furies.
The eager multitude, who never yet
Knew why to love or hate, but only pleased   770
T'express their rage of power, no sooner heard
The murmur of Sejanus in decline,
But with that speed and heat of appetite
With which they greedily devour the way
To some great sports, or a new theatre,   775
They filled the Capitol, and Pompey's Cirque;
Where, like so many mastiffs, biting stones,
As if his statues now were sensive grown
Of their wild fury, first they tear them down;
Then fastening ropes, drag them along the streets,   780
Crying in scorn, 'This, this was that rich head
Was crowned with garlands and with odours, this
That was in Rome so reverencèd! Now

---

775. theatre,] corr. F; Theatre; Q; theatre; uncorr. F.   776. Capitol,] F, corr.
Q; Capitoll; uncorr. Q.   778. sensive grown] corr. F; sensitive Q, uncorr. F.
779. fury,] corr. Q, corr. F; fury; uncorr. Q, uncorr. F.   781. 'This] No quotation marks in Q, F.   782. garlands] uncorr. F; Gyrlonds Q; gyrlands corr. F.

---

766. states] sorts of people (O.E.D. state, sb., 21).

767. soft] compassionate (O.E.D. soft, a., 8).

772. murmur] rumour.

774. devour the way] O.E.D., devour, 8.b, gives Shakespeare, 2H4, I.i.47
('He seem'd in running to devour the way') as its first example (1597). Cf.
Catullus, Poems, xxxv.7, 'if he is wise he will devour the way [viam vorabit]
with haste'.

775.] H.&S. cite Seneca, Hercules Furens, 838–9, 'Great as the host that
moves through city streets, eager to see the spectacle in some new theatre;
great as that which pours to ... the sacred games'.

776. Pompey's Cirque] his theatre, built c. 55 B.C. See the reference to
Sejanus's 'statue / In Pompey's theatre', I.519–20.

778–80.] From Dio, Roman History, LVIII.11.3, 'They hurled down, beat
down, and dragged down all his images, as though they were thereby treating
the man himself with contumely'.

778. sensive] capable of sensation. O.E.D., sensive, a., 2, cites as its one
and only example E.M.I., II.iii.65–7, 'the infection / ... spreads itself, /
Confusedly, through every sensiue part'.

781–6.] Jonson cites Juvenal Satires, X.61–4, 'And now the flames are
hissing, and amid the roar of furnace and of bellows the head of the mighty
Sejanus, the darling of the mob, is burning and crackling, and from that face,
which was but lately second in the entire world, are being fashioned pipkins,
basins, frying-pans and slop-pails!'

The furnace and the bellows shall to work,
The great Sejanus crack, and piece by piece,   785
Drop i'the founder's pit.'
Lepidus.   O popular rage!
Terentius. The whilst the Senate, at the temple of Concord,
    Make haste to meet again, and thronging cry,
    'Let us condemn him, tread him down in water,
    While he doth lie upon the bank. Away!'   790
    Where some, more tardy, cry unto their bearers,
    'He will be censured ere we come. Run, knaves!'
    And use that furious diligence, for fear
    Their bondmen should inform against their slackness,
    And bring their quaking flesh unto the hook.   795
    The rout, they follow with confusèd voice,
    Crying, they'are glad, say they could ne'er abide him;
    Enquire, what man he was? What kind of face?
    What beard he had? What nose? What lips? Protest

---

784. furnace] *Q;* fornace *F.*   784. to] *corr. Q;* too *uncorr. Q, F.*
784. work,] *Edd.;* worke *Q, F.*   786. pit.'] *Barish ends quotation after*
reverencèd! *No quotation marks in Q, F, for* 789–90, 792.   792. Knaves !']
knaves; *corr. F;* Knaves, *Q;* knaves, *uncorr. F.*

787–8. *the Senate ... again*] Jonson cites Dio, *Roman History*, LVIII.11.4,
'that very day, the senate assembled in the temple of Concord not far from the
jail, when they saw the attitude of the populace ..., and condemned him to
death'.

789–95.] From Juvenal, *Satires*, X.85–8, '"Let us rush headlong and
trample on Caesar's enemy, while he lies upon the bank!"—"Ay, and let our
slaves see that none bear witness against us, and drag their trembling master
into court with a halter round his neck"'.

790. *upon the bank*] of the Tiber, where bodies of the executed were
displayed.

791. *their bearers*] those who carry them through the streets.

795. *the hook*] see II.416n.

798–814.] Jonson cites Juvenal, *Satires*, X.67–77: '"What a lip the fellow
had! What a face!"—"Believe me, I never liked the man!"—"But on what
charge was he condemned? Who informed against him? What was the
evidence, who the witnesses, who made good the case?"—"Nothing of the
sort; a great and wordy letter came from Capri."—"Good; I ask no more."
And what does the mob of Remus say? It follows fortune, as it always does,
and rails against the condemned. That same rabble, if Nortia [Etruscan
Fortune] had smiled upon the Etruscan [Sejanus, b. in Volsinii, Etruria], if the
aged Emperor had been struck down unawares, would in that very hour have
conferred upon Sejanus the title of Augustus.' The opening scornful excla-
mations, as Gifford pointed out, are misunderstood by Jonson to be questions.

They ever did presage h'would come to this—   800
They never thought him wise nor valiant; ask
After his garments, when he dies? What death?
And not a beast of all the herd demands,
What was his crime? Or, who were his accusers?
Under what proof or testimony he fell?   805
'There came', says one, 'a huge, long, worded letter
From Capreae against him.' 'Did there so?
O!'—they are satisfied; no more.
Lepidus.   Alas!
They follow Fortune, and hate men condemned,
Guilty or not.
Arruntius.   But had Sejanus thrived   810
In his design, and prosperously oppressed
The old Tiberius, then, in that same minute,
These very rascals, that now rage like furies,
Would have proclaimed Sejanus emperor.
Lepidus. But what hath followed?
Terentius.   Sentence, by the Senate, 815
To lose his head—which was no sooner off,
But that and th'unfortunate trunk were seized
By the rude multitude; who, not content
With what the forward justice of the state
Officiously had done, with violent rage   820
Have rent it limb from limb. A thousand heads,
A thousand hands, ten thousand tongues and voices,
Employed at once in several acts of malice!

---

805. proof] *Q, corr. F;* roofe *uncorr. F.*   807. Capreae] *Capreae F; Capraeae
Q.*   808. O!'] *This ed.; O, Q, F. Bolton excludes from quotation. No quotation
marks in Q, F, for 806–8.*   816. lose] *F;* loose *Q.*   822. voices,] *F;* voices
Q.

---

811. *prosperously oppressed*] successfully struck down.

813. *rascals*] rabble.

815–6. *Sentence ... head*] Jonson cites the passage in Dio quoted above,
V.787–8n.

817–21. *that ... from limb*] Jonson quotes Seneca, *On Tranquility of Mind,*
xi.11, 'Yet on the day on which the senate played the escort, the people tore
him to pieces!'

818. *rude*] ignorant.

819. *forward*] eager.

823. *several*] different.

Old men not staid with age, virgins with shame,
Late wives with loss of husbands, mothers of children,   825
Losing all grief in joy of his sad fall,
Run quite transported with their cruelty—
These mounting at his head, these at his face,
These digging out his eyes, those with his brain,
Sprinkling themselves, their houses, and their friends.   830
Others are met, have ravished thence an arm,
And deal small pieces of the flesh for favours;
These with a thigh; this hath cut off his hands;
And this his feet; these, fingers, and these, toes;
That hath his liver; he his heart; there wants   835
Nothing but room for wrath, and place for hatred.
What cannot oft be done is now o'erdone.
The whole, and all of what was great Sejanus,
And next to Caesar did possess the world,
Now torn and scattered, as he needs no grave;   840
Each little dust covers a little part.

826. Losing] *F;* Loosing *Q.*   834. these, fingers] *F2;* these fingers *Q, F.*
834. these, toes] *F2;* these toes *Q, F.*

824–42.] The source for this passage, Claudian's *Against Rufinus*, II.
410–53, is not acknowledged by Jonson, who rearranges the material. See
Appendix A.

825. *staid*] sober; a pun on 'stayed'.

828. *mounting*] *H.&S.*, along with other editors, think the word hopelessly
inappropriate in its context. Whalley, cited by *H.&S.*, noted an earlier suggested emendation to 'minting'—'aiming blows'—but *O.E.D.*'s examples for
this sense of the verb 'mint' are mainly Scottish. There is perhaps something to
be said for 'mounting', given that Jonson carefully supervised the printing of
both *Q* and *F* texts. The excited citizens in the passage in Claudian which is
the source for Jonson's description of events here—see preceding note—throw
stones at the head of Rufinus which is carried *above* them, and it is hard not to
imagine them jumping up at it (and perhaps scrambling over each other), like
dogs at proffered meat; in fact Claudian likens them to a pack of savage
Molossian hounds. Jonson's distinction between the head and the face, which
H.&S. find a further confusion, makes sense if one takes note of the syntax of
ll. 828 and 829. In 829, 'These digging out his eyes' are the second group
mentioned in 828—i.e. the group concerned to get particularly at the face—
while 'those with his brain' are the first-mentioned group in 828—i.e. the
group merely concerned to get at the head (as the seat of the brain), for the
word 'those' in 829, gramatically speaking, must refer to the first group in
the preceding line.

835–6. *there ... hatred*] i.e., wrath and hatred burst all bounds.

841. *little dust*] small amount of dirt.

So lies he nowhere, and yet often buried.

[*Enter*] NUNTIUS.

Arruntius. More of Sejanus?
Nuntius.   Yes.
Lepidus.   What can be added?
   We know him dead.
Nuntius.   Then there begin your pity.
   There is enough behind to melt ev'n Rome   845
   And Caesar into tears—since never slave
   Could yet so highly'offend, but tyranny,
   In torturing him, would make him worth lamenting.
   A son and daughter to the dead Sejanus,
   Of whom there is not now so much remaining   850
   As would give fast'ning to the hangman's hook,
   Have they drawn forth for farther sacrifice;
   Whose tenderness of knowledge, unripe years,
   And childish silly innocence was such
   As scarce would lend them feeling of their danger;   855

842.1. [*Enter*] NUNTIUS.] NVNTIVS. &c. *Q;* ARRVNTIVS, NVNTIVS, LEPIDVS,
TERENTIVS. *F.*   843. *Arruntius.*] ARR. *Q; not in F.*   844. pity.] *F;* pitty, *Q.*
846. since] *F;* though *Q.*   847. highly'offend] *Q, H.&S.;* highly offend *F.*
852. farther] farder *Q, F.*

845. *behind*] still to come.
849–67. *A son ... Gemonies*] Jonson cites Tacitus, *Annals*, VI.v.9: 'It was
then determined that the surviving children of Sejanus should pay the penalty,
though the anger of the populace was nearly spent and the majority of men had
been placated by the earlier executions. They were therefore carried to the
dungeon, the boy conscious of the fate in store for him, the girl so completely
ignorant that she asked repeatedly what her offence had been and to what place
they were dragging her: she would do wrong no more, and she could be
cautioned with the usual childish beating. It is recorded by authors of the
period that, as it was considered an unheard-of thing for capital punishment to
be inflicted on a virgin, she was violated by the executioner with the halter
beside her: they were then strangled, and their young bodies thrown on to the
Gemonian Stairs'. Jonson also cites Dio, *Roman History*, LVIII.11.5, 'His
children also were put to death by decree, the girl (whom he had betrothed to
the son of Claudius) having been first outraged by the public executioner on
the principle that it was unlawful for a virgin to be put to death in the prison'.
But see below, V.859–60n.
850–1.] Jonson cites Seneca, *On Tranquility of Mind*, xi.11, 'Of the man
who had had heaped upon him all that gods and men were able to bestow
nothing was left for the executioner to drag to the river!'
854. *silly*] simple.

The girl so simple, as she often asked,
Where they would lead her? For what cause they dragged
  her?
Cried, she would do no more. That she could take
Warning with beating. And because our laws
Admit no virgin immature to die,   860
The wittily and strangely cruel Macro
Delivered her to be deflow'red and spoiled
By the rude lust of the licentious hangman,
Then to be strangled with her harmless brother.
Lepidus. O act most worthy hell and lasting night,   865
To hide it from the world!
Nuntius.   Their bodies thrown
Into the Gemonies, I know not how
Or by what accident returned, the mother,
Th'expulsèd Apicata, finds them there;
Whom when she saw lie spread on the degrees,   870
After a world of fury on herself,
Tearing her hair, defacing of her face,

---

872. hair] *corr. Q, F;* heare *uncorr. Q.*

859–60. *our laws . . . die*] Jonson notes that the law was concerned that no *immature* virgin, as opposed to virgins generally, should so die; its concern was over age rather than technical virginity. He cites a note in Lipsius to this effect. The point is important, since it explains 'wittily, and strangely cruel' in the following line.

861. *wittily and strangely cruel*] see preceeding note. 'Strangely' = unnaturally.

865–6. *O . . . world*] *H.&S.* cite Seneca, *Thyestes*, 1094–5, 'cover with endless darkness boundless crimes'.

868–87. *the mother . . . Drusus*] Jonson cites Dio, *Roman History*, LVIII.11.6: 'His wife Apicata was not condemned, to be sure, but on learning that her children were dead, and after seeing their bodies on the Stairway, she withdrew and composed a statement about the death of Drusus, directed against Livilla, his wife, who had been the cause of a quarrel between herself and her husband, resulting in their separation; then, after sending this document to Tiberius, she committed suicide. It was in this way that Tiberius came to read her statement; and when he had obtained proof of the information given, he put to death Livilla and all the others therein mentioned.'

869. *expulsèd*] divorced, as Barish notes, rather than exiled, as Bolton has it. Not in *O.E.D.* Latin *expulsa*, rejected (as a wife, among other senses).

870. *degrees*] steps. Jonson's note reminds his reader that the custom was to expose the bodies of executed criminals on the Gemonian steps, leading from the Capitol to the Forum Romanum.

Beating her breasts and womb, kneeling amazed,
Crying to heaven, then to them; at last,
Her drownèd voice gat up above her woes,   875
And with such black and bitter execrations
As might affright the gods, and force the sun
Run backward to the east—nay, make the old
Deformèd Chaos rise again, t'o'erwhelm
Them, us, and all the world—she fills the air,   880
Upbraids the heavens with their partial dooms,
Defies their tyrannous powers, and demands
What she and those poor innocents have transgressed,
That they must suffer such a share in vengeance,
Whilst Livia, Lygdus, and Eudemus live—   885
Who, as she says, and firmly vows to prove it
To Caesar and the Senate, poisoned Drusus.
Lepidus. Confederates with her husband?
Nuntius.   Ay.
Lepidus.   Strange act!
Arruntius. And strangely opened. What says now my monster,
The multitude? They reel now, do they not?   890
Nuntius. Their gall is gone, and now they 'gin to weep
The mischief they have done.
Arruntius.   I thank 'em, rogues!

875. gat] gate *Q, F.*   887. Drusus.] *Drusus? Q;* DRVSVS? *F.*   890. now,]
now? *Q, F.*   892. *Arruntius.*] ARR. *corr. Q;* AKR. *uncorr. Q.*

---

873. *amazed*] distraught.
875. *drownèd . . . woes*] i.e., her voice overcame her tearful sobbing.
877–9. *force . . . again*] references, as *H.&S.* point out, to Seneca's *Thyestes*, 784ff., where the sun moves backwards and darkness envelopes the earth and it seems that 'once more gods and men' will 'be o'erwhelmed by formless chaos'.
881. *partial*] unfair.
885.] another note citing the passage in Dio quoted at V.868–87n.
889–92. *monster . . . have done*] Cf. Marston, *Malcontent*, ed. G. K. Hunter (London, 1975), III.iii.5–6, 'that beast with many heads, / The staggering multitude'; and other examples in Tilley, M 1308. On the contradictory nature of a mob, cf. Livy, XXIV.xxv.8: 'either it is a humble slave or a haughty master. As for freedom, which is the mean, they know no moderation either in assuming or in keeping it'.
890. *reel*] sway unsteadily as a result of intoxication.
891–2. *now . . . done*] Riddell, 'Seventeenth-Century Identifications', p. 208, provides Seneca, *Troades*, 1119, 'the throng of Greeks wept for the crime it wrought'.

Nuntius. Part are so stupid, or so flexible,
    As they believe him innocent. All grieve.
    And some, whose hands yet reek with his warm blood,   895
    And gripe the part which they did tear of him,
    Wish him collected, and created new.
Lepidus. How Fortune plies her sports, when she begins
    To practise 'em! Pursues, continues, adds!
    Confounds, with varying her impassioned moods!   900
Arruntius. Dost thou hope, Fortune, to redeem thy crimes?
    To make amends for thy ill-placèd favours
    With these strange punishments? Forbear, you things
    That stand upon the pinnacles of state,
    To boast your slippery height. When you do fall,   905
    You pash yourselves in pieces, ne'er to rise,
    And he that lends you pity is not wise.
Terentius. Let this example move th'insolent man
    Not to grow proud, and careless of the gods.
    It is an odious wisdom to blaspheme,   910
    Much more to slighten or deny their powers.
    For whom the morning saw so great and high,
    Thus low and little, 'fore the'even, doth lie.   [*Exeunt.*]

FINIS

---

901. crimes?] *F;* crimes, *Q.*   910–911. *Both lines preceded by gnomic pointing, Q.*   913. the'even, doth] the'Euen doth *corr. Q;* the 'Evendoth *uncorr. Q;* the'euen doth   *F.* FINIS] *Q;* THE END.*F.*

---

893. *flexible*] easily influenced (Latin *flectere*, to turn).

898–9. *How ... practise 'em*] Cf. Horace, *Satires*, II.viii.62–3, on Fortuna who 'dost ever delight to make sport of the life of man'. Loeb ed., tr. H. R. Fairclough (London, 1947).

903–7. *Forbear ... wise*] another debt to the passage in Claudian used in V.824–42 above: 'Put not your trust in prosperity; learn that the gods are inconstant and heaven untrustworthy'. See also V.442n. The idea that the greater the tower, the more heavily it crashes, is commonplace (Briggs cites Horace, *Odes*, II.x.10; Juvenal, *Satires*, X.106; and Seneca, *Hercules Furens*, 201).

906. *pash*] dash.

910. *wisdom*] exercise of wit—a sense not recorded in *O.E.D.*

912–3.] Briggs cites Seneca, *Thyestes*, 613–14, 'Whom the rising sun hath seen high in pride, him the setting sun hath seen laid low'; and *Hercules Oetaeus*, 641–2, 'Whom Cynthia saw in happiness, the new-born day sees wretched'.

This tragedy was first
acted in the year
1603

by the King's Majesty's
SERVANTS.   5

The principal tragedians were

RICHARD BURBAGE   WILLIAM SHAKESPEARE
AUGUSTINE PHILLIPS   JOHN HEMMINGES
WILLIAM SLY   HENRY CONDELL

Add. 1–11. This tragedy ... REVELS.] *F; not in Q.*   Add. 1. tragedy]
Tragoedie *F.*   Add. 6. tragedians] Tragoedians *F.*   Add. 7–10. RICHARD
... COOKE] *F prints in two columns but with names abbreviated:* RIC.
BVRBADGE. / AVG. PHILIPS. / WILL. SLY. / IOH. LOWIN. *second column:*
WILL. SHAKE-SPEARE. / IOH. HEMINGS. / HEN. CONDEL. / ALEX. COOKE.

6–10.] On possible roles, see Introduction, pp. 37–8.

7. *RICHARD BURBAGE*] Born *c.* 1567, son of James Burbage, who built
the Theatre in 1576. Member of the Chamberlain's (later King's) Men from
1594. Jonson pays tribute to him in *B.F.*, V.iii.86–8, 'which is your *Burbage*
now? ... Your best *Actor*'. Also heads the cast lists in *F* for *E.M.O.*, *Volp.*,
Alc., and *Cat.*, and played, among other parts, Richard III, Hamlet, Othello,
Lear and Macbeth.

7. *WILLIAM SHAKESPEARE*] With the Chamberlain's-King's Men
from 1594. Also acted in *E.M.I.*, and of course in his own plays and those of
other dramatists. He was a part-owner of the Globe and the Blackfriars, and
eight or nine years Jonson's senior.

8. *AUGUSTINE PHILLIPS*] Long-time member of the company, an
original Globe shareholder, and actor in Shakespeare's plays. Heywood
praised his talents *c.* 1608, by which time he was dead.

8. *JOHN HEMMINGES*] Another long-term member of the company,
shareholder in the Globe and Blackfriars theatres. With Henry Condell he
supervised the publication of the first folio of Shakespeare's plays in 1623; d.
1630. Also acted in *E.M.I.*, *E.M.O.*, *Volp.*, *Alc.*, and *Cat.*

9. *WILLIAM SLY*] Longstanding member of the company, also acting in
E.M.I., *E.M.O.*, and *Volp.* Marston presents him (as William Sly) in the
Induction to *The Malcontent* (1605); d. 1608.

9. *HENRY CONDELL*] Longstanding member of the company, shareholder in the Globe and Blackfriars theatres, and with Hemminges edited the
Shakespeare first folio. Played the Cardinal in Webster's *Duchess of Malfi* and
appeared in *E.M.I..*, *Volp.*, *Alc.*, as well as *Sej.*, and in several of Shakepeare's
plays.

JOHN LOWIN   ALEXANDER COOKE   10

With the allowance of the Master of REVELS.

---

10. *JOHN LOWIN*] Joined the company shortly before the first production of *Sej.*, at the age of 27. Also in *Volp.*, *Alc.*, *Cat.* Played comic and villain roles, had a high reputation and, at least in the physical sense, a formidable presence; d. 1653.

10. *ALEXANDER COOKE*] Entered the company at about the same time as Lowin, and played in some of Shakespeare's plays as well as in *Sej.*, *Volp.*, *Alc.*, and *Cat.*; d. 1614.

11. Master of *REVELS*] Edmund Tilney when *Q* was published in 1605, Sir George Buc when *F* was published in 1616. The Master of the Revels organised entertainments at court, licensed plays for performance and (after 1607) for printing, and was paid out of the royal purse.

Longer passages from classical sources cited in the Commentary Notes

I.128–54. Tacitus, Annals, *II.lxxii–lxxiii*

Foreign nations and princes felt the pang—so great had been his courtesy to allies, his humanity to enemies: in aspect and address alike venerable, while he maintained the magnificence and dignity of exalted fortune, he had escaped envy and avoided arrogance. His funeral, devoid of ancestral effigies or procession, was distinguished by eulogies and recollections of his virtues. There were those who, considering his personal appearance, his early age, and the circumstances of his death, —to which they added the proximity of the region where he perished, —compared his decease with that of Alexander the Great:-'Each eminently handsome, of famous lineage, and in years not much exceeding thirty, had fallen among alien races by the treason of their countrymen. But the Roman had borne himself as one gentle to his friends, moderate in his pleasures, content with a single wife and the children of lawful wedlock. Nor was he less a man of the sword; though he lacked the other's temerity, and, when his numerous victories had beaten down the Germanies, was prohibited from making fast their bondage. But had he been the sole arbiter of affairs, of kingly authority and title, he would have overtaken the Greek in military fame with an ease proportioned to his superiority in clemency, self-command, and all other good qualities'.

III.407–60. Tacitus, Annals, *IV.xxxiv–xxxv*

'Conscript Fathers, my words are brought to judgement—so guiltless am I of deeds! Nor are they even words against the sole persons embraced by the law of treason, the sovereign or the parent of the sovereign: I am said to have praised Brutus and Cassius, whose acts so many pens have recorded, whom not one has mentioned save with honour. Livy, with a fame for eloquence and candour second to none, lavished such eulogies on Pompey that Augustus styled him "the Pompeian": yet it was without prejudice to their friendship. Scipio, Afranius, this very Cassius, this Brutus—not once does he describe them by the now fashionable titles of brigand and parricide, but time and again in such terms as he might apply to any distinguished patriots. The works of Asinius Pollio transmit their character in noble colours; Messalla Corvinus gloried to have served under Cassius: and Pollio and Corvinus lived and died in the fulness of wealth and honour! When Cicero's book praised Cato to the skies, what did it elicit from the dictator Caesar but a written oration as though at the bar of public opinion? The letters of Antony, the speeches of Brutus, contain invectives against Augustus, false undoubtedly yet bitter in the extreme; the poems—still read—of Bibaculus and Catullus are packed with scurrilities upon the Caesars: yet even the deified Julius, the divine Augustus himself, tolerated them and left them in peace; and I hesitate whether to ascribe their action to forbearance or to wisdom. For things contemned are soon things forgotten: anger is read as a recognition.

'I leave untouched the Greeks; with them not liberty only but licence itself went unchastised, or, if a man retaliated, he avenged words by words. But what above all else was absolutely free and immune from censure was the expression of an opinion on those whom death had removed beyond the range of rancour or of partiality. Are Brutus and Cassius under arms on the plains of Philippi, and I upon the platform, firing the nation to civil war? Or is it the case that, seventy years since their taking-off, as they are known by their effigies which the conqueror himself did not abolish, so a portion of their memory is enshrined likewise in history? —To every man posterity renders his wage of honour; nor will there lack, if my condemnation is at hand, those who shall remember, not Brutus and Cassius alone, but me also!'

III.503–29. Tacitus, Annals, *IV.xxxix*
Meanwhile Sejanus, blinded by over-great good fortune and fired to action by feminine passion as well—Livia was demanding the promised marriage—drafted a memorial to the Caesar: it was a convention of the period to address him in writing even when he was in the capital. The gist of the document was that 'owing to the benevolence of the prince's father Augustus, followed by so many expressions of approval from Tiberius, he had formed the habit of carrying his hopes and his vows to the imperial ears as readily as to the gods. He had never asked for the baubles of office: he would rather stand sentry and work like the humblest soldier for the security of the emperor. And yet he had reached the supreme goal—he had been counted worthy of an alliance with the Caesar. This had taught him to hope; and since he had heard that Augustus, when settling his daughter, had to some extent considered the claims even of Roman knights, so, if a husband should be required for Livia, he begged that Tiberius would bear in mind a friend who would derive nothing from the connection but its glory. For he did not seek to divest himself of the duties laid on him: it was enough, in his estimation, if his family was strengthened against the unfounded animosities of Agrippina; and that simply for the sake of his children. As to himself, whatever the term of years he might complete under such a sovereign, it would be life enough and to spare!

III.530–76. Tacitus, Annals, *IV.xl*
In reply, Tiberius praised Sejanus' devotion, touched not too heavily on his own services to him, and asked for time, in order, he said, to consider the matter fully and freely. Then he wrote again:- 'With other men, the standpoint for their decisions was what was in their own interests: the lot of princes was very different, as their weightiest affairs had to be regulated with an eye upon public opinion. Therefore he did not take refuge in the answer which came most readily to the pen—that Livia could determine for herself whether she ought to marry after Drusus or rest content with her old home, and that she had a mother and grandmother who were more natural advisers. He would deal more openly: and first with regard to Agrippina's enmity, which would blaze out far more fiercely if Livia's marriage divided, as it were, the Caesarian house into two camps. Even as matters stood, there were outbreaks of feminine jealousy, and the feud was unsettling his grandchildren. What then if the strife was accentuated by the proposed union?'—'For, Sejanus,' he continued, 'you

delude yourself, if you imagine that you can keep your present rank, or that the Livia who has been wedded successively to Gaius Caesar and to Drusus will be complaisant enough to grow old at the side of a Roman knight. Assuming that I myself consent, do you suppose the position will be tolerated by those who have seen her brother, her father, and our ancestors, in the supreme offices of state? You wish, for your own part, to stop short at the station you hold: but those magistrates and men of distinction who take you by storm and consult you on any and every subject make no secret of their opinion that you have long since transcended the heights of the equestrian order and left the friendships of my father far behind; and in their envy of you they censure myself as well. —You make the point that Augustus considered the possibility of bestowing his daughter on a Roman knight. Astonishing, certainly, that, tugged at by every sort of anxiety, and foreseeing an immense accession of dignity to the man whom he should have raised above his peers by such an alliance, his conversation ran on Gaius Proculeius and a few others, remarkable for their quietude of life and implicated in none of the business of that state! But, if we are to be moved by the hesitancy of Augustus, how much more cogent the fact that he affianced her to Marcus Agrippa and later to myself! —I have spoken openly, as was due to our friendship; but I shall oppose neither your decisions nor those of Livia. Of the result of my own reflections, and the further ties by which I propose to cement our union, I shall at present forbear to speak. One point only I shall make clear: no station, however exalted, would be unearned by your qualities and your devotion to myself; and when the occasion comes, either in the senate or before the public, I shall not be silent.'

IV.93–232. Tacitus, Annals, IV.lxviii–lxx
[As A.D. 28 opened,] the great Roman knight, Titius Sabinus, was dragged to the dungeon to expiate his friendship with Germanicus. For he had abated nothing of his scrupulous attentions to the widow and children of the dead, but remained their visitor at home, their companion in public—the one survivor of that multitude of clients, and rewarded, as such, by the admiration of the good and the hatred of the malevolent. He was singled out for attack by Latinius Latiaris, Porcius Cato, Petilius Rufus, and Marcus Opsius, ex-praetors enamoured of the consulate: an office to which there was no avenue but through Sejanus, while the complaisance of Sejanus was only to be purchased by crime.... [Latiaris proceeded to gain Sabinus's confidence with] eulogies on the constancy of Sabinus, who, unlike the rest, had not abandoned in its affliction the house to which he had been attached in its prosperity, ... [referring] to Germanicus in terms of honour, and to Agrippina in a strain of pity.... [Sabinus, losing control of his emotions,] broke into tears coupled with complaints, ... grew bolder and showered reproaches on Sejanus, his cruelty, his arrogance, his ambition. Even Tiberius was not spared.

[Having won the confidence of the man, Latiaris now proceeded to betray him.] ... Between roof and ceiling—an ambuscade as humiliating as the ruse was detestable—three senators inserted themselves, and applied their ears to chinks and openings.... [Latiaris entered with Sabinus, rehearsing the growing evil of the times.] Sabinus replied in the same vein, but at greater length: for grief, when once it has overflowed, becomes more difficult to repress. The accusation was now hurried forward; and in a letter to the Caesar the associates exposed the sequence of the plot.

[Sabinus was charged by Tiberius in a letter read to the Senate on New Year's Day] ... with the corruption of several of his freedmen, and with designs upon himself.... Vengeance was decreed without loss of time; and the doomed man was dragged to his death, crying with all the vigour allowed by the cloak muffling his head and the noose around his neck, that 'these were the ceremonies that inaugurated the year, these the victims that bled to propitiate Sejanus!'

V.545–659. Dio, Roman History, LVIII.10.1–5:
In the meantime the letter was read. It was a long one, and contained no wholesale denunciation of Sejanus, but first some other matter, then a slight censure of his conduct, then something else, and after that some further objection to him; and at the close it said that two senators who were among his intimate associates must be punished and that he himself must be kept under guard. For Tiberius refrained from giving orders outright to put him to death, not because he did not wish to give such orders, but because he feared that some disturbance might result from such a course. At any rate, he pretended that he could not with safety even make the journey to Rome, and therefore summoned one of the consuls to him. Now the letter disclosed no more than this; but one could observe both by sight and hearing many and various effects produced by it. At first, before it was read, they had been lauding Sejanus, thinking that he was about to receive the tribunician power, and had kept cheering him, anticipating the honours for which they hoped and making it clear to him that they would concur in bestowing them. When, however, nothing of the sort appeared, but they heard again and again just the reverse of what they had expected, they were at first perplexed, and then thrown into deep dejection. Some of those seated near him actually rose up and left him; for they now no longer cared to share the same seat with the man whom previously they had prized having as their friend. Then praetors and tribunes surrounded him, to prevent his causing any disturbance by rushing out, as he certainly would have done, if he had been startled at the outset by hearing any general denunciation. As it was, he paid no great heed to the successive charges as they were read, thinking each one a slight matter which stood alone, and hoping that, at best, no further charge, or, in any event, none that could not be disposed of, was contained in the letter; so he let the time slip by and remained in his seat.

V.824–42. Claudian, Against Rufinus, II.410–53
They stamp on that face of greed and while yet he lives pluck out his eyes; others seize and carry off his severed arms. One cuts off his foot, another wrenches a shoulder from the torn sinews; one lays bare the ribs of the cleft spine, another his liver, his heart, his still panting lungs. There is not space enough to satisfy their anger nor room to wreak their hate. Scarce when his death had been accomplished do they leave him; his body is hacked in pieces and the fragments borne on the soldiers' spears. Thus red with blood ran the Boeotian mountain when the Maenads caused Pentheus' destruction or when Latona's daughter seen by Actaeon betrayed the huntsman, suddenly transformed into a stag, to the fury of her Molossian hounds.... The citizens leave the town and hasten exulting to the spot from every quarter, old men and girls among them whom nor age nor sex could keep at home. Widows whose

husbands he had killed, mothers whose children he had murdered hurry to the joyful scene with eager steps. They are fain to trample the torn limbs and stain their deep pressed feet with the blood. So, too, they eagerly hurl a shower of stones at the monstrous head, nodding from the summit of the spear that transfixed it as it was carried back in merited splendour to the city.... See, he who owns the world lies denied six foot of earth, half covered with a sprinkling of dust, given no grave yet given so many.

APPENDIX B

Collations of 1605 Quarto and 1616 Folio

I. 1605 QUARTO (COPY-TEXT) COLLATION (ARRANGED BY FORMES)

Key to copies collated

 1. New York Public Library
 2. Yale University
 3. Harvard 1
 4. Harvard 2
 5. Folger
 6. Nat. Lib. of Scotland
 7. British Lib. (Ashley 3464)
    (ex-Wise)
 8. British Lib. (644. b. 53)
 9. Huntington (ex-Huth)
10. Bodleian (Malone 222.7)
11. Bodleian (Malone 184)
12. John Wolfson 1 (sold 1983)
13. John Wolfson 2

14. Victoria and Albert Mus.
    (Dyce 1)
15. Victoria and Albert Mus.
    (Dyce 2)
16. Victoria and Albert Mus.
    (Dyce 3)
17. Chapin Lib.
18. Pforzheimer Lib.
19. Newberry Lib.
20. Earl of Verulam
21. New College, Oxford
22. St John's College, Cambridge
23. Turnbull Lib., N.Z.

There are five copies which I was unable to collate: one in Corpus Christi College, Oxford; two in King's College, Cambridge; one in Dartmouth College, Hanover, New Hamsphire; and one at the Pierpont Morgan Library. Information was kindly provided on three of these by librarians at Kings and at Dartmouth College, allowing me to assign their formes to the categories 'uncorrected state', 'first corrected state' and 'second corrected state' on the basis of my collation of the twenty-three. No anomalies were noted. My thanks are especially due to the libraries and individuals who provided microfilm or photocopies.

1. *Prelims (outer)*
There are two stages of correction:
(*a*) *Stage 1: Uncorrected:* 2
            Corrected: the rest

	Uncorrected	Corrected
sig. ¶1r	Writen	Written

(*b*) *Stage 2: Uncorrected:* 2, 3, 10, 15
            Corrected: the rest, but see note

	Uncorrected	Corrected
sig. ¶1r	Ellde	Elld

(Note: leaf ¶1 missing in 11, 12, 13, 21, 22, 23)

2. *Prelims (inner)*
Uncorrected: 2, 3, 10, 12, 15, 16

269

Corrected: the rest

sig. ¶2r, 'To the Readers', l. 14	*Uncorrected* Horace,	*Corrected* Horace

(Note: leaf ¶2 misssing in 11, 23)

sig. ¶3v, 'In SEIANVM', ll. 31	*thy s ubiect*	*thy subiect*
34	*Semicircle*	*Semi-circle*
35	*Sphaere*	*Sphaere,*
36	*Liues,*	*Liues:*
46	*And ... waters*	*And, ... waters,*
58	*presence*	*Presence*
62	*faltter*	*falter*
sig. ¶4r, ll. 67	*eye ... flame*	*eye, ... flame,*
69	*truly,*	*truly*
70	*inspireth*	*inspireth:*
71	*unduly,*	*unduly*
85	*others*	*Others*
92	*emminence*	*emminence,*
93	*one*	*One*
94	*another*	*Another*
95	*life,*	*Life*
95	*knowne.*	*knowne:*
96	*all Degrees,*	*all Degrees.*
100	*deseruing.*	*deseruing:*

(Note: leaves ¶3 and 4 missing in 23)

3. Sheet A (inner)
There are two stages of correction:
(a) Stage 1: Uncorrected: 19
       Corrected: the rest

	Uncorrected	*Corrected*
sig. A1v, 'In SEIANVM', ll. 175–8	not indented	indented
sig. A2r, 'For ... Author', ll. 3	ambitions	Ambition's
4	heau'd	heaue
6	Kings	*Kings*
13	Time's	Times
'To ... Author', ll. 6	grace,	grace;
8	greatnesse;	greatnesse,
12	*Tragedians*	*Tragedians,*
sig. A3v, 'To ... subiect', l. 8	And ... conceat.	(And ... conceat.)
'To ... Poet', ll. 1	When ... worlds	Whē ... Worlds (line less crowded)
15	ED.B.	Ev. B.
sig. A4r, 'THE ARGVMENT', ll. 13	sussesful	successful
18	selfe	selfe,
18	meanes	meanes;
25	life	Life

Probably as a result of an accident during the last of these changes, *Tiberius* in the following line became *Tiberias*, which was put back to rights in the following stage.

(b) *Stage 2: Uncorrected:* 1, 7, 8, 9, 14, 15, 18, 20
    Corrected: the rest, 19 excepted

	Uncorrected	*Corrected*
sig. A4r, 'THE ARGVMENT', l. 26	*Tiberias*	*Tiberius*

(Note: sigs. A1r–A3v missing in 23)

4. *Sheet B (outer)*
There are two stages of correction:
(a) *Stage 1: Uncorrected:* 12, 23
    Corrected: the rest

	Uncorrected	*Corrected*
sig. B1r, I.11	ᶜWe did by	We did byᶜ
14	ᵈThat we	That weᵈ

(b) *Stage 2: Uncorrected:* 5, 12, 23
    Corrected: the rest

	Uncorrected	*Corrected*
sig. B2v, I.123	(He	(he
141	Lands	lands
sig. B3r, I.146	*Macedons*	Macedon's
	Lou'd	lou'd

5. *Sheet B (inner)*
Uncorrected: 1, 5, 7, 9, 12, 14, 16, 21, 23
Corrected: the rest

	Uncorrected	*Corrected*
sig. B3v, I.195	On?	On.

6. *Sheet C (outer)*
Uncorrected: 18, 20
Corrected: the rest

	Uncorrected	*Corrected*
sig. C4v, I.581.1	M. CHORVS.	MV. CHORVS.

(Note: sheet C missing in 19)

7. *Sheet E (outer)*
No correction. *H.&S.* distinguish between *clarescere* and *clareseere* on sig. E2v, but only poor inking obscures the fact that all copies read *clarescere*.

8. *Sheet E (inner)*
There are two stages of correction:
(a) *Stage 1: Uncorrected:* 3, 12, 15, 23
    Corrected: the rest

	Uncorrected	*Corrected*
sig. E1v, II.363	he (must	(he must
sig. E3v, II.493	noyse	noyse,

III.5	do it	do it,
sig. E4r, III.16	noble-lookers	noble Lookers

(b) Stage 2: Uncorrected: 1, 2, 3, 4, 5, 7, 9, 10, 11, 12, 13, 14, 15, 16, 21, 23
       Corrected: the rest

	Uncorrected	Corrected
sig. E2r, II.403	saftly	safety

9. *Sheet F (outer)*
There are two states of correction
Uncorrected: 6, 19
Corrected (1st state): 11
Corrected (2nd state): the rest

	Uncorrected	Corrected (1)	Corrected (2)
sig. F1r, III.96	now?	now!	as for (1), but
sig. F2v, III.213	dignity	dignity,	notes correct,
221	Nay I	Nay, I	first referring
sig. F3r, III.236	of *State*	of the *State*	to Tacitus,
sig. F4v, III.354	ô that	ô, that	second to
360	Informers	Informers,	Tacitus and
	both notes absent	notes present but	Dio
		elements	
		reversed, first	
		referring to Dio,	
		second twice to	
		Tacitus	

10. *Sheet G (outer)*
Uncorrected: 3, 5, 21
Corrected: the rest

	Uncorrected	Corrected
sig. G2r, III.487	Beneath	Betweene
sig. G4r, III.635	more,	more
636	hates,	hates

11. *Sheet H (outer)*
There are two stages of correction, with two states of the second stage, involving introduction of error and its correction.
(a) *Stage 1: Uncorrected:* 4, 8, 20
       Corrected: the rest

	Uncorrected	Corrected
sig. H1r, III.706	stild	stil'd
sig. H2v, IV.48	Spelunca	*Spelunca
	no note*	note * present
sig. H3r, IV.67	oppose:	oppose;
77	trust and Grace	trust, and grace
93	Lord *Seianus*	Lord ª *Seianus*
98	speed:	speed.
sig. H4v, IV.182	look't	look't,
187	in her,	in her;
189	her.	her:

190	Frownes	frownes
190	Iealousies	iealousies
191	Hatred	hatred
191	bursl	burst
204	Sonne	Sonne,
206	ambitious	ambitious,
207	clings	clasp's
210	him in	him, in
211	him, in	him, by

(b) *Stage 2: Uncorrected:* 2, 4, 8, 10, 13, 20
 Corrected (1st state): 17
 Corrected (2nd state): the rest

	Uncorrected	Corrected (1) (with error introduced)	Corrected (2) (error eliminated)
sig. H3r, IV.82	most	must	must
78	then	hem (error)	then

12. *Sheet I (outer)*
Uncorrected: 6, 11, 19
Corrected: the rest

	Uncorrected	Corrected
sig. I3r, IV.363	Night-ey d	Night-ey'd

13. *Sheet I (inner)*
Uncorrected: 1, 7, 8, 9, 14
Corrected: the rest

	Uncorrected	Corrected
sig. I3v, IV.414	MAR.	MIN.

14. *Sheet K (inner)*
Uncorrected: 4, 8, 11, 13, 17, 18, 20
Corrected: the rest

	Uncorrected	Corrected
sig. K3v, V.170.2	TIRENTIVS	TERENTIVS
175	vessels	Vessels
175	offrings	Offrings

15. *Sheet L (outer)*
There are two stages of correction:
(a) *Stage 1: Uncorrected:* 13
 Corrected: the rest

	Uncorrected	Corrected
sig. L2v, V.333	nr	nor

(b) *Stage 2: Uncorrected:* 2, 3, 5, 10, 12, 13, 15, 16, 21, 23
 Corrected: the rest

	Uncorrected	Corrected
sig. L4v, V.479.3	AANQVINIVS	SANQVINIVS
488	SAM.	SAN.

16. *Sheet L (inner)*
Uncorrected: 3, 5, 13, 15, 16, 21, 23
Corrected: the rest

	Uncorrected	*Corrected*
sig. L2r, note b	*Meridie . . . vid*	*Meridies . . . vid.*

(Note: side-notes cropped on 12)

17. *Sheet M (outer)*
There are three stages of correction:
(*a*) *Stage 1: Uncorrected:* 18, 20
            Corrected: the rest

	Uncorrected	*Corrected*
sig. M1r, V.510	elbow	elbow,
sig. M2v, V.626	remooue	remooue—
sig. M3r, V.667	HAYLES	HAYLES,

(*b*) *Stage 2: Uncorrected:* 6, 10, 13, 15, 18, 19, 20, 22
            Corrected: the rest

	Uncorrected	*Corrected*
sig. M1r, V.503	state	State
525–6	MAY WHAT I AM	MAY WHAT I AM
	TO VTTER, TVRNE	TO VTTER, TVRNE
	GOOD AND HAPPY	GOOD AND
	FOR THE	HAPPY
	COMMON	FOR THE
	VVEALTH	COMMON
		VVEALTH
note a	*de formut.*	*de formul.*
sig. M2v, V.627	off!	off,
627	winde.	winde!
636	There's	Here's
660	O the	O, the
sig. M3r, V.666	friends	friend
673	An . . . man,	(An . . . man)
678	forth	forth,
683	downe	downe,
686	nostrils.	nostril:
694	Gainst	'Gainst
695	sonnes	Sonnes

(Note: at 686, 'nostrils' was improperly 'corrected'. It received its intended form in the next stage.)

	Uncorrected	*Corrected*
sig. M4v, V.769	Eager	eager
776	*Capitoll;*	*Capitoll,*
776	Circke,	Circke:
777	*Mastiues*	Mastiues
779	fury;	fury,
784	too	to
794	slacknesse	slacknesse,

(*c*) *Stage 3: Uncorrected or improperly corrected:* 2, 3, 5, 6, 10, 12, 13, 15, 17, 18, 19, 20, 21, 22, 23

Corrected: the rest

	Improperly corrected (Stage 2)	*Corrected*
sig. M3r, V.686	nostril:	nostrills:

(Note: sheet M missing in 8)

18. *Sheet N (inner)*
There are two stages of correction:
(*a*) *Stage 1: Uncorrected:* 2, 3, 23
        Corrected: the rest

	Uncorrected	*Corrected*
sig. N1v, V.872	heare	haire
sig. N2r, V. 913	'Euendoth	'Euen doth

(*b*) *Stage 2: Uncorrected:* 2, 3, 4, 6, 7, 14, 18, 23
        Corrected: the rest

	Uncorrected	*Corrected*
sig. N2r, V.892	AKR.	ARR.

(Note: sheet N missing in 8, 12, 13)

II. 1616 FOLIO COLLATION (ARRANGED BY FORMES)

Key to copies collated

1. Harvard 1
2. Harvard 2
3. Durham Univ. (Cosin AA.III.30)
4. Durham Univ. 2 (Cosin W.III.27)
5. Folger (STC 14751) 1
6. Aberdeen Univ.
7. Newberry Lib.
8. British Lib. (G11630)
9. British Lib. (C.39.k9)
10. Bodleian (AA 83 Art)
11. Bodleian (Douce I.302)
12. Bodleian (U.16.5)
13. Manchester Univ.
14. Trinity Coll. Dublin

1. Sig. Gg5v
State 1: 3
State 2: 9, 13
State 3: the rest

		State 1	*State 2*	*State 3*
'THE ARGUMENT'	2	court:	court:	court;
	7	dislikes, it ... out	dislikes, it ... out,	dislikes (it ... out)
	14	and more	& more	& more
	15	Em-/pire: where	Empire: / where	Empire: / where
	16	and hard, / in respect	& hard, in re-/spect	& hard, in re-/spect
	17	in hope) he	in hope for the suc-/cession) he	in hope for the suc-/cession) he
	18–19	and instill's into his/eares	& instill's in-/to his eares	& instill's in-/to his eares
	19–20	and their/mother	and/their mother	and/their mother

21	coue-/tously	co-/uetously	co-/uetously
22–3	he labours to marry Li-/uia	he labours to marry Li-/uia	Seianus labours to marry / Liuia
25	separated	retyred	retyred
28	eares . . . there	feares . . . there,	feares . . . there,
36	with one letter, and in one/day	with one letter, and in one/day	and with a long doubtfull / letter, in one day
37	torne in pieces, by/the	torne in pieces, by/the	torne/in pieces by the

2. Sig. Ii4*v*
Uncorrected: 1, 3, 6, 8
Corrected: the rest

		Uncorrected	*Corrected*
	II.289	Sacrouir	SACROVIR

3. Sig. Kk2*r*
Uncorrected: 9, 14
Corrected: the rest

		Uncorrected	*Corrected*
	III.82	go'ds	gods,

4. Sigs. Ll1*v* and Ll6*r*
Uncorrected: 5, 7, 9, 13, 14
Corrected: the rest

		Uncorrected	*Corrected*
sig. Ll1*v*,	III.532	we faintly, such,	we, faintly, such,
	539	marrie	marrie,
	547	forth;	forth:
	551	LIVIA who was wife	LIVIA, first the wife
	552	to DRVSVS	my DRVSVS
	570	vs,	vs;
	571	Only	Only,
	572	Beleeue	Beleeue,
	574	merit;	merit.
sig. Ll6*r*,	IV.164	soueraigne;	soueraigne,
	172	SEIANVS?	SEIANVS!
	177	Empire	empire
	194	That	that
	198	The	the
	200	comment:	comment;
	201	there,	there;

5. Sigs. Ll2*r* and Ll5*v*
Uncorrected: 1, 3, 5, 9, 11, 12, 13
Corrected: the rest

	Uncorrected	*Corrected*
sig. Ll2r, III.586	shall. Dull	shall: dull
sig. Ll5v, IV.123	wife	wife,
124	hate,	hate;
140	*Vultures,*	vultures,
141	first	first,
146	fooles	fooles,
154	facile	readie

6. Sigs. Ll3r and Ll4v
Uncorrected: 2, 3, 4, 6, 8, 11, 12, 13, 14
Corrected: the rest

	Uncorrected	*Corrected*
sig. Ll3r, III.662	awhile!) when	awhile.) When
663	your	our
665	choise	choise,
667	ambition,	ambition:
673	*Capua;* Th'other	*Capua,* th'other
681	eare;	eare,
682	DRVSVS;	DRVSVS,
685	him:	him.
690	too much humour	too fit matter
693	apprehends:	apprehends.
695	nature:	nature.
696	Affections	Affections,
702	Thinke,	thinke,
sig. Ll4v, IV.34	they	they,
39	For	for
52	Others	others

7. Sig. Mm6v
Uncorrected: 2, 10, 11
Corrected: the rest

	Uncorrected	*Corrected*
V.185	away	away!

8. Sigs. Mm1v and Mm6r
Uncorrected: 1, 2, 3, 10, 11, 12, 13
Corrected: the rest

	Uncorrected	*Corrected*
sig. Mm1v, IV.288	men.	men!
290	*patriot*	patriot
sig. Mm6r, V.148.1	*no s.d.*	*s.d.: Returnes.*
153	palace;	palace,
156	By	by
157	Let	let
163	me,	me:
165	colleague;	colleague,
172	*farre; Farre*	*farre. Farre*
173	now;	now,

		Uncorrected	Corrected
	173	s.d.: These sound, / while the *Fla-/men* washeth.	s.d.: Sound, while / the *Flamen* washeth.
	174	*minds:*	*minds.*

9. Sigs. Mm3r and Mm4v
Uncorrected: 1, 5, 10, 11, 12, 13
Corrected: the rest

		Uncorrected	Corrected
sig. Mm3r, IV.414		MAR.	MIN.
	420	mention:	mention;
	434	choke (him.)	choke him,
	435	*line absent*	That . . . ARRVNTIVS.)
	438	CASTOR . . . POLLVX	POLLVX . . . HERCVLES
	444	owne;	owne,
	445	*s.d. absent*	*s.d.: They whisper with Terentius.*
	449	Mixing	Mingling
	455	strong,	strong;
	456	deuotion,	deuotion;
sig. Mm4v, V.19		So	so
	23	fortune	fortune,
	24	strife	strife:
	26	No	no
	30	furnace	fornace
	31	you, goe see	(you, goe see)
	33	'tis	'tis—
	33	imposture	imposture,
	34	*s.d. absent*	*s.d.: To them.*
	37	serpent.	serpent!
	48	lord?	lord!
	54	vs,	vs;
	57	ominous:	ominous!

10. Sigs. Nn2v and Nn5r
Uncorrected: 1, 2, 7, 13
Corrected: the rest

		Uncorrected	Corrected
sig. Nn2v, V.339		Which	With
	347	MACRO,	MACRO!
sig. Nn5r, V.544		*s.d.: The Epistle / is read.*	*The Epistle is / read.*
	561	*libels*	*libels,*

11. Sig. Oo1v
Uncorrected: 1, 4, 7, 9, 13, 14
Corrected: the rest

		Uncorrected	Corrected
	V.775	theatre;	theatre,

776	circke,	circke;
778	sensitiue	sensiue growne
779	furie;	furie,
782	garlands	gyrlands
783	reuerenced.	reuerenced!
792	knaues,	knaues;
801	Aske	aske
805	roofe	proofe

12. Sig. Oo3r
Uncorrected: 2, 3, 5, 7, 11, 14
Corrected: the rest

	Uncorrected	*Corrected*
V.906	rise,	rise:
912	For	For,

Glossarial Index to the Commentary